Beijing

"All you've got to do is decide to go
and the hardest part is over.

So go!"

TONY WHEELER, COFOUNDER – LONELY PLANET

THIS EDITION WRITTEN AND RESEARCHED BY
David Eimer
Trent Holden

Contents

(left) **Wángfǔjǐng Snack Street p76**
Barbecued skewers

(above) **The Great Wall p169** The Bādálǐng section of the Wall in winter

(right) **Temple of Heaven Park p106**
Traditional Ming architectural design

Summer Palace & Hǎidiàn
p150

Sānlǐtún & Cháoyáng
p132

Drum Tower & Dōngchéng North
p83

Běihǎi Park & Xīchéng North
p113

Forbidden City & Dōngchéng Central
p52

Dashilar & Xīchéng South
p124

Temple of Heaven Park & Dōngchéng South
p104

Welcome to Běijīng

Constantly reimagining itself as it races towards the future, yet inextricably linked to its glorious, notorious past, Běijīng is as compelling as it is complex.

Food Heaven

Food is an obsession for the Chinese and the dazzling array of different dishes you'll encounter in Běijīng reflects the sheer joy locals take in eating. Dining out is the main social activity; it's in restaurants that Běijīngers hang out with friends, romance each other, hold family reunions and do business, and the sheer variety of restaurants here is mind-boggling. Menus will have you salivating over succulent Peking duck, delicious dumplings and awesome noodles, but there's food from every corner of China (and beyond) to be sampled too. From fiery Sìchuānese to Turkic–inspired Uighur cuisine, Běijīng's 60,000-plus restaurants cover every base.

Imperial Delights

Few places on Earth can match the extraordinary historical panorama on display in Běijīng. There are six Unesco World Heritage Sites in this city alone (just one less than the whole of Egypt). At its heart is the magnificent Forbidden City, a royal palace on a scale like no other. Běijīng is also home to sublime temples, while the city centre is criss-crossed by enchanting *hútòng:* ancient alleyways that teem with life today, as they did hundreds of years ago. And, to cap it all, the awe-inspiring Great Wall snakes its way across the hills north of town.

Architectural Ambition

It's not just the ancient architecture that wows tourists. Běijīng is also home to some of the world's most innovative modern buildings. The world's leading architects clamber for the chance to make their mark on this global powerhouse, and jaw-dropping structures such as the CCTV Building, Galaxy Soho, the NCPA concert hall and the Olympic Stadium are clear signs that Běijīng is not shy about proclaiming its status as China's capital. Like the temples and palaces of the ancient past, and the imposing socialist-realist monuments of the 1950s, these latest additions are built on a scale that screams, 'Look at me!'.

Acrobats & Artists

Běijīng isn't just the political centre of China – it's the cultural heart of the country too. The nation's top artists, writers, movie-makers and musicians converge here, making this *the* place to take the pulse of China's ever-evolving cultural scene. With top-class museums, galleries galore, and an increasing number of music venues, there's enough to keep you busy day and night. Whether it's the mystique of Peking opera, tumbling acrobats or the graceful lines of Chinese classical dance that entrances you, the capital has it and more.

Why I Love Běijīng

By David Eimer, Writer

I am endlessly intrigued by Běijīng's ability to reinvent itself. To spend time here is to be on a permanent journey of discovery, where eye-popping buildings appear seemingly overnight, historic *hútòng* are transformed into hip hang-outs, and new venues open all the time. But some things never change in Běijīng and that is equally enticing. The food is always outstanding and the parks and temples remain oases of peace. Above all, I love being surrounded by the tangible evidence of China's amazing, dramatic history, whether it's the Forbidden City or the Great Wall. It's never boring here.

For more about our writers, see p288

Top: Performers at the Húguǎng Guild Hall (p129)

Běijīng's
Top 13

The Great Wall *(p162)*

1 China's most famous landmark, and one of the world's superlative sights, the Great Wall snakes its way across 17 provinces of China, but nowhere beats Běijīng as a base for mounting your assault. Scattered throughout the municipality are more than a dozen fragmented stretches, from the perfectly chiselled, to the charmingly dilapidated. You can get to them by bus, by train, by taxi...even by bicycle. And the adventurous can hike along it for days. The question isn't whether to see the Great Wall; it's how. BELOW LEFT: THE GREAT WALL AT JĪNSHĀNLĬNG (P168)

⊙ *The Great Wall*

Forbidden City *(p54)*

2 The largest palace complex in the world, the Forbidden City encapsulates imperial Chinese grandeur, with imposing halls, splendid gates and age-old relics. No other place in Běijīng is invested with so much history, legend and intrigue. You could spend hours wandering its vast squares and high-walled passageways, which lead to delightful courtyards, gardens and minimuseums, while contemplating the enormity of shuffling your way around the place that 24 emperors of China called home.

⊙ *Forbidden City & Dōngchéng Central*

3

4

Tiān'ānmén Square (p62)

3 The world's largest public square is a vast concrete desert at the heart of Běijīng. It's also a poignant epitaph to China's hapless democracy movement, which got a drubbing from the People's Liberation Army here in June 1989. The stringent security can be off-putting, but such is its iconic status, few visitors leave Běijīng without coming here. Get up early and watch the dawn flag-raising ceremony, or wander by later on to see the surrounding buildings lit up at night.

⊙ *Forbidden City & Dōngchéng Central*

Hútòng (p209)

4 The heart and soul of Běijīng are its *hútòng:* the alleyways that crisscross the centre of the city. Still home for many locals, these intoxicating, unique lanes not only tie the capital to its historic past – some lanes date back almost 800 years – but offer the chance to experience Běijīng street life in all its raucous glory. Wandering or cycling the *hútòng* during the day, and returning at night to the many bars and restaurants that now inhabit them, is an essential part of any visit to Běijīng.

⊙ *Historic Hútòng*

Temple of Heaven Park (p106)

5 The ultimate expression of the eternal Chinese quest for order, Temple of Heaven Park is geometric perfection: a series of stunning shrines – including the iconic Hall of Prayer for Good Harvests – where the sons of heaven, China's emperors, came to pray for divine guidance. Everything about them – colour, shape, sound – has an esoteric significance that's extraordinary to contemplate. Surrounding them is a delightfully soothing park, where locals come to stroll and dance, or to sit under the many ancient and gnarled cypress trees.

⊙ *Temple of Heaven Park & Dōngchéng South*

Summer Palace (p152)

6 The summer playground for China's emperors, the Summer Palace is a beguiling, superbly landscaped collection of temples, pavilions, gardens, lakes, bridges and corridors. Less formal than the Forbidden City, there is still more than enough elegance and beauty in its many structures to take your breath away. Clamber up Longevity Hill, pausing at the various temples that dot it, for splendid views across Běijīng, or promenade around Kūnmíng Lake and imagine what it must have been like to have had this place all to yourself.

👁 *Summer Palace & Haidian*

Peking Duck (p35)

7 You can't leave Běijīng without sampling its most iconic dish. Once reserved for emperors and mandarins, Peking duck began to feature on the menus of the lower orders at the beginning of the 20th century. Now there are a number of specialist *kǎoyā* (roast duck) restaurants and the dish – juicier and more flavoursome than the crispy duck you get back home – is as much a part of Běijīng's identity as the streets themselves. RIGHT: PEKING DUCK SERVED WITH SIDES

🍴 *Eating*

Lama Temple (p85)

8 Central Bĕijīng's largest, most important and atmospheric Buddhist temple, the serene Lama Temple used to be home to legions of monks from Mongolia and Tibet and was where the reincarnation of the Panchen Lama was determined. These days it is still an active temple, although tourists now outnumber the monks. There are five beautiful central halls, the last of which houses the world's largest sandalwood Buddha. LEFT: STATUE OF TSONG KHAPA IN THE HALL OF THE WHEEL OF THE LAW (P86)

◉ *Drum Tower &*
Dōngchéng North

Chinese Performing Arts (p220)

9 Whether it's the chance to experience the intricate, highly stylised Peking opera, or tumbling, spinning and high-wire-walking acrobats, to say nothing of shaven-headed Shàolín Monks showing off their supreme fighting skills, Běijīng is a great place to catch a show. There are performances every night of the week, giving you no excuse to miss out. And don't be put off by the language barrier: most shows are easy to follow. Acrobatics in particular is a stunning spectacle. BELOW: PERFORMERS AT THE HÚGUǍNG GUILD HALL (P129)

⭐ *Arts*

Hòuhǎi Lakes (p117)

10 These three inter-connected lakes are one of the great outdoor areas in Běijīng and a prime spot to watch, and join, the locals at play. Ringed by bars and restaurants, the lakes themselves provide much of the entertainment. In summer, flotillas of pedalos take to the water. During winter, the lakes are the best place in the capital to ice-skate. Then there's fishing, kayaking and swimming (for the brave). But perhaps the best option is simply meandering around them, enjoying the sight of Beijingers kicking back.

◉ *Běihǎi Park & Xīchéng North*

Drum & Bell Towers (p87)

11 Standing watch over one of the most charming corners of Běijīng, these two magnificent ancient towers, facing each other on either side of a small public square, used to be the city's official timekeeper, with drums and bells beaten and rung to mark the times of the day. Climb the Drum Tower to listen to a body-rumbling performance played out on replica drums or ascend either tower for a bird's-eye view of the surrounding *hútòng*.

◉ *Drum Tower & Dōngchéng North*

Pānjiāyuán Market *(p147)*

12 Save some time at the end of your trip to visit this treasure-filled outdoor market and head home with armfuls of unusual souvenirs. Pānjiāyuán Market is packed at the weekends as both locals and visitors congregate here from the early morning in search of that elusive Ming dynasty vase. It is by far the best place in Běijīng to shop for arts, crafts and (mostly fake) antiques. Even if you don't want to buy anything, it's fun to see what's on offer and the market is perfect for people-watching.

🛍 *Sānlǐtún & Cháoyáng*

798 Art District *(p134)*

13 Housed inside the cavernous buildings of a disused electronics factory, 798 has become the city's premier art district. It celebrates its proletarian roots via retouched red Maoist slogans decorating gallery interiors and statues of burly, lantern-jawed workers dotting the lanes, while the voluminous factory workshops are ideally suited to ambitious projects requiring lots of space. Cafes dot the streets, making this a pleasant spot for lunch before you plunge into the world of Chinese contemporary art.

ARTIST AND POET FAN XUEYI (SUNLIGHT) IN HER STUDIO IN THE 798 ART DISTRICT

👁 *Sānlǐtún & Cháoyáng*

What's New

Bike-Sharing Scheme
Běijīng's bike-sharing scheme is now open to foreigners, as well as locals, enabling visitors to rent a bike for a measly ¥1 an hour. All you need to do is go to Dongzhimen subway station, get an ordinary Běijīng travel card for the subway and activate it for bike-rental use.

Uber
Yes, they have it in Běijīng too now, although you'll wait longer for a ride here than in other cities thanks to fewer drivers and heavy traffic. It is available in English, but if you don't speak Chinese you're reliant on the driver's sat nav to get to your destination.

Antismoking Law
In June 2015, the capital introduced the toughest antismoking legislation in China, in an effort to stop smoking inside restaurants, clubs, bars, hotels and offices. Not every place is complying, but Běijīng now has far more smoke-free venues than ever before.

WeChat
WeChat (www.wechat.com) is now the most popular instant-messaging system in China; it's worth downloading it as your new Chinese friends will ask for your ID straightaway. An English version is available and you can use it for paying bills too.

New Subway Lines
The city's already extensive and impressive subway system continues to expand – you can get to the Ming Tombs by subway now – with new lines completed in the last couple of years and 12 more due to open by 2021.

Public Transport Price Hike
Běijīng has followed Shànghǎi in changing its subway and bus fares to a journey distance model, rather than the flat fare of old. But it's still supercheap: the most you'll pay for a subway ride is ¥8.

Pollution Red Alert
Since December 2015, Běijīng now issues a red alert if pollution levels go off the scale (as they often do, especially in winter). Stay off the streets if you can when the alert is in effect, as it means that the smog is very bad indeed.

For more recommendations and reviews, see **lonelyplanet. com/china/beijing**

Need to Know

For more information, see Survival Guide (p229)

Currency
Yuán (¥; 元)

Language
Mandarin

Visas
Passengers in transit are allowed 72 hours without a visa. Otherwise, visas are required for almost all nationals. A 30-day visa is standard. One extension is usually possible.

Money
Most ATMs accept foreign cards. Most large banks change money. Credit and debit cards are now used more widely than before, especially in hotels, shopping malls and upmarket restaurants, but cash remains king in Běijīng, so carry money with you at all times.

Mobile Phones
Local SIMs can be used in unlocked phones. Local phones are cheap. Smartphones can use China's 3G and 4G networks (with roaming charges) or Běijīng's many free wi-fi spots.

Time
China Standard Time (GMT/UTC plus eight hours)

Tourist Information
Tourist information offices are aimed at domestic tourists. Foreigners are better off using hotels or, better still, hostels.

Daily Costs

Budget:
Less than ¥250
→ Hostel dorm: ¥60–80
→ A meal in a local restaurant: ¥20–40
→ Subway tickets: ¥3–8

Midrange: ¥250–800
→ Standard private room: ¥260–500
→ A meal in a midrange restaurant: ¥40–80
→ Short taxi trip: ¥15
→ Admission to main sights: ¥20–60

Top end:
More than ¥800
→ Luxury accommodation: from ¥1000
→ A meal at an international restaurant: from ¥100
→ Drinks at cocktail bars: ¥60–80
→ Guided tours: ¥200–1000

Advance Planning

Three months before Check your vaccinations are up to date. Sort out your visa. Start learning some Mandarin phrases.

One month before Decide which neighbourhood to base yourself in. Scout around for hotel deals. Look into possible tours and courses.

One week before Book your accommodation, tours and courses. Consider possible day trips.

Useful Websites

The Beijinger (www.thebeijinger.com) Eating and entertainment listings, blog posts and forums.

Timeout Běijīng (www.timeoutbeijing.com) The best listings mag and a useful, well-designed website.

Běijīng Cream (http://beijingcream.com) Lighthearted Běijīng-based blog covering China-wide current affairs.

Sinica Podcast (http://popupchinese.com) Popular, uncensored current-affairs podcast based in Běijīng.

Air Pollution (http://aqicn.org/city/beijing) Real-time Air Quality Index (AQI) for Běijīng (and other cities).

Lonely Planet (lonelyplanet.com/china/beijing) Destination information, hotel bookings and more.

WHEN TO GO

April to May and October to November are most pleasant. December to February is dry and very cold. June to September (peak season) is very hot, but rainstorms offer respite.

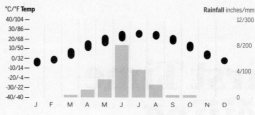

Arriving in Běijīng

Běijīng Capital International Airport The Airport Express (¥25, 30 minutes, 6.30am to 11pm) links up with the subway system (Lines 10 and 2). If taking a taxi (¥90 to ¥120), use the official taxi rank only.

Běijīng Train Station On subway Line 2.

Běijīng West Train Station On subway Line 9.

Běijīng South Train Station On subway Line 4.

For much more on **arrival** see p230

How Much?

➡ *Bāozi* (steamed dumpling) from street stall: ¥2

➡ One hour in internet cafe: ¥3 to ¥5

➡ Large bottle of local beer from a shop: ¥4

➡ Small bottle of local beer from a bar: ¥20

➡ Half-litre bottle of mineral water: ¥2

➡ Lamb skewer: ¥2 to ¥3

➡ Bananas from a market stall: ¥4 per *jīn* (500g)

➡ Bicycle rental per day: ¥30 to ¥50

➡ Repairing a puncture: ¥5

For much more on **getting around** see p236

Sleeping

Hostels are best value, with traveller-friendly facilities and staff with good English-language skills. Courtyard hotels are wonderfully atmospheric, and plant you right in the thick of the *hútòng* action, but they lack the facilities (pool, gym etc) of top-end hotels in similar price brackets. You can book rooms directly through hotel websites, or over the phone.

Useful Websites

Ctrip (www.english.ctrip.com) Discounted hotels.

China Homestay (http://china homestay.org) Homestays.

Lonely Planet (lonelyplanet. com/china/beijing/hotels) Recommendations and bookings.

For much more on **sleeping** see p181

MONEY-SAVING TIPS

Travel Card (一卡通; *yīkǎtōng;* deposit ¥20) Saves 50% on all bus fares. Obtained from subway stations.

Museum Pass (博物馆通票; Bówùguǎn Tōngpiào; ☑010 6222 3793; www.bowuguan.com.cn; annual pass ¥120) Worth it if you're staying a while. Gets you either complimentary access or discounted admission (typically 50%) to 112 tourist attractions.

First Time Běijīng

For more information, see Survival Guide (p229)

Checklist

➡ Secure your visa

➡ Make hotel bookings

➡ Have the name and address of your hotel printed out in Chinese characters

➡ Put your name down for any classes or courses

➡ Check your mobile phone is unlocked, so that you can use a local SIM card

➡ Tell your bank you'll be using your cards in China

What to Pack

➡ Phrasebook and/or Chinese dictionary

➡ Skin moisturiser (Běijīng can be incredibly dry)

➡ Smog mask

➡ Sun hat and sun cream in summer

➡ Woollies in winter

➡ Shoes with good grip for Great Wall hikes

➡ Small rucksack for day trips

Top Tips for Your Trip

➡ Learn as much Chinese (Mandarin) as you can before you come.

➡ Rent a bike. Běijīng is as flat as a mah-jong table and a great city to explore on two wheels.

➡ Have the name and address of wherever you're going each day written down in Chinese characters before you go out. And always bring your hotel business card with you, so you can find your way home.

➡ Try as wide a variety of Chinese food as you can. Běijīng has every culinary base covered, from Peking Duck to spicy Sichuānese, so grab some chopsticks and tuck in. Oh, and don't listen to anyone who tells you to avoid the street food – terrible advice.

What to Wear

Jeans and shirt or T-shirt are fine for much of the year. Shorts are OK in summer. It gets very hot in midsummer, so don't forget a sun hat (as well as sun cream and mosquito repellent) and a lightweight raincoat for sudden downpours. Winter is a different ball game. Wear plenty of layers: thermal underwear, thick shirt, jumper, gloves, woollie hat and a decent jacket or coat – plus thick-soled shoes or boots. At any time of year, you'll need shoes with good grip for Great Wall hiking.

Be Forewarned

➡ Air quality can be a problem, especially if you're particularly sensitive to pollution. Consider wearing a smog mask, and check the air-quality index (www.aqicn.org).

➡ Try to avoid visiting during national holidays (especially May Day and National Day) as the main sights can get ridiculously crowded. Conversely, Chinese New Year is relatively quiet, as most people spend time with their families.

Money

ATMs are everywhere, and many accept foreign bank cards. Visa and MasterCard are most readily accepted. Don't expect to be able to use a foreign card to make purchases (the exceptions are at hotels, upmarket restaurants and modern shopping malls) – always carry cash too.

For more information, see p245.

Bargaining

Bargaining is common in shops (apart from supermarkets), and expected in markets. But there are no hard and fast rules. In shops, you'll only be able to knock a small amount off the asking price, but in markets – especially souvenir markets – you can bargain your socks off. Remember to keep negotiations lighthearted, and be prepared to walk away; that's usually when you'll hear the genuine 'last price'.

Tipping

Tips are never asked for, or expected. The only time you should ever consider tipping is in top-end luxury hotels or in top-end international restaurants, although they usually tack a 10% to 15% service charge onto the bill anyway. Taxi drivers don't expect tips. Don't be pressured into tipping tour guides – giving them extra on top of their fee is entirely optional.

Language

Fewer people than you think speak English in Běijīng, and most people speak none at all (taxi drivers, for example). However, many people who work in the tourist industry do speak at least some English (particularly in hotels and hostels), so, as a tourist, you'll be able to get by without speaking Chinese. That said, you'll enrich your experience here hugely, and gain the respect of the locals, if you make a stab at learning some Chinese before you come.

1 **Where would you go for dumplings?**
哪里的饺子好？ Nǎlǐ de zǎjiǎozi hǎo?

When in Běijīng, make sure you find the right place for what has to be northeastern China's favourite comfort food: dumplings. They come steamed, fried or in delicious broth.

2 **Please bring a knife and fork.**
请拿一副刀叉来。 Qǐng ná yī fù dāochā lái.

Don't be afraid to ask for cutlery at a restaurant if you haven't quite mastered the art of eating with chopsticks.

3 **Can I get a discount (for the room)?**
这（房间）能打折吗？ Zhè (fángjiān) néng dǎzhé ma?

You can bargain for the price in many Chinese hotels. Discounts of 10% to 50% off the rack rate are the norm, available by simply asking at reception.

4 **I'd like to hire a bicycle.**
我想租一辆自行车。 Wǒ xiǎng zū yīliàng zìxíngchē.

Bikes are a great option for getting around Chinese cities and tourist sites. They can also be invaluable for exploring the countryside.

5 **Can you write that in pinyin for me?**
请用拼音写。 Qǐng yòng pīnyīn xiě.

If you find Chinese script intimidating, pinyin (the official system for writing Mandarin in the Roman alphabet) is your next best option.

Etiquette

Generally speaking, China is pretty relaxed when it comes to etiquette.

➡ **Greetings and goodbyes** Shake hands, but never kiss someone's cheek. Say 'nǐ hǎo' to greet someone, and 'zài jiàn' to say goodbye.

➡ **Asking for help** To ask for directions, say 'qǐng wèn…' ('can I ask…'). Say 'duìbuqǐ' ('sorry') to apologise.

➡ **Eating and drinking** Help fill your neighbour's plate or bowl at the dinner table. Toast the host and others at the table. At the start of dinner, wait until toasting begins before drinking from your glass. Offer your cigarettes around if you smoke. Always offer to pay for the meal, or for drinks at a bar, but don't fight too hard over the tab if someone else wants to pay.

Getting Around

For more information, see Transport (p230)

Bicycle

The most fun and often the quickest way to get around. Almost every road has a bike lane. Bike rental per day is around ¥50, or take advantage of Běijīng's bike-sharing scheme.

Walking

The best way to see Běijīng's *hútòng*.

Subway

Quick, modern and easy to use (all signage is in Chinese and English), but often crowded, so don't expect a seat. Fares range from ¥3 to ¥8.

Bus

Dirt cheap and they go everywhere, but difficult for non-Chinese speakers to negotiate, and often overcrowded. Per trip ¥2; with travel card ¥0.8.

Motor Rickshaw

Fares have to be negotiated (rickshaws don't have meters) and tourists are often heavily overcharged. We don't recommend using them.

Taxi

Cheap by Western standards but at certain times hard to find, and traffic jams can really slow things down. Flag fall is ¥13.

Key Phrases

dǎ dī (打的) To take a taxi (colloquial)

dǎ biǎo (打表) To use the meter

qù _____ duōshǎo qián? How much to _____ ?

zuò chē (坐车) To take a bus

qù _____ ma? Does this go to _____ ?

mǎi piào (买票) To buy a ticket

yīkǎtōng (一卡通) Travel card

shuā kǎ (刷卡) To swipe a travel card

xià chē (下车) To get off any vehicle

dào le! (到了) We've arrived!

kuài dào le (到了) We're nearly there

dǔ chē (堵车) Traffic jam

zū zìxíngchē (租自行车) To rent a bicycle

yǒu suǒ ma? (有锁吗?) Do you have a bike lock?

dǎ qì (打气) To pump up a tyre

Key Routes

Buses 专1 & 专2 These two handy buses do clockwise circuits of the Forbidden City, looping south to Qiánmén, via Tiān'ānmén Sq.

Subway Lines 1 & 2 For 30 years, until 2002, these were Běijīng's only two subway lines. They're still the most useful for tourists, as between them they get you to the Forbidden City, Tiān'ānmén Sq, the Drum Tower, the Lama Temple, the main train station and the shopping hubs of Xīdān and Wángfǔjǐng.

How to Hail a Taxi

➡ It's almost always best to simply hail a passing taxi from the side of the road.

➡ A red '空车–for hire' sign will be illuminated in the front windscreen when a taxi is free.

➡ Your hotel may be able to help arrange a taxi for day trips out of town.

TOP TIPS

➡ Go right to the very end of subway carriages for a bit more breathing space (but probably still no seat).

➡ Every subway platform has public toilets at one end.

➡ If a taxi driver refuses to *dǎ biǎo* (use the meter), get out and find another one.

➡ Taxi drivers don't speak English, so always have the name and address in Chinese characters of the place you're going to. And don't forget your hotel's business card, so you can find your way home again.

When to Travel

➡ **Rush hour** Roughly 7.30am to 8.30am and 6pm to 7pm. This is when the subway is heaving, but it's also very tough to find an available taxi. Avoid these times if you can, or cycle.

➡ **Rainstorms** Taxis are always elusive when it's raining.

➡ **Evening** In areas where there are lots of bars and restaurants, it can be hard to find a taxi from around 8pm to 10pm.

Etiquette

➡ Do give up your seat for children or the elderly, even if it seems as though others aren't prepared to do so.

➡ Passengers of all ages (not just kids) rush to any spare seats the moment the subway doors open.

➡ Don't expect people to let you off your subway carriage before they get on.

➡ Bus and subway passengers expect to be allowed to move next to the door in preparation for getting off at the next stop.

Tickets & Passes

➡ It's worth getting a free travel card (一卡通; *yīkǎtōng*; deposit ¥20) at any subway station or large bus station. It makes subway travel more convenient and gives you 60% off all bus rides, including those out to the Great Wall. You can recharge them at most (but not all) subway stations and bus-station ticket kiosks.

➡ Children shorter than 1.2 metres travel for free, but each must be accompanied by a fee-paying adult.

For much more on **getting around** see p236 ➡

DRIVING IN BĚIJĪNG

China does not recognise the International Driving Permit, but it is relatively straightforward to obtain a temporary driving licence that allows you to drive in Běijīng and the surrounding area.

Cars in China drive on the right-hand side of the road. Even skilled drivers will be unprepared for China's roads: cars lunge from all angles and chaos abounds.

Given the relatively low cost of hiring a car with a driver, or a taxi for the day, few visitors self-drive.

Top Itineraries

Day One

Temple of Heaven Park & Dōngchéng South (p104)

 You're jet-lagged anyway, so what the heck? Get up at the crack of dawn and head straight for **Temple of Heaven Park**. Běijīng is blessed with some fabulous city parks, but this is arguably the most captivating of them all, and early morning, when it's filled with locals rather than tourists, is the best time to visit. Don't miss the park's crowning edifice, the magnificent **Hall of Prayer for Good Harvests** – Ming dynasty architectural perfection.

Lunch It's time to try Běijīng's most famous dish at Liqún Roast Duck Restaurant (p111).

Temple of Heaven Park & Dōngchéng South (p104)

Join the crowds of domestic tourists on their pilgrimage-like tour of China's most famous public space, **Tiān'ānmén Square**, before spending the afternoon exploring the immense palace grounds of the **Forbidden City**.

Dinner It's only a short walk to cute courtyard restaurant Little Yúnnán (p76).

Forbidden City & Dōngchéng Central (p52)

 Start your evening with cocktails in **Mao Mao Chong Bar**, north of Little Yúnnán, before catching some live music at **School Bar** or **Yúgōng Yìshān**.

Day Two

Drum Tower & Dōngchéng North (p83)

 Ease yourself into day two with a calming stroll around the incense-filled courtyards of the **Lama Temple** before visiting the equally peaceful and historic **Confucius Temple**. Grab a coffee at nearby **Cafe Confucius** before lunch.

Lunch Try lunch at the serene Bǎihé Vegetarian Restaurant (p94), popular with the monks from the Lama Temple.

Drum Tower & Dōngchéng North (p83)

Stroll through the *hútòng* to the magnificent **Drum Tower**. Catch one of the drumming performances here before hopping across the square to climb the equally majestic **Bell Tower**. In the late afternoon, locals congregate in the square for formation dancing and you're welcome to join in.

Dinner Head to hip *hútòng* restaurant 4corners (p120), a short walk from the Drum Tower.

Běihǎi Park & Xīchéng North (p113)

 Join the knowledgeable crowd who gather at the nearby **East Shore Jazz Café** to listen to the best local jazz musicians, as well as overseas bands, before drinking the night away by the lakeside on the **Hòuhǎi Bar Strip**.

PLAN YOUR TRIP TOP ITINERARIES

Dragon boats on Kūnmíng Lake (p152)

Day Three

The Great Wall (p162)

 Make an early start. You're heading for the Great Wall at **Zhuàngdàokǒu**. It's not the most remote section of the Wall, but it still takes a while to get there by bus, via Huáiróu.

> ✗ **Lunch** Stop for lunch at Zǎoxiāng Yard (p168), a small village guesthouse.

The Great Wall (p162)

Leave the village, and follow the stony pathway up to the Great Wall. When you hit the Wall, turn right and begin the steep, 45-minute hike to the top (where you'll get fabulous views of the Wall snaking off into the distance), before descending (15 minutes) to the main road by **Huánghuā Chéng Great Wall**. You can climb another section of the Wall here, if you like, or just catch a bus back to Huáiróu.

> ✗ **Dinner** Authentic Běijīng eats at Bàodǔ Huáng (p139), near the bus terminus.

Sānlǐtún & Cháoyáng (p132)

 If you still have any energy left, head to one of Sānlǐtún's buzzing cocktail bars: try **Janes + Hooch** or **Parlor**.

Day Four

Summer Palace & Hǎidiàn (p150)

 Head to the western outskirts for a morning trip to the **Summer Palace**. The imperial court used to decamp here to flee Běijīng's midsummer heatwaves. Food options are poor (although it's great picnic territory), so have lunch at **798 Art District**, where you'll be spending the afternoon.

> ✗ **Lunch** Try the Japanese and Western menu at Timezone 8 (p135), one of the key 798 hangouts.

Sānlǐtún & Cháoyáng (p132)

 Spend the rest of the afternoon at **798 Art District**: wander the galleries, stop for coffee and chat to young artists, while keeping your eye out for quirky souvenirs.

> ✗ **Dinner** Head to Gǒubùlǐ (p128) for quality dumplings.

Dashilar & Xīchéng South (p124)

☾ Spend your last evening in Běijīng being wowed by the city's best performance artists. If it's Peking opera you fancy, there's nowhere better than **Húguǎng Guild Hall**. Acrobatics more your thing? Head to **Tiānqiáo Acrobatics Theatre**. Can't decide? Try the mixed-performance shows at **Lao She Teahouse**.

If You Like...

Imperial Architecture

Forbidden City Sitting at the very heart of Běijīng, this vast 9000-room palace made up of hundreds of buildings is China's best-preserved reminder of its imperial past. (p54)

Temple of Heaven Park This fabulous imperial park is home to the sublime Hall of Prayer for Good Harvests – the most-intact surviving example of Ming dynasty architecture. (p106)

Summer Palace A harmonious marvel of landscaping on the outskirts of the city that features hilltop temples and elegant pavilions all set around a lake. (p152)

Drum & Bell Towers Dating back to the Mongol occupation of Běijīng and still standing guard over the surrounding *hútòng* (narrow alleyways). (p87)

Gate of Heavenly Peace Chairman Mao's portrait may adorn it, and he proclaimed the founding of the People's Republic of China (PRC) from atop it, but this was the largest gateway to the old imperial city. (p68)

Workers Cultural Palace Not a very promising name, but this little-visited, pleasant park was once an important place of worship for China's emperors and is home to some superb imperial-era halls. (p64)

Southeast Corner Watchtower Splendid Ming dynasty structure that rises above the last remaining stretch of the former city walls. (p109)

Prince Gong's Residence The finest surviving example of a

Long Corridor (p153) in the Summer Palace

traditional courtyard house, only on a very grand scale. (p118)

Foreign Legation Quarter Imperial, but in the Western fashion rather than the Chinese; an incongruous slice of colonial-era European architecture in Běijīng. (p72)

Ming Tombs The Unesco-protected final resting place of 13 of the 16 Ming dynasty emperors showcases some of Běijīng's largest and most impressive imperial structures. (p175)

Parks

Fragrant Hills Park Superb in the early autumn, when Beijingers flock here to see the maple leaves turn red against the green backdrop of the hills. (p158)

Běihǎi Park Hire a boat and spend a lazy day floating on the lake, or just amble around watching the locals at play. (p115)

Temple of Heaven Park A prime spot for people-watching, as Běijīng's senior citizens dance or practise taichi in the shade of thousands of ancient cypress trees. (p106)

Jǐngshān Park Climb the human-made hill for fine views over the Forbidden City. (p68)

Rìtán Park A soothing escape from the hustle of the nearby CBD; fly a kite by the altar to the sun that's located here. (p136)

Dìtán Park Home to Běijīng's most popular temple fair during the Spring Festival. (p89)

Hòuhǎi Lakes Not strictly a park, but still one of the most happening open spaces in Běijīng; a playground by day, and nightlife hub come sundown. (p117)

Markets

Pānjiāyuán Market Hands down the most fun market in the city; a chaotic jumble of antiques, calligraphy, carpets, curios, furniture and Mao memorabilia. (p147)

Mǎliándào Tea Market All the tea in China, or at least most of it, with tea shops galore around it for those in search of tea sets. (p131)

Silk Market Still one of the essential stops for many visitors to the capital, its collection of counterfeit clothes and bags is as popular as the genuine silk sold here. (p148)

Hóngqiáo (Pearl) Market Pearls and more pearls, of wildly different quality, as well as all manner of ephemera. (p112)

Temples

Lama Temple A former royal palace that is now home to chanting monks, this impressive, ornate complex is Běijīng's most popular Buddhist temple. (p85)

Confucius Temple Lovely, tranquil retreat from the hustle of Běijīng's chaotic streets and surrounded by atmospheric *hútòng*. (p89)

Dōngyuè Temple Perhaps the strangest temple in the capital, certainly the most morbid, this thought-provoking and very active Taoist shrine has halls dedicated to ghosts and the god who manages the 18 levels of hell. (p136)

White Cloud Temple Founded in AD 739 and tended by top-knotted Taoist monks, White Cloud Temple is the HQ for China's Taoists and home to a fabulous temple fair during the Spring Festival. (p118)

For more top Běijīng spots, see the following:
➡ Eating (p34)
➡ Drinking & Nightlife (p42)
➡ Entertainment (p44)
➡ Shopping (p46)

Fǎyuán Temple Secluded and very ancient shrine, dating to the 7th century AD, and still busy with worshippers. (p126)

Wǔtǎ Temple A distinct oddity, with its five striking pagodas, and more reminiscent of an Indian temple than a Chinese one. (p155)

Fine Dining

Temple Restaurant A contemporary European menu and a fabulous location in the grounds of a former temple. (p78)

Lost Heaven The subtle flavours of Yúnnán province served up in the swanky surrounds of the former Foreign Legation Quarter. (p76)

Duck de Chine A France-meets-China take on the capital's favourite bird in industrial-chic surroundings. (p142)

Capital M Classic Mediterranean meets North African dishes and views over Tiān'ānmén Sq at this Běijīng outpost of a celebrated Shànghǎi restaurant. (p111)

Běijīng Dàdǒng Roast Duck Restaurant Ultramodern restaurant promising the leanest roast duck in the capital. (p78)

O'Steak Relaxed, French-run steakhouse with superior cuts of meat and a top-class wine list. (p142)

Okra Minimalist in design, but the best sushi in the capital. (p142)

Museums & Galleries

Capital Museum Běijīng's finest, containing superbly informative galleries on the evolution of the city and its customs, and all in a bright, user-friendly environment. (p117)

798 Art District A maze of galleries devoted to the weird and wonderful world of Chinese contemporary art; be prepared to be alternatively bemused and captivated. (p134)

Poly Art Museum The place to see some of the ancient treasures, including incredible bronzes, that weren't pillaged by invading armies in the 19th century. (p69)

Běijīng Police Museum Brothels, opium dens, class traitors, gangsters and spies; the past and present Běijīng underworld revealed in all its fascinating, sometimes gruesome, glory. (p72)

Military Museum A propaganda exercise perhaps, but plenty of detail on China's martial past and lots and lots of guns, swords, tanks, missiles and planes. (p157)

Běijīng Ancient Architecture Museum Little-visited but excellent museum housed in a former Ming dynasty temple; it offers a great guide to how the imperial city was built. (p126)

Red Gate Gallery The first Běijīng gallery devoted to modern Chinese art, and still showcasing some of the best of the capital's artists. (p109)

National Museum of China Much improved museum that offers an extensive trawl through 5000 years of Chinese history and culture. (p64)

Chinese Performing Arts

Tiānqiáo Acrobatics Theatre Probably the finest tumbling, spinning, high-wire-walking show in town, and less touristy than other venues. (p129)

Húguǎng Guild Hall Fantastic, historic venue for Peking opera, with the audience close to the action and superb balconies overlooking the stage. (p129)

National Centre for the Performing Arts One of the key hubs of Běijīng cultural life, as well as one of the city's most striking buildings, with China's top orchestras and classical-dance troupes as regular performers. (p80)

Lao She Teahouse A little bit of everything takes place here on a nightly basis: Peking opera, shadow-puppet and folk-music performances especially, but also crosstalk: traditional Běijīng stand-up comedy. (p129)

China Puppet Theatre Shadow play and puppetry every weekend, and a great place to take kids who've had enough of sightseeing. (p101)

Live Music

Yúgōng Yíshān Chinese and foreign bands and electronic knob-twiddlers, as well as an audience-friendly vibe, make this the top venue for seeing live music in the capital. (p100)

East Shore Jazz Café The number-one spot in town for jazzers, with a prime location by the side of the Hòuhǎi Lakes; a relaxed feel and cool tunes late into the night. (p123)

School Bar Hipsters, punks and indie kids congregate at this deliberately grungy venue that hosts some of the capital's best bands. (p100)

Jiāng Hú Intimate courtyard venue for local indie and rock bands. (p100)

Temple Bar The owners are tattooed, pierced, and metal and punk fiends, but all sorts of bands take to the stage at this friendly place. (p100)

What? Bar Years ago this tiny place was just about the only venue in town; it still has loads of character and it's a good place to see up-and-coming new bands. (p80)

Month By Month

January

Běijīng shivers, with temperatures dipping to –10°C or below. But there are far fewer visitors in town, so this is a great time to see the Forbidden City without the crowds. Head to the Hòuhǎi Lakes for ice skating.

Western New Year

With the Spring Festival as their New Year bash, the Chinese treat the Western New Year (元旦; Yuándàn) on 1 January as an excuse just to party and have fun. But don't expect any fireworks.

February

Not a good month for air pollution, and it can be bitterly cold, but the arrival of Spring Festival means winter is drawing to a close.

Spring Festival

Like Christmas in the West, the family-oriented, 15-day-long Spring Festival (春节; Chūn Jié) is the most joyous celebration of the year, with fireworks and nonstop firecrackers. Celebrate with a Chinese family or visit a temple fair (庙会; miàohuì), such as Dōngyuè Temple (p136). 2018: 16 February. 2019: 5 February.

Lantern Festival

Celebrated on the final day of Spring Festival, Lantern Festival (元宵节; Yuánxiāo Jié) is among the tastiest of festivities, as locals devour delicious yuánxiāo (glutinous rice dumplings with sweet fillings), while fireworks and firecrackers explode all over town.

Valentine's Day

While China has its own festival for lovers (Qīxī; 七夕; held on the seventh day of the seventh month of the lunar year), it's not as popular as the Western Valentine's Day (请人节; Qíngrén Jié), held here on 14 February too. Buy your Valentine 11 roses, not 12.

March

It's almost time to put away the winter wardrobe. The domestic tourists who came for the Spring Festival have gone, but foreign ones are arriving in numbers.

International Literary Festival

The International Literary Festival (国际文学节; Guójì Wénxué Jié) sees writers and bibliophiles convening at the Bookworm (www.chinabookworm.com) for a two-week bonanza of

---

THE CHINESE CALENDAR

China follows both the *yánglì* (Gregorian) and the *yīnlì* (lunar) calendars. Traditional Chinese festivals are calculated according to the lunar calendar and fall on different days each year according to the Gregorian calendar.

readings and talks. With a strong line-up of international authors and local writers, it's one of the key cultural events of the year. Get tickets early.

✻ Guanyin's Birthday

Held on the 19th day of the second moon, the birthday of Guanyin (观世音生日; Guānshìyīn Shēngrì), the Buddhist Goddess of Mercy, is a fine time to visit Buddhist temples. 2018: 4 April. 2019: 25 March.

April

One of the nicest months of the year to be in Běijīng, as a fresh wind keeps the sky clear and snowflake-like poplar seeds and willow catkins (liǔxù) flutter through the air. It's getting warmer.

✻ Tomb Sweeping Day

A day for worshipping ancestors, Tomb Sweeping Day (清明节; Qīngmíng Jié) falls on 5 April (4 April in leap years). People clean the graves of their departed relatives, place flowers on tombs and burn ghost money for the departed on pavements. It's an official public holiday.

✻ Midi Festival

China's longest-running music festival, Midi (迷笛音乐节; Mídí Yīnyuè Jié) normally takes place in Hǎidiàn (or sometimes Tōngzhōu on the eastern outskirts of Běijīng) on the last weekend of April. Domestic and international bands and electronic acts play. It's a great chance to

mingle with local music fans.

◉ Spring Flower Shows

Flower-loving locals flock to Zhōngshān Park (p70) and Jǐngshān Park (p68) in April and May for spring flower shows (花展; Huā Zhǎn), when the parks' tulip and peony flower shows are in full bloom.

May

The temperature starts to rise as the fiercely hot and humid Běijīng summer approaches. May also marks the beginning of the peak tourist season.

✻ May Day

May Day (五一; Wǔyī) on 1 May kicks off a much-needed three-day national holiday for the locals, who swamp tourist sights across the nation.

June

Hot and sweaty days and balmy nights. But this month is also the peak time for rainfall in Běijīng. The main tourist sites are packed.

🔒 SURGE Art Běijīng

Held at different venues from year to year, this art fair (北京艺术节; Běijīng Yìshùjié; www.surgeart. com) showcases emerging contemporary Chinese artists and acts as a platform for them to sell their art at affordable prices.

✻ Dragon Boat Festival

On the fifth day of the fifth month of the lunar year

(usually June), dragon-boat festival (端午节; Duānwǔ Jié) races are sometimes staged on Běijīng's reservoirs. You'll see people scoffing zòngzi (parcels of sticky rice and meat or veggies in a bamboo leaf). 2017: 30 May. 2018: 18 June. 2019: 7 June.

September

The crowds are thinning out a little at the main tourist sites and the heat has mercifully relented. But this month sometimes sees major gatherings of the Chinese Communist Party (CCP) in the capital, which means enhanced security around Tiān'ānmén Sq.

✻ Mid-Autumn Festival

Also known as the Moon Festival, the Mid-Autumn Festival (中秋节; Zhōngqiū Jié) is marked by eating yuèbǐng (moon cakes), gazing at the full moon and family reunions. 2017: 4 October. 2018: 24 September.

October

Autumn is a fine time to visit Běijīng as it enjoys clear skies and perhaps its best weather of the year. It can feel crowded, though, as domestic visitors descend on the capital during the Golden Week holiday.

✻ National Day

Crowds flock to Tiān'ānmén Sq for a huge party on National Day (国庆节; Guóqìng Jié) on 1 October, followed by a massive weeklong national holiday

(Top) Paper sculpture, Spring Festival (p27)

(Bottom) *Yuèbĭng* (moon cakes) for the Mid-Autumn Festival

OPERATION SHOOTING / SHUTTERSTOCK ©

SOFIAWORLD / SHUTTERSTOCK ©

where the Chinese blow their hard-earned savings on travelling and enjoying themselves in what is known as Golden Week.

✺ Běijīng Music Festival

Usually staged from mid-October, classical-music Běijīng Music Festival (北京国际音乐节; Běijīng Guójì Yīnyuè Jié; www.bmf. org.cn) showcases foreign orchestras and musicians and has become increasingly high profile in recent years. It's a must for Běijīng culture vultures.

December

Běijīng can feel gloomy once winter descends and it becomes relentlessly cold. But a white Christmas is a real possibility, and you can strap on the ice skates and take to the Hòuhǎi Lakes, although sometimes they don't freeze sufficiently until January.

✺ Christmas Day

Not an official Chinese festival perhaps, but Christmas (圣诞节; Shèngdàn Jié) is a significant event on the commercial calendar, when Běijīng's big shopping zones sparkle with decorations and younger Chinese get into the Yuletide spirit.

p282, G2; admission free; ☉6am-10pm;
Ⓢ Chaoyang Park) FREE .

With Kids

The Chinese have a deep and uncomplicated love of children and openly display their affection for them. Běijīng may have less child-friendly facilities than equivalent-sized cities in the West, but the locals will go out of their way to accommodate your kids.

Need to Know

Discounts Kids often half price; or free if shorter than 1.2 metres.

Nappies Supermarkets stock baby essentials.

Smoking Some restaurants are smoky. Sit outside, or near the door.

Bike seats Rent baby seats and helmets from Bike Běijīng (p236).

Seatbelts Only in the front of taxis, so sit there with your child on your lap.

Getting lost Always arm your child with your hotel's business card.

Cots Only available in top-end hotels.

Toddlers

Parks

Toddlers will love running around Běijīng's parks, exploring their dinky pathways and dancing along to bands of local singers. They're also perfect for family picnics. Try Temple of Heaven Park (p106), Jǐngshān Park (p68), Rìtán Park (p136) or **Cháoyáng Park** (朝阳公园; Cháoyáng Gōngyuán; Map

Young Kids

Lakes

Historic Běihǎi Park (p115) has a large boating lake. The lakes at Hòuhǎi (p117) also provide pedal-boat action and, come winter, they freeze over and become central Běijīng's biggest playground. Rent ice skates, ice bikes and even ice bumper cars. The rest of the year, try Le Cool Ice Rink (p149) inside the China World Shopping Mall.

Swimming

For water slides, try the outdoor pools at Cháoyáng Park, Tuánjiéhú Park (p137) with its minibeach, or Qīngnián Hú Park (p103). For something bigger, head to the huge indoor Happy Magic Water Park (p148).

Toys

Head to Wangfujing Dajie (p81) for big toy shops selling gadgets that whiz, whir, beep and flash.

Arts & Crafts

Take them to Jīngchéng Bǎixìng (p102) where they can have a go at painting, or even making, their own traditional Chinese clay figures.

Kite Flying

Buy a handmade kite at Three Stone Kite Shop (p123) and head to one of the parks to join Běijīng's legion of kite-flying enthusiasts.

Museums & Shows

Try the vast China Science & Technology Museum (p137) or the Běijīng Natural History Museum (p110), which has dinosaurs. Kids will love the China Puppet Theatre (p101) or an acrobatics show.

Teenagers

Hiking & Cycling

Older kids will love the adventure of hiking along the Great Wall; just be sure they know the dangers. Cycling tours around the *hútòng* (narrow alleyways) can also be fun. Try hooking up with Bike Běijīng (p236).

Like a Local

Eat pancakes from a cycle rickshaw, squat on your heels while waiting for a bus, play keepie-uppies with a shuttlecock, roll your shirt up to reveal your belly in the summer (if you're male) and walk backwards, barefoot, along pebbled pathways. You're in Běijīng now, where people do things differently.

TONYV3112 / SHUTTERSTOCK ©

aichi in Běijīng (p137)

Eating
Běijīng Cuisine

Běijīng has pretty much every type of world cuisine covered – be it Chinese or international – but there are still a few restaurants knocking out genuine old-school Běijīng tucker.

Breakfast

Skip the expensive fry-up and coffee in your hotel and head to any restaurant between 6am and 8.30am that has bamboo baskets stacked up at its entrance. This indicates that they do dumplings. Order *yītì bāozi* (一屉包子; a basket of dumplings) with *yīwǎn zhōu* (一碗粥; a bowl of rice porridge), and tuck in. Other favourite breakfast combos here include *yóutiáo* (油条; fried dough sticks) with *dòujiāng* (豆浆; soy milk); and *húntún* (馄饨; wonton soup) with *shāobǐng* (烧饼; sesame-seed roasted bun).

Snacks & Street Food

Things to look out for in the evenings include *yángròu chuàn* (羊肉串; lamb skewers) – any place with a large red neon 串 sign does them. During the day, look for *jiānbǐng* (煎饼; savoury pancakes), sometimes cooked off the back of a cycle rickshaw.

Food Markets

Western-style supermarkets are increasingly popular, but wander through the *hútòng* in central Běijīng and you can still see the locals haggling over fresh fruit and vegetables, fish and meat at streetside minimarkets.

Park Life
Group Dancing

Locals often congregate in parks for a hearty singsong or a good old dance. Large, group formation dancing, accompanied by heavily amplified, patriotic songs, is the order of the day, and passers-by are always welcome to join in. Note, it isn't just parks that attract group dancing. Any large paved area of the city, especially public squares (although not Tiān'ānmén Sq) and apartment compounds, are prime locations come early evening.

Flying Kites

The all-time classic Chinese pastime is as popular as ever and Běijīng's parks are a great place to join in. Buy a kite – try Three Stone Kite Shop (p123) – then head to any park; the northeast corner of Temple of Heaven Park (p106) is a good spot.

Games

Card games are very popular, as is *jiànzi:* an oversized shuttlecock that's used for keepie-uppies. Older people enjoy the soothing nature of *róuliqiú* (taiji softball). Whatever the game, locals are almost always happy for you to join in. So, don't just stand there taking photos; play!

Working Out

All Běijīng parks have exercise areas with low-tech apparatus, such as pull-up bars and leg curls. Hòuhǎi Exercise Park (p119) is a popular lakeside version. Some areas include a pebble path. Try walking barefoot along them; good for your circulation, apparently, especially if you do it backwards.

Taichi

You'll notice some trees in parks have a worn out ring of bare ground around the base of their trunk. This marks out the tree as a taichi spot. Every day, usually early in the morning, someone will come to this tree to perform his or her preferred taichi movements. It's fascinating to watch.

Other Activities

Cycling

Cyclist numbers are declining, but they are still huge, and cycling along with the masses is a great way to feel like you are a part of the everyday city flow. It's also the perfect way to explore Běijīng's *hútòng* (narrow alleyways).

Table Tennis

It's easy to understand how China dominates world table tennis when you see the facilities devoted to it. Schools have whole floors of buildings dedicated to table tennis, and there are free-to-use tables dotted around the city, in most parks and most residential areas. If you fancy being on the wrong end of a ping-pong thrashing, head to Jīngshān Table Tennis Park (p82). Hòuhǎi Exercise Park (p119) also has tables.

Ice Swimming

Every day of the year, a group of dedicated Beijingers go swimming in the lakes at Hòuhǎi (p117). Nothing strange about that, until it gets to December, when temperatures plummet and the lake freezes over. Instead of taking a winter break, they rise early each morning, smash a hole in the ice and go for the coldest swim imaginable. Head to Hòuhǎi Exercise Park (p119) if you want to watch or, heaven forbid, take a plunge yourself.

Nightlife

KTV

Bars and clubs are a Western influence. Most locals just go for a slap-up meal if they fancy a night out. If they do go anywhere after dinner, it's usually to a karaoke joint, aka KTV. You're locked away in your own private room, so it's pretty boring on your own, but if you get the chance to join a group of Chinese friends, take it; the local enthusiasm for belting out pop classics is incredible, and most KTV joints have an English song list available too.

Báijiǔ

We recommend you go easy with this stuff – it is lethal – but Beijingers who are serious drinkers tend only to drink *báijiǔ* (白酒), a potent liquor made from sorghum. If you do get goaded into a *báijiǔ* session at a local restaurant (no one drinks *báijiǔ* in bars), take care. The protocol is to down glassfuls in one hit, while declaring '*gānbēi!*' ('dry glass!'), so it doesn't take long to get legless.

For Free

Běijīng may not appear at first sight to be a city overburdened with freebies. But dig a little deeper and you'll find a plethora of places to see, things to do and worthwhile experiences to be had that don't involve cash changing hands.

Free Activities

Hòuhǎi Lakes
Join the locals as they promenade around the lakes (p117); offer them advice on their kite-flying technique, or scrounge a bat and play a game of table tennis.

Hútòng
Walk your shoes off through the myriad ancient alleyways that criss-cross Běijīng.

Parks
Jǐngshān Park (p68), Zhōngshān Park (p70), Dìtán Park (p89) and Workers Cultural Palace (p64) are not completely free, but as good as, fun to explore, and cost just ¥2 to ¥5 to enter.

798 Art District
One of the very best freebies in town is spending a day perusing the numerous galleries of this art district (p134), inhabiting a former electronics factory.

Free Museums & Galleries
All you have to do to get into the following for free is bring your passport.

Capital Museum
The best museum (p117) in the city, with a host of galleries and exhibits relating to Běijīng's history.

Military Museum
Guns, planes, rockets and tanks at this museum (p157).

National Museum of China
At this excellent museum (p64), get a crash course on 5000 years of Chinese history.

Chinese Art Museum
Absorbing art exhibitions from across China at the National Art Museum (p71).

Shǐjiā Hútòng Museum
Tells the story of one of Běijīng's most historic *hútòng* neighbourhoods (p71).

Lu Xun Museum
The life and times (and former courtyard residence) of the father of modern Chinese literature, at the Lu Xun Museum (p118).

Free Sights

Tiān'ānmén Square
Stroll with the hordes of domestic visitors, catch the flag-raising and lowering ceremonies at dawn and dusk, and watch the kite flying in the world's largest public square (p62).

Chairman Mao Memorial Hall
It doesn't cost a thing to shuffle reverently past the Great Helmsman's mummified remains in this memorial hall (p64).

Foreign Legation Quarter
Enjoy a free walk past the imposing European architecture of the Former Foreign Legation Quarter (p72).

Ming City Wall Ruins Park
See the sole remaining section of the Ming dynasty city walls (p110) that once enclosed Běijīng.

Free Wednesdays
On Wednesdays, the first 200 visitors through the door get free entrance to Zhìhuà Temple (p69), Xiānnóng Altar (p126), Wǔtǎ Temple (p155) and Wànshòu Temple (p154). Due to low visitor numbers, in practice this means they are free all day.

Wángfǔjǐng Snack Street (p76)

Eating

Běijīng is a magnificent place for culinary adventures. With upwards of 60,000 restaurants here, you can enjoy the finest local dishes, as well as eating your way through every region of China. Some of your most memorable Běijīng experiences will take place around the dining table. So do as the locals do – grab those chopsticks and dive in.

Běijīng Dàdŏng Roast Duck Restaurant (p78)

NEED TO KNOW

Price Ranges

The following price ranges represent the cost of a meal for one person.

$ less than ¥40

$$ ¥40–100

$$$ more than ¥100

Opening Hours

Běijīng restaurants are mostly open from around 10am to 11pm, although there are quite a few that run 24/7. Many shut after lunch and reopen at 5pm. Generally, the Chinese eat much earlier than Westerners, lunching from 11am and having dinner at about 6pm.

Menus

Be warned that some restaurants in tourist areas still fob off foreigners with an English menu (英文菜单; *yīngwén càidān*) that has higher prices than the Chinese menu (中文菜单; *zhōngwén càidān*). Generally, though, most places have picture and/or English menus.

Service

With the exception of upmarket restaurants, service can often be erratic and/or lackadaisical. Unless you're in a restaurant serving foreign food, don't expect the waiting staff to speak English.

Smoking

There are nonsmoking signs in almost all Běijīng restaurants these days, but that doesn't mean they are adhered to. Smoking is still commonplace in some eateries.

Tipping

Tipping is not standard practice in Běijīng. Leave a tip in a local restaurant and the waiter will likely come after you saying you've forgotten your change. Some upmarket Western places, though, do tack on a service charge to the bill, as do high-end hotel restaurants.

Peking Duck

You'd have to be quackers to leave Běijīng without trying Peking duck (北京烤鸭; *Běijīng kǎoyā*), the capital's most iconic dish. Its origins go back as far as the 13th century and the Yuan dynasty, when it was listed in royal cookbooks. But it wasn't until imperial rule in China came to an end in 1911 that most ordinary people got the chance to try it, as the former palace cooks set up roast-duck restaurants around Běijīng.

Chefs go through a lengthy process to prepare the duck. First the birds are inflated by blowing air between the skin and body. The skin is then pricked and boiling water poured all over the duck. Sometimes the skin is rubbed with malt sugar to give it an amber colour, before being hung up to air-dry and then roasted in the oven. When roasted, the flesh becomes crispy on the outside and juicy on the inside. The bird is then meticulously cut into slices and served with fermented-bean paste, light pancakes, sliced cucumbers and green onions.

Vegetarians & Vegans

China has a 1000-year-plus tradition of Taoist and Buddhist philosophers who abstained from eating animals. But with an equally long history of poverty and famine in China, eating meat is a sign of status and many Chinese regard vegetarianism as a strange Western concept.

However, there are an increasing number of vegetarian (吃素的人; *chīsùderén*) eateries, while many Buddhist temples also have vegetarian restaurants. Nevertheless, vegetarian food consists often of 'mock-meat' dishes made from tofu, wheat gluten and vegetables. Some of the dishes are almost works of art, with the ingredients

Top: Yúnnán cuisine at Dàlǐ Courtyard (p96)
Left: Pork steamed dumplings

sculpted to look like spare ribs or fried chicken and 'bones' created from carrots and lotus roots.

Etiquette

Strict rules of etiquette don't really apply to Chinese dining, with the notable exception of formal banquets. Table manners are relaxed and get more so as the meal unfolds and the drinks flow. By the end, the table can resemble a battlefield, with empty bottles, stray bones and other debris strewn across it.

Many foreigners get asked if they mind dishes that are *là* (辣; spicy). If you don't want very spicy then say '*bú yào tài là*' (not too spicy). The Chinese believe that a mix of tastes, textures and temperatures is the key to a good meal, so they start with cold dishes and follow them with a selection of hot meat, fish and vegetable dishes. Waiters will expect you to order straightaway after sitting down and will hover at your shoulder until you do. If you want more time, say '*wǒ huì jiào nǐ*' ('I'll call you').

Rice often arrives at the end of the meal but if you want it before, just ask. The mainland Chinese dig their chopsticks into communal dishes, or spoons will be used to ladle out the food, but don't root around for a piece of food. Instead, identify it first and go directly to it without touching what's around it. Bones can be deposited in your side dish, or even on the table itself. If you're in doubt about what to do, just follow the example of the people around you.

CHOPSTICKS

Most people get to grips with chopsticks quickly out of necessity (it's either that or go on an involuntary crash diet), but don't feel embarrassed if you struggle at first; there's no shame in dropping a dumpling.

Until recently, only posh places handed out their own, reusable chopsticks, while cheap joints relied on disposable wooden ones. The disposable ones are more hygienic but with China producing close on 60 billion pairs of them a year, which is an awful lot of bamboo, they are not environmentally friendly. If you don't want to use them but are worried about cleanliness, consider carrying your own chopsticks.

Regional Cuisines

All of China's cuisines converge on Běijīng, from far-flung Tibet to the hardy northeast, the arid northwest and the fecund south.

The most popular cooking styles are from Sìchuān, Shànghǎi, Hong Kong, Guǎngdōng (Cantonese) and Běijīng itself. If you want to explore China's full compendium of cuisines, Běijīng is *the* place to start.

BĚIJĪNG

Běijīng's native cuisine (京菜; *jīngcài*) is classified as a 'northern cuisine' and is in one of the four major styles of cooking in China. Peking duck apart, many popular dishes, such as hotpot (火锅; *huǒguō*), have their origins in Mongolia and arrived in the wake of Genghis Khan. Běijīng's bitter winters mean that warm, filling dishes are essential. Typically, they are made with wheat or millet, whose most common incarnations are delicious dumplings (饺子; *jiǎozi*) or noodles, which are preferred to rice in the capital. Vegetables are more limited, so there is a heavy reliance on freshwater fish and chicken. Cabbage and turnips, as well as yams and potatoes, are some of the most ubiquitous vegetables found on menus.

Two of the region's most famous culinary exports – Mongolian barbecue and Mongolian hotpot – are adaptations from Mongol field kitchens. Animals that were hunted on horseback could be dismembered and cooked with wild vegetables and onions using soldiers' iron shields on top of hot coals as primitive barbecues. Alternatively, each soldier could use his helmet as a pot, filling it with water, meat, condiments and vegetables to taste. Mutton is now the main ingredient in Mongolian hotpot.

Roasting was once considered rather barbaric in other parts of China and is still more common in the northern areas. The main methods of cooking in the northern style, though, are steaming, baking and 'explode-frying' (爆炒; *bàochǎo*), a rapid method of cooking in which the wok is superheated over a flame and the contents tossed in for a swift stir-frying.

SÌCHUĀN

Famed as China's fieriest food, Sìchuān cuisine (川菜) should be approached with caution along with lots of chilled H2O or beer. A concoction of searing red chillis (introduced by Spanish traders in the early Qing dynasty), star anise, peppercorns and pungent 'flower pepper' (花椒; *huājiāo*), a numbing herb peculiar to this cuisine, Sìchuān dishes are simmered to allow the chilli peppers time to seep into the food. Meats are often marinated, pickled or otherwise processed

Eating by Neighbourhood

Summer Palace & Hǎidiàn
Korean and Japanese eateries in Wǔdàokǒu

Xiba River

Xīhǎi Lake

Drum & Bell Towers

Hòuhǎi Lake

Qiánhǎi Lake **Nanluogu Xiang**

Drum Tower & Dōngchéng North
Courtyard restaurants, vegetarian and hotpot on Ghost St

Liangma River

Běihǎi Park & Xīchéng North
Local and foreign places around Hòuhǎi Lakes

Běihǎi Park

Jǐngshān Park

Sānlǐtún & Cháoyáng
Largest selection of foreign and fusion restaurants

Yùyuāntán

Zhōnghǎi Lake

Forbidden City

Nánhǎi Lake

Forbidden City & Dōngchéng Central
Foreign places, dumpling joints and Sìchuān

Tiān'ānmén Square

Tonghui River

Dashilar & Xīchéng South
Lamb kebabs in the local Muslim Huí community

Temple of Heaven

Temple of Heaven Park & Dōngchéng South
Peking duck and Western food

---

before cooking, which is generally by stir- or explode-frying.

Landlocked Sìchuān is a long way from the coast, so pork, poultry, legumes and *dòufu* (豆腐; bean curd) are commonly used, and supplemented by a variety of wild condiments and mountain products, such as mushrooms and other fungi, as well as bamboo shoots. Seasonings are heavy: the red chilli is often used in conjunction with Sìchuān peppercorns, garlic, ginger and onions. Hallmark dishes include camphor-smoked duck (樟茶鸭; *zhāngchá yā*), Granny Ma's bean curd (麻婆豆腐; *Mápó dòufu*) and spicy chicken with peanuts (宫保鸡丁; *gōngbǎo jīdīng*).

CANTONESE

Cantonese cuisine (粤菜) is what non-Chinese consider to be 'Chinese' food, largely because most émigré restaurateurs originate from Guǎngdōng or nearby Hong Kong. Cantonese flavours are generally more subtle than other Chinese styles and there are very few spicy dishes. Sweet-and-sour and oyster sauces are common. The Cantonese are almost religious about the importance of fresh ingredients, which is why so many restaurants are lined with tanks full of finned and shelled creatures. Stir-frying is by far the favoured method of cooking, closely followed by steaming. Dim sum (点心; *diǎnxīn*), now a worldwide Sunday institution, originated in this region; to go *yum cha* (饮茶; Cantonese for 'drink tea') still provides most overseas Chinese communities with the opportunity to get together at the weekend. Dim sum can be found in restaurants around Běijīng.

Expensive dishes – some that are truly tasty, others that appeal more for their 'face' value – include abalone (鲍鱼; *bàoyú*), shark's fin (鱼翅; *yúchì*) and bird's nest (燕窝; *yànwō*). Very few Westerners, though, eat shark's fin soup, as preparing the dish involves cutting the fin off the shark and then throwing the shark back into the water for it to die a painful and lingering death. Pigeon (鸽子; *gēzi*) is a Cantonese speciality served in various ways but most commonly roasted.

SHÀNGHĂI

Generally sweeter and oilier than China's other cooking styles, Shànghǎi cuisine (上海菜) features plenty of fish and seafood, especially cod, river eel and shrimp. Fish is usually *qīngzhēng* (清蒸; steamed) but can be stir-fried, pan-fried or grilled. Crab-roe dumplings (蟹黄饺子; *xièhuáng jiǎozi*) are another Shanghainese luxury. *Dàzháxiè* (大闸蟹; hairy crabs) are a Shànghǎi speciality between October and December. They are eaten with soy, ginger and vinegar and downed with warm Shàoxīng rice wine. They are delicious but can be fiddly to eat. The body opens via a little tab on the underside (don't eat the gills or the stomach).

Several restaurants specialise in cold salty chicken, while drunken chicken gets its name from being marinated in Shàoxīng rice wine. *Bāo* (煲; clay pot) dishes are braised for a long time in their own casserole dish. Shànghǎi's most famous snack is *xiǎolóngbāo* (小笼包), small dumplings containing a meaty interior bathed in a scalding juice.

Vegetarian dishes include *dòufu mèn* (焖; braised cabbage in cream sauce); and various types of mushrooms, including *xiānggū báicài* (香菇白菜; mushrooms surrounded by baby bok choy). Tiger-skin chillies (虎皮尖椒; *hǔpí jiānjiāo*) are a delicious dish of stir-fried green peppers seared in a wok and served in a sweet chilli sauce. Fried pine nuts and sweet corn (松子炒玉米; *sōngzǐ chǎo yùmǐ*) is another common Shanghainese dish.

UIGHUR

Uighur cuisine (新疆菜) reflects Xīnjiāng's chequered past. Despite centuries of sporadic Chinese and Mongol rule, the strongest influence on ingredients and methods is still Turkic or Middle Eastern, which is evident in the reliance on mutton

for protein and wheat as the staple grain. When rice is eaten, it is often in the Central Asian version of pilau *(plov)*. Nevertheless, the infusion of Chinese culinary styles and ingredients makes Xīnjiāng probably the most enjoyable region of Central Asia in which to eat.

Uighur bread resembles Arabic *khoubz* (Indian naan) and is baked in ovens based on the *tanour* (Indian tandoor) model. It is often eaten straight from the oven and sprinkled with poppy seeds, sesame seeds or fennel. Uighur bakers also make excellent *girde nan* (bagels). Wheat is also used for a variety of noodles. *Laghman* (拌面; *bàn miàn*) are the most common: noodles cooked al dente, thick and topped with a combination of spicy mutton, peppers, tomatoes, eggplant, green beans and garlic. *Suoman* are noodle squares fried with tomatoes, peppers, garlic and meat, sometimes quite spicy. *Suoman goshsiz* is the vegetarian variety.

Kebabs, both shashlik (羊肉串; *yángròu chuàn*) and tandoori styles, are common, as they are throughout the Middle East and Central Asia. *Samsas* or *samsis* (烤包子; *kǎo bāozi*) are the Uighur version of samosas: baked envelopes of meat. Meat often makes an appearance inside *chuchura* (dumplings; 饺子汤; *jiǎozi tāng*), which can be steamed or fried.

MĂIDĀN!

The Chinese pride themselves on unwavering generosity in public and the arrival of the bill (买单; *mǎidān*) among a group of diners is an excuse for some elaborate histrionics. People push each other aside and almost fight for the right to pay, but generally it is the host who does and if he didn't he would lose face.

Splitting the bill is less common here than in the West, so if you invite someone out for dinner, be prepared to foot the bill. And remember that most places will expect you to settle it in hard cash; only top-end restaurants take credit cards.

Lonely Planet's Top Choices

Dàlǐ Courtyard (p96) Beautiful courtyard restaurant with an ever-changing menu of subtly flavoured Yúnnán specialities.

Běijīng Dàdǒng Roast Duck Restaurant (p78) The leanest duck in town in a busy and bright setting.

Nàjiā Xiǎoguǎn (p141) Old-school Běijīng place with an esoteric menu of Manchu favourites.

Duck de Chine (p142) Peking duck with a French flavour in a swish environment and with super service.

Bǎihé Vegetarian Restaurant (p94) Inventive dishes at one of Běijīng's few veggie eateries.

Best by Budget

$

Tàn Huā Lamb BBQ (p93) Roast your own leg of lamb at this *hútòng* hang-out.

Zhāng Māma (p90) Super-popular Sìchuān restaurant and excellent value.

Bocata (p139) Fine sandwiches and salads and fantastic chips at this popular lunch spot.

Bāozi Pù (p93) Come to this long-standing place for dumplings and noodles.

Yàn Lán Lóu (p138) Great hand-pulled noodles at this landmark Muslim restaurant.

$$

Jīn Dǐng Xuān (p95) Tasty dim sum and open 24 hours.

Xiǎo Wáng's Home Restaurant (p141) Běijīng institution with a China-wide menu.

Vineyard Café (p95) Family-friendly, expat fave. Great Western breakfasts.

Jīngzūn Peking Duck (p140) Not just duck but a huge variety of dishes.

$$$

Duck de Chine (p142) Stand-out Peking duck in an artfully designed space.

Temple Restaurant (p78) Fantastic setting, flawless food and service.

Lost Heaven (p76) Top-notch Yúnnán dishes in the delightful surroundings of the former legation quarter.

Capital M (p111) Relaxed but upmarket restaurant specialising in Mediterranean classics.

Best by Cuisine

Best Peking Duck

Lìqún Roast Duck Restaurant (p111) Ramshackle setting but serves a superb bird.

Biànyífāng (p112) Old-school Peking duck; sees fewer foreigners than other places.

Duck de Chine (p142) Fancy-pants Peking-meets-Paris duck.

Jīngzūn Peking Duck (p140) An unpretentious introduction to Běijīng's most famous dish.

Qiánmén Quánjùdé Roast Duck Restaurant (p112) Always crowded but the duck is top quality.

Best Dumplings

Din Tai Fung (p140) Famed Taiwanese restaurant and shrine to dumplings in all their forms.

Bǎoyuán Dumpling Restaurant (p139) Multicoloured dumplings that delight the kids.

Dōuyīchù (p111) Serving up seasonal favourites since the Qing dynasty.

Hángzhōu Xiǎochī (p76) Cheap eats close to the Forbidden City.

Gǒubùlǐ (p128) Eight different types to choose from and all delicious.

Best Hotpot

Yáng Fāng Lamb Hotpot (p92) Classic Běijīng-style hotpot.

Lǎo Chē Jì (p158) Dry hotpots are the house speciality.

Róng Tiān Sheep Spine (p84) Down-to-earth eatery but delicious food.

Mǎn Fú Lóu (p77) Mongolian-style non-spicy hotpot.

Best Regional

Crescent Moon Muslim Restaurant (p73) Arguably the finest Uighur eatery in Běijīng.

Jíxiángniǎo Xiāngcài (p139) Spicy Húnán cuisine and always busy.

Chuān Bàn (p74) Fire fiends love this authentic, tongue-numbing Sìchuān place.

In & Out (p137) The best of southwestern China's many great dishes are on offer here.

Golden Peacock (p157) Southeast Asian–influenced Dai cuisine from the deep south of Yúnnán Province.

Best Noodles

Yàn Lán Lóu (p138) Dishes from China's northwestern noodle heartland.

Liú Family Noodles (p126) Cheap and cheerful, but excellent noodles.

Old Běijīng Zhájiàng Noodle King (p111) Traditional noodles and a local hotspot.

Lǐjì Fēngwèi Měishí Cāntīng (p121) Great for Chinese Muslim-style beef noodles.

Punk Rock Noodles (p90) Delicious hand-pulled noodles served up by punk rock musicians.

Best Běijīng

Yáojì Chǎogān (p93) Come here for *zhájiàng miàn*, the capital's signature noodle dish.

Bàodǔ Huáng (p139) True local's joint for those brave enough to eat like a real Beijinger.

Zuǒ Lín Yòu Shè (p76) No frills, but real-deal Běijīng eats.

Hóng Lú (p140) Běijīng specialities in a fresh and clean environment.

Xiǎodiàolítāng (p157) Dishes inspired by the cuisine of the Mandarins of the Qing dynasty.

Best Foreign

Taco Bar (p140) Mexican street-style food and great for brunch too.

Mosto (p142) Justly popular and stylish Mediterranean-themed restaurant.

O'Steak (p142) Succulent steaks served French-style.

Georg (p95) Fine dining with a Scandinavian twist.

Best Asian

Purple'Isle (p141) Hip Thai restaurant that doesn't hold back on the spices.

Desert Rose (p141) The best kebabs in the city and a genuine Central Asian feel.

Café Sambal (p95) Cute and cool courtyard restaurant serving Malaysian favourites.

4corners (p120) Vietnamese and Southeast Asian fusion food in a *hútòng* setting.

Khan Baba (p157) Fine Pakistani and Indian food and a generous lunchtime buffet deal.

Best Places to Eat Like a Local

Tàn Huā Lamb BBQ (p93) Eat outside in an authentic *hútòng* surrounded by unrestrained diners.

Yáng Fāng Lamb Hotpot (p92) Down-to-earth hotpot and no English spoken.

Yáojì Chǎogān (p93) A top spot for *zhájiàng miàn*, Běijīng's favourite noodles.

Bāozi Pù (p93) No frills, but great dumplings and noodles.

Bàodǔ Huáng (p139) Intestines and tripe are the top picks and they're so good the locals queue up for them.

Best for Kids

Din Tai Fung (p77) They have a dedicated area for kids to play in.

Bǎoyuán Dumpling Restaurant (p139) Dumplings in different colours that intrigue children.

Xiǎo Wáng's Home Restaurant (p141) Family-friendly and a menu big enough to satisfy any kiddies' cravings.

Vineyard Café (p95) A favourite with local and expat families.

Drinking & Nightlife

It's amazing to contemplate, as you sip a martini in the latest hot spot or dance to a big-name European DJ, but until 30 years ago there weren't any bars or nightclubs, outside a few hotels, in Běijīng at all. Now, as more and more locals take to partying after dark, the capital is home to an increasing number of sophisticated nightspots.

Hútòng Bar-crawling

In the last few years, a whole host of bars have sprung up in the ancient heart of the city with former courtyard homes converted into some of the finest and liveliest drinking destinations in town. They range from bohemian joints to distinctly chic cocktail bars. Nanluogu Xiang lane led the way in making the *hútòng* (narrow alleyways) an integral part of the city's nightlife; now many *hútòng* across Dōngchéng North are almost as popular.

Drink Like a Local

Although wine and whisky are gaining ground among the middle classes, the two most popular alcoholic drinks in Běijīng remain *píjiǔ* (beer) and *báijiǔ*, a pungent, potent white spirit with a unique taste that few foreigners can stomach. The commonest brews are Yanjing Beer (the local favourite), Běijīng Beer and Tsingtao. None are very distinguished, and all are weaker than most foreign beers. You can pick up a large bottle of Yanjing or Tsingtao, the closest to a European-style lager, for around ¥4 on the streets; Běijīng Beer is usually served on tap.

Běijīng Clubland

Most of the capital's nightclubs are as much places for drinking as they are for dancing so, despite the increasing numbers of international DJs who fly in, many local punters aren't too interested in what is on the turntables. Much of what you hear will be mainstream house and hip-hop. But a few local DJs do their best to promote more eclectic sounds and stage parties in various venues around town. Check the local listings magazines for details.

Karaoke

Karaoke is the number-one leisure pastime in China and there are well over 100,000 karaoke, or KTV, joints across the country. As alien as it can seem to be singing along to a TV in front of people, karaoke is one of the best ways of getting to know the locals.

If you speak Mandarin, you can sing along to the latest Mando-pop hits. English speakers will have to content themselves with a smaller and older selection of tunes, but you'll always find something you can sing. Prices depend on the size of the room you want and the time of day. It's always advisable to book ahead at weekends.

Drinking & Nightlife by Neighbourhood

⇒ **Drum Tower & Dōngchéng North (p97)** *Hútòng* bars and cafes on and off Gulou Dongdajie.

⇒ **Běihǎi Park & Xīchéng North (p122)** The shores of the Hòuhǎi Lakes are awash with bars.

⇒ **Sānlǐtún & Cháoyáng (p142)** Clubbing central and also home to upmarket cocktail bars.

⇒ **Summer Palace & Hǎidiàn (p159)** The Wǔdàokǒu district of Hǎidiàn is Běijīng's student heartland and buzzes come nightfall.

Lonely Planet's Top Choices

Distillery (p97) Hidden-away gem of a *hútòng* bar.

Lantern (p144) The best DJs in town and an authentic, sweaty underground vibe.

Janes + Hooch (p144) Wildly popular with both locals and Westerners.

Jing A Brewing (p143) Home base of Běijīng's finest brewers.

Best Hútòng Bars

El Nido (p99) Brilliant in the summer, when you can drink outside.

Ball House (p99) One of the most unique drinking spaces in Běijīng.

Great Leap Brewing (p97) Craft beers in a courtyard setting.

Capital Spirits (p97) *Báijiǔ*-based drinks for those in the know.

Distillery (p97) Speakeasy-style bar that makes its own hooch.

Best Cocktail Bars

Tiki Bungalow (p97) Polynesian-style bar with vintage cocktail recipes.

Parlor (p143) A 1920s Shànghǎi speakeasy-style bar, deliberately tucked away.

Revolution (p144) Mao-themed cubbyhole of a bar with knowledgeable bartenders.

Janes & Hooch (p144) Hip hang-out for cashed-up locals and expats.

Best for Craft Beers

Great Leap Brewing (p143) Běijīng's original brew masters.

Slow Boat Brewery Taproom (p78) A dozen draft beers available.

NBeer Pub (p122) Big range of imported beers and there are local ones on tap.

Arrow Factory Brewing (p143) Stellar selection of IPAs and pale ales.

Panda Brew (p98) Produces a dozen beers on-site.

Best Neighbourhood Bars

Tree (p146) Great range of foreign brews and excellent pizzas too.

Paddy O'Shea's (p145) The best spot to catch live sport in the capital.

Anchor (p144) Pint-sized, traditional English pub.

The Local (p143) The name says it all: craft beers, great food and live sport.

Best Cafes

Await Cafe (p122) Heavenly coffee and cakes in a superb space.

Alley Coffee (p80) Courtyard cafe that's ideal for a Forbidden City coffee break.

Bridge Café (p157) A 24-hour hang-out with decent drinks and food, and friendly staff.

Voyage Coffee (p98) Trendy roaster in the heart of *hútòng*-land.

Oasis Cafe (p78) One of the city's top spots for coffee and traditional Běijīng food.

Best Clubs

Spark (p144) True hot spot and rammed at the weekend.

NEED TO KNOW

Opening Hours

Most bars in Běijīng open in the late afternoon and close at 2am. But many stay open longer, especially on weekends, while others shut up shop around midnight. Cafes open much earlier and sometimes close early, too. Clubs can go all night, depending on their mood.

Prices

The cost of drinking in Běijīng's bars depends very much on your personal tastes. If you want to gargle with a Guinness, you'll pay more (¥40 to ¥50) than if you drink a bottle of Tsingtao (¥20 to ¥25). Mixed drinks start at around ¥35 in most bars, but in a swanky place expect to pay Western prices, ¥60 and up, for a proper cocktail. Many bars, though, have happy hours (usually 5pm to 8pm) when you can imbibe more cheaply.

Lantern (p144) Genuine underground club vibe and top DJs.

Destination (p145) Běijīng's only real gay club.

Mix (p144) Mainstream hip-hop for a younger crowd.

Chocolate (p146) Gloriously over-the-top Russian-style nightclub that gets going after midnight.

Entertainment

Běijīng is the cultural capital of China and by far the best place to be if you're interested in seeing anything from ballet and contemporary dance, to jazz or punk bands. Then there are the traditional local pastimes such as Peking opera (jīngjù) and acrobatic shows, as well as movies, theatre and Běijīng's various sports teams.

Acrobatics & Běijīng Opera

Two thousand years old, Chinese acrobatics (杂技; *zájì*) is one of the best shows in town and there are daily performances at a number of different theatres. Look out too for the legendary, shaven-headed Shàolín monks, who pass through the capital regularly to put on displays of their fearsome fighting skills.

Far more sedate, but equally intriguing, is Peking opera, also known as Běijīng opera. It might seem impenetrable to foreigners, its mystique reinforced by the costumes, singing style and, of course, the language, but live performances are actually relatively easy to follow. Plot lines are simple (rather like Shakespearean tragedy, including the low comic relief) and the shows are a more interactive experience than you might imagine.

Live Music

While there might be an instinctive Chinese fondness for K-pop and Taiwanese boy bands, Beijingers have always been at the forefront of the more soulful end of the Chinese music scene. Now, you can find all sorts of bands – indie, alternative, punk, metal, folk and jazz – lifting roofs every night of the week in venues that range from Qing dynasty courtyards, to open-air cinemas. Come summer and Běijīng hosts the odd open-air festival too. Sadly, though, the capital remains a backwater for international rock and pop acts, very few of whom make it out here.

Spectator Sports

The Chinese are avid football (*zúqiú*) fans, with many supporting the top teams in England, Italy and Spain. Now, the China Super League is emerging as a force of its own in Asia, with increasing numbers of foreign players arriving to lift standards. The local heroes are the Běijīng Guo'an, who play their home games at the Workers Stadium in front of some of China's most vocal fans.

Even more popular than football is basketball. A number of Chinese players have followed in the footsteps of national icon Yao Ming to play in the NBA. The capital's team is the Běijīng Ducks, Chinese champions for three of the last five years. They draw a big crowd at the 18,000-seat Wǔkēsōng Arena in Hǎidiàn.

Entertainment by Neighbourhood

➡ **Forbidden City & Dōngchéng Central (p80)** Prime district for culture vultures, with classical music, opera and theatre venues.

➡ **Drum Tower & Dōngchéng North (p100)** Home to many of the best live-music venues in town.

➡ **Běihǎi Park & Xīchéng North (p123)** Key cultural hub thanks to the impressive National Centre for the Performing Arts.

➡ **Dashilar & Xīchéng South (p129)** The Húguǎng Guild Hall is the most atmospheric Peking-opera venue of them all.

➡ **Sānlǐtún & Cháoyáng (p146)** Acrobatics shows galore and movie multiplexes.

Lonely Planet's Top Choices

Yúgōng Yíshān (p100) Great space and super booking policy make this the number-one spot for live music.

National Centre for the Performing Arts (p80) Extraordinary building that is now Běijīng's cultural centre.

Tiānqiáo Acrobatics Theatre (p129) The most agile and graceful acrobats in town.

Húguǎng Guild Hall (p129) Beautiful and historic venue to watch Peking opera in.

School Bar (p100) Hang with the hipsters, indie kids and punks on one of the capital's most happening *hútòng*.

Best for Classical Music & Dance

Forbidden City Concert Hall (p80) Superb acoustics and a romantic ambience.

Poly Plaza International Theatre (p146) Ambitious venue that stages both Chinese and Western plays, ballet, opera and folk music.

National Library Arts Centre (p159) A top spot for Chinese classical dance.

Best for Folk & Jazz

East Shore Jazz Café (p123) The most amenable place in town to catch local and foreign jazzers.

Jiāng Hú (p100) Lovely, intimate courtyard setting to hear Chinese bands.

Modernista (p98) Hipster hangout with live jazz and swing dancing.

Best for Alternative, Punk & Metal

School Bar (p100) Grungy but hip venue that attracts the best of Běijīng's indie and punk bands.

Temple Bar (p100) Local and foreign bands of all varieties at this raucous spot.

What? Bar (p80) Pint-sized club that's good for catching up-and-coming acts.

13 Club (p159) Metal fans flock to this suitably grimy place.

Hot Cat Club (p100) Everything from electronica to guitar-slinging local heroes.

Best for Běijīng Opera

Cháng'ān Grand Theatre (p80) *The* place for true Peking opera aficionados.

Húguǎng Guild Hall (p129) This magnificent, historic venue is the most atmospheric in all Běijīng.

Mei Lanfang Grand Theatre (p123) Traditional performances in a modern setting.

Líyuán Theatre (p130) A good place for your first Peking-opera experience.

Lao She Teahouse (p129) Peking opera, but also shadow plays and traditional folk music.

Best for Acrobatics & Plays

Cháoyáng Theatre (p146) Touristy but the show is consistently impressive.

Red Theatre (p112) Nonstop kung-fu fighting as a boy learns how to be a warrior monk.

China Puppet Theatre (p101) Shadow plays and puppets; very family-friendly.

Shopping

Whether you're a diehard shopaholic or a casual browser, you'll be spoiled for choice in Běijīng. Join the locals in their favourite pastime at any number of shiny shopping malls, markets and specialist shopping streets. Then there are the pavement vendors and itinerant hawkers. All ensure that keeping your cash in your pocket is increasingly difficult.

Arts, Crafts & Antiques

Běijīng is a great place to pick up curios such as embroidered purses, paper cuttings, wooden and bronze Buddhas, paper lanterns, Chinese musical instruments and kites. Carpets, jade and pearls of varying quality can be found in abundance too.

Remember it's not just DVDs and clothes that are pirated in China: antiques, ceramics and carpets get the facsimile treatment too, so be wary before paying for that supposed Ming dynasty vase. Be aware, too, that technically items dating from before 1795 cannot be exported from China.

Clothing

Sīchóu (silk) is an important commodity in Běijīng and excellent prices for both silk fabrics and clothing can be found. If you have the time, there are excellent tailors who will turn your silk into made-to-measure clothing, such as traditional Chinese gowns (*qípáo*, or *cheongsam* in Cantonese). *Yángróngshān* (cashmere) from Inner Mongolia is also a good buy in Běijīng.

Contemporary Art

With Chinese contemporary art still in demand from collectors around the world, artwork can be a great investment. If you're here in June, the annual SURGE Art Fair is a fine place to find reasonably priced work. Otherwise, visit reputable galleries such as Red Gate Gallery. Realistically, you'll need to spend at least $1000 for a piece from an up-and-coming artist that is likely to increase in value.

Tea

You can pick up any of China's huge variety of teas in Běijīng, as well as the tea sets you'll need to sample them in the proper local fashion. Prices range dramatically, depending on the type of tea, or the design of the tea set. But no matter your budget, you'll be able to find a brew to sip long after you've returned home.

Shopping by Neighbourhood

⇒ **Forbidden City & Dōngchéng Central (p81)** Wangfujing Dajie is Běijīng's premier shopping street.

⇒ **Drum Tower & Dōngchéng North (p101)** Trendy and offbeat boutiques abound in this area.

⇒ **Temple of Heaven Park & Dōngchéng South (p112)** Come here for Hóngqiáo Market and its oceans of pearls, as well as the refurbished Qiánmén shopping street.

⇒ **Dashilar & Xīchéng South (p130)** Some of the city's oldest emporiums, and the antiques, arts and crafts hub of Liúlichǎng.

⇒ **Sānlǐtún & Cháoyáng (p146)** Malls galore and home to most of Běijīng's finest markets.

Lonely Planet's Top Choices

Shard Box Store (p147) Utterly unique exquisite shard boxes in all sizes.

Ruìfúxiáng (p130) Purveyors of all kinds of silk in every conceivable pattern.

Plastered 8 (p101) Ironic T-shirts with Běijīng-centric themes.

Pottery Workshop (p101) Beautiful, handmade ceramics from a collective of young artists.

Best for Art

798 Art District (p134) Galleries galore in Běijīng's art-world centre.

Red Gate Gallery (p109) The first contemporary-art gallery in the capital.

Róngbǎozhāi (p131) Traditional scroll and ink paintings, as well as inks, brushes and paper.

UCCA Design Store (p147) Prints and paintings from some of China's best-known artists.

Best for Clothes

Silk Market (p148) The silk is one of the few genuine items on sale at this Běijīng institution.

Sānlǐtún Village (p147) Eye-catching mall with both midrange and high-end brands.

3.3 Shopping Centre (p148) Trendy boutiques and accessories for the style-conscious.

Sanlipop (p147) Hipster boutique with hard-to-find brands.

Best for Tea

Mǎliándào Tea Market (p131) All the tea in China and cheap tea sets nearby too.

Famous Tea of China (p101) Tiny but friendly emporium where the tea comes in pre-wrapped parcels.

Ten Fu's Tea Culture House (p72) A museum showcasing Chinese tea and a good place to buy it too.

Slow Lane (p81) Elegant, handmade teaware and quality tea.

Best Buys

Shard Box Store (p147) Porcelain fragments from antique vases reshaped into boxes and jewellery.

Jīngchéng Bǎixìng (p102) Traditional clay figurines, and you can mould and paint your own one too.

Plastered 8 (p101) Fun and stylish Běijīng-themed T-shirts.

Three Stone Kite Shop (p123) Beautiful hand-painted kites.

Xián Yàn Tāng (p130) Traditional shadow puppets, framed or ready for play.

Best Markets

Pānjiāyuán Market (p147) By far the best place in town for arts, crafts and antiques.

Mǎliándào Tea Market (p131) A great place to wander for anyone interested in China's favourite drink.

Hóngqiáo (Pearl) Market (p112) Famed for its pearls, but good for clothes and bags too.

Centergate Como (p159) Come here for computers, software and phones.

Best Shopping Streets

Wangfujing Dajie (p81) The capital's most prestigious shopping street.

NEED TO KNOW

Opening Hours

Most shops in Běijīng open earlier than in the West and close later; they usually open between 8am and 8.30am and shut between 9pm and 10pm. Open-air markets generally run from dawn to around sunset, but might open later and close earlier.

Bargaining

Always remember that foreigners are likely to be quoted an inflated price in Běijīng. Prices in malls are fixed, but haggling is standard practice in markets. It's always best to bargain with a smile on your face. Remember, the point of the process is to achieve a mutually acceptable price, not to screw the vendor into the ground.

Paying

Most large department stores take Western credit cards, but many smaller ones only accept Chinese ones. Markets deal in cash only.

Liulichang Xijie (p130) Antiques, calligraphy and Chinese-ink and scroll paintings.

Dashilar (p126) Home to some of the capital's oldest stores.

Nanluogu Xiang (p102) Crazy at weekends, but fine for souvenir hunting.

Qianmen Dajie (p111) Increasingly busy, refurbished street with midrange brands and some silk.

Yandai Xiejie (p123) Souvenirs and fake antiques, as well as a few more quirky outlets, but fun browsing.

48

Explore Běijīng

BĚIJĪNG'S
TOP SIGHTS

*Sculpture of soldiers fighting, located at
the entrance of the Mausoleum of Mao
Zedong, Tiān'ānmén Square (p62)*

Neighbourhoods at a Glance

① Forbidden City & Dōngchéng Central p52

This historic neighbourhood is the very heart of Běijīng. Packed with essential sights, and some fabulous accommodation options, it is the area where you'll likely be spending much of your time. Imperial palaces, temples, socialist-realist architecture, parks and museums jostle for space here, but it's also where you'll find the capital's most famous shopping street, Wangfujing Dajie.

② Drum Tower & Dōngchéng North p83

The *hútòng* (narrow alleyways) in this part of town are the most numerous and best pre-

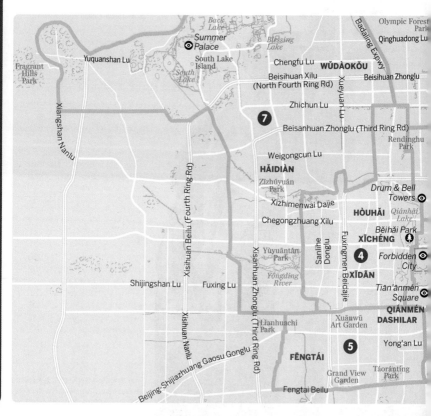

served and offer a fantastic insight into local life. Many, like Wudaoying Hutong, are also home to an ever-increasing number of hip bars and restaurants. With some lovely courtyard hotels to stay in and key sights scattered around too, it's the most visitor-friendly neighbourhood in all Běijīng and makes a great base.

❸ Temple of Heaven Park & Dōngchéng South p104

The neighbourhood of Dōngchéng South (东城南) is dominated by the magnificent Temple of Heaven Park, but it's also a place where ordinary Beijingers have long resided. Now, it's also home to some of the finest Peking-duck restaurants in the capital, as well as posh Western dining options, and the restored shopping street of Qianmen Dajie.

❹ Běihǎi Park & Xīchéng North p113

Northwest of the Forbidden City, Běihǎi Park and the adjacent Hòuhǎi Lakes act as one big playground for Beijingers. During the day, they are a great spot to kick back, while at night, locals carouse at the bars and restaurants that surround them. Also a temple- and *hútòng*-rich neighbourhood, Xīchéng North has some fun accommodation hidden away in its alleyways. It's also where you'll find the Capital Museum, one of Běijīng's finest.

❺ Dashilar & Xīchéng South p124

With the historic shopping street of Dashilar providing a focus, and the many hostels in the nearby *hútòng* making it Běijīng's backpacker central, this neighbourhood southwest of Tiān'ānmén Sq is handy for the major sights and has plenty of character. Formerly known as Xuanwu district, it's also home to the best acrobatics and opera shows in town.

❻ Sānlǐtún & Cháoyáng p132

Big and brash and a key nightlife zone, with many of the most popular bars, clubs and restaurants clustered in the Sānlǐtún area. While Cháoyáng lacks the history of other districts, most of the city's top-end hotels and shops are also located here. Further out, the 798 Art District is the centre of the Chinese contemporary art scene.

❼ Summer Palace & Hǎidiàn p150

As well as museums and parks, Hǎidiàn (海淀) is home to many of Běijīng's universities. The buzzing student district of Wǔdàokǒu makes for a fine contrast with the regal Summer Palace, or the tranquil, rural delights of the Fragrant Hills, which occupy Hǎidiàn's northwestern edge.

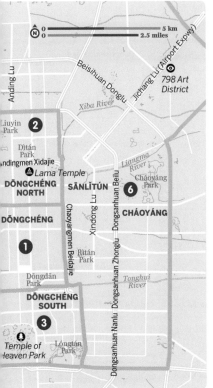

Forbidden City & Dōngchéng Central

Neighbourhood Top Five

1 **Forbidden City** (p54) Marvel at the might, splendour and sheer scale of the world's largest palace complex and the place 24 consecutive emperors of China called home.

2 **Tiān'ānmén Square** (p62) Place yourself at the symbolic heart of the Chi-

nese universe with a visit to this quintessential Běijīng sight.

3 **National Centre for the Performing Arts** (p69) Enjoy a show or just stare open-mouthed at the sci-fi architecture itself.

4 **Jǐngshān Park** (p68) Rise early to get the most

out of this area's wonderful imperial parks.

5 **National Museum of China** (p64) Peruse the galleries of the city's best museum with exquisite ceramics, calligraphy and artefacts.

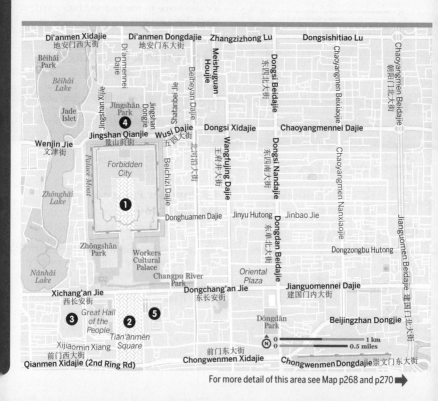

For more detail of this area see Map p268 and p270 ➡

Explore Forbidden City & Dōngchéng Central

The most historically significant part of Běijīng, Dōngchéng Central comprises much of what was once the Imperial City, at the heart of which lay the Forbidden City, from where emperors ruled China for more than 500 years.

The *hútòng* (narrow alleyways) fanning out to the north and east of the Forbidden City were where the members of the imperial court once lived, and are fascinating places to explore on foot or by bicycle. You can even base yourself here by settling in to one of this area's charming courtyard hotels.

You'll need at least a couple of days to visit all the best sights in this history-rich neighbourhood; figure on half a day for the Forbidden City alone.

Food options are strong, with cuisine from across China well represented, as well as street markets and some of the capital's more unusual fine-dining establishments. Nightlife is relatively thin on the ground, though.

Local Life

➡ **Food** Tuck into authentic Běijīng grub at Zuǒ Lín Yòu Shè (p76) or Yuèbīn Fànguǎn (p74). The street-food markets near Wángfǔjǐng (p76) may be fun, but locals find them touristy and overpriced. Enjoy your barbecued skewers from a hole-in-the-wall *hútòng* joint instead; spot the red neon 串 sign, and you're good to go.

➡ **Parks** Jǐngshān Park (p68) and Zhōngshān Park (p70) are two of Běijīng's most colourful – and locals, particularly the elderly, love to spend their mornings in them; dancing, singing and exercising with their friends. April and May are particularly popular as both parks burst into bloom during their annual flower fairs.

➡ **Formation Dancing** Join the legions of fitness-conscious, middle-aged women who meet at public squares (although not Tiān'ānmén) early evening, for a spot of line dancing. St Joseph's Church square (p72) is popular.

Getting There & Away

➡ **Subway** Tian'anmen West, Tian'anmen East, Wangfujing and Denghshikou are all useful subway stations. Once the extension of Line 8 is complete, it will run south to the Chinese Museum of Art.

➡ **Bus** The very handy buses 专1 and 专2 do clockwise circuits of the Forbidden City, looping south to Qiánmén, via Tiān'ānmén Sq. Bus 5 runs between Déshèngmén Gateway and Qiánmén, passing the Drum Tower, Jǐngshān Park, the Forbidden City and Tiān'ānmén Sq. The **airport bus** (机场大巴; Jīchǎng Dàbā; Map p270; ☎010 6457 3891; Jinbao Jie; ⏰9am-9pm; [S]Line 5 to Dengshikou, exit C) departs from the Regent Hotel to all terminals of Capital Airport (¥24, every 30 minutes).

Lonely Planet's Top Tip

Be very wary of rickshaw riders outside the north gate of the Forbidden City; they regularly trick tourists into paying over the odds (a common scam is saying 'three'. You think they mean 3 yuán. Later, they say they meant 300!). As a rough indicator, you shouldn't be paying much more than ¥20 per rickshaw to get from here to the Drum Tower or the Hòuhǎi Lakes.

🍴 Best Places to Eat

➡ Little Yúnnán (p76)
➡ Crescent Moon Muslim Restaurant (p73)
➡ Zuǒ Lín Yòu Shè (p76)
➡ Temple Restaurant Bites (p77)
➡ Běijīng Dàdǒng Roast Duck Restaurant (p78)

For reviews, see p73.➡

🍷 Best Places to Drink

➡ Slow Boat Brewery Taproom (p78)
➡ Oasis Cafe (p78)
➡ Láijīnyǔxuān Teahouse (p78)
➡ What? Bar (p80)

For reviews, see p78.➡

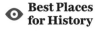

👁 Best Places for History

➡ Forbidden City (p54)
➡ National Museum of China (p64)
➡ Front Gate (Qiánmén) (p70)
➡ Gate of Heavenly Peace (p68)
➡ Workers Cultural Palace (p64)

For reviews, see p54.➡

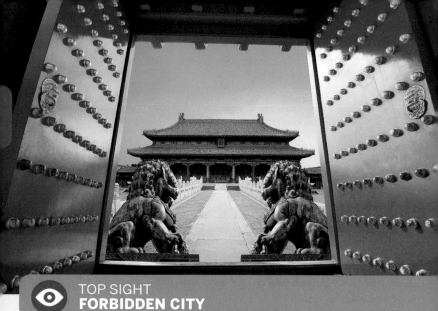

TOP SIGHT
FORBIDDEN CITY

Home to 24 Chinese emperors and more than 500 years, the astonishing Forbidden City (known as Gù Gōng; 故宫; ancient palace) is the largest palace complex in the world and a must-see sight for most visitors to Běijīng.

Located at the geographical centre of China's capital, the palace occupies a primary position in the Chinese psyche. To communists, it's a contradictory symbol: a politically incorrect yarn from a pre-Revolutionary dark age, but also one spun from the very pinnacle of Chinese civilisation. Violent forces during the Cultural Revolution wanted to ruin the place. But Premier Zhou Enlai, perhaps hearing the distant tinkle of the tourist dollar, stepped in to calm down the Red Guards.

Although you can explore the Forbidden City in a few hours, a full day will keep you occupied and the enthusiast will make several trips. A significant part of the complex is closed to the public, but a massive chunk remains, focusing mainly on the hugely impressive ceremonial halls, which line the central axis. Marvel at these by all means, but don't miss the delightful courtyards, pavilions and mini-museums within them on each side of the central axis. This is where the emperors actually lived, and it's fun to explore the passageways and courtyards that link them.

History

Constructed on the site of a palace dating to Kublai Khan and the Mongol Yuan dynasty, the Ming emperor Yongle established the basic layout of the Forbidden City between 1406 and 1420, basing it on the now-ruined Ming dynasty palace in Nánjīng. The grandiose emperor employed battalions of labourers and craftspeople – by some estimates there may have been up to a million of them – to build the Forbidden City. The palace once lay at the heart of

DON'T MISS

→ Clock Exhibition Hall
→ Ceramics Gallery
→ Belvedere of Pleasant Sounds
→ Eastern Palaces

PRACTICALITIES

→ 紫禁城; Zǐjìn Chéng
→ Map p268, B2
→ ☑ 010 8500 7114
→ www.dpm.org.cn
→ Nov-Mar ¥40, Apr-Oct ¥60, Clock Exhibition Hall ¥10, Hall of Jewellery ¥10, audio guide ¥40
→ ⊙ 8.30am-5pm Apr-Oct, to 4.30pm Nov-Mar, last entry 1hr prior to closing, closed Mon
→ S Line 1 to Tian'anmen West or Tian'anmen East

the Imperial City, a much larger, now-vanished walled enclosure reserved for the use of the emperor and his personnel. The wall enclosing the Forbidden City – assembled from 12 million bricks – is the last intact surviving city wall in Běijīng.

This gargantuan palace complex – China's largest and best-preserved cluster of ancient buildings – sheltered two complete dynasties of emperors (the Ming and the Qing), who didn't stray from their pleasure dome unless they absolutely had to. So highly rarefied was the atmosphere that nourished its elitist community, it was as if a bell jar had been dropped over the whole spectacle. A stultifying code of rules, protocol and superstition deepened its otherworldliness, perhaps typified by its twittering band of eunuchs. From here, the emperors governed China, often erratically and haphazardly, with authority occasionally drifting into the hands of opportunistic court officials and eunuchs. It wasn't until 1911 that revolution eventually came knocking at the huge doors, bringing with it the last orders for the Manchu Qing and dynastic rule.

Its mystique diffused (the Běijīng authorities prosaically call the complex the Palace Museum, or *gùgōng bówùguǎn;* 故宫博物馆), the palace is no longer off limits. In former ages, the price for uninvited admission would have been instant death; these days ¥40 to ¥60 will do.

Most of the buildings you see now are post-18th century. The largely wooden palace was a tinderbox and fire was a constant hazard – a lantern festival combined with a sudden gust of Gobi wind would easily send flames dancing in unexpected directions, as would a fireworks display. Fires were also deliberately lit by court eunuchs and officials who could get rich off the repair bills. It wasn't just buildings that burned, but also rare books, paintings and calligraphy. Libraries and other palace halls and buildings housing combustible contents were tiled in black; the colour represents water in the *wǔxíng* (five-element) theory, and its symbolic presence was thought to prevent conflagrations. Originally water was provided by 72 wells in the palace (only 30 have been preserved), while a complex system took care of drainage.

In the 20th century, there were two major lootings of the palace by Japanese forces and the Kuomintang (KMT; Chiang Kaishek's Nationalist Party, the dominant political force after the fall of the Qing dynasty). Thousands of crates of relics were removed and carted off to Taiwan, where they remain on display in Taipei's National Palace Museum (worth seeing). Some say this was just as well, since the Cultural Revolution reduced much of China's precious artwork to confetti.

Layout

Ringed by a picturesque 52m-wide moat that freezes over in winter, the rectangular palace is laid out

ENTRANCE

Tourists can only enter the Forbidden City via the south gate, known as **Meridian Gate**. It's a massive U-shaped portal that in former times was reserved for the use of the emperor. Gongs and bells would sound imperial comings and goings, while lesser mortals used lesser gates: the military used the west gate, civilians the east gate. The emperor also reviewed his armies from here, passed judgement on prisoners, announced the new year's calendar and oversaw the flogging of troublesome ministers.

Note that although tourists can only enter via Meridian Gate (the south gate), they are allowed to exit the Forbidden City via the south, north or east gates. There are places to lock bicycles by the south and northeast gates of nearby Zhōngshān Park.

CLOSED MONDAYS

The Forbidden City is usually closed on Mondays, apart from July and August when it's open every day.

roughly symmetrically on a north–south axis, bisected by a line of grand gates and ceremonial halls that straddle the very axis that cleaves Běijīng in two. The palace is so unspeakably big (more than 1 million sq metres, with 800 buildings and 9000 rooms) that restoration is a never-ending work in progress, and despite the attentions of restorers, some of the hall rooftops still sprout tufts of grass. Many halls have been repainted in a way that conceals the original pigment; other halls, such as the **Hall of Mental Cultivation** (养心殿; Yǎng Xīn Diàn; Map p268), however, possess a more threadbare and faded authenticity.

Entering the Complex

After passing through **Meridian Gate** (午门; Wǔ Mén; Map p268) – the only one of the four gateways now used as an entrance to the Forbidden City – you enter an enormous courtyard. Up top is the **Meridian Gate Gallery**, which hosts temporary cultural exhibitions of traditional Chinese arts and collections from abroad.

From here, you cross the Golden Stream (金水; Jīn Shuǐ) – shaped to resemble a Tartar bow and spanned by five marble bridges – on your way to the magnificent **Gate of Supreme Harmony** (太和门; Tàihé Mén; Map p268). This courtyard could hold an imperial audience of 100,000 people. Today it holds a tourist information desk where you can pick up a handy free map, and audio guide (¥40).

First Side Galleries

Before you pass through the Gate of Supreme Harmony to reach the Forbidden City's star attractions, veer off to the east of the huge courtyard to visit the exceptional **Ceramics Gallery**, housed inside the **Hall of Literary Brilliance** (文化殿; Wén Huà Diàn; Map p268), with more than 400 exquisite ceramic pieces displayed chronologically, dating from 6000 BC. To the west is the **Calligraphy and Painting Gallery** inside the **Hall of Martial Valor** (武英殿; Wǔ Yīng Diàn; Map p268).

Three Great Halls

Raised on a three-tier marble terrace with balustrades are the **Three Great Halls** (三大殿; Sān Dàdiàn), the glorious heart of the Forbidden City. The recently restored **Hall of Supreme Harmony** (太和殿; Tàihé Diàn; Map p268) is the most important and largest structure in the Forbidden City. Built in the 15th century and restored in the 17th century, it was used for ceremonial occasions, such as the emperor's birthday, coronations and the nomination of military leaders. Inside the Hall of Supreme Harmony is a richly decorated **Dragon Throne** (龙椅; Lóngyǐ), from which the emperor would preside over trembling officials. The entire court had to touch the floor nine times with their foreheads (the custom known as kowtowing) in the emperor's presence. At the back of the throne is a carved Xumishan, the Buddhist paradise, signifying the throne's supremacy. Today you can only view it from the outside, and it virtually involves a rugby scrum to view it.

Behind the Hall of Supreme Harmony is the **Hall of Central Harmony** (中和殿; Zhōnghé Diàn; Map p268), which was used as the emperor's transit lounge. Here he would make last-minute preparations, rehearse speeches and receive ministers. On display are two Qing dynasty sedan chairs, the emperor's mode of transport around the Forbidden City. The last of the Qing emperors, Puyi, used a bicycle and altered some features of the palace grounds to make it easier to get around.

The third of the Great Halls is the **Hall of Preserving Harmony** (保和殿; Bǎohé Diàn; Map p268), used for banquets and later for imperial examinations. The hall has no support pillars, and to its rear is a 250-tonne marble imperial carriageway carved with dragons and clouds, which was transported into Běijīng on an ice path. The outer housing surrounding the Three Great Halls was used for storing gold, silver, silks, carpets and other treasures.

Palace of Heavenly Purity

A string of side halls on the eastern and western flanks of the Three Great Halls usually, but not always, houses a series of excellent exhibitions.

Other Central Halls

The basic configuration of the Three Great Halls is echoed by the next group of buildings, which is accessed through **Gate of Heavenly Purity** (Map p268). Smaller in scale, these buildings were more important in terms of real power, which in China traditionally lies at the back door or, in this case, the back gate.

The first structure is the **Palace of Heavenly Purity** (乾清宫; Qiánqīng Gōng; Map p268), a residence of Ming and early Qing emperors, and later an audience hall for receiving foreign envoys and high officials.

Immediately behind it is the **Hall of Union** (交泰殿; Jiāotài Diàn; Map p268), which contains a clepsydra – a water clock made in 1745 with five bronze vessels and a calibrated scale. There's also a mechanical clock built in 1797 and a collection of imperial jade seals on display. The **Palace of Earthly Tranquillity** (坤宁宫; Kūnníng Gōng; Map p268) was the imperial couple's bridal chamber and the centre of operations for the palace harem.

Imperial Garden

At the northern end of the Forbidden City is the **Imperial Garden** (御花园; Yù Huāyuán; Map p268), a classical Chinese garden with 7000 sq metres of fine

TOP TIPS

➡ In 2015, the palace introduced a cap of 80,000 visitors per day, so aim to get here early during peak season.

➡ Official guides can be booked at an office just outside the entrance, costing between ¥200 and ¥400 (for up to five people), depending on what level of detail you're after. Otherwise pick up an audio guide for ¥40.

➡ Don't confuse the Gate of Heavenly Peace with the Forbidden City entrance. Some visitors purchase a Gate of Heavenly Peace admission ticket by mistake, not realising that this admits you only to the upstairs portion of that gateway.

➡ Restaurants, cafes, ATMs and toilets can be found within the Forbidden City.

➡ Wheelchairs (¥500 deposit) are free, as are pushchairs (¥300 deposit).

After an epic day exploring the Forbidden City, you'll definitely need to take a break. Exiting from the north gate, take a right and head towards Oasis Cafe (p78) for fantastic coffees. Its attached restaurant does inexpensive local food specialities.

Forbidden City

WALKING TOUR

After entering through the imperious Meridian Gate, resist the temptation to dive straight into the star attractions and veer right for a peek at the excellent **Ceramics Gallery ❶** housed inside the creaking Hall of Literary Glory.

Walk back to the central complex and head through the magnificent Gate of Supreme Harmony towards the Three Great Halls: first, the largest – the **Hall of Supreme Harmony ❷**, followed by the **Hall of Middle Harmony ❸** and the **Hall of Preserving Harmony ❹**, behind which slopes the enormous Marble Imperial Carriageway.

Turn right here to visit the fascinating **Clock Exhibition Hall ❺** before entering the **Complete Palace of Peace & Longevity ❻**, a mini Forbidden City constructed along the eastern axis of the main complex. It includes the beautiful **Nine Dragon Screen ❼** and, to the north, a series of halls, housing some excellent exhibitions and known collectively as The Treasure Gallery. Don't miss the **Pavilion of Cheerful Melodies ❽**, a wonderful three-storey opera house.

Work your way to the far north of this section, then head west to the **Imperial Garden ❾**, with its ancient cypress trees and pretty pavilions, before exiting via the garden's West Gate (behind the Thousand Year Pavilion) to explore the **Western Palaces ❿**, an absorbing collection of courtyard homes where many of the emperors lived during their reign.

Exit this section at its southwest corner before turning back on yourself to walk north through the Gate of Heavenly Purity to see the three final Central Halls – the **Palace of Heavenly Purity ⓫**, the **Hall of Union ⓬** and the **Palace of Earthly Tranquility ⓭** – before leaving via the North Gate.

Water Vats
More than 300 copper and brass water vats dot the palace complex. They were used for fighting fires and in winter were prevented from freezing over by using thick quilts.

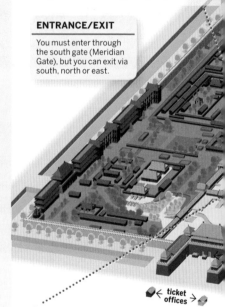

ENTRANCE/EXIT

You must enter through the south gate (Meridian Gate), but you can exit via south, north or east.

← ticket offices →

Guardian Lions
Pairs of lions guard important buildings. The male has a paw placed on a globe (representing the emperor's power over the world). The female has her paw on a baby lion (representing the emperor's fertility).

ZHAO JIAN KANG / SHUTTERSTOCK ©

Kneeling Elephants

At the northern entrance of the Imperial Garden are two bronze elephants kneeling in an anatomically impossible fashion, which symbolise the power of the emperor; even elephants kowtowed before him.

Nine Dragon Screen

One of only three of its type left in China, this beautiful glazed dragon screen served to protect the Hall of Imperial Supremacy from evil spirits.

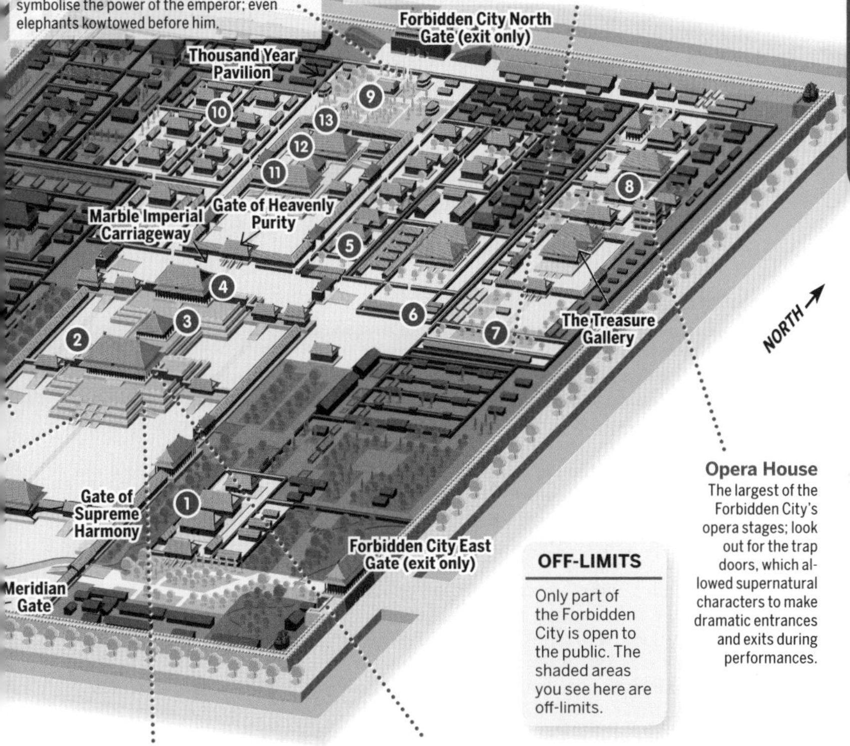

Forbidden City North Gate (exit only)
Thousand Year Pavilion
9
10
13
12
11
8
Gate of Heavenly Purity
Marble Imperial Carriageway
5
4
3
2
6
7
The Treasure Gallery
NORTH
1
Gate of Supreme Harmony
Forbidden City East Gate (exit only)
Meridian Gate

Opera House

The largest of the Forbidden City's opera stages; look out for the trap doors, which allowed supernatural characters to make dramatic entrances and exits during performances.

OFF-LIMITS

Only part of the Forbidden City is open to the public. The shaded areas you see here are off-limits.

Roof Guardians

The imperial dragon is at the tail of the procession, which is led by a figure riding a phoenix followed by a number of mythical beasts. The more beasts, the more important the building.

Dragon-Head Spouts

More than a thousand dragon-head spouts encircle the raised marble platforms at the centre of the Forbidden City. They were – and still are – part of the drainage system.

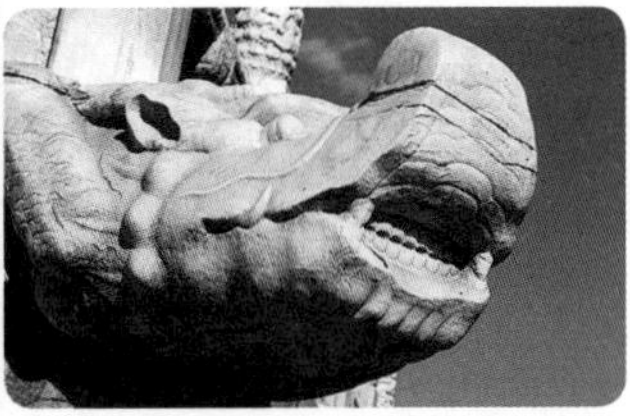

ELLIE MATSANOVA / SHUTTERSTOCK ©

landscaping, including rockeries, walkways, pavilions and ancient, carbuncular cypresses. At its centre is the double eaved **Hall of Imperial Peace** (Qin'an dian; Map p268). Before you reach the **Gate of Divine Prowess** (神武们; Shénwǔ Mén; Map p268), note the pair of **bronze elephants** (Map p268) whose front knees bend in an anatomically impossible fashion just before you reach **Shùnzhēn Gate** (顺贞门; Shùnzhēn Mén; Map p268). They signify the power of the emperor; even elephants kowtow before him!

Western & Eastern Palaces

A dozen smaller palace courtyards lie to the west and east of the three lesser central halls. It was in these smaller courtyard buildings that most of the emperors actually lived and many of the buildings, particularly those to the west, are decked out in imperial furniture.

Of the six **eastern palaces**, the four that are open to the public have exhibitions displaying cultural relics from ceramics, temple musical instruments to ceremonial bronze vessels. The most unusual is the **Palace of Prolonging Happiness** (延禧宫; Yánxǐ Gōng; Map p268), which features an unfinished 20th-century Western-style building with an intricately carved white marble facade and cast-iron roof.

Many of the six western palaces were closed for renovation at the time of research. The **Palace of Gathered Elegance** (储秀宫; Chǔxiù Gōng; Map p268) contains some interesting photos of the last emperor, Puyi, who lived here as a child ruler at the turn of the 20th century.

Palace Quirks

Attached to buildings, or standing incongruously in the corners of courtyards, are quirky objects that can easily go unnoticed.

The huge **copper and brass vats** that dot the Forbidden City were once full of water for dousing fires. There are 308 in total, all in various states of disrepair. They used to be draped in quilts or warmed with fires in winter to keep them from freezing over.

Pairs of stone or bronze **guardian lions** protect important buildings, with two particularly fine specimens in front of the Gate of Supreme Harmony. The male always has a paw placed on a globe (representing the emperor's power over the world), while the female has a paw placed on a baby lion (representing the fertility of the emperor's court).

More than a thousand **dragon-head spouts** encircle the raised marble platforms at the centre of the Forbidden City. They were, and still are, part of the drainage system. If you are unlucky enough to visit on a day of torrential rain, you will at least get to see water spouting out of their mouths.

Roof guardians adorn many important historic buildings in Běijīng. Here too, on the upturned eaves of significant halls, you'll find processions of mythical creatures leading and protecting the imperial dragon, which lies at the tail end of the line. The more mythical beasts in the procession, the more important the building, with nine guardians being the maximum.

From the back of the Hall of Preserving Harmony slopes the largest of the city's **marble imperial carriageways**. This beautifully carved, 250-ton block of marble, transported to the palace in winter on sheets of ice, was one of a few that acted as VIP access ramps for the raised hallways. Sedan-chair bearers would walk up the steps on each side, while the emperor was carried over a celestial scene of marble-carved clouds and dragons.

Bronze turtles like the large one in front of the Hall of Supreme Harmony symbolise longevity and stability. It has a removable lid, and on special occasions incense was lit inside it so that smoke billowed from its mouth.

Sundials also dot the complex. You can find one to the east of the Hall of Supreme Harmony. To the west of the hall, on a raised terrace, is a small pavilion with a **bronze grain measure**; both objects are symbols of imperial justice.

Also look out for the round, football-sized **tether stones** dotted around the weed-covered corners of the large central courtyards. It is assumed that these were used for tethering horses.

Clock Exhibition Hall

The **Clock Exhibition Hall** (钟表馆; Zhōngbiǎo Guǎn; Map p268; admission ¥10; ⊙8.30am-4pm summer, to 3.30pm winter) is one of the unmissable highlights of the Forbidden City. Located in the **Hall for Ancestral Worship** (奉先殿; Fèngxiān Diàn), the exhibition contains an astonishing array of elaborate timepieces, many of which were gifts to the Qing emperors from overseas. Many of the 18th-century examples are crafted by James Cox or Joseph Williamson (both of London) and imported through Guǎngdōng from England; others are from Switzerland, America and Japan. Exquisitely wrought, fashioned with magnificently designed elephants and other creatures, they all display astonishing artfulness and attention to detail. Standout clocks include the Gilt Copper Astronomy Clock equipped with a working model of the solar system, and the automaton-equipped Gilt Copper Clock with a robot writing Chinese characters with a brush. The Qing court must surely have been amazed by their ingenuity.

Treasure Gallery

In the northeastern corner of the complex is a mini Forbidden City known as the Treasure Gallery (or Complete Palace of Peace and Longevity; 宁寿全宫; Níng Shǒu Quán Gōng). During the Ming Dynasty, the Empress Dowager and the imperial concubines lived here. Today it comprises a number of atmospheric halls, pavilions, gardens and courtyard buildings that hold a collection of fine museums. Among the many exhibitions, highlights include the beautiful glazed **Nine Dragon Screen** (九龙壁; Jiǔlóng Bì; Map p268; admission included in through ticket), one of only three of its type left in China, and the **Belvedere of Pleasant Sounds** (畅音阁; Chàngyīn Gé; Map p268), a three-storey wooden opera house, which was the palace's largest theatre. Across is the **Hall for Viewing Opera** where the emperor and empress watched the show, and today houses a collection of opera artefacts and clothing.

CLOCK PERFORMANCE

Time your arrival for 11am or 2pm to see the clock performance in the Clock Exhibition Hall, in which choice timepieces strike the hour and give a display to wide-eyed children and adults.

Enter the Treasure Gallery from the south – not far from the Clock Exhibition Hall; afterwards you'll be popped out at the northern end of the Forbidden City.

TOP SIGHT
TIĀN'ĀNMÉN SQUARE

Flanked to the east and west by stern 1950s Soviet-style buildings and ringed by white perimeter fences that channel the hoi polloi towards periodic security checks and bag searches, the world's largest public square (440,000 sq metres) is a vast desert of paving stones at the heart of Běijīng. The square is also a poignant epitaph to China's hapless democracy movement, which got a drubbing from the People's Liberation Army (PLA) in June 1989. The stringent security and round-the-clock monitoring hardly make it the most relaxing of tourist sights, but such is its iconic status that few visitors leave Běijīng without seeing Tiān'ānmén Sq (天安门广场; Tiān'ānmén Guǎngchǎng). In any case, there's more than enough space to stretch a leg and the view can be breathtaking, especially on a clear, blue day or at nightfall when the square is illuminated.

DON'T MISS

➡ Chairman Mao Memorial Hall

➡ Front Gate (Qiánmén)

➡ Flag-raising ceremony

PRACTICALITIES

➡ 天安门广场; Tiān'ānmén Guǎngchǎng

➡ Map p268, B7

➡ admission free

➡ S Line 1 to Tian'anmen West, Tian'anmen East, or Line 2 to Qianmen

History

Tiān'ānmén Sq as we see it today is a modern creation and there is precious little sense of history. During Ming and Qing times, part of the Imperial City Wall (Huáng Chéng) called the Thousand Foot Corridor (Qiānbù Láng) poked deep into the space today occupied by the square, enclosing a section of the imperial domain. The wall took a 'T' shape, emerging from the two huge, now absent, gates that rose up south of the Gate of Heavenly Peace – Cháng'ān Zuǒ Gate and Cháng'ān Yòu Gate – before running south to the vanished Dàmíng Gate (Dàmíng Mén). Called Dàqīng Gate during the Qing dynasty and Zhōnghuá Gate during the Republic, the Dàmíng Gate had three watchtowers and upturned eaves and was guarded by a pair of stone lions. It was pulled down after 1949, a fate similarly reserved for Cháng'ān Zuǒ Gate and Cháng'ān Yòu Gate. East and west of the Thousand Foot Corridor stood official departments and temples, including the Ministry of Rites, the Ministry of Revenue, Honglu Temple and Taichang Temple.

Mao Zedong conceived the square to project the enormity of the Communist Party. During the Cultural Revolution, the chairman, wearing a Red Guard armband, reviewed parades of up to a million people here. The 'Tiān'ānmén Incident' is the term given to the near riot in the square that accompanied the death of Premier Zhou Enlai in 1976. Another million people jammed the square to pay their last respects to Mao in September that year. His mausoleum lies on Běijīng's north–south axis of symmetry on the footprint of Zhōnghuá Gate (Zhōnghuá Mén), a vast and ancient portal flattened during the communist development of Tiān'ānmén Sq.

Layout

The square is laid out on a north–south axis, however you can only enter via the four designated security gates positioned at the middle and north corner points. The ceremonial gates are Qiánmén (p70) and the Gate of Heavenly Peace (p68) – the latter lies on the other side of the main road.

Sitting innocuously in the middle of the square is the Chairman Mao Memorial Hall (p64), which thousands of domestic tourists visit each morning. In the square, one stands in the symbolic centre of the Chinese universe. The rectangular arrangement, flanked by halls to both east and west, to some extent echoes the layout of the Forbidden City. As such, the square employs a conventional plan that pays obeisance to traditional Chinese culture, but its ornaments and buildings are largely Soviet-inspired.

Activities

Early risers can watch the **flag-raising ceremony** at sunrise, performed by a troop of PLA soldiers drilled to march at precisely 108 paces per minute, 75cm per pace. The soldiers emerge through the Gate of Heavenly Peace to goosestep faultlessly across Dongchang'an Jie as traffic is halted. The same ceremony in reverse is performed at sunset. Ask at your hotel for flag-raising/-lowering times so you can get there early, as crowds can be intense.

Bicycles can no longer be ridden, or even walked, across Tiān'ānmén Sq, although you can ride along the north–south avenues on either side of the square. Kite flying has also been banned.

1989 Protests

Tiān'ānmén Sq is best known in the West for the tragic events of 4 June 1989, when live television pictures showed the army forcing pro-democracy demonstrators out of the square. Although it is generally agreed that no one was actually killed within the square itself, it is likely that hundreds were killed in the surrounding streets as the military opened fire on protestors. During the 10th anniversary of the 1989 protests, the square was shut for renovations, and every year around 4 June, security is stepped up a notch.

TOP TIPS

➡ The designated points of access come with security checks on entry, so expect lengthy queues.

➡ Just say no to the 'poor' art students press-ganging tourists to view their exhibitions; fending them off can be draining. Avoid invitations to teahouses, unless you want to pay an extortionate amount for the experience.

Despite being a public place, the square remains more in the hands of the government than the people; it is monitored by closed-circuit TV cameras, Segway-riding policemen and plain-clothes officers who move like lightning at the first sign of any disruption.

TAKE A BREAK

Your best bet for a feed is Lost Heaven (p76), with delicious Yúnnán cuisine and quality cocktails in a building that was once part of the foreign legation quarter.

⊙ SIGHTS

FORBIDDEN CITY   HISTORIC SITE
See p54.

TIĀN'ĀNMÉN SQUARE   SQUARE
See p62.

NATIONAL MUSEUM OF CHINA   MUSEUM
Map p268 (中国国际博物馆; Zhōngguó Guójì Bówùguǎn; http://en.chnmuseum.cn; Guangchang-dongce Lu, Tiān'ānmén Sq; 天安门，广场东侧路; audio guide ¥30; ⊗9am-5pm Tue-Sun, last entry 4pm; 🔊; **S**Line 1 to Tian'anmen East, exit D) **FREE** Běijīng's premier museum is housed in an immense 1950s communist-style building on the eastern side of Tiān'ānmén Sq, and is well worth visiting. The **Ancient China** exhibition on the basement floor is outstanding. You could easily spend a couple of hours in this exhibition alone. It contains dozens and dozens of stunning examples of ceramics, calligraphy jade and bronze pieces dating from prehistoric China through to the Qing dynasty. It's all displayed beautifully in modern, spacious, low-lit exhibition halls. You'll need your passport to gain entry.

In this basement exhibition, look out for the 2000-year-old jade burial suit, made for the Western Han dynasty king Liu Xiu, and the life-sized bronze acupuncture statue, dating from the 15th century. The 2000-year-old rhino-shaped bronze *zūn* (wine vessel) is another stand-out piece. The Ancient Chinese Money exhibition on the top floor, and the Bronze Art and Buddhist Sculpture galleries, one floor below, are also worth seeing.

The ground floor has a number of Salvador Dalí sculptures, and a new room dedicated to socialist-realism art with the epic *Birth of New China* ink painting, which depicts Mao Zedong addressing the nation to announce the establishment of the People's Republic of China in 1949.

The museum, which is vast and energy-sapping, also has a ground-floor cafe (sandwiches from ¥20) and a teahouse. There's a refreshing ban on selfie sticks.

WORKERS CULTURAL PALACE   PARK
Map p268 (Imperial Ancestral Temple; 劳动人民文化宫; Láodòng Rénmín Wénhuà Gōng; ☑tennis court 010 6512 2856; park entrance ¥2, Sacrificial Hall ¥15; ⊗6.30am-7.30pm; **S**Line 1 to Tian'anmen East, exit A) Despite the prosaic name and its location at the very heart of town, this reclusive park, between Tiān'ānmén Sq and the Forbidden City, is one of Běijīng's best-kept secrets. Few visitors divert here from their course towards the main gate of the Forbidden City, but this was the emperor's premier place of worship and contains the **Sacrificial Hall** (Front Hall; 太庙, Tài Miào; Map p268; admission ¥15); as exquisite as any temple you'll find in Běijīng.

If you find the Forbidden City either too colossal or crowded, the temple halls here are a cheaper, more tranquil and more manageable alternative. Enter the temple area of the park through the striking **Glazed Gate** (琉璃门; Liúlí Mén). Then, rising up to the splendid Sacrificial Hall are three flights of steps. Only gods could traverse the central plinth; the emperor was consigned to the left-hand flight. Note how the plaque above the Sacrificial Hall is inscribed in both Chinese and Manchu. Its space is now used to host temporary cultural exhibitions; be sure to look up to admire its beautifully carved interior roofing.

The northern perimeter of the park abuts the palace moat, where you can find a bench and park yourself in front of a fine view. There's also a south gate, for Tiān'ānmén Sq, and a northwest gate, for the Forbidden City, and east gate for restaurants.

**CHAIRMAN MAO
MEMORIAL HALL**   MAUSOLEUM
Map p268 (毛主席纪念堂; Máo Zhǔxí Jìniàntáng; Tiān'ānmén Sq; bag storage ¥10, electonics storage per device ¥10; ⊗7am-noon Tue-Sun; **S**Line 1 to Tian'anmen West or Tian'anmen East or Line 2 to Qianmen) **FREE** No doubt one of Běijīng's more surreal spectacles is the sight of Mao Zedong's embalmed corpse on public display within his mausoleum. The Soviet-inspired memorial hall was constructed soon after Mao died in September 1976, and is a prominent landmark in the middle of Tiān'ānmén Sq. He is still revered across much of China, as evidenced by the perpetual snaking queues of locals here clutching flowers to pay their respects; some are reduced to tears but most are in high spirits, treating it like any other stop along their Běijīng tour.

Mao's body lies in a crystal cabinet, draped in an anachronistic red flag emblazoned with hammer and sickle, as guards in white gloves impatiently wave visitors on towards further rooms where a riot of Mao kitsch – lighters, bracelets, statues, key rings, bottle openers, you name it – ensues. Directly outside the mausoleum are some

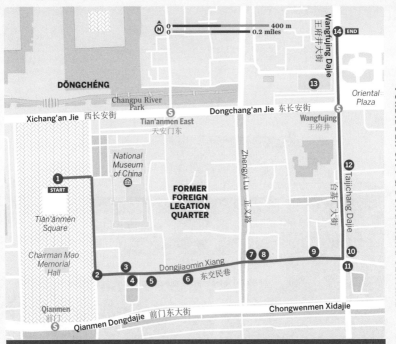

FORBIDDEN CITY & DŌNGCHÉNG CENTRAL

🏃 Neighbourhood Walk
Tiān'ānmén Square & Foreign Legation Quarter

START TIĀN'ĀNMÉN SQ
END RAFFLES BĚIJĪNG HOTEL
LENGTH 2KM; ONE HOUR

From ❶ **Tiān'ānmén Square** (p62), cross the road and climb the steps into ❷ **Dongjiaomin Xiang** (东交民巷). The red-brick building on your left was the former ❸ **French Hospital**.

Through a sometimes-closed, grey-brick archway on your right, stands the elegant former ❹ **Legation Quarter** (p72) of ash-grey architecture, now a collection of trendy restaurants facing onto a grass quadrangle, and accessed from the south.

Behind a wall a short walk east rises a green-roofed building at No 40, which was once the ❺ **Dutch Legation**.

Further along on your right stands a building with massive pillars, the erst-while address of the First National City Bank of New York (花旗银行; Huāqí Yín-háng), now the quirky ❻ **Běijīng Police Museum** (p72).

Keep walking east to the domed building on the corner of Zhengyi Lu (正义路) and Dongjiaomin Xiang, once the ❼ **Yokohama Specie Bank**.

The grey building at No 19 is the ❽ **former French post office** (p73), before you reach the former ❾ **French Legation**, at No 15, with its large red entrance.

Backing onto a small school courtyard, the twin spires of the Gothic ❿ **St Michael's Church** rise ahead at No 11, facing the green roofs and ornate red brickwork of the old ⓫ **Belgian Legation**.

Stroll north along Taijichang Dajie and hunt down the brick street sign embedded in the northern wall of Taijichang Toutiao (台基厂头条), carved with the old name of the road. ⓬ **Rue Hart**. Located along the north side of Rue Hart (at No 3) was the Austro-Hungarian Legation.

Reaching the north end of Taijichang Dajie, across busy Dongchang'an Jie, is the ⓭ **Raffles Běijīng Hotel** (built 1900), which is just a stone's throw from the famous ⓮ **Wangfujing Dajie** shopping strip.

1

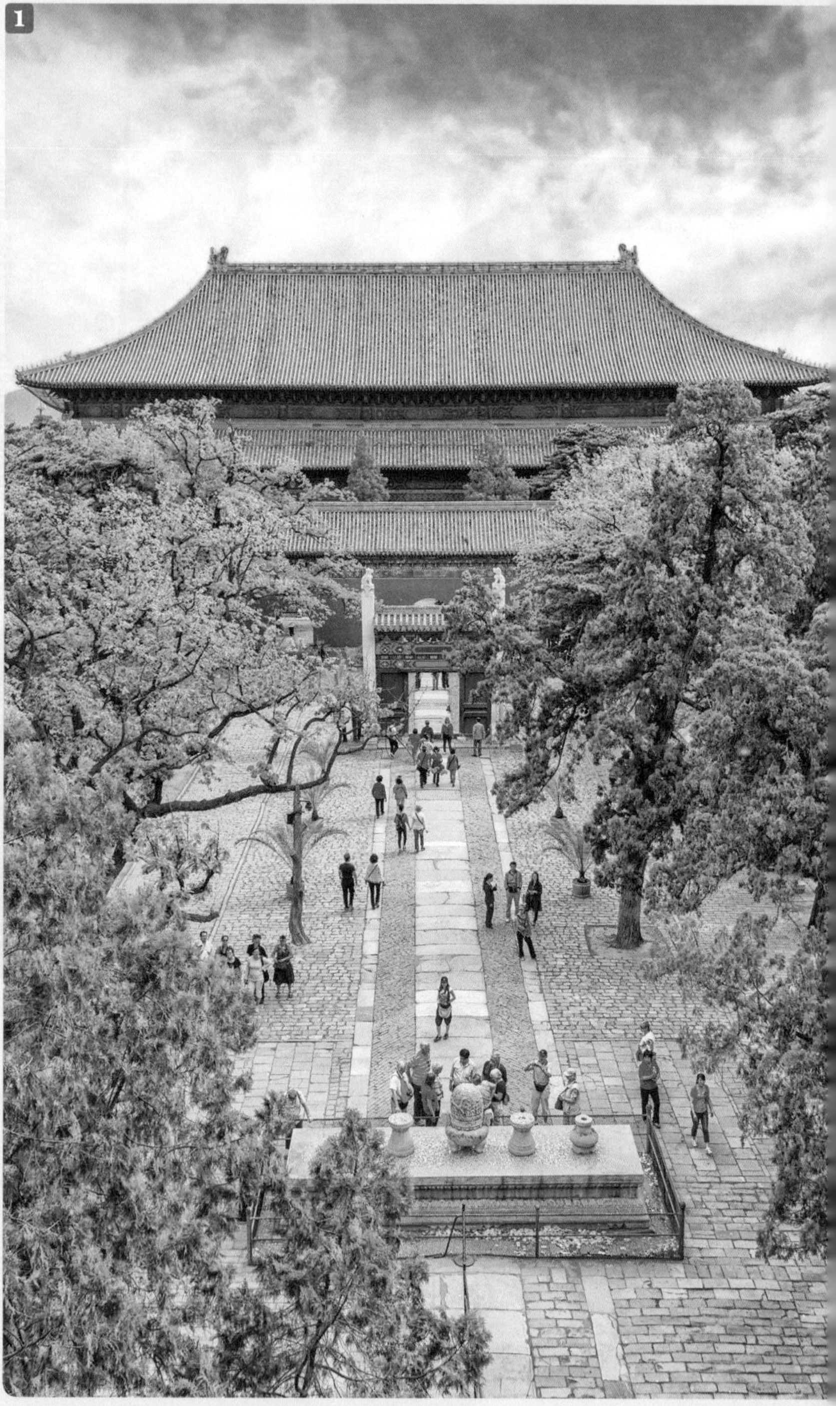

MATT MUNRO / LONELY PLANET ©

MATT MUNRO / LONELY PLANET ©

Forbidden City (p54)
plore the largest palace complex in
e world

2. Tiān'nānmén Square (p62)
View the Gate of Heavenly Peace from this
iconic square

3. Hútòng (p209)
Be sure to tour these fast-disappearing
remnants of old Běijīng

stirring socialist-realism war memorials that make for good photo ops.

Mao is one of a pantheon of world communist/personality-of-cult leaders to be embalmed, along with Vladimir Lenin, Ho Chi Minh and North Korea's Kim Il Sung and Kim Jong-il, who are also on public display in their respective countries.

Before you join the queue, all bags and cameras need to be deposited at the onsite building just east of Zhèngyáng Gate within Tiān'ānmén Sq towards Qianmen; collect them before 2pm. And don't forget your passport. You won't be let into the hall without it. Note, the queues may seem impossibly long, but they are constantly moving (visitors aren't allowed to stop inside the hall), so they go down relatively quickly.

Be aware that opening hours can vary; occasionally it can open later at 9am or close earlier at 11am.

JĪNGSHĀN PARK   PARK
Map p268 (景山公园; Jǐngshān Gōngyuán; Jingshan Qianjie; adult/child ¥10/5; ⏰6.30am-9pm; Ⓢ Lines 6, 8 to Nanluoguxiang, exit A) The domi-nating feature of Jǐngshān – one of the city's finest parks – is one of central Běijīng's few hills; a mound that was created from the earth excavated to make the Forbidden City moat. Called Coal Hill by Westerners during Legation days, Jǐngshān also serves as a feng shui shield, protecting the palace from evil spirits – or dust storms – from the north. Clamber to the top for a magnificent panorama of the capital and princely views over the russet roofing of the Forbidden City.

On the eastern side of the park, a locust tree stands in the place where the last of the Ming emperors, Chongzhen, hanged himself as rebels swarmed at the city walls. The rest of the park is one of the best places in Běijīng for people-watching. Come early to see (or join in with) elderly folk going about their morning routines of dancing, singing, performing taichi or playing *jiànzi*, a traditional game of keepie-uppies played with an oversized shuttlecock. In April and May, the park bursts into bloom with fabulously colourful peonies and tulips forming the focal point of a very popular flower fair. The park has three gates: the south is directly

⦿ TOP SIGHT
GATE OF HEAVENLY PEACE

Decorated wtih a giant framed portrait of Chairman Mao, and guarded by two pairs of Ming dynasty **stone lions**, the double-eaved Gate of Heavenly Peace, north of Tiān'ānmén Sq, is a potent national symbol. Built in the 15th century and restored in the 17th century, the gate was formerly the largest of the four gates of the Imperial City Wall, and it was from this gate that Mao proclaimed the People's Republic of China on 1 October 1949. Today's political coterie watches mass troop parades from here.

Climb the gate for excellent views of the square, and peek inside at the impressive beams and overdone paintwork; in all there are 60 gargantuan wooden pillars and 17 vast lamps suspended from the ceiling. Within the gate tower there is also a fascinating photographic history of the gate (but only captioned in Chinese) and Tiān'ānmén Sq, and video footage of military parades.

There's no fee for walking through the gate, en route to the Forbidden City, but if you climb it you'll have to pay.

The **ticket office** (Map p268) is on the north side of the gate; here you'll need to stow all bags before entering. For Forbidden City tickets, keep walking about 600m further north.

The nearby Láijīnyǔxuān Teahouse (p78) is an atmospheric spot to drop by for a cuppa tea within the grounds of Zhōngshān Park.

DON'T MISS
→ Mao's giant portrait
→ Views of Tiān'ānmén Sq
→ Impressive interior beams
→ Photography exhibition

PRACTICALITIES
→ 天安门; Tiān'ānmén
→ Map p268, B5
→ Xichang'an Jie; 西长安街
→ admission ¥15, bag storage ¥3-6
→ ⏰8.30am-4.30pm, to 4pm Nov-Mar
→ Ⓢ Line 1 to Tian'anmen West, exit B or Line 1 Tian'anmen East, exit A

opposite the Forbidden City's north gate (exit only), the west leads towards Běihǎi Park's east gate, while the east gate has a couple of nice cafes outside it.

NATIONAL CENTRE FOR THE
PERFORMING ARTS (NCPA) ARCHITECTURE

Map p268 (国家大剧院; Guójiā Dàjùyuàn; ☑010 6655 0000; www.chncpa.org/ens; 2 W Chang'an Ave; admission ¥30, concert tickets ¥80-400; ☺9am-4.30pm Tue-Sun; Ⓢ Line 1 to Tian'anmen West, exit C) Critics have compared it to a shiny metallic egg (although it looks more like a massive mercury bead), while modernists love it to bits. Plonked in the middle of an artificial lake, the sci-fi looking NCPA, also known as the National Grand Theatre, is a surreal location in which to catch a show.

Examine the bulbous interior, including the titanic steel ribbing of interior bolsters (each of the 148 bolsters weighs 8 tonnes), and tour the three halls. See the website for details on concerts.

ZHÌHUÀ TEMPLE BUDDHIST TEMPLE

Map p270 (智化寺; Zhìhuà Sì; 5 Lumicang Hutong; 禄米仓胡同5号; adult ¥20, audio guide ¥10, Wed free; ☺8.30am-4.30pm, closed Mon; Ⓢ Lines 1, 2 to Jianguomen, exit A or Lines 2, 6 to Chaoyangmen, exit G) Běijīng's surviving temple brood has endured casual restoration that often buried authenticity. But this rickety non-active temple, hidden down a rarely visited *hútòng*, is thick with the flavours of old Peking, having eluded the Dulux treatment that invariably precedes entrance fee inflation and stomping tour groups.

You won't find the coffered ceiling of the **Zhìhuà Hall** (it's in the USA), and the Four Heavenly Kings have vanished from **Zhìhuà Gate** (智化门; Zhìhuà Mén), but the **Scriptures Hall**, off to one side of the central courtyard, encases a unique, eight-sided, Ming dynasty wooden library topped with a seated Buddha and a magnificently unrestored ceiling. The highlight, the **Ten Thousand Buddhas Hall** (Tathagata Hall & Wanfo Pavilion; 万佛殿; Wànfó Diàn), is right at the back of the complex, and is an enticing two floors of miniature niche-borne Buddhist effigies and cabinets for the storage of sutras. Its entrance is dominated by three stunning, wood-carved deities (a 20ft-tall Tathagata Buddha, flanked by Brahma and Indra). Unfortunately, visitors are no longer allowed to climb to the 2nd floor of this hall.

Try to time your visit to coincide with the free, 15-minute, **musical performances**, which take place in Zhìhuà Hall at 10am and 3pm each day. Performers use traditional Chinese instruments associated with Buddhist worship. Also, note the surreal juxtaposition of this 15th-century temple with the swirling, space-age curves of the Galaxy Soho buildings, which now loom over this historic *hútòng* neighbourhood.

GALAXY SOHO ARCHITECTURE

Map p270 (银河Soho; Chaoyangmennei Dajie; 朝阳门内大街; Ⓢ Lines 2, 6 to Chaoyangmen, exit G) Along with the CCTV Tower and the Bird's Nest, Běijīng's striking Galaxy Soho has announced itself as one the capital's modern architectural landmarks. Opening in 2012, it stands in direct juxtaposition to the adjoining *hútòng* housing (which was controversially cleared for its development). It was designed by acclaimed British-Iraqi architect the late Zaha Hadid (1950–2016), and typical of her work, it's characterised by its flowing, sleek contours and an interconnected design with adjoining walkways and space-age Modernist facade.

Its interior is equally as impressive with streamlined, undulating curves. The space is a mix of office and commercial space, including cafes, bars and even a live music venue (p80).

POLY ART MUSEUM MUSEUM

Map p270 (保利艺术博物馆; Bǎolì Yìshù Bówùguǎn; ☑010 6500 8117; www.polymuseum.com; 9th fl, Poly Plaza, 14 Dongzhimen Nandajie; 东城区东直门南大街14号保利大厦9层; admission ¥20, audio guide ¥10; ☺9.30am-5pm, closed Sun; Ⓢ Line 2 to Dongsi Shitiao, exit D) This small but exquisite museum displays a glorious array of ancient bronzes from the Shang and Zhou dynasties, a magnificent high-water mark for bronze production. Check out the intricate scaling on the '*Zūn* vessel in the shape of a Phoenix' (偁季凤鸟尊) or the '*Yǒu* with Divine Faces' (神面卣), with its elephant head on the side of the vessel. The detailed animist patterns on the *Gangbo You* (橺柏卣) are similarly vivid and fascinating.

In an attached room are four of the Western-styled 12 bronze animals plundered during the sacking of the Old Summer Palace: which have been acquired by the museum: pig, monkey, tiger and ox. The last room is populated with a wonderful collection of standing Bodhisattva statues, dating from the Northern Qi, Northern Wei and Tang dynasties.

TOP SIGHT
FRONT GATE (QIÁNMÉN)

Qiánmén (前门) or Front Gate, actually consists of two gates. The northernmost of the two gates is the 40m-high **Zhèngyáng Gate** (正阳门城楼; Zhèngyáng Mén Chénglóu; Tiān'ānmén Sq; admission ¥20, audio guide ¥20; ⏲9am-4.30pm Tue-Sun, last entry 4pm; [S]Line 2 to Qianmen, exit A), which is within the gates of Tiān'ānmén Sq. It dates from the Ming dynasty and was the largest of the nine gates of the Inner City Wall separating the inner, or Tartar (Manchu), city from the outer, or Chinese, city. Partially destroyed in the Boxer Rebellion around 1900, the gate was once flanked by two temples that have since vanished. With the disappearance of the city walls, the gate sits out of context, but it can be climbed for decent views of Tiān'ānmén Sq and of Arrow Tower, immediately to the south.

Inside its upper levels are some fascinating historical photographs, showing the area as it was at the beginning of the last century, before the city walls and many of the surrounding gates and temples were demolished. Explanatory captions are in English as well as Chinese.

The second gate, the **Zhèngyáng Gate Arrow Tower** (正阳门箭楼; Zhèngyángmén Jiànlóu; Map p268; Qianmen St; [S]Line 2 to Qianmen, exit C or B), directly south, can't be climbed. It also dates from the Ming dynasty and was originally connected to Zhèngyáng Gate by a semicircular enceinte (enclosing wall), demolished last century.

DON'T MISS

- Fascinating historical photographs
- Views of Tiān'ānmén Sq

PRACTICALITIES

- 前门; Zhèngyáng Mén
- Map p268, B8
- admission ¥20, audio guide ¥20
- ⏲9am-4pm Tue-Sun
- [S]Line 2 to Qianmen, exit B or C

GALLERY@TEMPLE — GALLERY

Map p270 (☎010 8401 5680; www.thetemplehotel.com; 23 Shatan Beijie, off Wusi Dajie; 五四大街，沙滩北街23号; [S]Lines 6, 8 to Nanluoguxiang, exit B or Lines 5, 6 to Dongsi, exit E) A unique space within the Temple Hotel's (p184) stunning reconstruction of the 250-year-old Zhīzhù Sì (智珠寺; Temple of Wisdom), this gallery hosts regular exhibitions of contemporary painting, sculpture and photography. Some enchanting open-air sculptures dot the site, and the atmospheric temple itself hosts film screenings on Sunday evenings.

Across the way is the **Gathered Sky** installation by acclaimed American light artist James Turrell. It's a unique piece that's viewed at sunset, lying or sitting down looking up at the ceiling of the 'Skyspace' chamber, where LED lights interplay with natural light. It's held on Sundays. Tickets cost ¥100.

ZHŌNGSHĀN PARK — PARK

Map p268 (中山公园; Zhōngshān Gōngyuán; adult ¥3, Spring Flower & Tulips Show ¥10; ⏲6am-9pm; [S]Line 1 to Tian'anmen West, exit B) Named after Sun Zhongshan (Sun Yatsen), the father of modern China, this peaceful park sits at the southwest corner of the Forbidden City and partly looks out onto the palace's moat (you can rent pedal-boats here) and towering walls. A refreshing prologue or conclusion to the magnificence of the Forbidden City, the park was formerly the sacred Ming-style **Altar to the God of the Land and the God of Grain** (北京社稷坛; Shejitan; Map p268; Zhōngshān Park; [S]Line 1 to Tian'anmen West, exit B), where the emperor offered sacrifices. The Square Altar remains, bordered on all sides by walls tiled in various colours.

Near the park's south entrance stands a towering dark-blue-tiled *páilou* (traditional Chinese archway) with triple eaves that originally commemorated the German Foreign Minister Baron von Ketteler, killed by Boxers in 1900. Just off to the right (east) is the 100-year-old Láijīnyǔxuān Teahouse (p78). North of here, also in the eastern section of the park, is the Forbidden City Concert Hall (p80). As with Jǐngshān Park,

April and May is a beautiful time to visit thanks to the hugely colourful Spring Flower and Tulips Show. The northeast exit of the park brings you out by Meridian Gate, from where you can enter the Forbidden City. The south exit brings you out near Tiān'ānmén Sq. There is also a west gate.

SHĬJIĀ HÚTÒNG MUSEUM — MUSEUM

Map p270 (史家胡同博物馆; Shǐjiā Hútòng Bówùguǎn; 24 Shijia Hutong; 史家胡同24号; ⏲9.30am-4.30pm Tue-Sun; [S]Line 5 to Dengshikou) [FREE] Within a pleasant, renovated double courtyard, which used to be a local kindergarten, is this small museum that explains the history of Shǐjiā Hútòng, and of Běijīng's *hútòng* districts in general. There are interesting large-scale models, old photos and a range of artefacts, all with excellent English captions throughout.

NATIONAL ART MUSEUM OF CHINA — MUSEUM

Map p270 (中国美术馆; Zhōngguó Měishùguǎn; www.namoc.org/en; 1 Wusi Dajie; 五四大街1号; ⏲9am-5pm, last entry 4pm; [S]Lines 5, 6 to Dongsi, exit E) [FREE] This revamped museum has received a healthy shot of imagination and flair, with absorbing art exhibitions from across China and abroad promising doses of colour and vibrancy. Běijīng's art-lovers have lapped up some top-notch presentations here, from the cream of Italian design to contemporary artworks from the Taipei Fine Arts Museum and exhibitions of paintings from some of China's ethnic minority groups. It's one of the capital's best galleries for 20th-century Chinese modern art.

Lifts allow for wheelchair access. There's a cafe on the ground floor. Bring your passport to gain entry.

GREAT HALL OF THE PEOPLE — NOTABLE BUILDING

Map p268 (人民大会堂; Rénmín Dàhuìtáng; Renda Huitang W Rd; adult ¥30, bag deposit ¥2-5; ⏲8.15am-4pm, times vary; [S]Line 1 to Qinamen, exit A, or Line 1 to Tian'anmen West, exit C) On the western side of Tiān'ānmén Sq, on a site previously occupied by Taichang Temple, the Jinyiwei (Ming dynasty secret service) and the Ministry of Justice, the Great Hall of the People is the venue of the legislature, the National People's Congress (NPC). The 1959 Soviet-style architecture (which features on the ¥100 note) is monolithic and intimidating, and a fitting symbol of China's huge bureaucracy. The ticket office is down the south side of the building; bags must be checked in but cameras are admitted.

Inside you can peek into 29 of its lifeless rooms named after the provinces of the Chinese universe. Also here is the banquet room where US president Richard Nixon dined in 1972, and the 10,000-seat auditorium with the communist red star embedded in a galaxy of ceiling lights – though you'll have to pay an extra ¥40 to get your photo taken in order to see the ceiling itself.

CHINA NUMISMATIC MUSEUM — MUSEUM

Map p268 (中国钱币博物馆; Zhōngguó Qiánbì Bówùguǎn; ☎010 6608 4178; 17 Xijiaomin Xiang; 西交民巷17号; admission ¥10; ⏲9am-4pm Tue-Sat; [S]Line 2 to Qianmen, exit C) Appropriately located in a former 1930s bank, this three-floor museum follows the evolution of money production in China. You'll see spade-shaped coins of the Spring and Autumn period, chunky gold-nugget coins and 'money necklaces' containing strings of small bronze knives. All coinage and paper currency used during the Cultural Revolution are displayed, including all five sets of the modern-day rénmínbì, only two of which are still in circulation.

ANCIENT OBSERVATORY — OBSERVATORY

Map p270 (古观象台; Gǔ Guānxiàngtái; Jianguomen Bridge, East 2nd Ring Rd; 二环东路建国门桥; Erhuandong Lu, Jianguomen Qiao; adult ¥20; ⏲9am-5pm Tue-Sun, last entry 4.30pm; [S]Lines 1, 2 to Jianguomen, exit A) This unusual former observatory is mounted on the battlements of a watchtower lying along the line of the old Ming City Wall and originally dates back to Kublai Khan's days, when it lay north of the present site. Kublai, like later Ming and Qing emperors, relied heavily on astrologers to plan military endeavours. The present observatory – the only surviving example of several constructed during the Jin, Yuan, Ming and Qing dynasties – was built between 1437 and 1446 to facilitate both astrological predictions and seafaring navigation.

At ground level is a pleasant courtyard flanked by halls housing displays (with limited English captions). Also within the courtyard is an armillary sphere dating to 1439, supported by four dragons.

Clamber the steps to the roof of the watchtower to admire a mind-boggling array of Jesuit-designed astronomical instruments, embellished with sculptured bronze dragons and other Chinese flourishes – a kind of East and West astronomical fusion.

ℹ️ CON 'ARTISTS' & THE TEAHOUSE SCAM

We receive a number of emails from those unfortunate enough to be scammed in Běijīng. By far the most notorious is the tea-ceremony scam: tourists are invited (often by young ladies, and sometimes under the guise of an on-the-spot guided tour) to drink tea at a teahouse, after which the traveller is hit with a bill for hundreds of dollars. Many travellers pay up and only realise later that they have been massively conned. Tiān'ānmén Sq and Wangfujing Dajie are the two most notorious locations where foreigners are targeted. As a guide, a pot of tea (for at least four people) will normally cost between ¥100 and ¥400, depending on the grade of tea. As a rule, always double-check the price of anything you eat or drink before you order it.

Foreigners at Tiān'ānmén Sq and Wangfujing Dajie are also routinely hounded by 'art students' who rope visitors into going to exhibitions of overpriced art. Be suspicious if you are approached by anyone who speaks good English on the street until you are sure all they want is to chat.

ST JOSEPH'S CHURCH   CHURCH

Map p270 (东堂; Dōng Táng; 74 Wangfujing Dajie; ⏰services 6.30am & 7am Mon-Sat, 7am Sun; 🚇Line 5 to Dengshikou, exit A) FREE A crowning edifice on Wangfujing Dajie, and one of Běijīng's four principal churches, St Joseph's is known locally as Dōng Táng (East Cathedral). Originally built during the reign of Shunzhi in 1655, it was damaged by an earthquake in 1720 and reconstructed. The luckless church also caught fire in 1807, was destroyed again in 1900 during the Boxer Rebellion and restored in 1904, only to be shut in 1966. Now fully repaired, the church is a testament to the long history of Christianity in China.

A large square in front swarms with kids skateboarding, newlyweds posing for photographs and elderly folk meeting up in the early evening for formation dancing. Unless you're here for an early morning service, it's not open to visitors. Mass is held in English every Sunday at 7am.

FORMER FOREIGN
LEGATION QUARTER   HISTORIC BUILDING

Map p268 (租界区; 🚇Line 2 to Qianmen, exit A or Lines 2, 5 to Chongwenmen, exit A1) The former Foreign Legation Quarter, where the 19th-century foreign powers flung up their embassies, schools, post offices and banks, lies east of Tiān'ānmén Sq. Apart from the Běijīng Police Museum and a complex of trendy restaurants facing onto a grass quadrangle, accessed from the south, you can't enter most of the buildings. Many are now used as government buildings, but a stroll along the streets here (Dongjiaomin Xiang, Taijichang Dajie and Zhengyi Lu) gives you a hint of the area's former European flavour.

BĚIJĪNG POLICE MUSEUM   MUSEUM

Map p268 (北京警察博物馆; Běijīng Jīngchá Bówùguǎn; 📞010 8522 5018; 36 Dongjiaomin Xiang; 东交民巷36号; adult ¥5, through ticket ¥20; ⏰9am-4pm Tue-Sun, last entry 3.30pm; 🚇Line 2 to Qianmen, exit A) Propaganda aside, this is an interesting exposé of Běijīng's *dà gài mào* (slang for the constabulary). Learn how Běijīng's first Public Security Bureau (PSB) college operated from the Dōngyuè Temple (p136) in 1949 and find out how officers tackled the 'stragglers, disbanded soldiers, bandits, local ruffians, hoodlums and despots...' planted in Běijīng by the Kuomintang (KMT).

There are also eye-opening accounts of how KMT spies Li Andong and Yamaguchi Takachi planned to mortar the Gate of Heavenly Peace, and an analysis of how the Běijīng PSB was destroyed during the Cultural Revolution. For police weapons, head to the 4th floor. The through ticket includes some laser-shooting practice (if it's up and running) and a souvenir.

SHÈNG XĪ FÚ HAT MUSEUM   MUSEUM

Map p270 (368 Dongsi Beidajie; 东四北大街 368号; ⏰8.30am-7pm; 🚇Line 5 to Zhangzizhonglu, exit C) FREE This branch of the famous Shèng Xī Fú Hat Store (p81) has a quirky, free-to-visit hat museum out the back, detailing the history of the company and of hats in China.

TEN FU'S TEA CULTURE HOUSE   MUSEUM

Map p270 (天福茶文化馆; Tiānfú Chá Wénhuàguǎn; 3 Jinyu Hutong; 金鱼胡同3号; ⏰9am-10pm; 🚇Line 5 to Dengshikou) Head upstairs above the tea shop for the Ten Fu tea brand to get an overview of the history and processes involved in Chinese tea production, including some miniature moving models of tea-making machinery. Downstairs you can sample, and buy, teas from across China. It sells neat, slim, gift packs of tea (¥20 to ¥30), or else buy it by the *liǎng* (50g).

IMPERIAL GRANARIES   HISTORIC SITE
Map p270 (Nan Xincang Cultural Leisure St; 南新仓; Nán Xīncāng; ⓢ Line 2 to Dongsi Shitiao, exit D) Those interested in Ming dynasty architecture should check out the Imperial Granaries, comprising of nine restored storehouses dating from 1409. They once contained grain and rice for Běijīng's royalty; they now house posh restaurants and art galleries.

LAO SHE MUSEUM   HISTORIC BUILDING
Map p270 (老舍纪念馆; Lǎo Shě Jìniànguǎn; www.bjlsjng.com; 19 Fengfu Hutong; 丰富胡同19号; ⏱9am-4pm Tue-Sun, last entry 3.40pm; ⓢ Line 5 to Dengshikou, exit A) 𝗙𝗥𝗘𝗘 Brimful of uncomplicated charm, this renovated courtyard house off Dengshikou Xijie was the home of Lao She (1899–1966), one of Běijīng's best-loved 20th-century writers. The life of Lao She – author of *Rickshaw Boy* and *Tea House*, and former teacher at London's School of Oriental and African Studies – is detailed in a modest collection of halls, via newspaper cuttings, first-edition books, photographs and personal effects.

The exhibition falls at the final hurdle, giving perfunctory mention to perhaps the most significant aspect of Lao She's life: his death by drowning in Taiping Lake on 24 August 1966 after a nasty beating by vituperative Red Guards the day before. Captions are largely in Chinese.

MONUMENT TO THE PEOPLE'S HEROES   MONUMENT
Map p268 (人民英雄纪念碑; Rénmín Yīngxióng Jìniànbēi; Tiān'ānmén Sq; ⓢ Lines 1 to Tian'anmen West, Tian'anmen East or Line 2 Qianmen) North of Mao's mausoleum, and also in the centre of Tiān'ānmén Sq, the Monument to the People's Heroes was completed in 1958. The 37.9m-high obelisk, made of Qīngdǎo granite, bears bas-relief carvings of key patriotic and revolutionary events, as well as calligraphy from communist bigwigs Mao Zedong and Zhou Enlai.

DŌNG'ĀN MÉN REMAINS   RUINS
Map p270 (明皇城东安门遗址; Míng Huáng Chéng Dōng'ānmén Yízhǐ; Imperial Wall Foundation Ruins Park, cnr Donghuamen Dajie & Beiheyan Dajie; ⏱24hr; ⓢ Line 5 to Dengshikou) 𝗙𝗥𝗘𝗘 In two roadside pits, a couple of metres below the road surface on the north and south side of the crossroads here, are the remains of the once magnificent Dōng'ān Mén – the east gate of the Imperial City – as well as parts of the imperial city wall and parts of a bridge that used to cross the city canal (now a road).

The ruins are little more than small piles of bricks, but they are brought to life by a carved map fastened to one wall, showing what the area once looked like. Before being razed, the gate was a single-eaved, seven-bay-wide building with a hip-and-gable roof capped with yellow tiles. All that's left of it now are two layers of 18 bricks.

FORMER FRENCH POST OFFICE   HISTORIC BUILDING
Map p270 (19-1 Dongjiaomin Xiang; 东交民巷19-1号; ⓢ Line 2 to Qianmen, exit A) This small grey brick building was the French Post Office in the early 20th century. It was recently a Sìchuān restaurant but now stands empty.

PǓDÙ TEMPLE   BUDDHIST TEMPLE
Map p268 (普渡寺; Pǔdù Sì; Pudusi Dongxiang, off Nanheyan Dajie; 南河沿大街普渡寺东巷; ⓢ Line 1 to Tian'anmen East, exit A) This inactive Ming dynasty temple can't be entered, but the square in front of it, which forms part of a small park, is a peaceful place to rest up after a shopping spree on Wangfujing Dajie. The structure of the main hall is unusual in its Manchu style, and from the park's elevated position you get views of the surrounding *hútòng*.

🍴 EATING

★CRESCENT MOON MUSLIM RESTAURANT   XINJIANG $
Map p270 (新疆弯弯月亮维吾尔穆斯林餐厅; Xīnjiāng Wānwānyuèliàng Wéiwú'ěr Mùsīlín Cāntīng; 16 Dongsi Liutiao Hutong; 东四六条胡同16号, 东四北大街; dishes from ¥18; ⏱11am-11pm; ❄🛜; ⓢ Line 5 to Zhangzizhonglu, exit C) You can find a Chinese Muslim restaurant on almost every street in Běijīng. Most are run by Huí Muslims, who are Hàn Chinese, rather than ethnic-minority Uighurs from the remote western province of Xīnjiāng. Crescent Moon is the real deal – owned and staffed by Uighurs, it attracts many Běijīng-based Uighurs and people from Central Asia, as well as a lot of Western expats.

It's more expensive than most other Xīnjiāng restaurants in Běijīng, but the food is consistently good, and it has an English menu. The speciality is the barbecued leg of lamb (¥128). The lamb skewers (¥6) are also delicious, and there's naan bread (¥5), home-made yoghurt (¥12) and plenty of noodle options (¥18 to ¥25). You can also get Xīnjiāng tea (¥30 per pot), beer (¥15) and wine (¥95).

CHUĀN BÀN
SICHUAN $

Map p270 (川办餐厅; 28 Dongzongbu Hutong, off Chaoyangmen Nanxiaojie; 朝阳门南小街东总部胡同28号; dishes from ¥20; ⏱11am-2pm & 5-9pm Mon-Fri, 11am-11pm Sat & Sun; ⒮Lines 1, 2 to Jianguomen, exit A) Every Chinese province has its own official building in Běijīng, complete with a restaurant for cadres and locals working in the capital who are pining for a taste of home. Often they're the most authentic places for regional cuisines. This restaurant in the Sìchuān Government Offices is always crowded and serves up just about every variety of Sìchuān food you could want.

It's very much a place for fire fiends: almost every dish comes loaded with chillies and mouth-numbing Sìchuān peppercorns, whether it's bamboo shoots, Sìchuān specials such as *làzi jī* (here called 'young chicken Chongqing style'), or steamed fish with pepper and taro (here called 'boiled fish in spicy and hot pepper'). There are also dishes with rabbit and frog, both regional delicacies. There's an English menu with photos, but no English sign; it's housed in an office block of a building, with the entrance around the back.

GRANDMA'S
HÁNGZHŌU $

Map p270 (外婆家; Wàipó Jiā; 6th fl, Beijing apm shopping mall, 138 Wangfujing Dajie; 王府井大街138号apm6楼; mains ¥10-45; ⏱10am-2.30pm & 4-9pm; ⒮Line 5 to Dengshikou) Handy for shoppers on Wangfujing Dajie, but worth making the trip to from any part of the city, the Běijīng branch of this hugely successful Hángzhōu chain is a big hit in the capital. It's excellent value and is clean and bright, with comfy booth seating, so very popular with families. The menu is in English, although you might need a magnifying glass to read it.

Dishes we heartily recommend include Grandma's Pork (a juicy, braised pork dish, known in Hángzhōu as *Dōngpō ròu*; 东坡肉), tea-flavoured chicken (cooked with Hángzhōu's famous Lóngjǐng green tea), potatoes on a sizzling iron plate, the grilled eggplant and the organic cauliflower. But anything with a red thumbs-up icon next to it on the menu is a safe bet.

This place is so popular you can expect to wait an hour on midweek evenings; two hours at weekends. Lunchtimes are less busy. You can't reserve in advance; you have to come to the entrance and take a ticket (like in a bank). As you do so, you need to enter your details on the touch screen. In the first box, enter your mobile telephone number. In the second box, enter the number of people there are in your group. Then click on the left-hand red button that reads: 领号 (meaning, receive a number), and take your ticket. Armed with your mobile number, the restaurant will then text you about five minutes before your table is ready. If you don't have a local phone, you'll have to keep coming back to check what they're up to.

YUÈBĪN FÀNGUǍN
BEIJING $

Map p270 (悦宾饭馆; 43 Cuihua Hutong, off Wusi Dajie; 五四大街翠花胡同43号; mains ¥18-58; ⏱11am-9pm; ⒮Lines 5, 6 to Dongsi, exit D) Post-1949, this was the first privately owned restaurant to open in Běijīng. It's so minimalist that it still has an old canteen-like feel to it, but the focus here, as with many of China's best restaurants, is on the food, not the decor. This is a proper locals' joint, so ignore the cigarette smoking and the fish-bone spitting, pull up a chair, order a bottle of Yanjing beer (燕京啤酒; Yānjīng píjiǔ), and tuck in.

The menu, naturally, is in Chinese only. House specialities include: *guōshāo yā* (锅烧鸭; fried duck – the first dish ever served here, apparently), *suànní zhǒuzi* (蒜泥肘子; pork shoulder in garlic and vinegar), *miànjīn pá báicài* (面筋扒白菜; glutinous braised cabbage), *qīngchǎo xiārén* (清炒虾仁; stir-fried shrimp) and *wǔ sī tǒng* (五丝筒; chicken-and-veg egg rolls, served with pancakes, leeks and hoisin sauce). Note, check how much your beer costs before they open it for you. Some are cheap, but some cost almost ¥20 a bottle.

WǓGĒ JĪCHÌ
BARBECUE $

Map p270 (五哥鸡翅; 5 Nanbanqiao Hutong, off Dongsi Batiao; 东四八条,南板桥胡同5号; chicken wings ¥6; ⏱3pm-midnight; ⒮Line 5 to Zhangzizhonglu, exit C) Not the friendliest place, but the fabulously tasty chicken wings in this tiny hole-in-the-wall joint are worth the grumpy reception. No menu and no English spoken, but it doesn't matter; all they usually do here are chicken wings (鸡翅; jī chì; ¥6 each), so you've just got to convey how many you want, and whether you want them spicy (辣; là) or not (不辣; bù là).

To find it, head east along Dongsi Batiao then turn left at the tiny *hútòng* crossroads

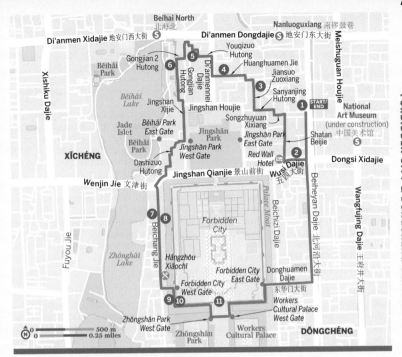

Neighbourhood Bike Tour
Imperial City Bike Tour

START BIKE BĚIJĪNG
END BIKE BĚIJĪNG
LENGTH 6KM; 1½ HOURS

Pick up a bike at **1 Bike Běijīng** (p81) and head south, turning right on to the imperial *hútòng* Wusi Dajie, passing the 1918 **2 Hóng Lóu** (Red Building), the former Peking University where Mao Zedong once worked as a librarian.

Turn right into Shatan Beijie (沙滩北街) then left into Songzhuyuan Xixiang (嵩祝院西巷). Bear right, then turn left into Sanyanjing Hutong (三眼井胡同). Note the elaborately carved Qing dynasty doorway on your right, now blocked up and turned into a wall and window. Just before the end, turn right into Jiansuo Zuoxiang (吉安所左巷). No 8 was **3 Mao Zedong's former home**.

At the end, turn left, take the second right and turn left onto Huanghuamen Jie (黄花门街). No 43 is the **4 former courtyard home of imperial eunuch Li Lianyin**, a favourite of Empress Dowager Cixi. At the end, turn right then left under an arch in

part of the old imperial city wall, into Youqizuo Hutong (油漆作胡同).

Follow the wiggly **5 hútòng** to Gongjian Hutong (恭俭胡同). Soon after, turn right into Gongjian 2 Hutong (恭俭二胡同), a quiet residential alleyway, which hugs the **6 eastern wall of Běihǎi Park**.

Follow Jingshan Xijie (景山西街) to Jǐngshān Park west gate, turn right, then cycle under the car-park arch and into Dashizuo Hutong (大石作胡同), which wiggles its way to Jingshan Qianjie (景山前街), and the Forbidden City moat. Follow Beichang Jie (北长街), past the former entrance to the **7 Longevity and Prosperity Temple** (now houses) and the also-closed **8 Fúyòu Temple**.

Turn left to the west gate of the Forbidden City, and follow the **9 Forbidden City moat** and towering **10 palace walls** around to **11 Meridian Gate**. Cross the square in front of the gate, and follow the moat eastward. Pass the palace's east gate before crossing onto Donghuamen Dajie (东华门大街), into Beiheyan Dajie (北河沿大街) and returning to Bike Běijīng.

and the unmarked restaurant will be on your left. If, when walking along Dongsi Batiao, you reach Slow Boat Brewery (at No 56), you've gone slightly too far.

ZUǑ LÍN YÒU SHÈ
BEIJING $

Map p270 (左邻右舍褡裢火烧; 50 Meishuguan Houjie; 美术馆后街50号; dumplings per liang ¥7, dishes ¥10-30; ⏰11am-9.30pm; ⓢLines 6, 8 to Nanluoguxiang, exit B or Line 5 to Zhangzizhonglu, exit D) This small, no-frills restaurant focuses on Běijīng cuisine. The speciality is dàlián huǒshāo (褡裢火烧), golden-fried finger-shaped dumplings stuffed with all manner of savoury fillings; we prefer the pork ones, but there are lamb, beef and veggie choices too. They are served by the liǎng (两), with one liǎng equal to three dumplings, and they prefer you to order at least two liǎng (二两; èr liǎng) of each filling to make it worth their while cooking a batch.

Other specialities include the pickled fish (酥鲫鱼; sū jì yú), the spicy tofu paste (麻豆腐; má dòufu) and the deep-fried pork balls (干炸丸子; gān zhá wánzi), while filling bowls of millet porridge (小米粥; xiǎo mǐ zhōu) are served up for free. No English sign (look for the wooden signboard), and no English spoken, but most parts of the menu have been translated into English.

HÁNGZHŌU XIǍOCHĪ
DUMPLING $

Map p268 (杭州小吃; Hángzhōu Xiǎochī; 76 Beichang Jie; 北长街76号; mains ¥5-10; ⏰6.30am-8pm; ⓢLine 1 to Tian'anmen West, exit B) Lao Li, the eccentric manager of What? Bar, two doors from here, swears by the boiled dumplings (蒸饺; zhēng jiǎo) in this simple restaurant. They come by the basket and are perfect for lining your stomach before you delve into the cheap beer at What? Bar.

You can also get fluffier, steamed dumplings (小笼包; xiǎolóng bāo) for the same price (¥6 per basket), as well as soups (seaweed, 紫菜汤; zǐcài tāng; wonton, 馄饨, hún dùn; egg, 鸡蛋汤, jīdàn tāng) and noodles (beef, 牛肉面, niúròu miàn; spicy glass noodles, 酸辣粉, suān là fěn). No English sign or menu.

DŌNGZI LǓRÒU HUǑSHĀO
HEBEI $

Map p270 (冬子驴肉火烧; 193-7 Chaoyangmen Nanxiaojie; 朝阳门南小街193-7号; mains from ¥8; ⏰7.30am-11pm; ⓢLine 5 to Dengshikou) Small, no-nonsense, but clean restaurant serving some of the best lǘròu huǒshāo (驴肉火烧; donkey-meat pastry pockets; ¥8) in Běijīng; though the donkey portraits on the

wall don't help to sell it! Bowls of xiǎomǐ zhōu (小米粥; millet porridge) make an ideal accompaniment, or else just grab a large beer (啤酒; píjiǔ; ¥5). No English sign or menu, and no English spoken.

WÁNGFǓJǏNG SNACK STREET
STREET FOOD $

Map p270 (王府井小吃街; Wángfǔjǐng Xiǎochījiē; west off Wangfujing Dajie; 王府井大街西侧; dishes & snacks ¥10; ⏰9.30am-10pm; ⓢLine 1 to Wangfujing, exit C2) Fronted by an ornate archway, this pedestrianised lane is lined with cheap and cheerful food stalls that are always busy. There are dishes from all over China, including málà tàng (a spicy soup from Sìchuān) and zhájiàngmiàn (Běijīng noodles in fried bean sauce), savoury pancakes, oodles of noodles and novelty items such as scorpion skewers. Not all stalls have prices listed, but most things cost around ¥10 for a portion.

XĪN TIĀN YUÀN
CHINESE $

Map p268 (新天苑; Tiān'ānmén Sq, east side; 天安门广场东边; meals ¥25-37; ⏰5.15am-7.30pm; ⓢLine 2 to Qianmen, exit A) An uninspired option, but convenient for a quick, cheap bite close to Tiān'ānmén Sq is this branch of the Chinese fast-food chain that does cheap bowls of noodles or rice meals. It even does cans of beer (¥8).

★LITTLE YÚNNÁN
YUNNAN $$

Map p270 (小云南; Xiǎo Yúnnán; ☎010 6401 9498; 28 Donghuang Chenggen Beijie; 东皇城根北街28号; mains ¥26-60; ⏰10am-10pm; ⓢLines 6, 8 to Nanluoguxiang, exit B or Line 5 to Zhangzizhonglu, exit D) Run by young, friendly staff and housed in a cute courtyard conversion, Little Yúnnán is one of the more down-to-earth Yúnnán restaurants in Běijīng. The main room has a rustic feel to it, with wooden beams, flooring and furniture. The tables up in the eaves are fun, and there's also some seating in the small open-air courtyard by the entrance.

Dishes include some classic southwest China ingredients, with some tea-infused creations as well as river fish, mushroom dishes, fried goat's cheese and là ròu (腊肉; cured pork – south China's answer to bacon). It also serves a variety of Yúnnán wines (rice, pine and plum), rice-wine-based cocktails and the province's local beer.

★LOST HEAVEN
YÚNNÁN $$

Map p268 (花马天堂; Huāmǎ Tiāntáng; ☎010 8516 2698; www.lostheaven.com.cn; 23 Qianmen

LOCAL KNOWLEDGE

THE EVOLUTION OF 23 QIANMEN DONGDAJIE

Known today for its restaurants, including Lost Heaven (p76), and the site of exclusive fashion shows, 23 Qianmen Dongdajie is host to far more than just top chefs and supermodels. The elegant buildings in a neoclassical style set around a quadrangle have a unique history, having been built in 1903 to house the US embassy. The original American legation was located on nearby Dongjiaomin Xiang and was badly damaged during the 1900 Boxer Rebellion when it, and other foreign embassies, came under siege for months.

The address stayed as the US embassy until 1949 and the communist takeover of China, when the American diplomats decamped to Taiwan. The next resident was the Dalai Lama; it was his official Běijīng home until he too fled China for India in 1959. Later, the buildings became part of the Chinese foreign ministry and were the venue for secret talks between the US and China in 1971 that led to President Nixon's historic visit to China the next year, and the beginning of the normalisation of relations between Běijīng and Washington.

Dongdajie; 前门东大街23号; dishes ¥50-130; ⏲11am-2pm & 5.30-10.30pm; [S]Line 2 to Qianmen, exit A) The Běijīng branch of the famed Shànghǎi restaurant, Lost Heaven specialises in the folk cuisine of Yúnnán province. While the spices have been toned down, the flavours remain subtle and light and are guaranteed to transport you to China's balmy southwest. The location in the elegant former Legation Quarter is an added bonus, and there's an outside roof terrace for the summer.

Try the Dai-style roast pork in banana leaf (¥68), or one of the many splendid salads, such as the marinated beef salad and peppers or the Burmese tea leaves salad. But all the dishes on the extensive menu are enticing, and the service is attentive. The cocktails are another reason to stop by; the extortionately priced beer is its only downside. Book ahead in the evenings.

DIN TAI FUNG — DUMPLING $$

Map p270 (鼎泰丰; Dǐng Tài Fēng; ☎010 6512 8019; www.dintaifung.com.cn; 6th fl, Beijing apm shopping mall, 138 Wangfujing Dajie; 王府井大街138号apm6楼; 5/10 dumplings from ¥25/49; ⏲11.30am-2.30pm & 5-10pm Mon-Thu, 11am-10pm Fri-Sun; ❄📶; [S]Line 1 to Wangfujing, exit C2 or Line 5 to Dengshikou) One of several Běijīng branches of this world-famous Taiwainese dumpling house.

MǍN FÚ LÓU — MONGOLIAN, HOTPOT $$

Map p270 (满福楼; 38 Di'anmennei Dajie; 地安门内大街38号; raw ingredients ¥9-66; ⏲11am-10pm; [S]Lines 6, 8 to Nanluoguxiang, exit A) This grand-looking but inexpensive 20-year-old hotpot restaurant serves up Mongolian hotpot – the less spicy, mutton-based variety which owes its origins to a time, centuries ago, when Mongolia and China were almost one and the same. Here each diner gets their own, mini, conical brass pot in which to boil their food. Choose the clear broth (*qīng tāng;* 清汤; ¥12), which isn't spicy, then pick portions of raw ingredients from the menu (in English and with photos).

Each person should also order a small bowl of sesame-paste dipping sauce (小料; *xiǎo liào*), which you dip your cooked food into before eating it. There should be a pot of chilli oil (辣椒油; *làjiāo yóu*) on your table (if not, ask for it), which can be mixed into the sesame paste to spice things up a bit. It also does great *shāobǐng* (sesame-seed buns) stuffed with meat, as well as hand-pulled noodles.

★TEMPLE RESTAURANT BITES — EUROPEAN $$$

Map p268 (TRB; ☎010 8400 2232; www.trb-cn.com; 95 Donghuamen Dajie; 东华门大街95号; 3/4/5 courses ¥198/258/298; ⏲11.30am-10.30pm Mon-Fri, 10.30am-10pm Sat & Sun; [S]Line 1 to Tian'anmen East, exit A) A peerless location, housed in a Qing dynasty building beside the Forbidden City moat, Ignace Lecleir's new offering is a more casual version of his upmarket Temple Restaurant (p78). The service is flawless, and the contemporary European food – salmon, lobster, pigeon, veal – is sheer quality. Here you order by customising your own meals, picking three or more items from whatever section of the menu takes your fancy.

Reservations are recommended, especially if you want a table overlooking the moat (the walls beside it are lit up in the evening). There's rooftop terrace seating in the warmer months.

★ BĚIJĪNG DÀDŎNG ROAST DUCK RESTAURANT PEKING DUCK $$$

Map p270 (北京大董烤鸭店; Běijīng Dàdŏng Kǎoyādiàn; ☑010 8522 1111; 5th fl Jinbao Place, 88 Jinbao Jie; 东城区EA金宝街88号金宝汇购物中心5层; roast duck half/whole ¥134/268; ◐11am-10pm; ✳🐢; 🅂Line 5 to Dengshikou, exit C) Ultramodern Dàdŏng sells itself on being the only restaurant that serves Peking duck with all the flavour of the classic imperial dish, but less fat – the leanest roast duck in the capital. For some, it's hideously over-priced and far from authentic. For others, it's the best roast duck restaurant in China.

There are nine branches in Běijīng, but this is one of the most memorable with its swish decor. Note, it's not the roast duck that will necessarily break the bank; it's the other dishes, delicious though they are. You'll pay ¥102, for example, for a medium portion of sautéed bean sprouts. Order wisely.

TEMPLE RESTAURANT EUROPEAN $$$

Map p270 (嵩祝寺餐厅; Sōngzhù Sì Cāntīng; ☑010 8400 2232; www.trb-cn.com; Sōngzhù Temple, 23 Shatanbei Jie, off Wusi Dajie; 五四大街沙滩北街23号, 嵩祝寺; 3/4/5/6 courses ¥388/488/588/688; ◐11am-3pm & 5.30-11pm; ✳🐢; 🅂Lines 6, 8 to Nanluoguxiang, exit B or Lines 5, 6 to Dongsi, exit E) Housed within the beautifully renovated grounds of a disused, centuries-old temple, this was the first of the high-end restaurants set up by celebrated restaurateur Ignace Lecleir. The place is exquisite, with decor as sleek as a contemporary art gallery and fitted with Scandinavian furniture. The food is contemporary European with French influences.

It also has one of the best wine lists in town and can do a serious cocktail. Reservations recommended. Its new Temple Restaurant Bites (p77) near the Forbidden City is also one to seek out.

🍷 DRINKING & NIGHTLIFE

★ OASIS CAFE CAFE

Map p268 (绿洲咖啡; Lùzhōu Kāfēi; 2 Jingshan Qianjie; 景山前街2号; coffee from ¥15; ◐9am-7pm; 🅂Lines 6, 8 to Nanluoguxiang, exit A, or Line 5, 6 to Dongsi, exit E) Oasis' award-winning

owner/barista/coffee roaster, Duan, really knows his stuff. Not only does he nail the V60 drip-coffee pour overs, but he knocks out one of the best flat whites in the city. Its attached restaurant is also a great place for a feed, specialising in cheap traditional Běijīng dishes, including hand-pulled noodles and meat-filled *shāobǐng* (烧饼, sesame-seed rolls; ¥5).

Its location just up from the Forbidden City makes it the ideal spot to take a break after a long day of sightseeing.

★ SLOW BOAT BREWERY TAPROOM BAR

Map p270 (悠航鲜啤; Yōuháng Xiānpí; www.slowboatbrewery.com; 56-2 Dongsi Batiao; 东四八条56—2号; draft beer ¥25-55; ◐5pm-midnight Mon-Fri, 2pm-2am Sat, 11.30am-10pm Sun; 🐢; 🅂Line 5 to Zhangzizhonglu, exit C) One of the original breweries to get Běijīng's craft-beer scene kicking, Slow Boat continues to conjure up some of the city's finest. Well hidden away down a residential side street, it's a cool little bar in a converted *hútòng* house, with a selection of around 15 Slow Boat beers on tap. Get the critically acclaimed Fry Burger stuffed with fries.

Signature beers include the Captain's Pale Ale and Monkey's Fist IPA, but there's a long list of core and seasonal North American-style beers to make your way through. Check the website for specials, and its flagship brewpub opened in Sānlǐtún (p143) in 2016.

LÁIJĪNYŮXUĀN TEAHOUSE TEAHOUSE

Map p268 (来今雨轩茶社; Láijīnyǔxuān Cháshè; ☑010 6601 9978; inside Zhōngshān Park; 中山公园, Zhōngshān Gōngyuán; tea per cup from ¥40; ◐9am-9pm; 🅂Line 1 to Tian'anmen West, exit B) This 100-year-old teahouse, set in the east corner of the Zhōngshān Park, has a large terrace and is a pleasant place to sample a cup of China's finest. A number of well-known writers, intellectuals and revolutionaries used to hang out here. These days it's mostly tourists, of course.

You'll pay from ¥180 to ¥380 for a pot, but you can get a cup for around ¥40, which, as always, can be topped up with hot water as many times as you wish. The traditional Chinese biscuit-cakes are tasty accompaniments. English tea menu.

BIKING CAFE CAFE

Map p270 (双行咖啡; Shuāngxíng Kāfēi; ☑010 6455 3909; www.bikingcafe.com; 81 Beiheyan Dajie; 北河沿大街81号; coffee from ¥25; ◐8am-9pm; 🐢; 🅂Lines 6, 8 to Nanluoguxiang, exit B or

ALL THE TEA IN CHINA

Although most Chinese tea is produced thousands of miles away in south China, there are still plenty of opportunities for you to sample and buy tea here in Běijīng. In case you don't know your oolong from your *pǔ'ěr*, here's a quick-look guide to all the tea in China.

Tea Types

Green tea (绿茶; *lǜ chá*) The most common tea in China, this tea undergoes the least amount of oxidation.

Black tea (红茶; *hóng chá*) More commonly drunk outside China, the tea leaves are allowed to completely oxidise, resulting in a stronger tasting tea.

Oolong tea (乌龙; *wū lóng*) This tea's oxidation is stopped somewhere between the standards for green tea and black tea. Tea leaves are often individually curled into tiny balls after processing.

Post-fermented tea (黑茶; *hēi chá*) These teas are allowed to undergo a second oxidation after the fixation of the tea leaves, in a process not dissimilar to composting. The most famous type by far is *pǔ'ěr*, which is often compressed into 'bricks' or 'cakes' of tea.

White tea (白茶; *bái chá*) Young leaves or new-growth buds that have undergone minimal oxidation through a slight amount of withering before halting the oxidative processes by being baked dry.

Yellow tea (黄茶; *huáng chá*) Usually implies a special tea processed similarly to green tea, but with a slower drying phase, where the damp tea leaves are allowed to sit and yellow.

Scented tea (香片; *xiāng piàn*) Tea (usually green, but sometimes oolong) scented with flowers, the most common being jasmine (茉莉花; *mòli huā*). Sometimes the tea leaves are bundled together with the flower into large balls (sold individually) which then 'bloom' in your tea cup.

Flower tea (花茶; *huā chá*) These don't contain any actual tea leaves, and are therefore caffeine-free. Instead parts of flowers, such as chrysanthemum (菊花; *jú huā*), are used. Note, jasmine tea is not flower tea so does contain caffeine.

Where to Drink Tea

- **Láijīnyǔxuān Teahouse** (p78)
- **Tángrén Teahouse** (p122)
- **Qi Baishi's Former Residence** (p90)
- **Bell Tower Tea House** (p88)

Tea Tips

When buying tea, be aware that prices are usually marked by the *jīn* (斤; 500g), but that most people buy it by the *liǎng* (两; 50g); ask for *yī liǎng* (one *liǎng*).

When drinking tea in a teahouse, remember that you can fill up your cup or pot with hot water as many times as you wish for no extra cost. If you're not given a hot-water flask, ask them to help you '*jiā rè shuǐ*' (加热水; add hot water).

Line 5 to Zhangzizhonglu, exit D) Sharing space with Bike Beijing (p81) is this mellow cafe that does speciality hand-drip coffees, toasted sandwiches and breakfasts specifically designed for cyclists. There are Belgian beers waiting in the fridge upon your return. With its unhurried pace and abundance of power points, it's also well suited as a work space.

DRUNK BAR, CAFE

Map p270 (☎010 6526 7080; 249-5 Dongsii Nandajie; 东四南大街249-5号; ⏲9.30am-2am; [S]Line 5 to Dengshikou) While it may not be worth a trip here in its own right, if you happen to be in the area, Drunk's the kind of place you'd be happy to stumble upon. It brews 11 of its own ales, served on tap upstairs, while downstairs is more cafe with good coffee, homemade cakes and pub grub – including a 2kg giant burger (¥218) that feeds three!

ALLEY COFFEE
CAFE

Map p270 (寻常巷陌咖啡厅; Xúncháng Xiàngmò Kāfēi Tīng; 61 Shatan Houjie, 沙滩后街61号; food ¥20-58; ⊘8am-10.30pm; 🛜; §Lines 6, 8 to Nanluoguxiang, exit A) Perfect for a coffee break after a visit to the Forbidden City or Jǐngshān Park, this cute, traveller-friendly courtyard cafe, diagonally opposite Jǐngshān Park's east gate, has English-speaking staff and fresh coffee (from ¥28), overpriced cold beer and a mix of Chinese and Western food, including breakfast fry-ups (until 11am). Also rents bikes (per day ¥50, deposit ¥600) and has free wi-fi.

WHAT? BAR
BAR

Map p268 (什么酒吧; Shénme? Jiǔbā; ☑133 3111 2734; 72 Beichang Jie; 北长街72号, 故宫西门往北; beers from ¥25; ⊘3pm-midnight; §Line 1 to Tian'anmen West, exit B) If you like to get up close and personal with the bands you go and see, then visit this easy-to-miss venue. That doesn't mean it is groupie heaven here; rather, it's so small that the audience might as well be on stage with the musicians. Gigs are on Fridays and Saturdays (sometimes Thursdays and Sundays too), and it's a good place to hear up-and-coming local talent.

What? Bar is also the best bar within walking distance of the Forbidden City (exit through the West Gate). You could also just come here for a low-key, late-afternoon, streetside tipple. If there's a cover charge, it's usually around ¥30, but often includes a drink.

⭐ ENTERTAINMENT

★DDC
LIVE MUSIC

Map p270 (Dusk Dawn Club; 黄昏黎明俱乐部; Huánghūn Límíng Jùlèbù; ☑010 6407 8969; https://site.douban.com/237627; 14 Shanlao Hutong; 山老胡同14号; tickets free-¥60, beer from ¥30, cocktails from ¥35; ⊘noon-1am; §Lines 6, 8 to Nanluoguxiang, exit B, or Line 5 to Zhangzizhonglu, exit D) One of the capital's current favourite spots to catch Chinese indie, punk and metal bands, DDC is an intimate space located down a nondescript *hútòng*. Its courtyard bar is also a good place for a drink, with a wide selection of Běijīng craft beers on tap (including a few of their own brews) and cheap cocktails at its bar made up of Lonely Planet guidebooks.

DDC was established by a collective of Chinese musicians, artists and curators to foster a Běijīng underground subculture.

MODERNSKY LAB
LIVE MUSIC

Map p270 (☑010 5876 0143; http://m.modernsky.com; basement fl, D 5-108 Galaxy Soho; 朝阳门银河SOHO, D座B1层5-108; §Lines 2, 6 to Chaoyangmen, exit G) One of Běijīng's newest venues, Modernsky is run by a local music label of the same name, and has shows by local indie, rock and electro bands. It's in the basement of the Galaxy Soho building.

NATIONAL CENTRE FOR THE PERFORMING ARTS
CLASSICAL MUSIC

Map p268 (国家大剧院; Guójiā Dàjùyuàn; ☑010 6655 0000; www.chncpa.org/ens; 2 Xichang'an Jie; 西长安街2号; tickets ¥80-880; ⊘performances 7.30pm; §Line 1 to Tian'anmen West, exit C) Sometimes called the National Grand Theatre, this spectacular Paul Andreu–designed dome, known to Beijingers as the 'Alien Egg', attracts as many architectural tourists as it does music fans. But it's *the* place to listen to classical music from home and abroad. You can also watch ballet, opera and classical Chinese dance here.

CHÁNG'ĀN GRAND THEATRE
PEKING OPERA

Map p270 (长安大戏院; Cháng'ān Dàxìyuàn; ☑010 6510 1310; Chang'an Bldg, 7 Jianguomennei Dajie; 建国门内大街7号; tickets ¥50-800; ⊘performances 7.30pm; §Lines 1, 2 to Jianguomen, exit A) This large theatre, with its distinctive model of a Peking-opera mask standing outside, offers a genuine experience, with the erudite audience chatting away knowledgably among themselves during the daily performances of Peking opera classics – this is a place for connoisseurs, although they do usually have English captions on a screen to one side of the stage.

Matinees, when they have them, usually start at 2pm; evening shows at 7.30pm. Most shows last for around two hours. Buy tickets in person from the ticket office here. Shows rarely sell out, but the cheaper seats often do. Note, there are sometimes days, between a change of shows, when there are no performances.

FORBIDDEN CITY CONCERT HALL
CLASSICAL MUSIC

Map p268 (中山公园音乐堂; Zhōngshān Gōngyuán Yīnyuè Táng; ☑010 6559 8285; www.fc

chbj.com; Zhōngshān Park; 中山公园内; tickets ¥30-880; ⏲performances 7.30pm; [S]Line 1 to Tian'anmen West, exit B) Located on the eastern side of Zhōngshān Park, this is a wonderfully romantic venue for performances of classical and traditional Chinese music. It's also the best acoustically.

SHOPPING

★SLOW LANE
TEA, CLOTHING

Map p270 (细活裡; Xì Huó Lǐ; 13 Shijia Hutong; 史家胡同13号; ⏲10am-8pm; [S]Line 5 to Dengshikou, exit C) Secreted away down historic Shijia Hutong, this quietly seductive shop sells beautiful, handmade teaware and quality tea as well as elegant clothing, much of which is made from Tibetan yak wool. Tea sets start from around ¥680.

SHÈNG XĪ FÚ HAT STORE
FASHION & ACCESSORIES

Map p270 (盛锡福; Shèng Xī Fú; 196 Wangfujing Dajie; 王府井大街196号; ⏲8.30am-9pm; [S]Line 1 to Wangfujing, exit B) They used to say that a truly dignified person would only wear shoes made by Nèiliánshēng (p130), silk made by Ruìfúxiáng (p130) and hats made by Shèng Xī Fú. This is China's most famous hat producer. It was first established in the city of Qīngdǎo in 1911, and its hats have been warming the noggins of Chinese people ever since.

Chairman Mao used to get his famous berets from here, and you can pick up a good-quality replica for around ¥60. There are thick winter caps (from ¥160) – perfect for mid-January Běijīng – as well as Russian-style fur hats, some of which will set you back thousands of yuán. This Wangfujing Dajie branch is one of many. A branch further north has a small, free-to-enter hat museum (p72).

WANGFUJING DAJIE
SHOPPING STREET

Map p270 (王府井; Wangfujing Dajie; [S]Line 1 to Wangfujing, Exit C2 or B) Prestigious, but these days rather old-fashioned, this part-pedestrianised shopping street not far from Tiān'ānmén Sq is generally known as Wángfǔjǐng. It boasts a strip of stores selling well-known, midrange brands, and a number of tacky souvenir outlets. At its south end, Oriental Plaza is a top-quality, modern shopping mall. Further north, just before the pedestrianised section ends, is the well-stocked Foreign Languages Bookstore.

HÁOYUÁN MARKET
GIFTS & SOUVENIRS

Map p270 (豪园市场; Háoyuán Shìchǎng; west off Wangfujing Dajie; 王府井大街西侧; [S]Line 1 Wangfujing, exit C2) Branching off from Wángfǔjǐng Snack Street is this small, bustling souvenir market. It has lots of Mao memorabilia, pandas and Buddhas, as well as other tacky tourist tat, but if you're pushed for time and need a last-minute present, you might find something. Haggling is imperative.

FOREIGN LANGUAGES BOOKSTORE
BOOKS

Map p270 (外文书店; Wàiwén Shūdiàn; 235 Wangfujing Dajie; 王府井大街235号; ⏲9.30am-9pm; [S]Line 5 to Dengshikou) Stocks a good selection of English-language novels (ground floor) as well as lots of books on Chinese history, art and architecture. The kids' section (upstairs) is also decent. Has hundreds of Lonely Planet guides (although no China ones), and this is also a good place to pick up cards, postcards and maps of Běijīng,

ORIENTAL PLAZA
MALL

Map p270 (东方广场; Dōngfāng Guǎngchǎng; ☎010 8518 6363; 1 Dongchang'an Jie; 东长安街1号; ⏲10am-10.30pm; [S]Line 1 to Wangfujing, exit B) Vast, modern, hugely popular shopping mall filled with midrange and high-end clothing brands from Asia and the West, plus a range of food outlets and Western coffee shops.

SPORTS & ACTIVITIES

★BIKE BĚIJĪNG
CYCLING

Map p270 (康多自行车租赁; Kāngduō Zìxíngchē Zūlìn; ☎010 6526 5857; www.bikebeijing.com; 81 Beiheyan Dajie; 北河沿大街81号; ⏲8am-8pm; [S]Lines 6, 8 to Nanluoguxiang, exit B, or Line 5 to Zhangzizhonglu, exit D) Rents a range of good-quality bikes, offering mountain bikes (¥200), road bikes (¥400) and ordinary city bikes (¥100); helmets inclusive. It also runs popular guided bike tours around the city (half-day tours from ¥300 to ¥400 per person, depending on group size) and beyond, including bike-and-hike trips to the Great Wall (¥1800 per person, including hotel pickup and lunch).

Guides and shop assistants speak English. And they can also provide you with baby seats (¥50), children's trailers (¥100), and strong bike locks (free). Rental prices are for the first day, with prices halving for

LOCAL KNOWLEDGE

FALLING INTO LINE

Fitness dancing is as popular an activity in Běijīng as it is throughout China. Various forms exist, but the most common is a kind of line dance, which consists of a large number of people (usually middle-aged women) dancing in synchronicity to patriotic music played over a loudspeaker. The main purpose is fitness, but it is also done to continue and perform traditional dance moves, and to strengthen community spirit.

Groups congregate in parks or public squares, or even just on wide sections of pavement, either in the early morning or, more commonly, in the early evening. The dancers usually organise themselves into rank and file, with the most proficient at the front, while beginners (and foreign tourists) line up at the back, trying to copy their moves. Regulars are always happy for visitors to join in – just fall into line (at the back), and tag along.

Prime spots for formation dancing in central Běijīng include the square outside St Joseph's Church (p72), the small roadside square known as the **Imperial City Ruins Park** (皇城根遗址公园; Huángchénggēn Yízhǐ Gōngyuán; Map p270), and the large square situated between the Drum Tower and the Bell Tower.

any subsequent days and weekly discounts. Deposits range from ¥500 to ¥2000, depending on the bike. Alternatively, give staff a copy of your passport and details of where you are staying. Also here is their smart Biking Cafe (p78).

⭐**BLACK SESAME KITCHEN**   COOKING
Map p268 (黑芝麻厨房; Hēi Zhīma Chúfáng; ☎136 9147 4408; www.blacksesamekitchen.com; 28 Zhong Lao Hutong; 中老胡同28号; ⊗cooking classes 11am Wed & Sun, dinner 7pm Tue & Fri; Ⓢ Lines 6, 8 to Nanluoguxiang, exit A) Runs popular cooking classes with a variety of recipes from across China. Booking is essential; walk-in guests are not encouraged as this is a residential courtyard. You can also eat here at one of its communal dinners (set menu ¥300 per person, including wine and beer) – it gets rave reviews – but again you must book.

MÍLÚN KUNGFU SCHOOL   MARTIAL ARTS
Map p270 (弥纶传统武术学校; Mílún Chuántǒng Wǔshù Xuéxiào; ☎138 1170 6568; www. kungfuinchina.com; 36 Ganyu Hutong; 甘雨胡同 36号; per class ¥150, 10-class card ¥1100; ⊗7-8.30pm Mon & Wed; Ⓢ Line 5 to Dengshikou, exit A) Runs classes in various forms of traditional Chinese martial arts (from Shàolín kung fu to kickboxing) in a historic courtyard near Wángfǔjǐng shopping district. In summer, typically in August, classes are held in Rìtán Park. Has set-time drop-in classes, but can arrange individual schedules too. Instruction is in Chinese, but with an English translator. Taichi classes are also available.

JǏNGSHĀN TABLE TENNIS PARK   TABLE TENNIS
Map p270 (东城全民健身第一园; Dōngchéng Quánmín Jiànshēn Dìyī Yuán; Jingshan Houjie, 景山后街; ⊗6am-10pm; Ⓢ Lines 6, 8 to Nanluoguxiang, exit A) This small exercise park has five free-to-use outdoor table tennis tables, which attract some pretty hot pingpong. Only the tables are provided. Players need to bring their own net, bats and ball. Regulars – all too keen to show foreigners who rules the world when it comes to table tennis – will almost certainly let you join in using their equipment.

Drum Tower & Dōngchéng North

Neighbourhood Top Five

❶ Hútòng (p91) Lose yourself in the maze-like network of historic *hútòng*.

❷ Lama Temple (p85) Stroll the incense-filled halls and courtyards of Běijīng's largest and most impressive Buddhist temple.

❸ Drum Tower (p87) Listen to a drumming performance inside this mag-

nificent ancient building, before climbing its equally impressive neighbouring Bell Tower.

❹ Beijing Cultural & Art Centre (p89) Wander down the hipster enclave of Wudaoying Hutong and pop in to check out some contemporary art in a converted courtyard gallery.

❺ Hot Cat Club (p100) Catch a local band at one of the many excellent live-music venues in this part of town. This venue offers a bit of everything.

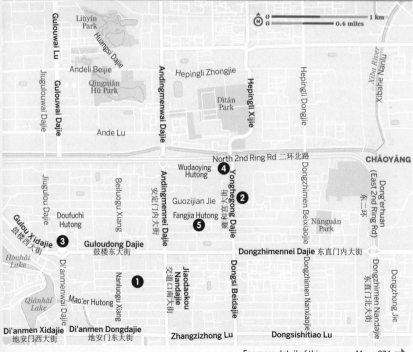

For more detail of this area see Map p274.

Lonely Planet's Top Tip

Rent a bike while you're here, or even buy a cheap secondhand one; you can give it away when you leave. Cycling is the best way to see the city, and is especially good for exploring this area's *hútòng*.

Best Places to Eat

➜ Bǎihé Vegetarian Restaurant (p94)

➜ Georg (p95)

➜ Dàlǐ Courtyard (p96)

➜ Punk Rock Noodles (p90)

➜ Toast (p94)

For reviews, see p90.➜

Best Places to Drink

➜ Capital Spirits (p97)

➜ Tiki Bungalow (p97)

➜ Great Leap Brewing (p97)

➜ Distillery (p97)

➜ Modernista (p98)

➜ 8-Bit (p98)

➜ Voyage Coffee (p98)

For reviews, see p97.➜

Best Places for Live Music

➜ School Bar (p100)

➜ Hot Cat Club (p100)

➜ Jiāng Hú (p100)

➜ Yúgōng Yíshān (p100)

➜ Temple Bar (p100)

For reviews, see p100.➜

Explore Drum Tower & Dōngchéng North

This *hútòng*-rich neighbourhood incorporates the northern section of Běijīng's historic Dōngchéng (东城) district and is the most pleasant area in which to base yourself during your stay in the capital. Book yourself into a *hútòng* hostel or a beautifully converted courtyard hotel, and make this most charming of neighbourhoods your new temporary home.

While there are fewer top-name sights here than in Dōngchéng Central, there is still some sightseeing to be done, although the main attraction is the chance to simply wander around the lanes getting lost.

Nanluogu Xiang is the most famous of the *hútòng* strips, and while it's worth a look, it's lost most of its charm since becoming so popular with tourists. There are much better options, such as happening Wudaoying Hutong, Beiluogu Xiang and Fangjia Hutong with cool cafes, coffee roasters and galleries in converted courtyards.

At night, this neighbourhood is the city's most enjoyable place to drink. Bars here are cool rather than brash and are often tucked away in hard-to-find *hútòng* locations, perfect for the number of speakeasies opening here. It's also the place to catch Běijīng's live-music scene, with a number of venues scattered around these backstreets.

Local Life

➜ **Food** To sample some authentic Běijīng tucker, first check our Běijīng Menu (p96) then head to Yáojì Chǎogān (p93) for some dumplings and pig's liver stew, or to **Róng Tiān Sheep Spine** (容天土锅羊羯子馆; Róngtiān Tǔguō Yángjiézi Guǎn; Map p274; 8 Jingtu Hutong, off Beiluogu Xiang; 北锣鼓巷净土胡同8号; sheep spine per jīn ¥38, other ingredients ¥6-12; ☉10am-10.30pm; Ⓢ Lines 2, 8 to Guloudajie, exit G) for a succulent sheep-spine hotpot.

➜ **Music** Tap into the city's underground music scene at live-music venues such as School Bar (p100), Jiāng Hú (p100) or Hot Cat Club (p100).

➜ **Parks** Head to Dìtán Park (p89) for a spot of kite flying, before cooling off with the masses at the outdoor swimming complex in Qīngnián Hú Park (p103).

Getting There & Away

➜ **Subway** Lines 8, 2, 6 and 5 all serve this neighbourhood well.

➜ **Bus** Bus 107 links the Drum Tower with Dongzhimen Transport Hub. Bus 5 runs south from the Drum Tower, past Běihǎi and Jǐngshān Parks, along the west side of the Forbidden City and on to Qiánmén at the south end of Tiān'ānmén Sq. Bus 113 runs south from Andingmennei Dajie then east to the Workers Stadium and Sānlǐtún.

TOP SIGHT
LAMA TEMPLE

Běijīng's foremost Buddhist temple, the Lama Temple is one of the most magnificent Tibetan Buddhist temples outside Tibet itself. With three richly worked archways and five main halls (each one taller than the preceding one), revolving prayer wheels (propel them clockwise), multicoloured glaze tiles, magnificent Chinese lions, tantric statuettes and hall boards decorated with Mongolian, Manchu, Tibetan and Chinese, the temple is a profound introduction to Tibetan Buddhist lore.

History

The temple was once the official residence of Count Yin Zhen, who became emperor in 1723 and traded up to the Forbidden City. His name changed to Yongzheng, and his former residence became Yōnghé Palace (Yōnghé Gōng). In 1744, it was converted into a lamasery (a monastery of lamas) and became home to legions of monks from Mongolia and Tibet.

In 1792, the Emperor Qianlong, having quelled an uprising in Tibet, instituted a new administrative system involving two golden vases. One was kept at the renowned Jokhang Temple in Lhasa, to be employed for determining the reincarnation of the Dalai Lama, and the other was kept at the Lama Temple for choosing the Panchen Lama. The Lama Temple thus assumed a new importance in ethnic minority control.

Premier Zhou Enlai stepped in when the Red Guards focused their iconoclastic attentions on the temple. Today the temple is an active place of worship, attracting pilgrims from across the land and thronging with worshippers, some of whom prostrate themselves at full length within its halls.

DON'T MISS

➡ 18m-tall sandalwood Buddha
➡ Exhibition in Jiètái Lóu
➡ Exhibition in Bānchán Lóu

PRACTICALITIES

➡ 雍和宫; Yōnghé Gōng
➡ Map p274, F3
➡ www.yonghegong.cn
➡ 12 Yonghegong Dajie; 北新桥雍和宫大街12号
➡ admission ¥25, English audio guide ¥50
➡ ⊙9am-4.30pm
➡ S Lines 2, 5 to Yonghegong-Lama Temple, exit C

Yōnghé Gate

The first hall, Yōnghé Gate (雍和门; Yōnghé Mén), houses a statue of Maitreya, the future Buddha, flanked by celestial guardians. Above it is a board inscribed with the characters 心

SIDE-HALL EXHIBITIONS

Don't miss the collection of bronze Tibetan Buddhist statues within **Jiètái Lóu** (戒台楼). Most effigies date from the Qing dynasty, from languorous renditions of Green Tara and White Tara to exotic tantric pieces (such as Samvara) and figurines of the fierce-looking Mahakala. Also peruse the collection of Tibetan Buddhist ornaments within the **Bānchán Lóu** (班禅楼): there's a fantastic array of *dorje* (Tibetan ritual sceptres), mandalas, tantric figures, and an impressive selection of ceremonial robes in silk and satin.

English-speaking guides (¥80) can be found in the office to the left of the entrance gate, or loitering near the entrance to the complex. Otherwise, pick up an audio guide for ¥50. Photography isn't permitted inside temple buildings, although you can snap away freely around the rest of the complex.

TAKE A BREAK

There are plenty of restaurants in the area, including Veggie Table (p94) and Vineyard Café (p95), as well as the streetfood stall Jiānbing Savoury Pancake Vendor (p92).

明妙现: 'If the heart is bright, the wonderful will appear'. In the courtyard beyond is a pond with a bronze mandala depicting Xumishan, the Buddhist paradise. Glimpses of the more abstruse nature of the temple can be seen in the hall on the right after Yōnghé Gate: the **Esoteric Hall** (密宗殿; Mìzōng Diàn) contains the fierce, multi-armed deity Deweidejingang. Opposite is the **Exoteric Hall** (讲经殿; Jiǎngjīng Diàn), where sutras were studied and recited.

Yōnghé Hall

With its air of peaceful reverence, the second hall, Yōnghé Hall (雍和殿; Yōnghé Diàn), contains a trinity of gilded effigies representing the past, present and future Buddhas.

Yǒngyòu Hall

The third hall, Yǒngyòu Hall (永佑殿; Yǒngyòu Diàn), contains statues of the Buddha of Longevity and the Buddha of Medicine (to the left). Peek into the **East Side Hall** (东配殿; Dōngpèi Dian) for its esoteric gathering of cobalt-blue Buddhas and two huge dog-like creatures. Note how the tantric statues have been partially draped to disguise their couplings.

Hall of the Wheel of the Law

The fourth hall, Hall of the Wheel of the Law (法轮殿; Fǎlún Diàn), houses a large bronze statue of a benign and smiling Tsong Khapa (1357–1419), founder of the Gelukpa, or Yellow Hat, sect, robed in yellow and illuminated from a skylight above. Also within the hall is a throne that seated the Dalai Lamas when they used to lecture sutras here.

Wànfú Pavilion

The final main hall, Wànfú Pavilion (万福阁; Wànfú Gé), has a stupendous 18m-tall statue of the Maitreya Buddha in his Tibetan form, clothed in yellow satin and reputedly sculpted from a single block of sandalwood. Smoke curling up from yak-butter lamps enhances the Tibetan-like atmosphere.

Behind the statue is the **Vault of Avalokiteshvara** (观音洞; Guānyīn Dòng), from where a diminutive and blue-faced statue of Guanyin peeks out. The Wànfú Pavilion is linked by an overhead walkway to the **Yánsuí Pavilion** (延绥阁; Yánsuí Gé), which encloses a huge lotus flower that revolves to reveal an effigy of the longevity Buddha.

Behind Wànfú Pavilion, worshippers gather to worship White Tara and Green Tara in the **Suíchéng Hall** (绥成殿; Suíchéng Diàn).

LEONID ANDRONOV / SHUTTERSTOCK ©

TOP SIGHT
DRUM TOWER

Along with the older-looking Bell Tower, which stands behind it, the magnificent red-painted Drum Tower used to be the city's official timekeeper, with drums and bells beaten and rung to mark the times of the day; effectively the Big Ben of Běijīng.

Originally built in 1272, the Drum Tower was once the heart of the Mongol capital of Dàdū, as Běijīng was then known. That structure was destroyed in a fire before a replacement was built, slightly to the east of the original location, in 1420. The current structure is a later Qing dynasty version of that 1420 tower.

You can climb the incredibly steep inner staircase for views of the grey-tiled rooftops in the surrounding *hútòng* alleys. Arguably the best view of the Drum Tower is from the top of the Bell Tower. Annoyingly, though, the view isn't reciprocated because visitors aren't allowed to walk round to the north-facing side of the Drum Tower's viewing balcony.

It's still well worth climbing the tower, though, especially if you can time it to coincide with one of the regular drumming performances, which are played out on reproductions of the 25 Ming dynasty watch drums that used to sound out across this part of the city. One of the original 25 drums – the Night Watchman's Drum (更鼓; Gēnggǔ) – is on display; now dusty, battered and worn. Also on display is a replica of a Song dynasty water clock, which was never actually used in the tower, but is interesting nonetheless.

The times of the drumming performances, which only last for a couple of minutes, are posted by the ticket office. At the time of research they were 9.30am, 10.30am, 11.30am, 1.30pm, 2.30pm, 3.30pm and 4.45pm.

There are a handful of excellent bars and cafes around the recently developed Drum & Bell Sq, including 1796 (p99) with a rooftop terrace overlooking the plaza. For typical Běijīng cuisine, head to Yáojì Chǎogān (p93) around the corner.

DON'T MISS

➡ Drumming performance

➡ Night Watchman's Drum

PRACTICALITIES

➡ 鼓楼; Gǔlóu

➡ Map p274, A5

➡ Gulou Dongdajie; 鼓楼东大街

➡ admission ¥20, both towers through ticket ¥30

➡ 🕒9am-5pm, last entry 4.40pm

➡ [S]Line 8 to Shichahai, exit A2

LEONID ANDRONOV / SHUTTERSTOCK ©

TOP SIGHT
BELL TOWER

The more modest, grey-stone structure of the Bell Tower is arguably more charming than its resplendent other half, the Drum Tower, after which this area of Běijīng is named. It also has the added advantage of being able to view its sister tower from a balcony.

Along with the drums in the Drum Tower, the bells in the Bell Tower were used as Běijīng's official timekeepers throughout the Yuan, Ming and Qing dynasties, and on until 1924. The Bell Tower looks the older of the two, perhaps because it isn't painted. In fact both are of similar age. The Bell Tower was also built during the Mongol Yuan Dynasty, in 1272, and was rebuilt in the 1440s after being destroyed in a fire. This current structure was built in 1745.

Like the Drum Tower, the Bell Tower can be climbed up an incredibly steep inner staircase. But the views from the top are even better here, partly because the structure is set back more deeply into the surrounding *hútòng,* and partly because you can get great photos of the Drum Tower from its viewing balcony. Marvel too at the huge, 600-year-old, 63-tonne bell suspended in the pleasantly unrestored interior. Note how Chinese bells have no clappers but are instead struck with a stout pole.

Inside the tower, on the ground floor (south side), is the **Bell Tower Tea House**, where you can sample a selection of Chinese teas (per person per hour ¥50) as well as buy tea and tea sets.

The Drum & Bell Sq, between the two towers, is a great people-watching area in which to while away some time, even if you don't climb either of the two towers. Both towers are lit up beautifully come evening.

DON'T MISS

- 63-tonne bell
- View of the Drum Tower

PRACTICALITIES

- 钟楼; Zhōnglóu
- Map p274, A4
- Gulou Dongdajie; 鼓楼东大街
- admission ¥20, both towers through ticket ¥30
- ⏰9am-5pm, last tickets 4.40pm
- [S] Line 8 to Shichahai, exit A2

SIGHTS

LAMA TEMPLE
BUDDHIST TEMPLE

See p85.

DRUM TOWER
HISTORIC SITE

See p87.

BELL TOWER
HISTORIC SITE

See p88.

CONFUCIUS TEMPLE & IMPERIAL COLLEGE
CONFUCIAN TEMPLE

Map p274 (孔庙、国子监; Kǒng Miào & Guózǐjiàn; 13 Guozijian Jie; 国子监街13号; admission ¥30, audio guide ¥30; ⏲8.30am-6pm May-Oct, to 5pm Nov-Apr, last entry 1hr before closing; [S]Lines 2, 5 to Yonghegong-Lama Temple, exit C) An incense stick's toss away from the Lama Temple, China's second-largest Confucian temple has had a refit in recent years, but the almost otherworldly sense of detachment is seemingly impossible to shift. A mood of impassiveness reigns and the lack of worship reinforces a sensation that time has stood still. However, in its tranquillity and reserve, the temple can be a pleasant sanctuary from Běijīng's often congested streets – a haven of peace and quiet.

Antediluvian *bìxì* (mythical tortoise-like dragons) glare from repainted pavilions while lumpy and ossified ancient cypresses claw stiffly at the Běijīng air. There's the Qianlong Stone Scriptures, a stone 'forest' of 190 stelae recording the 13 Confucian classics in 630,000 Chinese characters at the temple rear. Also inscribed on stelae are the names of successful candidates of the highest level of the official Confucian examination system.

Next to the Confucius Temple, but within the same grounds, stands the **Imperial College**, where the emperor expounded the Confucian classics to an audience of thousands of kneeling students, professors and court officials – an annual rite. Built by the grandson of Kublai Khan in 1306, the former college was the supreme academy during the Yuan, Ming and Qing dynasties. On the site is a marvellous, glazed, three-gate, single-eaved decorative archway called a *liúli páifāng* (glazed archway). The **Biyong Hall** (辟雍大殿, Pìyōng Dàdiàn) beyond is a twin-roofed structure with yellow tiles surrounded by a moat and topped with a splendid gold knob. Its stupendous interior houses a vermillion and gold lectern. The side pavilions house several interesting museums on Confucianism and the academy itself.

Some of Běijīng's last remaining *páilou* (decorated archways) bravely survive in the tree-lined street outside (Guozijian Jie) and the entire area of *hútòng* here is now dotted with small cafes, cute restaurants and boutique shops, making it an ideal place to browse in low gear. At the western end of Guozijian Jie stands a diminutive **Fire God Temple** (火神庙; Huǒshén Miào; Map p274; Guozijian Jie; 国子监街; [S]Lines 2, 5 to Yonghegong-Lama Temple, exit C), built in 1802 and now occupied by Běijīng residents.

BĚIJĪNG CULTURAL & ART CENTRE
GALLERY

Map p274 (BCAC, 北京文化艺术中心; Běijīng Wénhuà Yìshù Zhōngxīn; ☎010 8408 4977; www.bcac.org.cn; 3 Wudaoying Hutong; 五道营胡同3号; admission ¥10; ⏲10am-8pm Tue-Sun; [S]Lines 2, 5 to Yonghegong-Lama Temple, exit D) In a beautiful *hútòng* courtyard building along one of Beijing's coolest streets, this not-for-profit art gallery has three slick exhibition spaces that cover anything from contemporary and traditional arts to design, fashion and architecture. It generally shows a mix of local and international artists.

ARROW FACTORY
GALLERY

Map p274 (箭厂空间; Jiànchǎng Kōngjiān; www.arrowfactory.org.cn; 38 Jianchang Hutong, off Guozijian Jie; 国子监街，箭厂胡同38号; ⏲24hr; [S]Lines 2, 5 to Yonghegong Lama Temple or Line 2 to Andingmen) This tiny, 15-sq-metre, storefront gallery occupies a former vegetable shop and is now an independently run art space for avant-garde installations and modern-art projects designed to be viewed from the street, 24 hours a day, seven days a week. You can't enter the room, but its all-glass front means you can peer in whenever you walk past.

DÌTÁN PARK
PARK

Map p274 (地坛公园; Dìtán Gōngyuán; park ¥2, altar ¥5; ⏲6am-9.30pm, to 8.30pm Nov-Apr; [S]Lines 2, 5 to Yonghegong-Lama Temple, exit A) Directly north of the Lama Temple, but cosmologically juxtaposed with the **Temple of Heaven** (Tiāntán), the **Altar of the Moon** (Yuètán), the **Altar of the Sun** (Rìtán) and the **Altar to the God of the Land and the God of Grain** (Shèjìtán), Dìtán is the Temple of the Earth. The park, site of imperial sacrifices to the Earth God, lacks the splendour of Temple of Heaven Park but is certainly worth a stroll if you've just been to nearby Lama Temple.

You'll find locals flying kites, singing songs, strumming *èrhú* (two-stringed fiddle), practising taichi and keeping fit in the exercise park (northeast corner). The park's large, open-air altar (*fāngzé tán*) is square in shape, symbolising the earth. Sadly, recent renovation work has robbed it of some of its previous authenticity. During Chinese New Year, a huge (though rather commercialised) temple fair is held here. Note admission to the temple complex is an additional ¥5.

QI BAISHI'S FORMER RESIDENCE — MUSEUM

Map p274 (齐白石旧居纪念馆; Qí Báishí Jiùjū Jìniànguǎn; 13 Yu'er Hutong, off Nanluogu Xiang; 南锣鼓巷，雨儿胡同13号; admission ¥5; ⏲9am-5pm Tue-Sun, last entry 4pm; [S]Lines 6, 8 to Nanluoguxiang, exit E, or Line 8 to Shichahai, exit C) Known for the whimsical, often playful style of his watercolors, Qi Baishi (1864–1957) was an influential Chinese painter who lived in Běijīng from 1917 onwards. This particular courtyard residence – built on the site of the Qing dynasty home of Emperor Hong Taiji's fourth son, Ye Bushu (1627–90) – was his home for just the final two years of his life. Rooms here contain numerous examples of his scroll paintings, and one includes a detailed introduction (with English translations) to his life story.

MAO DUN'S FORMER RESIDENCE — HISTORIC BUILDING

Map p274 (茅盾故居; Máo Dùn Gùjū; 13 Houyuan Ensi Hutong; 后圆恩寺胡同13号; ⏲9am-4pm Tue-Sun; [S]Lines 6, 8 to Nanluoguxiang, exit E) [FREE] The lack of English captions is frustrating, but this small and unassuming museum does at least give visitors the chance to stroll around a trapped-in-time courtyard residence. Mao Dun was the pen name of Shen Yanbing (1896–1981), who was born into an elite family in Zhèjiāng province but educated in Běijīng. He lived at the back courtyard here from 1974 until his death.

🍴 EATING

This historic part of Běijīng has a huge range of dining options covering every type of Chinese cuisine, as well as plenty of international places. It's also home to some of the capital's most atmospheric restaurants, from beautifully converted courtyards, to the many hole-in-the-wall establishments scattered throughout the local *hútòng*. Locals also head to the very popular so-called Ghost Street (簋街; Gui Jie) for hotpot and seafood at all hours.

★PUNK ROCK NOODLES — NOODLES $

Map p274 (鼓楼吃面; Gǔlóu Chīmiàn; ☎010 8402 3180; 25 Donggong Jie, Loudong Dajie; 鼓楼东大街东公街25号; noodles from ¥25; ⏲noon-2am; [S]Line 5 to Beixinqiao, exit A) Run by owner Ma Yue, and her merry staff of punk rockers, this restaurant is equally popular with workers and students as it with skinheads, all drawn by the delicious hand-pulled noodles. It also does inventive dishes such as 'Punk's Not Dead' with sliced ox tongue, enjoyed by hard-core punk band the Exploited upon their visit. Tables are decked out in gingham and walls decorated in punk memorabilia.

It's a good place for a drink too, especially for its ¥10 cocktail happy hour (9pm to 10pm). Most staff are connected to the local Oi! punk band Misandao, whose frontman (and restaurant co-owner), Lei Jun, sadly passed away in 2015.

ZHĀNG MĀMA — SICHUAN $

Map p274 (张妈妈特色川味馆; Zhāng Māma Tèsè Chuānwèiguǎn; 76 Jiaodaokou Nandajie; 交道口南大街76号; mains ¥10-20; ⏲11am-10.30pm; [S]Line 5 to Beixinqiao, exit A) The original Zhāng Māma, on nearby Fensiting Hutong, was such a hit with Beijingers they were forced to also open this new, larger branch with two floors. At the smaller, original branch you have to wait up to an hour for a table. Here, they've cut that down to about 15 minutes. It's worth the wait. This is arguably Běijīng's best-value Sìchuānese restaurant.

The speciality is *málà xiāngguō* (麻辣香锅; ¥48 to ¥58), a fiery, chilli-laced broth with either chicken (香锅鸡; *xiāngguō jī*), prawns (香锅虾; *xiāngguō xiā*) or ribs (香锅排骨; *xiāngguō páigǔ*) simmering away inside, and with a variety of vegetables added into the mix. One pot is enough for two or three people. Also worth trying here is the *dàndàn miàn* (担担面; spicy dry noodles; ¥8) and the rice meals; the classic being the *gōngbào jīdīng gàifàn* (宫爆鸡丁盖饭; spicy chicken with peanuts; ¥12), which is lip-tinglingly delicious, thanks to the generous sprinkling of Sìchuān peppercorns. No English menu, so don't be shy about pointing to what fellow diners are eating. Chances are it'll be spicy, but delicious.

Neighbourhood Walk
Historic Hútòng Around Nanluogu Xiang

START NANLUOGUXIANG SUBWAY STATION
END DRUM & BELL TOWERS
LENGTH 2KM; ONE HOUR

Běijīng's *hútòng* are the heart and soul of the city.

Exit Nanluoguxiang subway station and turn right into Chaodou Hutong (炒豆胡同). Starting at No 77, the next few courtyards once made up the ❶**former mansion of Seng Gelinqin**, a Qing dynasty army general. Note the enormous *bǎogǔshí* (drum stones) at the entranceway to No 77, followed by more impressive gateways at Nos 75, 69, 67 and 63. After No 53, turn left up an unmarked winding alleyway then left onto Banchang Hutong (板厂胡同).

At No 19, turn right through an unusual ❷**hallway gate**, a connecting passageway leading to Dongmianhua Hutong (东棉花胡同). Turn right here, then left down an unnamed alley, which is signposted to Pénghāo Theatre.

Turn left onto Beibingmasi Hutong (北兵马司胡同) and cross Nanluogu Xiang into historic ❸**Mao'er Hutong** (帽儿胡同). Admire the entranceways, or if the gates are open, step into the charming courtyards at Nos 5 and 11. Further on, No 37 was the ❹**former home of Wan Rong**, who would later marry China's last emperor, Puyi.

Next, turn right down Doujiao Hutong (豆角胡同) and wind your way (past Great Leap Brewing) to Fangzhuanchang Hutong (方砖厂胡同) then Nanxiawazi Hutong (南下洼子胡同), with its small ❺**fruit & veg street market**, and continue north to Gulou Dongdajie (鼓楼东大街). Turn left here and then, just before you reach the imperious red-painted ❻**Drum Tower** (p87), turn right into Caochang Hutong (草厂胡同). Continue down the lane, then take the second left: you'll see the magnificent grey-brick ❼**Bell Tower** (p88) in front of you. Follow this wonderfully winding alley to the back of the Bell Tower, then walk around the tower to the recently redeveloped ❽**Drum & Bell Square**.

GHOST STREET

For a close-up look at how Beijingers treat their restaurants as party venues and not just places for a meal, take a trip to **Ghost Street** (簋街; Gui Jie; Map p274; Dongzhimennei Dajie; ⓢLine 5 to Beixinqiao, exit B). This 1.4km strip of Dongzhimennei Dajie is home to more than 150 restaurants that attract everyone from hipsters to office workers, man-bag-toting businessmen and families, as well as the odd celebrity.

It never closes, making it one of Běijīng's most buzzing streets, and it's especially fun on Friday and Saturday nights. Traffic slows to a crawl as the restaurant workers line the side of the road trying to entice passing cars to stop at their joint. Crowds of people spill out onto the pavement waiting for a free table while clacking open sunflower seeds, as the sweating staff rush around delivering food and beers to people celebrating the end of the week.

Most styles of Chinese cuisine are represented on Ghost Street, but it's best known for its hotpot and spicy seafood restaurants.

The giant Xiǎo Yú Shān (p93) is always jammed with people cracking open crayfish and shrimp. For classic Běijīng-style hotpot, try Supreme Hotpot (p94).

Ghost Street gets its English name from a mistranslation for the Chinese nickname of the street, Gui Jie (簋街). 簋 (pronounced 'guǐ') is an ancient bronze food vessel, a statue of which you can find at the far eastern end of Dongzhimennei Dajie, by the 2nd Ring Rd, but it's pronounced the same as 鬼 – Chinese for ghost.

Sadly its signature red lanterns, which for years lined both sides of the street, lending it a unique look, were torn down by overzealous local officials in 2014 – they were a fire risk, apparently.

PALMS LA KITCHEN & BAR   MEXICAN $

Map p274 (洛杉矶厨房和酒吧; Luòshānjī Chúfáng Hé Jiǔbā; ☑010 6405 4352; 14 Zhangwang Hutong; 西城区张旺胡同14号; 3 tacos ¥45; ⊙noon-2.30pm & 5.30-10.30pm Tue-Fri, 11.30am-10.30pm Sat & Sun; ❀🐱; ⓢLines 2, 8 to Gouloudajie, exit G) Bringing the LA food-truck craze of Korean-Mexican fusion to Běijīng, this small *hútòng* restaurant does kimchi tacos, K-town fries and soju cocktails. It makes its own hot sauce, but loses points for no soft corn masa tortillas. There's craft beers on tap and a good selection of cocktails.

PEBBLES COURTYARD   MEXICAN $

Map p274 (卵石庭院; Luǎnshí Tíngyuàn; ☑010 8404 0767; 74 Wudaoying Hutong; 五道营胡同74号; tacos ¥20, burritos ¥65; ⊙11am-11pm; ⓢLine 2 to Andingmen or Lines 2, 5 to Yonghegong-Lama Temple, exit D) While it doesn't have the street cred of other Běijīng hipster taquerias, don't be deceived by its kitschy decor, the tacos at Pebble's are the real deal. Soft corn tortillas come with a choice of classic chorizo, *al pastor* (marinated pork) or *carne asada* (beef), to go with Mexican beers (including zesty *micheladas)* and margaritas.

JIĀNBING SAVOURY
PANCAKE VENDOR   STREET FOOD $

Map p274 (煎饼; 154 Yonghegong Dajie; 雍和宫大街154号; pancakes ¥5-¥6; ⊙7am-7pm; ⓢLines 2, 5 to Yonghegong-Lama Temple, exit C) Hole-in-the-wall stall selling *jiānbing* (煎饼; savoury pancakes).

WǓ JĪN CAFE   BREAKFAST $

Map p274 (五金; Wǔjīn Kāfēi; 38 Jianchang Hutong, off Guozijian Jie; 国子监街，箭厂胡同38号; breakfast incl tea or coffee ¥10-30; ⊙8.30am-12.30pm Mon-Fri, 9am-3pm Sat & Sun; 🐱; ⓢLines 2, 5 to Yonghegong-Lama Temple, exit D, or Line 2 to Andingmen) This hole-in-the-wall cafe has one communal counter to enjoy thick-cut home-baked bread, with slow-poached 63°C eggs or, seasonal homemade jams and great value Yúnnán filter-coffee refills (¥15). Its very drinkable house wines are also a bargain at ¥15 a glass. It's run by the local Arrow Factory (p89) gallery.

YÁNG FĀNG
LAMB HOTPOT   MONGOLIAN HOTPOT $

Map p274 (羊坊涮肉; Yáng Fāng Shuàn Ròu; 270 Gulou Dongdajie; 鼓楼东大街270号; broth ¥8-15, dips & sauces ¥2-5, raw ingredients ¥6-25; ⊙11am-11pm; ⓢLine 8 to Shichahai, exit A2) There are two main types of hotpot in China: the ridiculously spicy one that comes from the fire-breathing southwestern city of Chóngqìng, and the milder version which is cooked in an unusual conical brass pot. Yáng Fāng is a salt-of-the-earth version of the latter, and is a real favourite with the locals round here.

First order the broth you want in your pot – clear (清汤锅底; *qīng tāng guōde;* ¥15), or spicy (辣锅底; *là guōde;* ¥20); clear is more common. Then ask for some sesame-paste dipping sauce (小料; *xiǎo liào;* ¥5); each person should have one. And, if you fancy it, order some freshly prepared chilli oil (鲜榨辣椒油; *xiān zhá là jiāo yóu;* ¥2) to mix into your dipping sauce; one bowl is enough for everyone to share.

Finally, select the raw ingredients you want to cook in your broth. Our favourites include wafer-thin lamb slices (鲜羊肉; *xiān yáng ròu;* ¥26), lotus root slices (藕片; *ǒu piàn;* ¥8), tofu slabs (鲜豆腐; *xiān dòufu;* ¥6), sweet potato (红薯; *hóng shǔ;* ¥6) and spinach (菠菜; *bō cài;* ¥6). No English sign; no English menu; no English spoken.

BĀOZI PÙ DUMPLING $

Map p274 (包子铺; 108 Gulou Dongdajie; 鼓楼东大街108号; dumplings per basket ¥5-7, noodles ¥10-12, rice meals ¥13-18; ⏲6am-9pm; [S]Line 5 to Beixinqiao, exit A, or Line 8 to Shichahai, exit A2) A local favourite, especially for breakfast, Bāozi Pù – literally 'dumplings shop' – has been on this corner for years. Steamed pork dumplings (包子; *bāozi;* ¥7 per basket) are the speciality; say *'sù bāozi'* if you want vegetable ones (¥5). The boiled dumplings (蒸饺; *zhēng jiǎo*) are also good. Wash it down with a traditional soy milk drink (豆浆; *dòu jiāng;* ¥3).

At lunchtimes, try the knife-sliced pork noodles (刀削面; *dāo xiāo miàn*), the spicy dry mincemeat noodles (担担面; *dàndàn miàn*), or one of the many rice meals (盖饭; *gài fàn*). It's had a big makeover, offering a much wider menu to cater for the explosion of Chinese tourists coming to the area, and has consequently lost much of its charm, but the hand-cut noodles arc still good.

YÁOJÌ CHĂOGĀN BEIJING $

Map p274 (姚记炒肝店; 311 Gulou Dongdajie; 鼓楼东大街311号; mains ¥8-20; ⏲6am-10.30pm; [S]Line 8 to Shichahai, exit A2) Proper locals' joint, serving Běijīng dishes in a noisy, no-nonsense atmosphere. The house speciality is *chǎogān* (炒肝; pig's liver stew; ¥10). This is also a good place to try *zhá guànchang* (炸灌肠; garlic-topped deep-fried crackers; ¥8) and *má dòufu* (麻豆腐; spicy tofu paste; ¥10).

Its steamed pork dumplings (包子; *bāozi;* ¥3.50 for two) are excellent, and are perfect for breakfast with a bowl of *xiǎomǐ zhōu* (小米粥; millet porridge; ¥2) or locals' favourite *dòuzhī* (豆汁; soy milk; ¥2). It also does a decent bowl of Běijīng's best-known noodle dish, *zhájiàng miàn* (炸酱面; ¥12). No English menu or English sign.

YĪ LÓNG ZHĀI XINJIANG $

Map p274 (伊隆斋; cnr Mao'er Hutong & Doujiao Hutong; 帽儿胡同和豆角胡同的路口; mains ¥15-30; ⏲9.30am-midnight; [S]Line 8 to Shichahai, exit C) Bright and boisterous, this no-frills restaurant specialises in the Turkic-influenced cuisine of Xīnjiāng province, in west China. So expect lots of tasty lamb dishes. The *kǎo yáng tuǐ* (烤羊腿; grilled leg of lamb; ¥25) is excellent, as are the *yáng ròu chuàn* (羊肉串; lamb skewers; ¥3). There's also a good selection of noodle dishes (¥12 to ¥18) in the photo menu.

Another signature dish here is the *dà pán jī* (大盘鸡; literally, 'big plate chicken'; ¥88), which is enough to feed four or five hungry mouths, especially when the sauce is mopped up with some *kǎo náng* (烤馕; naan bread; ¥6). If there's only two or three of you, go for the small portion (*xiǎo pán jī;* 小盘鸡; ¥55), which is still massive. Has patio seating out front in summer.

TÀN HUĀ LAMB BBQ BARBECUE $

Map p274 (碳花烤羊腿; Tàn Huā Kǎo Yángtuǐ; 63 Beixinqiao Santiao; 北新桥三条63号; lamb per jīn ¥52, side dishes ¥1-12; ⏲11am-midnight; [S]Line 5 to Beixinqiao, exit B) Meat-loving Beijingers flock to this raucous joint where you roast a leg of lamb on your own personal table-top barbecue spit before hacking away at the meatiest bits with a rudimentary, long-handled knife and fork. Tables spill out onto the lively *hútòng*, creating a party atmosphere of multi-barbecue revelry.

Order your leg of lamb (羊腿; *yáng tuǐ*) by the *jīn* (500g). Three *jīn* (三斤; *sān jīn*) is enough for two or three people. You'll then be given a selection of free cold dishes as accompaniments, plus a cumin-based dry dip to roll your lamb slices in. Other popular side dishes include barbecued naan bread (烤馕; *kǎo náng;* ¥6), soy fried rice (酱油炒饭; *jiàng yóu chǎo fàn;* ¥12) and noodle-drop soup (疙瘩汤; *gēda tāng;* ¥12).

XIĂO YÚ SHĀN SEAFOOD $

Map p274 (小渔山; 195 Dongzhimennei Dajie; 东直门内大街195号; mains ¥30-150; ⏲24hr; [S]Line 5 to Beixinqiao, exit B) A very popular fixture along the Ghost Street eating strip, this giant seafood restaurant is always jammed with people cracking open crayfish and shrimp.

LOCAL KNOWLEDGE

TRADITIONAL BĚIJĪNG YOGHURT

On your shopping wanders through the *hútòng*, you may notice intriguing rows of little clay pots, sealed with thin, white and blue paper tops, and lined up outside small corner shops. The pots contain *lǎo Běijīng suānnǎi* (老北京酸奶), traditional Běijing yoghurt, and make a perfect slurp-on-the-go street-side refreshment.

Prices vary slightly, but they tend to cost ¥3 or ¥4 if you drink them on the spot and return your pot, and ¥1 extra if you take them away.

SUPREME HOTPOT — CHINESE $

Map p274 (208 Dongzhimennei Dajie; 东直门内大街208号; hotpot ¥15, plus items from ¥10; ⏲11am-4am; [S]Line 5 to Beixinqiao, exit B) One of many hotpot places along this popular neon-lit restaurant strip, this smart little eatery does it all Beijing-style. For a local experience, come at night when things get rowdy.

CHEZ GÉRARD — DELI $

Map p274 (40 Jianchang Hutong, off Guozijian Jie; 国子监街，箭厂胡同40号; ⏲10am-10.30pm; [S]Line 2 to Andingmen or Lines 2, 5 to Yonghegong-Lama Temple, exit D) This tiny grocery store, located inside two adjacent shopfronts, is a decent place to grab picnic supplies. It stocks freshly baked breads, imported cheeses, a selection of cold meats, international packaged foods and well-priced imported wines and craft beers.

TOAST — MIDDLE EASTERN $$

Map p274 (☎010 8404 4818, 010 5799 0806; www.theorchidbeijing.com; 65 Baochao Hutong, Dulou Dongdajie; 鼓楼东大街宝钞胡同65号; mains from ¥88; ⏲10am-2.30pm & 6-10pm Wed-Mon; [S]Lines 2, 8 to Guloudajie, exit F or Line 8 to Shichahai, exit A2) Located at the boutique Orchid (p186) hotel is this stylish restaurant with a quality menu of Middle Eastern/North African/Indian–influenced cuisine. Dishes are shared plates and range from homemade bread and dips, poached egg kofte, roasted lamb ribs with hummus, to spicy clams. It's popular also for its quality breakfast and brunch menus, and rooftop cocktails when the sun's out.

STUFF'D — INTERNATIONAL $$

Map p274 (塞; Sāi; ☎010 6407 6308; www.stuff-d.com; 9 Jianchang Hutong, off Guozijian Jie; 国子监街，箭厂胡同9号; sausages from ¥30, pies ¥68, pizza ¥68, beer ¥40; ⏲11.30am-midnight Sun-Thu, to 1am Fri & Sat; 📶; [S]Line 2 to Andingmen or Lines 2, 5 to Yonghegong-Lama Temple, exit D) Handmade sausages and home-brewed beer. What more could you want? Set up by Arrow Factory brewery (which has a taproom out the back), this rustic space has a warm, cosy feel; almost like an English pub, only housed within a restored Chinese *píngfáng* (bungalow). The menu is all about the sausages and ale, but there are also pies and pizza.

BǍIHÉ VEGETARIAN RESTAURANT — CHINESE $$

Map p274 (百合素食; Bǎihé Sùshí; 23 Caoyuan Hutong; 东直门内北小街草园胡同甲23号; mains ¥25-60, tea per cup/pot from ¥25/45; ⏲11am-10pm; ✍; [S]Lines 2, 13 to Dongzhimen, exit A, or Line 5 to Beixinqiao, exit B) This peaceful, tastefully furnished, courtyard restaurant, which also serves as a delightful teahouse, has a wonderful air of serenity – it's not uncommon to see monks from nearby Lama Temple (p85) coming here for a pot of tea. The all-vegetarian menu (with English translations) includes imaginative mock-meat dishes as well as more conventional vegetable dishes and a range of tasty noodles.

With courteous service, this is one of Běijīng's more soothing dining experiences. There's also a separate and extensive tea menu – customers are welcome to come here just to sample the tea. To get here, walk north on Dongzhimen Beixiaojie from the junction with Ghost Street for 100m, then turn left into the first *hútòng*. The restaurant is on the right, although the sign is in Chinese only.

VEGGIE TABLE — VEGAN $$

Map p274 (吃素的; Chīsù De; ☎010 6446 2073; 19 Wudaoying Hutong; 五道营胡同19号; burgers ¥65; ⏲11.30am-11.30pm; ✍; [S]Lines 2, 5 to Yonghegong-Lama Temple, exit D) 🍃 With Wudaoying Hutong garnering a reputation as hipster central – craft beer, single-origin coffee, art/indie music venues, fixed-gear bike shops – you can add a vegan diner to the mix. The food is mainly Western, along the lines of shiitake mushroom burgers with dairy-free mayo, meze platters, soups and organic veggie salads.

LE LITTLE SAIGON
FRENCH, VIETNAMESE $$

Map p274 (西贡在巴黎; Xīgòng Zài Bālí; ☎010 6401 8465; www.lelittlesaigon.com; 141 Jiugulou Dajie; 旧鼓楼大街141号; mains ¥35-128; ⏲noon-10pm; 📶; Ⓢ Line 8 to Shichahai, exit A2) The menu at this stylish bistro – with a nice roof terrace in summer – is a mix of classic Vietnamese – *phở* (Vietnamese soup; ¥35), lemon chicken, shrimps in tamarind sauce – and French – beef bourguignon and foie gras. The desserts are especially good. The decor and decent wine list are decidedly Gallic, making it popular with French expats and anyone in search of a lovingly prepared cup of coffee, whether it's the European or Vietnamese variety.

CAFÉ DE LA POSTE
FRENCH $$

Map p274 (云游驿; Yúnyóu Yì; 58 Yonghegong Dajie; 雍和宫大街58号; mains ¥60-218; ⏲12.30-3pm & 6-11pm; 📶; Ⓢ Line 5 to Beixinqiao, exit B, or Lines 2, 5 to Yonghegong-Lama Temple, exit C) Just down the street from the Lama Temple, this long-time expat favourite, with a relaxed vibe and friendly service, is Běijīng's original French bistro. A small bar area opens into an intimate, nicely lit dining space, and the food (unlike many French restaurants) is unpretentious, affordable and authentic.

The steaks (from ¥60) are impressive cuts of meat, but there's also a good vegetarian selection, as well as imported French cheeses and delicious homemade desserts. There's a set lunch during the week, brunch at weekends, and an impressive wine list, including inexpensive house French wines for ¥90 per bottle. The bar stays open late and has clientele spilling out onto the pavement in summer.

VINEYARD CAFÉ
INTERNATIONAL $$

Map p274 (葡萄院儿; Pútáo Yuànr; www.vineyardcafe.cn; 31 Wudaoying Hutong; 五道营胡同31号; mains from ¥60; ⏲10.30am-11.30pm Sun-Thu, to 1am Fri & Sat; Ⓢ Lines 2, 5 to Yonghegong-Lama Temple, exit D) This laid-back, attractive, family-friendly cafe-restaurant was the first place to open its doors on the increasingly popular Wudaoying Hutong. It's a good spot to get your fix of Western food, doing cheeseburgers, pastrami on rye, steak and ale pies, sausages and pizza. There's Arrow Brewery beers on tap, a quality wine list and cocktails.

CAFÉ SAMBAL
MALAYSIAN $$

Map p274 (☎010 6400 4875; www.cafesambal.com; 43 Doufuchi Hutong; 旧鼓楼大街豆腐池胡同43号; mains ¥60-138; ⏲11am-11pm; Ⓢ Line 8 to Shichahai, exit A2, or Lines 2, 8 to Guloudajie, exit G) This rustic Malaysian restaurant located off Jiugulou Dajie is in a cleverly converted courtyard house at the entrance to Doufuchi Hutong. The minimalist bar opens into a narrow dining area that has a temporary roof during winter, but is open in summer. The food is classic Malaysian. Try the beef rendang (¥80), or deep-fried tofu with prawns, peanuts and sambal (¥58). The wine list is decent, as are the mojitos (¥55).

JĪN DǏNG XUĀN
CANTONESE $$

Map p274 (金鼎轩; 77 Hepingli Xijie; 地坛南门和平里西街77号; dim sum ¥10-20, mains ¥30-100; ⏲24hr; Ⓢ Lines 2, 5 to Yonghegong-Lama Temple,

BARBECUE SKEWERS

The red neon 串 signs that you see hanging outside restaurants come evening, are actually shaped as the Chinese character for *chuàn* (串; skewers) and signify that the restaurant serves barbecue skewers. They are often, but not always, Muslim-food restaurants, and sometimes they are simply a hole-in-the-wall outfit that only serves skewers. Either way, they're a favourite snack spot for locals; pull up a stool, order a bottle of local beer (啤酒; *píjiǔ;* ¥4 to ¥5) and join them for a barbecue pit-stop.

Chances are the staff won't speak a word of English, so to help you order, here's a list of the most common skewers and their usual prices:

lamb skewers 羊肉串, *yángròu chuàn*, ¥2

steamed buns 馒头片, *mántou piàn*, ¥1

chicken wings 鸡翅, *jī chì*, ¥4 to ¥6

lamb tendon 肉筋, *ròu jīn*, ¥1

roasted garlic 大蒜, *dà suàn*, ¥1

LOCAL KNOWLEDGE

BĚIJĪNG MENU

The following are all classic Běijīng dishes, many of which you'll only find at places specialising in Běijīng cuisine. Try **Zuǒ Lín Yòu Shè** (p76), **Yáojì Chǎogān** (p93) or **Bàodǔ Huáng** (p139). Many roast duck restaurants will have some of the other Běijīng specialities as well as roast duck.

Peking duck (烤鸭; *kǎo yā*) Roast duck, known in the West as Peking duck, is Běijīng's most famous dish. The duck here is fattier but much more flavoursome than the 'crispy duck' typically served in Chinese restaurants in the West. Like back home, though, it also comes with pancakes, cucumber slices and plum sauce.

zhá jiàng miàn (炸酱面) Běijīng's most famous noodle dish; thick wheat noodles with ground pork and cucumber shreds mixed together in a salty fermented soybean paste. Chilli oil (辣椒油; *là jiāo yóu*) is a popular optional extra.

dālian huǒshāo (褡裢火烧) Finger-shaped fried dumplings with a savoury filling.

má dòufu (麻豆腐) Spicy tofu paste.

zhá guànchang (炸灌肠) Deep-fried crispy crackers served with a very strong garlic dip.

chǎo gānr (炒肝) Sautéed liver served in a gloopy soup.

bào dǔ (爆肚) Boiled tripe, usually lamb. Sometimes served in a seasoned broth.

yáng zá (羊杂) Similar to *bào dǔ*, but includes an assortment of sheep's innards, not just tripe, and is always served in a broth.

ròu bǐng (肉饼) Meat patty, usually filled with pork or beef before being lightly fried.

jiāo quān (焦圈) Deep-fried dough rings, usually accompanied with a cup of *dòu zhī*.

dòu zhī (豆汁) Sour-tasting soy milk drink.

exit A) By the south gate of Dìtán Park, this giant, busy, neon-lit, 24-hour restaurant on three floors serves up good-value dim sum, as well as a selection of other mostly Cantonese dishes. Note, the dim sum (点心; *diǎn xin*) is in the second half of the menu, entitled 'North & South Snacks'.

★GEORG — INTERNATIONAL $$$

Map p274 (☎010 8408 5300; www.thegeorg.com/en; 45 Dongbuyaqiao Hutong; 东不压桥胡同45号; tasting plates from ¥130, set menu ¥450, cafe mains ¥58-78; ⏰restaurant 6.30-10.30pm Tue-Sun, cafe from 10.30am daily; ❄📶; [S]Lines 6, 8 to Nanluoguxiang, exit E, or Line 8 to Shichahai, exit C) In a city glaringly short on international fine dining, the Georg delivers with its gastronomic menu of fusion cuisine. It's an enterprise by Copenhagen designer Georg Jensen, creating a refined, intimate space with Danish design and heritage silverware. Tasting plates with a Scandinavian twist are creative and original.

Descriptors on the menu are left vague for the diner to dissect tastes of its weekly rotating dishes. Given the work put into the menu, it is very good value for less than ¥450 a head. Its Living Room cafe is open during the day with a more casual menu of brisket sandwiches, home-cured duck prosciutto, cheesecake and high tea. The location along a picturesque river is a nice area to stroll.

There's a Georg Jensen showroom on the 2nd floor with high-end silverware and jewellery. The Beijing Centre for the Arts (www.beijingcenterforthearts.com) gallery is next door.

DÀLǏ COURTYARD — YUNNAN $$$

Map p274 (大理; Dàlǐ; ☎010 8404 1430; 67 Xiaojingchang Hutong, Gulou Dongdajie; 鼓楼东大街小经厂胡同67号; set menu ¥150; ⏰noon-2pm & 6-10pm; [S]Line 2 to Andingmen, exit D, or Line 5 to Beixinqiao, exit A) The charming *hútòng* setting in a restored courtyard makes this one of Běijīng's more pleasant places to eat, especially in summer (in winter they cover the courtyard with an unattractive temporary roof). It specialises in the subtle flavours of Yúnnán cuisine. There's no menu. Instead, you pay ¥150 (drinks are extra), and enjoy whatever inspires the chef that day. He rarely disappoints.

From Gulou Dongdajie, turn north onto Xiaojingchang Hutong and look for the red lanterns down the first alley on the left.

DRINKING & NIGHTLIFE

This neighbourhood, and its network of historic *hútòng*, is many visitor's favourite place to drink in Běijīng. New bars are popping up (and closing) all the time, so take a wander and see what you stumble across. Top drinking strips include Wudaoying Hutong with both craft-beer taphouses and third-wave coffee roasters specialising in single-origin beans. Fangjia Hutong and Beiluogu Xiang are also happening strips with cool bars and live-music venues.

⭐**CAPITAL SPIRITS**   COCKTAIL BAR
Map p274 (首都酒坊; Shǒudū Jiǔfāng; www.capitalspiritsbj.com; 3 Daju Hutong; 大菊胡同3号; cocktails from ¥40; ⊗8pm-12.30am Tue-Sun; 🚇; ⓢLine 5 to Beixinqiao, exit C) Much maligned by non-Chinese drinkers, *báijiǔ* (白酒; literally 'white alcohol'; a face-numbing spirit) is often compared to consuming paint stripper. However, that's until you sample some of the top-shelf stuff, and that's where Capital Spirits step in with an entire speakeasy bar dedicated to quality *báijiǔs*. On a mission to dispel its poor reputation, here pro bartenders mix up *báijiǔ* cocktails along with tasting flights of four varietals (¥40) from across China.

Once you've figured out your tastes – which vary markedly according to distillery processes – there's a whole choice of flights to follow. The *báijiǔ* cocktails are definitely worth trying, from the Báijiǔ Sour to the Ma-La Rita margarita infused with Sìchuān peppercorns. If you're up for shots, there's a range of infused *báijiǔs*, from jalapeno to bottled snakes.

It's down a residential non-commerical *hútòng* within a nondescript building without signage and you can only enter from the back door; it's 20m from Dongzhimen Nanxiaojie. The tasting gift packs (¥260) make good souvenirs. Cash only.

⭐TIKI BUNGALOW   COCKTAIL BAR
Map p274 (34 Jiaodaokou; 东城区 交道口北三条34号; cocktails ¥60; ⊗7pm-late Tue-Sat; 🚇; ⓢLine 5 to Beixinqiao, exit A) From the palm leaves and Exotica soundtrack to the carved totem poles and Polynesian knick-knacks, this is your quintessential tiki bar down to the finest detail. However, of course, it's all about the drinks, which is where Tiki Bunglaow really shines, delivering some of the finest and most extravagant rum-based cocktails you'll taste. All are based on vintage tiki recipes from the 1930s to 1960s.

All the classics are made by owner Phil and his hard-working team, shaking up Mai Tais and Jet Pilots served in tiki mugs and coconut-shell cups. There's also a fascinating selection of obscure 'lost classic' cocktails, some that date back to the 19th century. A selection of rum flights and Cuban cigars round out a great night.

⭐**DISTILLERY**   COCKTAIL BAR
Map p274 (www.capitalspiritsbj.com/#the-distillery; 23 Xinsi Hutong; 辛寺胡同23号; cocktails ¥40-60; ⊗8pm-12.30am Mon-Sat; 🚇; ⓢLine 5 to Zhangzizhonglu, exit B) Down a residential *hútòng* alley, hidden behind a nondescript facade, is this fantastic bar that's so much your quintessential speakeasy that it even makes its own hooch. It's a classy dark-lit space, where they distill their own gin and vodka on-site, to go with a menu of original and classic cocktails.

It's run by the same team as Capital Spirits, and a free rickshaw runs between the two on Friday and Saturdays evenings.

⭐**GREAT LEAP BREWING**   BREWERY
Map p274 (GLB #6; 大跃啤酒, Dàyuè Píjiǔ; www.greatleapbrewing.com; 6 Doujiao Hutong; 豆角胡同6号; beer per pint ¥25-50; ⊗2-11pm Sun-Thu, to midnight Fri & Sat; ⓢLine 8 to Shichahai, exit C) Běijīng's original microbrewery, this refreshingly simple courtyard bar, set up by American beer enthusiast Carl Setzer, is housed in a hard-to-find, but beautifully renovated, 100-year-old Qing dynasty courtyard and serves up a wonderful selection of unique ales made largely from locally sourced ingredients. Sip on familiar favourites such as pale alcs and porters, or choose from China-inspired tipples like Honey Ma, a brew made with lip-tingling Sìchuān peppercorns.

All it serves here is ale (although it does hand out bottled water and spicy peanuts for free). If you want other drinks and bar food too, head to the larger branches (p143) out **Sānlǐtún** (GLB #45; 大跃啤酒; Dàyuè Píjiǔ; Map p282; ☎010 5947 6984; www.greatleapbrewing.com; 45-1 Xinyuan Lu; 新源街45-1号; ⊗11am-1am Sun-Thu, to 2am Fri & Sat; 🚇; ⓢLine 10 to Liangmaqiao, exit A) way specialising in burgers or pizzas. To get here, walk south out of Shichahai subway station, then left down Mao'er Hutong, then left down Doujiao Hutong, and you'll soon wind you way to the bar. From Nanluogu Xiang, walk west down Jingyang Hutong (景阳胡同), bearing right, then left, then right again before turning left down Doujiao Hutong.

★MODERNISTA   BAR

Map p274 (老摩; Lǎo Mó; ☎136 9142 5744; www.facebook.com/modernistabj; 44 Baochao Hutong; 宝钞胡同44号; ◉4pm-2am Mon-Fri, 11am-late Sat & Sun; ⓈLines 2, 8 to Guloudajie, exit G) Making full use of its space, bohemian Modernista is a mix of glamorous bar, eatery and live arts venue. Set up by a Barcelona expat, its front area is done up like an old-school Spanish tapas bar with polished wooden decor, bar stools and black-and-white checkered tiles. Its adjoining building is an atmospheric space that hosts cabaret shows, live jazz, and wildly popular swing and salsa dance classes.

Though not always open, its upstairs absinthe bar is another highlight with a collection you'll be hard to pressed to find anywhere in the world. There's also a rooftop terrace when the sun's out. Downstairs has good pinxtos and tapas at the bar (¥68 for two pieces), Estrella beer and IPAs on tap, spritz cocktails and postmidnight ¥10 shots. It's popular with fun-loving European expats here for a boozy night out.

PANDA BREW   MICROBREWERY

Map p274 (www.pandabrew.com.cn; 14 Dongsi Beidajie; 东四北大街14号; beers from ¥40; ◉10am-1am; ☎; ⓈLine 5 to Beixinqiao, exit C) Another reason to celebrate Běijīng's craft-beer scene, Panda Brew is a local microbrewery that produces a dozen beers on-site. Its equipment is on display in a cool industrial warehouse-like space, with couches downstairs and a rooftop terrace laid with Astroturf. There's a menu of pub grub (mains from ¥32) to go with its IPAs, and brown, golden and pale ales.

VOYAGE COFFEE   COFFEE

Map p274 (80 Beiluogu Xiang; 北锣鼓巷80号; ◉9am-9pm; ☎; ⓈLine 2 to Andingmen or Line 5 to Beixinqiao, exit C) Slotting in effortlessly along this happening strip is this chic third-wave coffee roaster decked out in exposed brick and blonde wood. Grab a stool to enjoy single-origin Chemex pour-overs, espressos or eight-hour cold brews. The VPN-enabled wi-fi makes it a good workspace.

8-BIT   BAR

Map p274 (☎010 8044 8229; www.facebook.com/beijing8bit/; 13 Beiluogu Xiang; 北锣鼓巷13号; ◉3pm-2am Tue-Sun, from 6pm Sat & Sun; ⓈLines 2, 8 to Guloudajie, exit G) A killer combo of beer and video games, 8-Bit is equipped with old-school consoles, which are all free to play for those here to eat or drink. Along with the original Nintendo, there are Super Nintendos, 64s, Sega, Wii and Playstations, all with an extensive catalogue of games and two-player controls. When it's time to give your thumbs a break, head upstairs to its

HIPSTER HÚTÒNG ALLEYS

Forget Brooklyn, Berlin, Portland or Melbourne, the *hútòng* alleys of North Dōngchéng is where it's at. Scattered among the residential backstreets are a growing number of courtyard houses converted into third-wave coffee roasters, craft-beer taphouses, avant-garde galleries, vegan restaurants, speakeasies, tiki bars, fixed-gear bike stores and even a place doing LA food-truck-style kimchi tacos. The neighbourhood is also home to Běijīng's underground music scene, with several venues hosting local Chinese bands playing anything from indie, punk, garage, metal and hip hop to electonica.

The current hot spots are the streets around Wudaoying Hutong, Fangjia Hutong and Beiluogu Xiang, where you'll find the cool kids hanging out. Such areas are refreshingly down to earth, and free of the pretension you'd get in similar parts of the world.

While heritage-preservation campaigners bemoan the gentrification of traditional residential *hútòngs* as a loss of cultural identity – others reason it's a better outcome than developers bulldozing them to build high-rise apartments. Though perils do loom, as with the case of the overcommerialisation of Nanluogu Xiang (p102): a decade has transformed it into a Disneyland-like spectacle where the masses descend daily.

bar and rooftop lined with pot plants and Astroturf.

There's a cool indie playlist, several Japanese beers on tap, cocktails, pickleback shots and tasty bar food.

MÀI BAR
BAR

Map p274 (麦; 40 Beiluogu Xiang; 北锣鼓巷40号; cocktails from ¥45, beers from ¥30; ⏲6pm-2am; [S]Lines 2, 8 to Guloudajie, exit G) Run by the same team as Parlor (p143) in Sānlǐtún, Mài Bar is a more intimate affair with its *hútòng* location in a beautifully renovated section of an old courtyard building. Cocktails here are similarly good, mixed by knowledgeable bartenders who concoct labour-intensive originals and smoky Manhattans and Negronis.

1796
CAFE

Map p274 (☎010 64087149; 60 Zhonglouwan Hutong; 钟楼湾胡同60号; beer from ¥25, cocktails from ¥45; ⏲noon-midnight; [S]Line 8 to Shichahai, exit A2) Set up within a charming 18th-century house, this relaxed cafe-bar boasts a stellar position overlooking the Drum & Bell Sq. There's a selection of teas, beers, cocktails and Western dishes (from ¥35) to enjoy on its leafy rooftop terrace or in its cosy tearoom interior.

ARROW FACTORY TAPROOM
MICROBREWERY

Map p274 (箭厂啤酒屋; Jiànchǎng Píjiǔ Wū; ☎010 6407 6308; www.arrowfactorybrewing.com; 9 Jianchang Hutong; 箭厂胡同9号"塞"餐厅院内; ⏲5pm-1am Mon-Thu, to 2am Fri, 11.30am-2am Sat, to 1am Sun; [S]Line 2 to Andingmen or Lines 2, 5 to Yonghegong-Lama Temple, exit D) Accessed by a shoddy slide door at the back of Stuff'd (p94), Arrow's tiny taproom is an appealing spit-and-sawdust minimalist space with a wooden bar, stools and a few tables. It has a wide choice of its beers on tap to go with a menu of homemade sausages and pies. Its flagship brewpub (p89) is north of Sānlǐtún.

BALL HOUSE
BAR

Map p274 (波楼酒吧; Bōlóu Jiǔbā, Lǎo Mó; 40 Zhonglouwan Hutong; 钟楼湾胡同40号; beers from ¥20, cocktails from ¥40.; ⏲2pm-2am; [S]Line 8 to Shichahai, exit A2) A bar for those in the know, Ball House is set back from the main *hútòng* (which circumnavigates the Bell Tower) at the end of a narrow pathway that looks like it leads to ordinary housing. There's washing hanging outside and bikes leant up against the wall, but if you push the door open at the end of the pathway, you enter an enormous, beautifully restored split-level room and one of the capital's most unusual drinking spaces.

There are pool tables (¥30 per hour) and table-football tables (free) dotted around the place – hence the name – but there are enough nooks and crannies to find your own quiet spot if you don't fancy the ball games.

PASS BY BAR
BAR

Map p274 (过客; Guòkè; 108 Nanluogu Xiang; 南锣鼓巷108号; ⏲10am-2am; 📶; [S]Lines 6, 8 to Nanluoguxiang, exit E) One of Beijing's longest running bars, Pass By is a local institution and offers respite from tourist-clogged Nanluogu Xiang. Run by common owners of NBeer (p122), here you'll get a selection from six of their beers on tap, as well as 100-odd brands in the fridge. There's an old-school backpackers' menu of pizzas, burgers and local dishes served in its light- and plant-filled courtyard or rooftop terrace.

If you're not a beer lover, there's wine by the bottle (from ¥98) and cocktails (from ¥28) too.

EL NIDO
BAR

Map p274 (爱妮岛; Ài Nī Dǎo; 59 Fangjia Hutong; 方家胡同59号; beers from ¥10; ⏲6pm-late; [S]Line 2 to Andingmen) One of the original bars to get this hipster enclave started, tiny El Nido is a friendly and intimate *hútòng* bar with an interchanging 12 beers on tap. There are plenty of imported beers in the fridge too, and a bar lined with jars of infused spirits. The streetside tables are the place to be come summer.

OTHER PLACE
CAFE

Map p274 (www.theotherplacebeijing.com; 1 Langjia Hutong; 朗家胡同1号; ⏲2pm-late; 📶; [S]Lines 2, 8 to Guloudajie, exit G) This *hútòng* bar is an expat favourite with cool staff, 40 different beers, specialist coffee and a charming tree-filled courtyard. Regular events are held here during the week.

SALUD
BAR

Map p274 (老伍; lǎowǔ; ☎010 6402 5086; 66 Nanluogu Xiang; 南锣鼓巷66号; beers from ¥15, cocktails from ¥38; ⏲8am-2am; 📶; [S]Lines 6, 8 to Nanluoguxiang, exit E) One of the biggest and liveliest spots on Nanluogu Xiang, Salud is a saloon-style bar that's expat-centric, but gets very busy on weekends with a mixed crowd of locals and foreigners who party well into the early hours. Its house-special infused flavoured rums (¥20) come in long shot glasses and are lethal.

FRESH BEAN COFFEE

Map p274 (13 Wudaoying Hutong; 五道营胡同13号; coffee from ¥35; ⏲9.30am-8pm; [S]Lines 2, 5 to Yonghegong-Lama Temple, exit D) One of several coffee roasters along Wudaoying Hutong, Fresh Bean has seasonal beans from Guatemala, Ethiopia and Indonesia. Pour-overs are its main speciality, along with an eight-hour cold brew. It has two cafes along here (also at 60 Wudaoying Hutong), the more atmospheric being this one with the VW Kombia counter inside a live house.

CAFE CONFUCIUS CAFE

Map p274 (秀冠咖啡; Xiù Guàn Kāfēi; 25 Guozijian Jie; 国子监街25号; ⏲8.30am-8.30pm; 📶; [S]Lines 2, 5 to Yonghegong-Lama Temple, exit C) This smart and friendly cafe has an understated Buddhist theme with a good tea selection, speciality coffee, lassis, juices, and Western and Chinese dishes.

MAO MAO CHONG BAR BAR

Map p274 (MMC; 毛毛虫; Máo Máo Chóng; 12 Banchang Hutong; 板厂胡同12号; beers from ¥35, cocktails ¥40-50; ⏲6pm-late Mon-Thu, noon-late Fri-Sun; [S]Lines 6, 8 to Nanluoguxiang, exit F) This small but lively expat favourite has a rustic interior, good-value cocktails and a no-smoking policy. Its pizzas also get rave reviews.

☆ ENTERTAINMENT

★HOT CAT CLUB LIVE MUSIC

Map p274 (热力猫俱乐部; Rèlìmāo Jùlèbù; 46 Fangjia Hutong; 方家胡同46号; ⏲10am-midnight; [S]Line 2 to Andingmen) Hot Cat Club is one of the city's most popular venues with its sticky-carpet pub feel and nightly roster of local and foreign guitar-slinging bands playing everything from rock 'n' roll to electronica. Gigs are usually free, but there are a few paid events. Walk behind the stage to access the grungy beer garden.

★SCHOOL BAR CONCERT VENUE

Map p274 (☎010 6402 8881; https://site.douban.com/school; 53 Wudaoying Hutong; 东城区五道营胡同53号; tickets around ¥50; ⏲6pm-2am; [S]Lines 2, 5 to Yonghegong-Lama Temple, exit D) Another reason why hip Wudaoying Hutong is too cool for school, this divey band venue is the best spot to tap into the capital's underground scene. Run by a couple of veteran Běijīng punks, it hosts quality gigs from local and touring punk, garage, indie and noise to hard-core and metal bands.

★JIĀNG HÚ LIVE MUSIC

Map p274 (江湖酒吧; Jiāng Hú Jiǔbā; 7 Dongmianhua Hutong; 东棉花胡同7号; admission ¥30-50; ⏲7pm-2am, closed Mon; [S]Lines 6, 8 to Nanluoguxiang, exit F) One of the coolest places to hear Chinese indie and rock bands, Jiāng Hú, run by a trombone-playing, music-loving manager, is housed in a small courtyard and packs in the punters on a good night. Intimate, cool, and a decent spot for a drink in a courtyard, even when no bands are playing. Beers from ¥25.

DADA CLUB

Map p274 (达达; Dádá; Bldg B, 206 Gulou Dongdajie; 鼓楼东大街206号; beers from ¥15; ⏲9am-2am; 📶; [S]Line 8 to Shichahai, exit A2) Since this cool Shànghǎi club arrived in Běijīng in 2012, it's remained one of the capital's best spots for electronic music with nightly DJs spinning house and techno. Drinks are cheap so things get loose.

YÚGŌNG YÍSHĀN LIVE MUSIC

Map p274 (愚公移山; ☎010 6404 2711; www.yugongyishan.com; 3-2 Zhangzizhong Lu, West Courtyard; 张自忠路3-2, 号段祺瑞执政府旧址西院; admission from ¥50; ⏲7pm-2am; [S]Line 5 to Zhangzizhonglu, exit A) Reputedly one of the most haunted places in Běijīng, this historic building has been home to Qing dynasty royalty, warlords and the occupying Japanese army in the 1930s. You could probably hear the ghosts screaming if it wasn't for the array of local and foreign bands, solo artists and DJs who take to the stage here every week.

With a very sound booking policy and a decent space to play with, this is one of the best places in town to listen to live music.

TEMPLE BAR LIVE MUSIC

Map p274 (坛酒吧; Tán Jiǔbā; ☎134 2607 0554; Bldg B, 206 Gulou Dongdajie; 鼓楼东大街206号; beers from ¥25, cocktails from ¥30; ⏲5pm-late; [S]Line 8 to Shichahai, exit A2) Large single-room space with a long bar in one corner, a low stage in another, and tables, chairs and sofas strewn across the rest of the floor. The three music-loving managers ensure decent billing from local bands playing most nights, and gigs are often free. Nightly happy hour (5pm to 10pm) has a buy-one-get-one-free deal on local beers.

It's above Dada (p100), and the two together form a sort of duel rock-electric nightlife experience, with punters often going between the two venues multiple times of an evening. Walk under the decorative archway by 206 Gulou Dongdajie, and continue to Building B, right at the back of the small car park.

CHINA PUPPET THEATRE   THEATRE
(中国木偶剧院; Zhōngguó Mù'ǒu Jùyuàn; ☑010 6425 4847; www.puppetchina.com; 北三环中路安华西里; ⓢLine 8 to Anhuaqiao, exit D1) Aimed at families, this theatre puts on shadow play, puppetry, music and dance events on weekends only. There are three theatres, however, there's no English.

The theatre is just inside the north 3rd Ring Rd. Come out of exit D1 of Anhuaqiao subway station (Line 8) and walk east along the main road for about 500m until you see the building that looks like a fairy-tale castle.

🛍 SHOPPING

The wildly popular *hútòng* of Nanluogu Xiang contains an eclectic mix of clothes and gifts, sold in trendy boutique shops. It can be a pleasant place to shop for souvenirs, but avoid summer weekends when the shopping frenzy reaches fever pitch and you can hardly walk down the street for the crowds. At its northern end, Gulou Dongdajie has for a while now been a popular place for young Beijingers to shop for vintage clothing, skater fashion and music gear. Yonghegong Dajie, the road the Lama Temple is on, is chock-full of Buddhist-themed shops, selling prayer flags, incense sticks and Buddha figurines to a backdrop of Tibetan-mantra music.

★PLASTERED 8   CLOTHING
Map p274 (创可贴T-恤; Chuàngkětiē Tìxù; ☑010 5762 6146; www.plasteredtshirts.com; 61 Nanluogu Xiang; 南锣鼓巷61号; ⓢ9.30am-10.30pm; ⓢLines 6, 8 to Nanluoguxiang, exit E) British-

owned, this iconic Nanluogu Xiang T-shirt shop prints ironic takes on Chinese culture onto its good-quality T-shirts and tops (from ¥168). Also stocks decent smog masks (from ¥225).

Opposite the entrance to the shop is a rare surviving (but very faded) slogan from the Cultural Revolution era, which exhorts the people to put their trust in the People's Liberation Army.

POTTERY WORKSHOP   CERAMICS
Map p274 (☑153 1380 5178; 80 Wudaoying Hutong; 五道营胡同80号; ⓢnoon-9pm; ⓢLine 2 to Andingmen or Lines 2, 5 to Yonghegong-Lama Temple, exit D) Featuring the work from a collective of six young artists, this wonderful, but small, ceramics store has a beautiful range of handmade, handpainted tea cups, tea sets, vases and incense holders. There's a good variation in techniques and glazes, and all are made in Jīngdézhèn – the pottery centre of China.

FAMOUS TEA OF CHINA   TEA
Map p274 (福建茶行; Fújiàn Cháháng; 123 Gulou Dongdajie; 鼓楼东大街123号; ⓢ8am-10pm; ⓢLine 5 to Beixinqiao, exit A, or Line 8 to Shichahai, exit A2) This small tea shop is run by a friendly couple who speak almost no English but are as accommodating as they can be towards foreign tourists. Most of the tea is sold by weight; priced by the *jīn* (500g), but more commonly sold by the *liǎng* (50g). They have a few tea sets for sale too.

They also sell tea in small pre-wrapped parcels (perfect for gifts), and have cute, tiny 'cakes' of *pǔ'ěr* tea, sold for ¥10 for 10 pieces; each piece is enough for one cup of tea. You can buy individual tea cups here (from as little as ¥3), as well as individual *gàiwǎn* (lidded cups, used as tea pots; from ¥20). Also look out for the smart little travel tea sets (旅行茶具; *lǚxíng chájù;* ¥60).

C ROCK   MUSIC
Map p274 (C Rock; 音乐光盘店; C Rock yīnyuè guāngpán diàn; 99 Gulou Dongdajie; 鼓楼东大街99号; ⓢ11am-10pm; ⓢLine 5 to Beixinqiao, exit A, or Line 8 to Shichahai, exit A2) This pocket-sized shop is the best place in the area to pick up albums produced by Chinese artists. The guy who runs it speaks enough English to help you decide and is happy to let you listen to an album that takes your fancy. There's music of all types from all over China (as well as some international stuff), but the

TRADITIONAL CLAY FIGURINES

Clay figurines are popular souvenirs in China, and you'll find them in gift shops across Běijīng. Try **Jīngchéng Bǎixìng** near the Lama Temple. The following are the three best-known types of figures you'll find:

Běijīng Rabbit Lord (兔儿爷; *tù ér yé*) These tall-eared rabbit figures have been around since the late Ming dynasty (17th century) and are supposed to represent the Rabbit Lord who was sent down to Běijīng by Chang'e (the Moon God) to protect the city from a deadly plague. The figurines now represent good health.

Tiānjīn Clay People (天津泥人; *Tiānjīn ní rén*) Characterised by plump, playful child-like figures, these originated in the city of Tiānjīn around 180 years ago, and were first created by a famous sculptor named Zhang Mingshen (1826–1906).

Shāndōng Roaring Tiger (山东泥叫虎; *Shāndōng ní jiào hǔ*) Originating from the town of Gāomì in Shāndōng province, these clay tigers have a piece of sheep skin connecting their front and hind legs, which makes a roaring sound when squeezed (young kids love these).

focus is on local rock and indie bands and folk music. CDs cost between ¥35 and ¥100.

RUÌFÚXIÁNG — SILK, CLOTHING

Map p274 (瑞蚨祥; Ruìfúxiáng; 50 Di'anmen Waidajie; 地安门外大街50号; ⏰10am-8.30pm; [S]Line A to Shichahai, exit A2) A relatively new branch of the 150-year-old Ruìfúxiáng silk store, this place does all manner of silk items, from scarves and shawls (from ¥158) to slippers and hats (from ¥50). It's a great place to come for Chinese-style clothing (women's cotton *qípáo* start at around ¥300, and silk from ¥2500), men's shirts and children's outfits.

JĪNGCHÉNG BǍIXÌNG — CERAMICS

Map p274 (京城百姓（泥塑陶艺）; 44 Guozijian Jie; 国子监街44号; ⏰9am-9pm; [S]Line 2 to Andingmen or Lines 2, 5 to Yonghegong-Lama Temple, exit C) This small shop on historic Guozijian Jie sells beautifully painted traditional clay figurines, which make wonderfully affordable China souvenirs. What makes this place stand out from other, similar shops, though, is that they also set up tables and chairs outside so customers can paint, and even mould, their own figurines. Young kids love it, although you'll often see adults mucking in too.

If you want make your own figurine, say: '*néng ní sù ma?*' (能泥塑吗? – Can I do some clay modelling?). If you just want to paint a figurine, say: '*néng cǎi huì ma?*' (能彩绘吗? – Can I do some painting?). It's completely free of charge to do either, but if you want to take away your creations, you'll have to pay ¥10 (more for larger figures).

The professionally painted figurines, which also cost from just ¥10 upwards, come in all sorts of shapes and sizes, but the main two types are the Běijīng Rabbit Lord (兔儿爷; *tù ér yé*) and the Shāndōng Roaring Tiger (山东泥叫虎; *Shāndōng ní jiào hǔ*).

GIANT — SPORTS & OUTDOORS

Map p274 (捷安特; Jié'āntè; ☎010 6403 4537; www.giant.com.cn; 4-18 Jiaodaokou Dongdajie; 交道口东大街4-18号; ⏰9am-7pm; [S]Line 5 to Beixinqiao, exit A) One of a string of decent bike shops on this stretch of road, Giant has the biggest range of new bicycles and bike equipment, such as helmets, locks and baby seats. Bikes start at around ¥850. Also rents good-as-new mountain bikes (per day ¥100 including helmet; deposit ¥1500). Chinese for bike rental is: 租车 (*zū chē*), pronounced 'zoo chuh'.

NANLUOGU XIANG — STREET

Map p274 (南锣鼓巷; Nanluogu Xiang; [S]Lines 6, 8 to Nanluoguxiang, exit E) Once neglected and ramshackle, strewn with spent coal briquettes in winter, and silent bar the hacking coughs of shuffling old-timers and the jangling of bicycle bells, the funky north–south alleyway of Nanluogu Xiang (literally 'South Gong and Drum Alley', and roughly pronounced '*nan-law-goo-syang*') has been undergoing an evolution since 1999 when Pass By Bar (p99) first threw open its doors, and was the subject of a complete makeover in 2006. Today, the alley is an insatiably bubbly strip of bars, wi-fi cafes, restaurants, hotels and trendy shops.

It is also a victim of its own success, though. Come here on a summer weekend to experience more people than you thought could possibly fit onto one street! With that in mind, don't miss exploring the quieter alleys, which fan out from the main lane and house Qing dynasty courtyards as well as hidden cafes, shops, restaurants and bars.

⚡ SPORTS & ACTIVITIES

★ THE HUTONG   COOKING

Map p274 (☏159 0104 6127; www.thehutong. com; 1 Jiudaowan Zhongxiang Hutong, off Shique Hutong; 北新桥石雀胡同九道弯中巷胡同1号; classes for members/nonmembers ¥260/300; ⏱9.30am-10pm; ⓢLine 5 to Beixinqiao, exit C) Down a maze of narrow alleys, the Hutong is a highly recommended Chinese-culture centre, run by a group of extremely knowledgeable locals and expats. Classes are held in a peaceful converted courtyard, and focus on cooking and guided tours. See its website for the schedule.

Its cookery classes focus on cuisine from around China, from *xiǎolóngbāo* to hand-pulled noodles. Its guided tours include the three-hour 'Hútòng Tour' (¥260) around the city's network of alleyways, the five-hour 'Tea Tour' (¥300), which includes a trip to Mǎliándào Tea Market, and the two-hour 'Culinary Market Tour' (¥200).

NATOOKE   CYCLING

Map p274 (耍 (自行车店); Shuǎ (Zìxíngchē Diàn); ☏010 8402 6925; www.natooke.com; 19-1 Wudaoying Hutong; 五道营胡同19−1号; ⏱11am-7pm; ⓢLines 2, 5 to Yonghegong-Lama Temple, exit D) The coolest bike shop in Běijīng, Natooke sells fixed-gear bikes (from ¥2900), but also rents a small range of secondhand bikes (24-hour hire ¥80, deposit per day ¥500). You can buy good-quality smog masks here too. It also organ-ises cycling events in and around Běijīng – check the website.

CULTURE YARD   LANGUAGE

Map p274 (天井越洋; Tiānjǐng Yuèyáng; ☏010 8404 4166; www.cultureyard.net; 10 Shique Hutong; 石雀胡同10号; ⏱9am-9pm Mon-Fri, 10am-4pm Sat; ⓢLine 5 to Beixinqiao, exit C) Tucked away down a *hútòng,* this cultural centre focuses on Chinese classes. Its main program is a six-week course (¥4500), but you can tailor courses to suit your needs. Its 'Survival Chinese' course is ideal for tourists.

MÀO'ÉR LǍOLǏ HEALTH CLUB   MASSAGE

Map p274 (帽儿老李足疗保健馆; Mào'ér Lǎolǐ Zúliáo Bǎojiàn Guǎn; 3 Mao'er Hutong; 帽儿胡同3号; ⏱noon-midnight; ⓢLines 6, 8 to Nanluoguxiang, exit E) Located intriguingly inside part of an old courtyard off historic Mao'er Hutong, this small massage parlour is great value. One-hour full-body massages start from ¥99. It also provides cupping therapy (¥49) and, if you dare, Tibetan 'fire-dragon' therapy (¥59) – actual flames are used. Not much English spoken, but the massage menu has English translations.

The sign outside No 3 Mao'er Hutong is in Chinese only, but has the word 'massage' on it. Walk through the gateway, and continue on through a beautiful old carved gateway into the back courtyard where you'll find the place on your left.

QĪNGNIÁN HÚ PARK   SWIMMING

Map p274 (青年湖公园; Qīngnián Hú Gōngyuán; Qingnianhu Lu, off Andingmenwai Dajie; 安定门外大街，青年湖路; adult/child ¥20/15; ⏱9am-7pm May-Sep; ⓢLine 2 to Andingmen, exit B) In summer, locals flock to Qīngnián Hú Park where there's an outdoor swimming complex with water slides and a shallow pool for young'uns. It's floodlit in the evening. You can buy all the swimming gear you need, and there are stalls selling grilled kebabs, snacks and even beer.

Temple of Heaven Park & Dōngchéng South

Neighbourhood Top Five

❶ Temple of Heaven Park (p106) Touring a simply stunning collection of halls and altars where China's emperors came to seek divine guidance; the surrounding park is equally special.

❷ Peking Duck (p111) Feasting on Běijīng's signa-ture dish at the restaurants where it originated.

❸ City Walls (p110) Stepping back in time to impe-rial China by strolling the last remaining stretch of the walls that once surrounded the capital.

❹ Hóngqiáo (Pearl) Market (p112) Trawling for pearls of all varieties, as well as jewellery and jade.

❺ Qianmen Dajie (p111) Joining the crowds of locals exploring the shops and restaurants of this restored Qing dynasty shopping street.

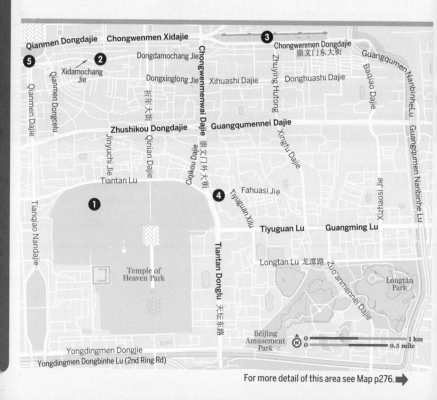

For more detail of this area see Map p276. ➡

Explore Temple of Heaven Park & Dōngchéng South

Ranging south and southeast of the Forbidden City, and encompassing the former district of Chóngwén, this neighbourhood is less fashionable than the rest of Dōngchéng (东城) – it's a nightlife desert – and has always been home to the *lǎobǎixìng* (common people).

Start at Temple of Heaven Park. After touring the sights, amble through the park itself before heading north to the Qiánmén area. Alternatively, shopaholics can hit the Hóngqiáo Market, a few hundred metres north of the park's east gate, where five floors of pearls, jewellery, jade and more await. The roof terrace offers fantastic views across the Temple of Heaven Park.

The last remaining stretch of Běijīng's city walls are a brief subway ride north of the Temple of Heaven. From there, wander west through the surviving *hútòng* (alleyways) of the neighbourhood towards Qiánmén, where museums and the popular pedestrian shopping street of Qianmen Dajie await. Nearby are some of Běijīng's oldest and most traditional Peking-duck restaurants, as well as high-class dumplings and upmarket Western eateries.

Local Life

➡ **Hútòng** Make sure to spend some time exploring the decaying alleyways and lanes to the east of Qianmen Dajie (p111), still home to many people.

➡ **Peking duck** If you want to eat Běijīng's best-known dish where the locals do, try Biànyífáng (p112).

➡ **Park life** Serene Lóngtán Park, to the east of Temple of Heaven Park, is one of the capital's best-kept secrets.

Getting There & Away

➡ **Subway** Line 2 stops at Qianmen station and Chongwenmen station, where the north–south Line 5 intersects with it. For Temple of Heaven Park, take Line 5 direct to the Tiantandongmen stop; get off at Chongwenmen for the Ming City Ruins Park and Southeast Corner Watchtower. Qianmen station serves Qianmen Dajie and the area around it.

➡ **Bus** Bus 20 journeys from Běijīng South train station via the Temple of Heaven and Qiánmén to Wángfǔjǐng, Dōngdān and Běijīng train station.

Lonely Planet's Top Tip

Do as the locals do and rise early to get to Temple of Heaven Park when it opens at sunrise. Not only will you see Běijīng's senior citizens at play – practising taichi and formation dancing – but the park is a superb, tranquil experience at this time of day, and you'll have the jump on the crowds when the sights open at 8am.

 **Best Places to Eat**

➡ Capital M (p111)

➡ Dōuyīchù (p111)

➡ Old Běijīng Zhájiàng Noodle King (p111)

➡ Lìqún Roast Duck Restaurant (p111)

For reviews, see p111.

 Best Peking Duck

➡ Lìqún Roast Duck Restaurant (p111)

➡ Biànyífáng (p112)

➡ Qiánmén Quánjùdé Roast Duck Restaurant (p112)

For reviews, see p111.

🔒 **Best Places to Shop**

➡ Hóngqiáo (Pearl) Market (p112)

➡ Red Gate Gallery (p109)

➡ Qianmen Dajie (p111)

For reviews, see p112.

TEMPLE OF HEAVEN PARK & DŌNGCHÉNG SOUTH

TOP SIGHT
TEMPLE OF HEAVEN PARK

Extraordinary to contemplate, the collection of halls and altars set within the delightful 276-hectare Temple of Heaven Park (天坛公园) is *the* most perfect example of Ming architectural design. Each year, the Chinese emperors – the sons of heaven – came here to seek divine clearance and good harvests and to atone for the sins of their people in an esoteric ceremony of prayers and ritual sacrifices.

Cosmology & Design

Everything about the complex is unique, with shape, colour and sound combining to take on symbolic significance. The park itself is equally harmonious, a true oasis amid Běijīng's bedlam. Don't expect to see worshippers in prayer; this is not so much a temple as an altar. Essentially Confucian in function, the cosmic overtones of the Temple of Heaven will delight numerologists, necromancers and the superstitious – not to mention acoustic engineers and carpenters. Seen from above the structures are round and the bases square, a pattern deriving from the ancient Chinese belief that heaven is round and earth is square. Thus the northern end of the park is semicircular and the southern end is square. Temple of the Earth, in the north of Běijīng, is on the northern compass point and Temple of Heaven is on the southern point.

There are four gates to the park, one on each point of the compass, and you can enter through any of them. The imperial approach to the temple was via **Zhāohēng Gate** (昭亨门; Zhāohēng Mén; Map p276) in the south. You can enter either with just the basic park ticket (¥10/15 winter/summer), then buy a ¥20 ticket that includes each major sight later, or buy the through ticket (¥35), which gets you into the park and all the sights.

DON'T MISS

- Hall of Prayer for Good Harvests
- Echo Wall

PRACTICALITIES

- 天坛公园; Tiāntán Gōngyuán
- Map p276, B4
- ☎010 6702 9917
- Tiantan Donglu; 天坛东路
- park/through ticket Apr-Oct ¥15/35, Nov-Mar ¥10/30, audio guide ¥40 (deposit ¥50)
- 🕒park 6.30am-10pm, sights 8am-5.30pm Apr-Oct, park 6.30am-8pm, sights 8am-5pm Nov-Mar
- [S]Line 5 to Tiantandongmen, Exit A

Round Altar

Constructed in 1530 and rebuilt in 1740, the 5m-high **Round Altar** (圜丘; Yuán Qiū; Map p276) once looked very different: its first incarnation was in deep-blue glazed stone before being redone in light green. The current white marble structure is arrayed in three tiers; its geometry revolves around the imperial number nine. Odd numbers were considered heavenly, and nine is the largest single-digit odd number. The top tier, thought to symbolise heaven, contains nine rings of stones. Each ring has multiples of nine stones, so that the ninth ring has 81 stones. The middle tier (earth) has the 10th to 18th rings. The bottom tier (humanity) has the 19th to 27th rings. The numbers of stairs and balustrades are also multiples of nine. If you stand in the centre of the upper terrace and say something, the sound bounces off the marble balustrades, making your voice sound louder (by nine times?).

Echo Wall

Just north of the Round Altar, surrounding the Imperial Vault of Heaven, is **Echo Wall** (回音壁; Huíyīn Bì; Map p276), 65m in diameter. Its form has unusual acoustic properties, enabling a whisper to travel clearly from one end to the other (unless a tour group or a loudmouth with a mobile phone gets in the way). In the courtyard are the **Triple-Sounds Stones** (三音石; Sānyīn Shí). It is said that if you clap or shout while standing on the stones, the sound is echoed once from the first stone, twice from the second stone and thrice from the third stone. Queues can get long here.

Imperial Vault of Heaven

The octagonal **Imperial Vault of Heaven** (皇穹宇; Huáng Qióng Yǔ; Map p276) was built at the same time as the Circular Mound Altar, and is structured along the same lines as the older Hall of Prayer for Good Harvests. The vault once contained spirit tablets used in the winter solstice ceremony. Behind the Imperial Vault of Heaven stands the Nine Dragon Juniper, a hoary tree with a trunk of sinewy and coiling knots. Proceeding north from the Imperial Vault is a 360m-long walkway called the **Red Stairway Bridge** (丹陛桥; Dānbì Qiáo; Map p276), leading to the Hall of Prayer for Good Harvests.

Hall of Prayer for Good Harvests

The crowning structure of the Temple of Heaven Park is the Hall of Prayer for Good Harvests, magnificently mounted on a three-tiered marble terrace and capped with a triple-eaved umbrella roof of purplish-blue tiles. Built in 1420, it was burnt to

TOP TIPS

Some of the key sights within the park get very crowded, making photo opportunities difficult. Get here as early as you can, preferably when the sights open at 8am, especially if you want to test the unique acoustic properties of the Echo Wall. And if at all possible, avoid the park on public holidays when it is rammed with domestic tourists.

Try the 2nd floor of Wedomé (p111), opposite the park's east gate, for a cheap coffee or tea break, as well as cakes and sandwiches. The delicious shāomài, or dumplings, at Dòuyīchù (p111) are just a short taxi or subway ride away.

LOCATION

Building Běijīng's principal shrine in the heart of the former Chóngwén district, a traditionally down-at-heel, working-class neighbourhood outside the walls of the Imperial City, might seem unusual at first. But the neighbourhood lies in the south, with an aspect facing the sun and indicative of *yáng* (the male and positive principle). Blessed with such positive feng shui (geomancy; literally 'wind and water'), it is not surprising that the Temple of Heaven was sited here.

THE WINTER SOLSTICE CEREMONY

The emperor, the Son of Heaven (天子; Tiānzǐ), visited the Temple of Heaven twice a year, but the most important ceremony was performed just before the winter solstice. The emperor and his enormous entourage passed down Qianmen Dajie in total silence to the Imperial Vault of Heaven. Commoners were not permitted to view the ceremony and remained cloistered indoors. The procession included elephant and horse chariots and long lines of lancers, nobles, officials and musicians dressed in their finest. The imperial 12m-long sedan was almost 3m wide and employed 10 bearers. The next day the emperor waited in a yellow silk tent at the southern gate while officials moved the sacred tablets to the Round Altar, where prayers and sacrificial rituals took place. It was thought that this ritual decided the nation's future; hence a hitch in any part of the proceedings was regarded as a bad omen.

The ritual was last attempted in 1914 by Yuan Shikai, who harboured unfulfilled ambitions of becoming emperor.

cinders in 1889 and heads rolled in apportioning blame (although lightning was the most likely cause). A faithful reproduction based on Ming architectural methods was erected the following year; the builders chose Oregon fir for the support pillars.

The four central pillars symbolise the seasons, the 12 in the next ring denote the months of the year, and the 12 outer ones represent the day, broken into 12 'watches'. Embedded in the ceiling is a carved dragon, a symbol of royalty. The patterning, carving and gilt decoration of this ceiling and its swirl of colour are a dizzying sight.

All this is made more amazing by the fact that the wooden pillars ingeniously support the ceiling without nails or cement – quite an accomplishment for a building 38m high and 30m in diameter. You can't enter so instead you'll have to settle for viewing it through the open door.

Other Buildings

With a green, glazed-tiled two-tier roof, the gated **Animal Killing Pavilion** (宰牲亭; Zǎishēng Tíng; Map p276) FREE was the venue for the slaughter of sacrificial oxen, sheep, deer and other animals, with copper boilers and cleaning sink on display; you'll need to show your passport for entry. Stretching out from here runs the **Long Corridor** (长廊; Cháng Láng; Map p276) where locals play cards, listen to the radio, and practise Peking opera, dance moves and hacky-sack. Sacrificial music was rehearsed at the **Divine Music Administration** (神乐署; Shényuè Shǔ; Map p276; ¥10) in the west of the park, while wild cats live in the dry moat of the green-tiled **Fasting Palace** (斋宫; Zhāi Gōng; Map p276) FREE.

The Park

There are around 4000 ancient, knotted cypresses (some 800 years old, their branches propped up on poles) providing much-needed shade. The parkland itself is typical of Chinese parks, with the imperfections and wild irregularity of nature largely eliminated and the harmonising hand of humans accentuated in its obsessively straight lines and regular arrangements. The resulting order, balance and harmony has a haunting but slightly claustrophobic beauty.

◉ SIGHTS

TEMPLE OF HEAVEN PARK　　　　PARK

See p106.

**SOUTHEAST CORNER WATCHTOWER &
RED GATE GALLERY**　　WATCHTOWER, GALLERY

Map p276 (东南角楼、红门画廊; Dōngnán Jiǎolóu & Hóngmén Huàláng; ☑010 6527 0574; www.redgategallery.com; ¥10; ☺8am-5.30pm; Ⓢ Jianguomen or Chongwenmen) This splendid fortification, with a green-tiled, twin-eaved roof rising imperiously south of the Ancient Observatory, dates to the Ming dynasty. Mount the battlements for views alongside camera-wielding Chinese trainspotters eagerly awaiting rolling stock grinding in and out of Běijīng Train Station. Make sure to hunt out the **signatures** etched in the walls by allied forces during the Boxer Rebellion.

You can make out the name of a certain P Foot; 'USA' is also scrawled on the brickwork. The international composition of the eight-nation force that relieved Běijīng in 1900 is noted in names such as André, Stickel and what appears to be a name in Cyrillic. One brick records the date 'Dec 16 1900'. Allied forces overwhelmed the redoubt after a lengthy engagement. Note the drainage channels poking out of the wall along its length. You can reach the watchtower from the west through the Railway Arch, which was built for the first railway that ran around Běijīng.

The watchtower is punctured with 144 archers' windows, as well as two forlorn stumps of flag abutments and a cannon or two. Attached to it is a 100m section of the original Inner City Wall, beyond which stretches the restored Ming City Wall extending all the way to Chóngwén Mén and north to Beijingzhan Dongjie. Inside the highly impressive interior is some staggering carpentry: huge red pillars that are topped with solid beams surge upwards. The 1st floor is the site of the **Red Gate Gallery**, one of Běijīng's long-established modern art galleries. The 3rd-floor gallery has a fascinating photographic exhibition on the old gates of Běijīng, while the 4th-floor gallery contains more paintings. Say you are visiting the Red Gate Gallery and the ¥10 entry fee to the watchtower is normally waived.

**BĚIJĪNG PLANNING
EXHIBITION HALL**　　　　MUSEUM

Map p276 (北京市规划展览馆; Běijīngshì Guīhuà Zhǎnlǎnguǎn; ☑010 6701 7074; 20 Qianmen Dong-dajie; 前门东大街20号。; ¥30; ☺9am-5pm Tue-Sun; Ⓢ Qianmen) It doesn't see much foot traffic, but a lot of thought has gone into making this modern museum a visitor-friendly experience. True, it strains every sinew to present Běijīng's gut-wrenching, *hútòng*-felling metamorphosis in the best possible light, but the 3rd floor houses a fantastic, giant scale model of the capital mounted on a series of even bigger satellite photos.

It's a great way to get a perspective of this ever-expanding city. There's also a scale model of the Forbidden City and 3D films touting the Běijīng of the future.

BĚIJĪNG RED STAR　　　　MUSEUM

Map p276 (红星; Hóngxīng; 97 Qianmen Dajie; 前门大街97号; ☺9am-9pm; Ⓢ Line 2 to Qianmen, exit B or C) **FREE** Set up by the government-owned Red Star *báijiǔ* (literally 'white alcohol'; a face-numbing spirit) company, this museum is dedicated to the 'drink for the people'. There are no English captions but it takes you through the distillation process using displays of dioramas, traditional equipment and old bottles (including an original 1949 vintage endorsed by the Chairman himself). You can do a tasting upstairs of the firewater-like spirit, and pick up a souvenir bottle from its store for ¥15.

The building here was a centuries old *báijiǔ* distillery before the Communist government acquired the business in 1949 to create the Red Star brand. It shares space with the Běijīng Tourist Information Office.

LOCAL KNOWLEDGE

CITY GATE TO SUBWAY STOP

The names of the subway stations of Qianmen, Chongwenmen and Jianguomen recall some of the Tartar City Wall's vast and imposing gates, which divided the Imperial City from the Chinese city beyond it. Today, Front Gate and the Southeast Corner Watchtower to the southeast are the only reminders of that wall. The road looping south from Jianguomen station, following the line of the city moat, marks the outline of the levelled Chinese City Wall, whose gates (*mén*) survive only in street names, such as Guangqumen Nanbinhe Lu, Zuo'anmen Xibinhe Lu and Yongdingmen Dongbinhe Lu. Vestiges of this wall can still be seen at the Ming City Wall Ruins Park (p110).

BĚIJĪNG RAILWAY MUSEUM MUSEUM

Map p276 (北京铁路博物馆; Běijīng Tiělù Bówùguǎn; ☎010 6705 1638; 2a Qianmen Dongdajie; 前门东大街2a号; ¥20; ⏲9am-5pm Tue-Sun; [S]Qianmen) Located in the historic former Qiánmén Railway Station, which once connected Běijīng to Tiānjīn, this museum offers an engaging history of the development of the capital and China's railway system, with plenty of photos and models. Its lack of space, though, means it doesn't have many actual trains, although there is a life-size model of the cab of one of China's high-speed trains to clamber into (¥10).

Hard-core trainspotters should make tracks to the **China Railway Museum** (中国铁道博物馆; Zhōngguó Tiědào Bówùguǎn; ☎010 6438 1317; north of 1 Jiuxianqiao Bei Lu, Chaoyang District; 朝阳区酒仙桥北路1号院北侧; ¥20; ⏲9am-4pm Tue-Sun; 🚌688) on the far north-eastern outskirts of Běijīng, which is vast and has far more loco action.

MING CITY WALL RUINS PARK CITY WALLS

Map p276 (明城墙遗址公园; Míng Chéngqiáng Yízhǐ Gōngyuán; Chongwenmen Dongdajie; 崇文門东大街; ⏲24hr; [S]Chongwenmen) [FREE] This slice of restored Ming Inner City Wall runs along the length of the northern flank of Chongwenmen Dongdajie and is attached to a slender strip of park. It's all that is left of the original 24km-long city wall, which started being demolished in the 1960s to make room for new roads and the subway system.

The wall stretches from the former site of Chóngwén Mén (崇文门; Chóngwén Gate), one of the nine gates of the Inner City Wall, to the Southeast Corner Watchtower and then turns north for a short distance along Jianguomen Nandajie to Beijingzhan Dongjie. Chóngwén Mén was also called Shuì Mén (税门; Tax Gate) as the capital tax bureau lay just outside the gate. You can walk the park's length, taking in its higgledy-piggledy contours and the interior layers of stone in parts of the wall that have collapsed. The restored sections run for just over 2km, rising to a height of around 15m and interrupted every 80m with buttresses extending to a maximum depth of 39m. The most interesting sections of wall are those closer to their original and more dilapidated state and some of the bricks come complete with bullet holes.

BĚIJĪNG NATURAL HISTORY MUSEUM MUSEUM

Map p276 (北京自然博物馆; Běijīng Zìrán Bówùguǎn; ☎010 6702 7702; 126 Tianqiao Nandajie; 天桥南大街126号; ⏲9am-5pm Tue-Sun, last entry 4pm; [S]Qianmen or Tiantandongmen) [FREE] The main entrance to this creeper-laden museum is hung with portraits of the great natural historians, including Darwin and

LOCAL KNOWLEDGE

THE LOST CITY WALLS OF BĚIJĪNG

As Běijīng continues to develop relentlessly, it's increasingly hard to believe that as recently as 40-odd years ago the capital was still surrounded by the city walls that had protected it from invaders for more than 500 years.

Two walls once guarded Běijīng: an outer wall and and inner wall. Now, nothing is left of the original outer wall, while only a few remnants of the inner city wall remain, most notably the stretch now known as the Ming City Wall Ruins Park. Their absence is perhaps the most conspicuous chunk of lost heritage in Běijīng.

The outer wall went first. Demolition started in the early 1950s and by 1961 half a millenia of history had vanished. The inner wall disappeared more slowly; as late as the mid-1970s, sections of wall and their gates and watchtowers were being torn down.

It was Mao Zedong who ordered the removal of the walls. The justification was that they stood in the way of the new roads being built, as well as the subway system (Line 2 follows the route of the old inner wall). But blotting out the grandeur of earlier dynasties may also have inspired Mao's decision to erase such a vital part of Běijīng's identity.

Opposition to the scheme was unusually vigorous, given Mao's dislike of public criticism. It was led by the late Liang Sicheng, a famed architect known as the father of modern Chinese architecture. Liang argued that Běijīng could still develop into a modern city while keeping its walls. He was almost certainly right. Nánjīng and Xī'ān are examples of Chinese cities that have evolved while retaining their walls.

But Liang failed to convince Mao and in a horrible irony, Liang's own *sìhéyuàn* (traditional courtyard house) disappeared under the wrecking ball in 2012.

Linnaeus. The contents range from dinosaur fossils and skeletons, including a *Mamenchisaurus jingyanensis* (a vast sauropod that once roamed China) to creepy-crawlies, an aquarium with Nemo-esque clown fish and an exhibition on the origins of life on Earth. Bring your passport for free entry.

QIANMEN DAJIE
HISTORIC SITE

Map p276 (前门大街; S Qianmen) Restored to resemble a late Qing dynasty street scene and wildly popular with domestic visitors, this ancient thoroughfare (once known as Zhengyangmen Dajie, or Facing the Sun Gate Street) is something of a tourist theme park. It is especially lively at its northern end, as more (overpriced) restaurants and shops open up, while the rebuilt Qiánmén Decorative Arch (the original was torn down in the 1950s) looks handsome.

EATING

OLD BĚIJĪNG ZHÁJIÀNG NOODLE KING
NOODLES $

Map p276 (老北京炸酱面大王; Lǎo Běijīng Zhájiàng Miàn Dàwáng; ☑010 6705 6705; 56 Dongxinglong Jie; 东兴隆街56号; noodles from ¥18; ☺10.30am-10pm; S Chongwenmen) Faux old-school Běijīng style – look for the two rickshaws parked outside the entrance – but always busy (especially at lunchtime) with locals sampling the signature noodles with bean-paste sauce on offer here. The sauce, scallions and your choice of meat or veggie options come on the side and you mix them with the noodles. Confusingly, the English sign to the restaurant says, 'Fortune Long Běijīng Bean Sauce Noodles'.

YĪZHĒN YUÁN
MUSLIM $

Map p276 (伊珍源饭庄; ☑010 6712 9856; 80 Xihuashi Dajie; 西花市大街80号; mains from ¥22; ☺10.30am-9pm; S Chongwenmen) A good spot for a lunch break in the area, this Muslim eatery offers juicy *yángròu chuàn* (羊肉串; lamb skewers, ¥5) and decent naan bread, as well as noodle and veggie dishes. No English spoken, but they do have a picture menu.

WEDOMÉ
CAFE $

Map p276 (味多美; Wèiduōměi; ☑010 6715 9205; 12 Tiyuguan Lu; 体育馆路12号; coffee & tea from ¥10; ☺7.30am-9pm; S Tiantandongmen) If you're looking for a place to rest your legs after shopping or sightseeing in the area, then retreat to the 2nd floor of this

citywide chain cafe opposite the east gate of the Temple of Heaven Park (p106). It offers a wide selection of coffee, tea and juices, as well as cakes and sandwiches.

DŌUYĪCHÙ
DUMPLING $$

Map p276 (都一处; ☑010 6702 1555; 38 Qianmen Dajie; 前门大街38号; dumplings ¥42-90; ☺7.30am-9.30pm; S Qianmen) Still located on the street where it opened during the mid-Qing dynasty, Dōuyīchù specialises in the delicate dumplings called *shāomài*. The shrimp-and-leek and veggie ones are especially good, and are presented very nicely, but it also has innovative seasonal variations, such as sweet corn and what the English menu calls 'honey bean' in the summer, or pork and bamboo shoots in the winter.

There are other, non-dumpling dishes on the menu too. No-frills service and be prepared to queue at weekends.

★ CAPITAL M
MEDITERRANEAN $$$

Map p276 (M餐厅; M Cāntīng; ☑010 6702 2727; www.m-restaurantgroup.com/capitalm; 3rd fl, 2 Qianmen Dajie; 前门步行街2号; mains from ¥208; ☺11.30am-3pm & 5.30-10.30pm; ☎; S Qianmen) The terrace of this swish but relaxed restaurant, with its unfussy menu of Mediterranean favourites, offers fine views over Qiánmén Gate and Tiān'ānmén Sq. The weekday lunch menu is decent value (¥188). It's down the first turning on the left at the beginning of Qianmen Dajie; look for the 'M' hanging off the side of the building. Book ahead.

The menu ranges across France, Italy, Greece, Turkey and north Africa and the signature leg-of-lamb dish remains as popular as ever. If you can't snaffle a table on the terrace, the large, light-filled dining room is almost as good a spot to enjoy your meal. There's a weekend brunch deal with two/three courses for ¥258/298.

★ LÌQÚN ROAST DUCK RESTAURANT
PEKING DUCK $$$

Map p276 (利群烤鸭店; Lìqún Kǎoyādiàn; ☑010 6702 5681, 010 6705 5578; 11 Beixiangfeng Hutong; 前门东大街正义路南口北翔凤胡同11号; roast duck for 2/3 people ¥240/285; ☺11am-10pm; S Qianmen) As you walk in to this compact courtyard restaurant, you're greeted by the fine sight of rows of ducks on hooks glowing in the ovens. The delectable duck on offer is in such high demand that it's essential to call ahead to reserve both a bird and a table (otherwise, turn up off-peak and be prepared to wait an hour).

Inside, it's a little tatty (no prizes for the toilets) and service can be chaotic, but the food more than makes up for that. Buried away in a maze of crumbling *hútòng* in east Qiánmén that have somehow survived demolition, look for the red-neon duck sign that points the way to the restaurant.

BIÀNYÍFĀNG — PEKING DUCK $$$

Map p276 (便宜坊烤鸭店; Biànyífāng Kǎoyādiàn; 010 6708 8680; 3rd fl, China New World Shopping Mall, 5 Chongwenmenwai Dajie; 崇文门外大街5号新世界商场二期三层; roast duck ¥198; 11am-9.30pm; Chongwenmen) Biànyífāng claims to be the original Peking duck restaurant – it cites a heritage that dates back to the reign of the Qing emperor Xianfeng. The birds here are roasted in the *mènlú* style (in a closed oven, as opposed to a half-open one where the duck hangs to cook) and the meat is nice and tender.

A half bird is ¥108 (trimmings are extra) a good deal in Běijīng now – and the menu also offers duck liver, heart and feet dishes. In fact, just about any part of the duck that is edible is available here. It's rather less touristy than the other duck options in the area.

QIÁNMÉN QUÁNJÙDÉ ROAST DUCK RESTAURANT — PEKING DUCK $$$

Map p276 (前门全聚德烤鸭店; Qiánmén Quánjùdé Kǎoyādiàn; 010 6701 1379; www.qmquanjude.com.cn; 30 Qianmen Dajie; 前门大街30号; roast duck ¥238; 11am-1.30pm & 4.30pm-8pm; Qianmen) This is the most popular branch of Běijīng's most famous destination for duck – check out the photos of everyone from Fidel Castro to Zhang Yimou. The duck, while not the best in town, is roasted in ovens fired by fruit-tree wood, which means the birds have a unique fragrance, as well as being juicy, if slightly fatty.

It's very much geared to the tourist hordes (both domestic and foreign) and the crowds mean it is wise to reserve ahead. Service can be peremptory, while the huge, two-floor venue lacks atmosphere.

 ENTERTAINMENT

RED THEATRE — ACROBATICS

Map p276 (红剧场; Hóng Jùchǎng; 010 6714 2473; 44 Xingfu Dajie; 幸福大街44号; tickets ¥200-880; performance 7.30pm; Tiantandongmen) The daily show is *The Legend of Kung Fu*, which follows one boy's journey to becoming a warrior monk. Slick, high-energy fight scenes are interspersed with more soulful dance sequences, plus plenty of 'how do they do that' balancing on spears and other body-defying acts. To find the theatre, look for the all-red exterior set back from the road.

SHOPPING

HÓNGQIÁO PEARL MARKET — MARKET

Map p276 (红桥市场; Hóngqiáo Shìchǎng; 010 6711 7429; 9 Tiantan Lu; 天坛路9号; 9.30am-7pm; Tiantandongmen) Besides a cosmos of clutter (shoes, clothing, cosmetics, electronics and bags), Hóngqiáo is home to more pearls than the South Sea. The range is huge (freshwater, seawater, white and black) and prices vary incredibly depending on quality. The 3rd floor has the cheaper pearls, mostly sourced from Zhèjiāng province, as well as other jewellery and jade.

The better-quality, pricier pearls can be found on the far more hushed 4th and 5th floors, where there's a roof terrace that offers an excellent overview of the Temple of Heaven. Prices are generally high, while the vendors, who all speak some English, are canny bargainers.

SPORTS & ACTIVITIES

Many Beijingers head to the Temple of Heaven Park to practise taichi, or to enjoy formation dancing and kite flying.

NTSC TENNIS CLUB — TENNIS

Map p276 (国家体育总局训练局网球俱乐部; Guójiā Tǐyù Zǒngjú Xùnliànjú Wǎngqiú Jùlèbù; 010 8718 3401; 50 Tiantan Donglu; 天坛东路50号; nonmembers per hr ¥500; 9am-9pm; Tiantandongmen) Tennis *(wǎng qiú)* is an increasingly popular sport in Běijīng, so phone in advance to book one of the inside courts at this professional complex where some of China's top players train. Nonmembers can only play on Wednesday and Thursday afternoons.

Běihǎi Park & Xīchéng North

Neighbourhood Top Five

❶ Běihǎi Park (p115) Once reserved for emperors only, this is one of the capital's most striking imperial parks, dominated by its namesake lake and dotted with temples.

❷ Hòuhǎi Lakes (p117) Sedate during the day and raucous at night, these lakes are one of the best places to escape the city sprawl.

❸ Capital Museum (p117) Spend a morning at this impressive museum to understand the evolution of this great city.

❹ Fuchengmennei Dajie (p117) Head down this road to explore its authentic *hútòng*, museums and Buddhist temples, including the peaceful Miàoyīng Temple White Dagoba.

❺ Mei Lanfang Grand Theatre (p123) Spend a night at the Peking Opera at this modern theatre named after a local legend.

For more detail of this area see Map p278.

Lonely Planet's Top Tip

Come nightfall, the Hòuhǎi Lakes become a madhouse of milling crowds and bar touts trying to entice you into their overpriced bars. If you want to experience a night out drinking, Chinese style, dive in. If you'd rather avoid the wailing karaoke, slip down the *hútòng* that run off the lakeshore, where you'll find quieter bars and cafes. The lanes on the southwest side of Silver Ingot Bridge are a good place to start.

 Best Places to Eat

➡ Royal Icehouse (p121)

➡ Kǎo Ròu Jì (p122)

➡ 4corners (p120)

➡ Meatball Company (p121)

➡ Wang Pang Zi (p121)

For reviews, see p120.

 Best Places to Drink

➡ 4corners (p120)

➡ NBeer Pub (p122)

➡ East Shore Jazz Café (p123)

➡ Tángrén Teahouse (p122)

For reviews, see p122. ➡

Best Places for People-watching

➡ Bĕihǎi Park (p115)

➡ Hòuhǎi Exercise Park (p119)

➡ Hòuhǎi Park (p119)

For reviews, see p117. ➡

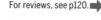

Explore Bĕihǎi Park & Xīchéng North

The majority of the Imperial City was in this part of Xīchéng (西城; literally 'West City'), lending it a regal grandeur that survives to this day. Less visited than Dōngchéng to the east, but equally endowed with ancient temples and charming *hútòng* (narrow alleyways), it's one of the most worthwhile neighbourhoods to visit in all Bĕijīng.

Any tour has to start at the lakes that dominate the eastern part of the district. Take in Bĕihǎi Park first, perhaps spending an hour or more floating around its lake, before striking out through the park's north gate to take in the sights and *hútòng* scattered around Qiánhǎi, Hòuhǎi and Xīhǎi Lakes, collectively known as either Shíchàhǎi or more commonly just Hòuhǎi. Once night falls, eat at one of the many restaurants close to the lakes and then join the crowds promenading around them, stopping in for a drink at the many bars and cafes that line their shores.

A second day here is more or less an imperative. Head to Fuchengmennei Dajie, a street lined with lesser-known temples; the most impressive being Miàoyīng Temple White Dagoba. Then dive into the *hútòng* behind them. The district's best temple, though, is southwest of here: the Taoist White Cloud Temple, which can be combined with a visit to nearby Capital Museum. Come evening, there's a wealth of venues in which to catch everything from jazz to classical music and Peking opera.

Local Life

➡ **Fly a kite** Bĕihǎi Park is prime kite-flying territory. Visit Three Stone Kite Shop (p123) to kit yourself out.

➡ **Hútòng** The alleyways and lanes here are far less commercial than any others in the city and a great introduction to Bĕijīng's tremendous street life. The *hútòng* behind Fuchengmennei Dajie are also fascinating.

➡ **Ice skating** When winter clamps the Hòuhǎi Lakes in its icy embrace, do as Beijingers do and strap on a pair of ice skates (you can hire them by the lakes).

Getting There & Away

➡ **Subway** Beihai North (Line 6) and Shichahai (Line 8) subway stations best serve Bĕihǎi Park and the Hòuhǎi Lakes, although you can also reach them from Line 2 (which circles the district) and Line 4 (which runs north–south). Line 1 cuts across the south of this district.

➡ **Bus** Bus 1 runs along Xichang'an Jie, Fuxingmennei Dajie and Fuxingmenwai Dajie, taking you to the Capital Museum. Bus 22 takes you from Tiān'ānmén West to Xīdān and then north to Xīnjiēkou.

LEONID ANDRONOV / SHUTTERSTOCK ©

TOP SIGHT
BĚIHǍI PARK

With an extraordinary history as the former palace of the great Mongol emperor Kublai Khan, and back garden for the subsequent Yuan dynasty emperors, Běihǎi Park is the principal oasis for Beijingers in this part of town. With the tranquil, willow-fringed lake of Běhǎi (literally, 'North Sea') at its centre, and temples, pavilions and spirit walls scattered around it, the park offers visitors a rare chance in Běijīng to combine sightseeing with fun, whether it's mucking around in a boat, having a picnic or just watching the dancing, taichi and the parade of humanity that passes through.

Jade Islet

Made out of the heaped earth scooped out to create Běihǎi Lake itself, which some attribute to Kublai Khan, and dominated by the 36m-high **White Dagoba** (白塔; Báitǎ; Map p278; incl in through ticket for Běihǎi Park; ⏲9am-5pm; [S]Line 6 to Beihai North or Nanluogu Xiang; or Line 4 to Xisi), which was originally constructed in 1651 for a visit by the Dalai Lama and then rebuilt in 1741 after being destroyed in an earthquake, Jade Islet sits in the southeastern corner of the lake. At its northern edge is the decorative curved **Long Corridor**, an elegant double-storey walkway with a colourful panelled ceiling and lattice woodwork. You can reach the island by a land bridge close to the South Gate and East Gate, or catch a boat (one way/return ¥10/15) from the northwestern shore if you come in by the North Gate. You can also hire pedalos (¥120 per hour, ¥200 deposit) from here as well.

Yǒngān Temple

The principal site on Jade Islet is the impressive **Yǒngān Temple** (Temple of Eternal Peace; 永安寺; Yǒngān Sì; Map p278; incl in through ticket for Běihǎi Park; [S]Line 6 to Beihai North or Nanluogu Xiang;

DON'T MISS

- Jade Islet
- Round City
- North Shore Temples

PRACTICALITIES

- 北海公园; Běihǎi Gōngyuán
- Map p278, D4
- ☎010 6403 1102
- www.beihaipark.com.cn/en
- high/low season ¥10/5, through ticket ¥20/15, audio guide ¥60
- ⏲6am-9pm, sights to 5pm
- [S]Line 6 to Beihai North or Nanluogu Xiang, or Line 4 to Xisi

TOP TIPS

➡ There's a lot to see, so build in half a day here into your itinerary.

➡ Hold on to your ticket as some sights require you to momentarily exit, so you'll need it to get back in.

Běihǎi Park isn't renowned for its culinary options, so if the weather's fine you could pack a picnic and find a quiet spot among the temples overlooking the lake. Otherwise Qìngfēng Steamed Dumpling Shop (p121), close to Yǒngān Temple, does quick, inexpensive stuffed dumplings such as *jiǎozi*, *bāozi* and wonton soups.

ENTERING THE PARK

You can enter or leave the park by its South Gate on Wenjin Jie, its North Gate on Di'anmen Xidajie or its East Gate, hidden among the *hútòng* between this park and Jǐngshān Park. There's also a rarely used West Gate, also on Wenjin Jie, which you can use if you wish to walk a complete circuit of the lake – you'll have to leave the park (hang on to your ticket) then re-enter again through the South Gate.

or Line 4 to Xisi), meaning Temple of Eternal Peace. Enter from the south, through the Hall of the Heavenly Kings (Tiānwáng Diàn), past the Drum and Bell Towers to the **Hall of the Wheel of the Law** (Fǎlún Diàn), with its central effigy of Sakyamuni and flanked by Bodhisattvas and 18 *luóhàn* (Buddhists, especially monks, who achieved Enlightenment and passed to Nirvana at death). At the rear of the temple you will find a bamboo grove and quite a steep flight of steps up through a decorative archway, which is emblazoned with the characters 'Lóng Guāng' (龙光) on one side and 'Zǐzhào' (紫照) on the other side. Head up more steps to the **Zhèngjué Hall** (Zhèngjué Diàn), which contains a statue of Milefo and Weituo.

Pǔ'ān Hall (Pǔ'ān Diàn), the next hall, houses a statue of Tsongkhapa, who was the founder of the Yellow Hat sect of Tibetan Buddhism, flanked by statues of the fifth Dalai Lama and the Panchen Lama. Eight golden effigies on either flank include tantric statues and the goddess Heinümu, adorned with a necklace of skulls. The final flight of steep steps brings you to the White Dagoba.

North Shore Temples

Located on the lake's northern shore, **Xītiān Fánjìng** (西天梵境; Western Paradise; Map p278; incl in through ticket for Běihǎi Park; Ⓢ Line 6 to Beihai North or Nanluogu Xiang) is one of the most interesting temples in Běijīng. It was closed for major renovations at time of research.

The nearby **Nine Dragon Screen** (九龙壁; Jiǔlóng Bì; Map p278; incl in through ticket for Běihǎi Park; Ⓢ Line 6 to Beihai North or Nanluogu Xiang), a 5m-high and 27m-long spirit wall, is a glimmering stretch of coloured glazed tiles.

Further west you'll find several attractive temples, including the unique **Xiaoxitian** (Little Western Heaven; 小西天; Map p278; incl in through ticket for Běihǎi Park; Ⓢ Line 6 to Beihai North or Nanluogu Xiang), the largest square pavilion-style palace in China.

The Palace of the Great Khan

Kublai Khan, the grandson of the even more dominant Genghis Khan, conquered China and established the Yuan dynasty in 1271. He chose what is now Běihǎi Park as the site of his palace. All that remains of his former home is a large jar made of green jade dating from 1265 in the **Round City** (团城; Tuán Chéng; Map p278; Běihǎi Park; inclusive of admission to Běihǎi Park; Ⓢ Line 6 to Beihai North or Nanluogu Xiang, or Line 4 to Xisi) near the park's southern entrance. At the top of the Round City is the splendid **Hall of Divine Light** (Chéngguāng Hall; Chéngguāng Diàn), where a 1.5m-tall, white-jade, jewel-encrusted statue of Sakyamuni from Myanmar (Burma) can be found. The side pavilions host temporary cultural exhibitions.

◉ SIGHTS

BĚIHĂI PARK   PARK
See p115.

CAPITAL MUSEUM   MUSEUM
(首都博物馆; Shǒudū Bówùguǎn; ☑010 6339 3339; www.capitalmuseum.org.cn; 16 Fuxingmenwai Dajie; 复兴门外大街16号; ⊗9am-5pm Tue-Sun, last entry 4pm; Ⓢ Line 1 to Muxidi, exit C1) **FREE** Behind the riveting good looks of the sleek Capital Museum are some first-rate galleries, including a mesmerising collection of ancient Buddhist statues and a lavish exhibition of Chinese porcelain. There is also an interesting chronological history of Běijīng, an exhibition that is dedicated to cultural relics of Peking opera, a fascinating Běijīng Folk Customs exhibition, and displays of ancient bronzes, jade, calligraphy and paintings. Bring your passport or photo ID for free entry and audio guide.

Come out of exit C1 of Muxidi subway station, and you'll soon see the museum on your right (200m).

HÒUHĂI LAKES   LAKE
Map p278 (后海, Hòuhǎi; Ⓢ Line 6 to Beihai North, exit B, Line 8 to Shichahai, exit A1, Line 2 to Jishuitan, exit B) **FREE** Also known as Shíchàhǎi (什刹海) but mostly just referred to collectively as Hòuhǎi, the Hòuhǎi Lakes are compromised of three lakes: Qiánhǎi (Front Lake), Hòuhǎi (Back Lake) and Xīhǎi (West Lake). Together they are one of the capital's favourite outdoor spots, heaving with locals and out-of-towners in the summer especially, and providing great people-spotting action.

During the day, senior citizens meander along, use the exercise machines scattered along the lakeshore, fish, fly kites or just sit and chew the fat. At night, the area turns into one of the more popular nightlife areas, as the restaurants, bars and cafes that surround the lakes spring into life. This is a night out, Chinese style, so be prepared for neon lights galore, and plenty of karaoke being blasted out onto the surrounding lanes. Meanwhile, as the midday sun disappears, the lakes become a mass of pedalos circling round and round.

It's great fun, and even if you find parts of the lakes too hectic (**Silver Ingot Bridge** (银锭桥; Yíndìng Qiáo; Map p278; Hòuhǎi Lake; Ⓢ Line 8 to Shichahai, exit A2) is a major bottleneck), it's easy enough to escape the crowds, by exploring the many *hútòng* that run both east and west of the lakes, or to just venture

further northwest towards the quieter Xīhǎi Lake. It's particularly good to cycle around and numerous places by the lakeshores hire out bikes by the hour (¥10 per hour, ¥200 deposit). There are many spots to rent pedalos too (¥120 per hour, ¥300 deposit), if you want to take to the water. Some locals swim in the lakes, even in midwinter!

The lakes look majestic in winter, when they freeze over and become the best place in Běijīng to ice skate (usually for around six weeks in January and February). Qiánhǎi Lake is most popular, although some people skate on Hòuhǎi Lake too; local vendors set themselves up with all the gear you need. You have to pay to enter the ice-skating area (weekdays/weekends ¥35/40 including skate hire). There's also chair sleds, ice bikes and even ice bumper cars to rent, and a giant ice slide.

MIÀOYĪNG TEMPLE
WHITE DAGOBA   BUDDHIST TEMPLE
Map p278 (妙应寺白塔; Miàoyīng Sì Báitǎ; ☑010 6616 0211; 171 Fuchengmennei Dajie; 阜成门内大街171号; adult ¥20; ⊗9am-5pm Tue-Sun; Ⓢ Line 2 to Fuchengmen, exit B, or Line 4 to Xisi, exit A) Originally built in 1271, the serene Miàoyīng Temple slumbers beneath its huge, distinctive, chalk-white Yuan dynasty pagoda, which towers over the surrounding *hútòng*. It was, when it was built, the tallest structure in Dàdū (the Yuan dynasty name for Běijīng), and even today it is the tallest Tibetan-style pagoda in China. The highlights of a visit here include the diverse collection of Buddhist statuary.

The main building is the **Hall of the Great Enlightened One** (大觉宝殿; Dàjué Bǎodiàn), which is glittered splendidly with hundreds of Tibetan Buddhist effigies and a superb coloured patterned roof. The **Hall of the Seven Buddhas** features golden-painted wooden statues of the Buddhas of the Three Realms which date from the 13th century and also has exquisite detailing in the roof with dragon carvings. At the time of research, the pagoda itself was closed for renovations.

After you finish here, exit the temple and wander the tangle of local alleyways for street-market action and earthy shades of *hútòng* life.

SONG QINGLING
FORMER RESIDENCE   MUSEUM
Map p278 (宋庆龄故居; Sòng Qìnglíng Gùjū; ☑010 6402 3195; 46 Houhai Beiyan; 后海北沿

46号; admission ¥20; ⊙9am-5.30pm Apr-Oct, to 4.30pm Nov-Mar; ⓢLine 2 to Jishuitan, exit B) Madam Song is lovingly venerated by the Chinese as the wife of Sun Yatsen, founder of the Republic of China. Set in a lovely garden, her mansion, the former home of the father of Puyi (China's last emperor) displays her personal items, pictures, clothing and books. The highlight, however, is the museum to the side, which houses a very comprehensive exhibition on Madam Song's fascinating life, including the car given to her by Stalin, which comes with good English captions.

Volunteers conduct free English tours within the house.

PRINCE GONG'S
RESIDENCE   HISTORIC BUILDING

Map p278 (恭王府; Gōngwáng Fǔ; ☑010 8328 8149; 14 Liuyin Jie; admission ¥40, tours incl short opera show & tea ceremony ¥70; ⊙8am-5pm Apr-Oct, 9am-4pm Nov-Mar; ⓢLine 6 to Beihai North, exit B) The historic courtyard home of Prince Gong's (aka Prince Kung) mansion is one of Běijīng's largest private residential compounds. It remains one of the capital's more attractive retreats, decorated with rockeries, plants, pools, pavilions and elaborately carved gateways, although it can get very crowded with tour groups. It's reputed to be the model for Chinese writer Cáo Xuěqín's 18th-century classic *Dream of the Red Mansions*.

TEMPLE OF ANCIENT
MONARCHS   TAOIST TEMPLE

Map p278 (历代帝王庙; Lìdài Dìwáng Miào; 131 Fuchengmennei Dajie; 阜成门内大街131号; ¥20; ⊙9am-4pm Wed-Sun; ⓢLine 4 to Xisi, exit A) Constructed in 1530 as a twin of a temple built in Nánjīng in the 14th century, this rarely visited ancestral temple was reopened in 2004 after extensive renovations. It had spent the previous 80-odd years housing various locals schools, having been abandoned after the fall of the Qing dynasty.

The scale of the complex is vast – the main hall, the massive Jing De Chong Sheng Palace is the second largest of its kind in Běijīng (after the Forbidden City's Hall of Supreme Harmony) – and although the atmosphere is somewhat lifeless, the architecture is impressive enough to warrant a quick side trip from your visit to nearby Miàoyīng Temple. Look out for the huge marble stele turtles and the glazed furnaces, used to burn paper and silk offerings.

WHITE CLOUD TEMPLE   TAOIST TEMPLE

(白云观; Báiyún Guàn; ☑010 6346 3887; 9 Baiyunguan Jie; 白云路白云观街9号; adult ¥10; ⊙8.30am-4.30pm May-early Oct, to 4pm early Oct-Apr; ⓢLine 1 to Muxidi, exit C1) White Cloud Temple, once the Taoist centre of northern China, was founded in AD 739, although most of the temple halls date from the Qing dynasty. It's a lively, huge and fascinating complex of shrines and courtyards, tended by Taoist monks with their hair gathered into topknots.

Near the temple entrance, worshippers rub a polished stone carving for good fortune. The halls at the temple, centre of operations for the Taoist Quanzhen School and abode of the China Taoist Association, are dedicated to a host of Taoist officials and marshals. The Hall of the Jade Emperor celebrates this most famous of Taoist deities, while Taoist housewives cluster earnestly at the Hall to the God of Wealth to divine their financial future. Depictions of the Taoist Hell festoon the walls of the Shrine Hall for the Saviour Worthy.

Drop by White Cloud Temple during the Spring Festival (Chinese New Year) and you will be rewarded with the spectacle of a magnificent temple fair (*miàohuì*).

The temple is about a 1km walk from Muxidi subway station. Come out of exit C1, walk past the Capital Museum, then turn right down Baiyun Lu. After crossing the canal, take the second left, down Baiyunguan Jie, and the temple will be on your left.

LU XUN MUSEUM   MUSEUM

Map p278 (鲁迅博物馆; Lǔ Xùn Bówùguǎn; ☑010 6616 4080; www.luxunmuseum.com.cn; 19 Gongmenkou Ertiao; 宫门口二条19号; ⊙9am-4pm Tue-Sun; ⓢLine 2 to Fuchengmen, exit B) FREE Lu Xun (1881–1936) is regarded as the father of modern Chinese literature. Born in Shàoxīng in Zhèjiāng province and buried in Shànghǎi, he lived in Běijīng for more than a decade. As a writer, Lu Xun, who first trained in medicine, articulated a deep yearning for reform by mercilessly exposing the foibles of the Chinese character in such tales as *Medicine* and *Diary of a Madman*. The modern two-storey museum here depicts his life in great detail. Entry is free but you need to bring your passport.

The exhibits are well presented and come with English captions. Don't miss visiting Lu Xun's small former courtyard home, off to the left as you face the museum. The room round the back, overlooking

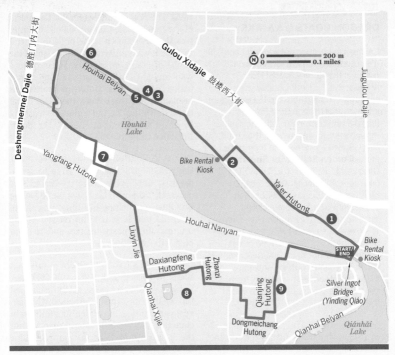

Neighbourhood Bike Tour
Houhai Lakes Bike Ride

START YÍNDÌNG QIÁO (SILVER INGOT BRIDGE)
END YÍNDÌNG QIÁO (SILVER INGOT BRIDGE)
LENGTH 3KM; ONE HOUR

There's a bike rental place beside Silver Ingot Bridge. You could easily walk this too.

Travelling north from the bridge, turn left down quiet Ya'er Hutong, where you'll soon reach the serene Buddhist ❶**Guānghuá Temple**, dating from the far-off Yuan dynasty, and open to the public. As the *hútòng* bears sharp right, turn left (at No 46) down a narrow alley, which will take you to the lakeside, past ❷**Dàzànglónghuá Temple** (on your left), built in 1719 and now a kindergarten.

Turn right at the lake and push on past ❸**Prince Zaifeng's former stables** (at No 43) and ❹**Prince Chun's Mansion** (at No 44), where China's last emperor, Puyi, was born. You'll also pass a bunch of locals on your left, working out, playing table tennis and swimming in the lake at ❺**Hòuhǎi Exercise Park** before you reach ❻**Song Qingliang's Former Residence**, once also part of Prince Chun's Mansion, and now a museum.

Follow the lake anticlockwise until you reach a small public square called ❼**Hòuhǎi Park**, a popular spot for formation dancing during the early morning and evening. Wheel your bike up the access ramp at the far right-hand corner of the square, then turn left into Yangfang Hutong, then right into Liuyin Jie and left into Daxiangfeng Hutong, following the huge grey-brick ❽**back wall of Prince Gong's Mansion**.

Now the wiggly-*hútòng* fun begins: turn right (still following the big wall) into Zhanzi Hutong, bear left, but then go straight on as the *hútòng* bears right, and turn right at the very end into the narrowest of narrow alleys. Wind your way down this alley, before taking the first left (Dongmeichang Hutong). Bear left, then right, then turn left at the *hútòng* crossroads onto Qianjing Hutong. The small, unmarked courtyard at No 8, on your right, was the ❾**former residence of Emperor Puyi's sister**, Yunxin.

Follow Qianjing Hutong back to the lakeside, where you can turn right towards Silver Ingot Bridge, past a plethora of bars and cafes.

LOCAL KNOWLEDGE

DRAGON BOATS & KAYAKS

Běijīng's general lack of water means it's not associated with dragon boat racing in the same way that Hong Kong is. But the Hòuhǎi Lakes are an exception and are home to the Běijīng International Dragon Boat Racing team, which comprises both locals and foreigners. Starting in April, they train every Sunday afternoon at their base at the **Golden Sail Water Sports Club** (金帆; Jīnfān; Map p278; ☎010 6401 2664; 81A Houhai Xiyan; 后海西沿 81A号; beer ¥30, cocktails ¥45, coffee ¥35; ☺9pm-6am, bar 6pm-midnight, summer only; Ⓢ Line 2 to Jishuitan, exit B). The owner also rents kayaks (April to September) and the club has a pleasant terrace overlooking Hòuhǎi Lake, where you can sit outside and enjoy a late afternoon beer well away from the far more crowded southern end of the lakes.

the yard, was his study. Just by the entrance to his home is a small bookshop where you can buy English translations of some of his works for around ¥35.

MEI LANFANG
FORMER RESIDENCE   MUSEUM
Map p278 (梅兰芳纪念馆; Méi Lánfāng Jìniàn Guǎn; ☎010 8322 3598; 9 Huguosi Jie; 护国寺街 9号; adult/child & senior ¥10/5; ☺9am-4pm Tue-Sun; Ⓢ Lines 4, 6 to Ping'anli, exit B, or Line 6 to Beihai North, exit A) Place of pilgrimage for Peking opera aficionados, this former *sìhéyuàn* (traditional courtyard house) of actor Mei Lanfang (1894–1961) is on the corner of a *hútòng* that's named after the nearby remains of Hùguó Temple (护国寺; Hùguó Sì; only one hall remains, and it's not open to the public).

Peking opera was popularised in the West by Mei Lanfang, who played *dàn* (female roles) and is said to have influenced Charlie Chaplin. His former residence has been preserved as a museum, replete with costumes, furniture, opera programs and video presentations of his opera performances.

SOUTH CATHEDRAL   CHURCH
Map p278 (南堂; Nántáng; 141 Qianmen Xidajie; 前门西大街141号; ☺Mass in English 10.30am & 3pm Sun; Ⓢ Lines 2, 4 to Xuanwumen, exit B2)

FREE The South Cathedral (aka Cathedral of the Immaculate Conception or Nántáng) was the first church to be built in central Běijīng. It was constructed on the site of the house of Jesuit missionary Matteo Ricci, who brought Catholicism to China. Since being completed in 1703, the church has been destroyed three times, including being burnt down in 1775, and endured a trashing by anti-Christian forces during the Boxer Rebellion in 1900.

GUĂNGJÌ TEMPLE   BUDDHIST TEMPLE
Map p278 (广济寺; Guǎngjì Sì; 25 Fuchengmennei Dajie; 阜城门内大街25号; ☺6am-4.30pm; Ⓢ Line 4 to Xisi, exit A) **FREE** Now the HQ of the Buddhist Association of China, this small, informal temple is a Ming rebuild of the original Jin dynasty temple, and is often busy with worshippers.

CATHEDRAL OF OUR SAVIOUR   CATHEDRAL
Map p278 (Běitáng; 救世主堂; ☎010 6617 5198; Xishiku Dajie; Ⓢ Line 4 to Xisi, exit B) Also called the Xishiku or North Cathedral, this august cathedral is one of Běijīng's four main churches and the only one located within the former grounds of the Imperial City. Built in 1887, the cathedral served as a factory warehouse during the Cultural Revolution. Despite being covered in gaudy grey, flaking paint, the cathedral is worth visiting, especially for those keen to glimpse the growing stature of Christianity in China.

DÉSHÈNGMÉN GATEWAY   LANDMARK
Map p278 (德胜门; Déshèngmén) A monumental landmark along the 2nd Ring Road is this Ming dynasty city gate and watchtower, which made up part of Běijīng's northern wall. The remaining structure is the archery tower, built in 1437, which stands over the city's northern moat. On the north side is where buses leave to the Ming Tombs and Bādálǐng Great Wall section.

The gate's name is a play on words, with an alternative meaning from its spoken name signifying 'gain victory'.

✕ EATING

★**4CORNERS**   INTERNATIONAL $
Map p278 (四角餐厅; Sìjiǎo Cāntīng; ☎010 6401 7797; http://these4corners.com; 27 Dashibei Hutong; 大石碑胡同27号; dishes from ¥40; ☺11am-late Tue-Sun; Ⓢ Line 8 to Shichahai, exit A2) Given this *hútòng* bar-restaurant is run

by a Canadian-Vietnamese expat, it makes total sense it's known for its phở and poutine. Everything is made from scratch, including the curds for its poutine and baked baguettes for the *bánh mì*, and everything is gluten-free. Its courtyard bar is also one of the area's best spots for a drink, with Běijīng craft beers on tap and quality cocktails.

Check its website for nightly events including live music, Tuesday quiz, Wednesday 'story-telling' nights and Thursday open mic.

MEATBALL COMPANY — SANDWICHES $

Map p278 (www.themeatballcompanybj.com; 27 Dashibei Hutong; 大石碑胡同27号; meatballs ¥40; ⌚noon-10pm Tue-Sat, 11.30am-9pm Sun; [S]Line 8 to Shichahai, exit A2) Though you may not come all the way to Běijīng to eat meatballs, this tiny hole-in-the-wall *hútòng* eatery is hard to resist with its juicy beef, pork, chicken and vegetarian balls. They come with a choice of homemade sauces in a toasted sub roll, or on a plate with sides. There's draft beer, cocktails and sangria too.

LǏJÌ FĒNGWÈI MĚISHÍ CĀNTĪNG — CHINESE, MUSLIM $

Map p278 (李记风味美食餐厅; Ya'er Hutong; 鸦儿胡同 (烟袋斜街西口); mains ¥20-40, snacks ¥1-10; ⌚5am-9pm; [S]Line 8 to Shichahai, exit A2) Known simply as Lǐjì (pronounced 'lee jee'), this popular place has two outlets close to each other on Ya'er Hutong, both of which serve great-value Chinese Muslim dishes and snacks.

The first one you come to, if walking from Silver Ingot Bridge, is the main sit-down restaurant (look for the long, green-and-yellow sign). It has an English menu, including grilled skewers, lamb dishes and noodles, and is basic but clean. Further on is a smaller, older branch, which specialises in boiled tripe (爆肚; *bàodǔ*) and has an adjacent takeaway-dumplings stall, which is very popular at breakfast time: try the beef and onion dumplings (牛肉大葱包子; *niúròu dàcōng bāozi;* ¥2 each). It also roasts very good sesame-seed buns (烧饼; *shāobing;* ¥1 each), which you can have filled with lamb (烧饼夹肉; *shāobing jiā ròu;* ¥7 each).

WANG PANG ZI — HEBEI $

Map p278 (王胖子驴肉火烧; Wáng Pàngzi Lǘròu Huǒshāo; 80 Gulou Xidajie; 鼓楼西大街80号; pastry pockets ¥11, soups ¥3-10; ⌚24hr; [S]Line 8 to Shichahai, exit A2, or Lines 2, 8 to Gulou Dajie, exit G) Lauded by many as the best donkey-meat place in town, this small 24-hour restaurant specialises in flaky pastry pockets, stuffed with lightly spiced shreds of donkey meat, known in Chinese as 驴肉火烧 (*lǘròu huǒshāo;* pronounced 'loo row hwore shaow').

Two per person, plus a soup, is plenty for lunch. Soups include 西红柿鸡蛋汤 (*xīhóngshì jīdàn tāng;* egg and tomato), 紫菜鸡蛋汤 (*zǐcài jīdàn tāng;* egg and seaweed), 小米粥 (*xiǎomǐ zhōu;* millet porridge-soup) and, of course, 驴肉汤 (*lǘròu tāng;* donkey-meat soup). English sign, but there's a picture menu in Chinese only.

QÌNGFĒNG STEAMED DUMPLING SHOP — DUMPLING $

Map p278 (庆丰包子铺; Qìngfēng Bāozi Pù; www.qing-feng.com/index.html; Jade Islet, Běihǎi Park; 北海公园; dumplings ¥3-16; ⌚9am-4.45pm; [S]Line 6 to Beihai North or Nanluogu Xiang, or Line 4 to Xisi) The best of the eating options at Běihǎi Park is this dumpling chain outside Yǒngān Temple (p115) that does *bāozi* (包子; steamed meat buns) and *jiǎozi* (饺子; stuffed dumplings) among other Chinese mains.

ROYAL ICEHOUSE — SHANDONG $$

Map p278 (皇家冰窖小院; Huángjiā Bīngjiào Xiǎoyuàn; ☎010 6401 1358; 5 Gongjian Wuxiang, Gongjian Hutong; 恭俭胡同5巷5号; mains ¥28-58; ⌚11.30am-2pm & 5.30-9.30pm; [S]Line 6 to Beihai North, exit B, or Lines 6, 8 to Nanluguxiang, exit A) Tucked away in the *hútòng* running alongside the east wall of Běihǎi Park, this intriguing restaurant is located inside one of the city's former royal ice houses – where, before the days of refrigeration, massive blocks of ice were stored for use in the imperial court during summer.

You can walk down into the underground ice cellars (which now keep the wine cool); look for the red arched door.

The main restaurant is decked out in old-Běijīng paraphernalia; look for the homemade *báijiǔ* (sorghum liquor) hanging in pig's bladders. The food is imperial cuisine, but with a heavy Shāndōng influence (the original chef was from Shāndōng province), so there is some crossover in dishes. All are very well done, though. The menu is in English. To find the restaurant, walk south down Gongjian Hutong from Di'anmen Xidajie, turn right into 5 Gongjian Wuxiang and you'll see it straight ahead of you.

KǍO RÒU JÌ CHINESE, MUSLIM $$

Map p278 (烤肉季; Qianhai Dongyan; 前海东沿银锭桥; mains ¥40-80; ⏲1st fl 11am-11pm, 2nd fl 11am-2pm & 5-9pm; [S]Line 8 to Shichahai, exit A2) This restaurant serves roast duck (including half portions for ¥92), and a range of China-wide dishes, but it's the mutton that everyone comes for – and the lake views from the 2nd floor.

This place has been around for years (it featured in our very first edition of *Lonely Planet China*, in 1984), and its choice location, overlooking Qiánhǎi Lake, makes it as popular as ever. It's pricier than it should be, but the atmosphere is fun, and the English menu with photos makes ordering easy. Bag a table by the window on the 2nd floor, and order the roast mutton (¥108), a hot plate from heaven. If you're stuck for cash, fill up on freshly roasted sesame-seed buns (¥2 each), called 'sesame cakes' on the menu.

🍷 DRINKING & NIGHTLIFE

★NBEER PUB BAR

Map p278 (牛啤堂; Niú Pí Táng; ☎010 8328 8823; www.nbcraftbrewing.com; Huguo Xintiandi, 85 Huguosi Dajie; 护国寺大街85号护国新天地一层; bottles from ¥25, draft ¥35-50; ⏲3pm-2am; 📶; [S]Lines 4, 6 to Ping'anli, exit B) In a scene dominated by North American expats, NBeer is an all-Chinese affair that produces some of Běijīng's best beers. It has a massive 37 ales on tap behind a bar made from Lonely Planet guidebooks! The majority are brewed on-site and include a variety of IPAs, pale ales, stouts and European-style ales. It also boasts the biggest fridge of beers in Běijīng. The food is also good, including excellent cheeseburgers and enormous, juicy kebabs. Visit before 7pm for 30% discounts on all draft beers.

It's on the ground floor of a multifloor complex known as Xīntiāndì, at the western end of Huguosi Dajie. You can sometimes sit on the patio out the back in summer and spy **Jīngāng Hall** (金刚殿; Jīngāng Diàn), originally built in 1284 and the only surviving feature of Hùguó Temple, which this *hútòng* is named after.

TÁNGRÉN TEAHOUSE TEAHOUSE

Map p278 (唐人茶道听茶轩; Tángrén Chádàoyǐn Cháxuān; 15 Qianhai Nanyan; 前海南沿15号; tea per cup from ¥40, pot ¥120; ⏲9.30am-1am; [S]Line 6 to Beihai North, exit B, or Line 8 to Shichahai, exit A1) Commanding fine views across Qiànhǎi Lake from its rooftop terrace, this cute teahouse is on a quieter stretch of the lake, away from the noisier bars, and is a delightful spot in which to sample Chinese tea.

Prices are high – you even have to pay extra for the spring water your tea is brewed in (from ¥10 per cup) – but the location, service and ambience compensate. The wooden decor is attractive, as is the tea menu – a bamboo scroll – which is translated into English. Teas are listed to the left of the tea type (oolong, green, black etc) they belong to. They have two cafes along this strip, only 100m from one another.

AWAIT CAFE CAFE

Map p278 (那间咖啡; Nàjiā Kāfēi; 59 Xisi Nandajie; 西四南大街59号; coffee ¥26, beer ¥18, mains ¥35-65; ⏲8am-midnight; 📶; [S]Line 4 to Xisi, exit D) One of the loveliest cafes in this part of Běijīng, Await stands next to a church and its main room has the feeling of a small nave, with its high ceilings and cool, calm atmosphere. The coffee is heavenly, the homemade cheesecakes are divine, and it does a range of Western main courses too (pastas, pizzas, salads, soups).

There are three rooms – each lovingly furnished – spread over two floors, plus a small 3rd-floor terrace which is open in summer. There are plenty of power points, so it's a good workspace too.

LOTUS CAFE & BAR CAFE

Map p278 (185 Fuchengmennei Dajie; 阜成门内大街185号, 3rd fl, Pagoda Light Hostel; ⏲10am-10pm; 📶; [S]Line 2 to Fuchengmen, exit B, or Line 4 to Xisi, exit A) At the top of the Pagoda Light (p187) hostel is this glass-enclosed rooftop cafe that overlooks the Miàoyīng Temple White Dagoba and surrounding *hútòng*. It's a smart, plant-filled space with designer furniture, good coffee, bottled beers and cocktails, as well as cakes, sandwiches and Western mains.

HÒUHǍI BAR STRIP BAR

Map p278 (Silver Ingot Bridge; 后海银锭桥; ⏲noon-late; [S]Line 8 to Shichahai, exit A2) Fabulously located, and with roof terraces overlooking the lakes, the neon-lit bars lining the lakes either side of Silver Ingot Bridge (银锭桥; Yíndìng Qiáo) are transformed into noisy guitar bars and karaoke joints come evening, and fitted with speakers facing out onto the lakeshore.

Inside, punters (mainly provincial Chinese tourists) sing songs, play dice games or just down shots until they have to be carried home. All the bars are similar, so it's best just to walk around and see which one takes your fancy. Drinks prices start high, but can be negotiated. The further you walk away from Silver Ingot Bridge, the quieter the bars become.

⭐ ENTERTAINMENT

MEI LANFANG
GRAND THEATRE   PEKING OPERA
Map p278 (梅兰芳大戏院, Méi Lánfāng Dàxiyuàn; ☏010 5833 1288; www.bjmlfdjy.cn; 32 Ping'anli Xidajie; 平安里西大街32号; tickets ¥30-300; ⏰performances 7.30pm; Ⓢ Lines 2, 6 to Chegongzhuang, exit C) Named after China's most famous practitioner of Peking opera, this theatre opened its doors in 2007 and has since become one of the most popular and versatile venues in town. Performances start at 7.30pm daily. Tickets have to be bought from the ticket office in the lobby between 9.30am and 8pm.

EAST SHORE JAZZ CAFÉ   JAZZ
Map p278 (东岸, Dōng'àn; ☏010 8403 2131; 2nd fl, 2 Shichahai Nanyan; 地安门外大街 什刹海南沿2号楼2层, 地安门邮局西侧; beers from ¥30, cocktails from ¥45; ⏰3pm-2am; Ⓢ Line 6 to Beihai North, exit B, or Line 8 to Shichahai, exit A1) Cui Jian's saxophonist, whose quartet plays here, opened this chilled venue just off Di'anmen Waidajie and next to Qiánhǎi Lake. It's a place to hear the best local jazz bands, with live performances from Wednesdays to Sundays (from 10pm), in a laid-back, comfortable atmosphere.

There's a small roof terrace open in summer with a nice view of the lake. No cover charge.

🛍 SHOPPING

YANDAI XIEJIE   GIFTS & SOUVENIRS
Map p278 (烟袋斜街; Yandai Xiejie, off Di'anmen Neidajie; 地安门内大街烟袋斜街; Ⓢ Line 8 to Shichahai, exit A2) If nearby Nanluogu Xiang (p102) is too hectic for you, you can find some of the same here, on a smaller scale. It's still busy at weekends, but more manageable.

Shops here, on this re-built 'old-Běijīng' *hútòng*, which leads down to the lakes, are almost exclusively souvenir shops – T-shirts, silk shawls, fabric slippers, paper fans, fake antiques etc – but it's more fun shopping for them here than in one of the city's big, multifloor souvenir markets. Walk south from the Drum Tower, along Di'anmenwai Dajie, and it's the first *hútòng* on the right.

THREE STONE KITE SHOP   ARTS & CRAFTS
Map p278 (三石斋风筝; Sānshízhāi Fēngzhēng; ☏010 8404 4505; www.cnkites.com; 25 Di'anmen Xidajie; 地安门西大街甲25号; ⏰9am-9pm; Ⓢ Lines 6, 8 to Nanluoguxiang, exit F) The great-grandfather of the owner of this friendly store used to make the kites for the Chinese imperial household. Most of the kites here are handmade and hand-painted, although the selection is limited these days, now that the owner uses half his shop to display other, admittedly attractive, souvenirs.

Kites start from around ¥150. You can also find all the gear you'll need to fly your new kite, as well as miniature framed kites, which make pretty gifts.

SANFO   SPORTS & OUTDOORS
(三夫户外; Sānfū Hùwài; ☏010 6201 5550; www. sanfo.com/en; 3-4 Madian Nancun; 北三环中路 马甸南村4之3–4号; ⏰9am-9pm; Ⓢ Line 10 to Jiandemen, exit D) With no less than three shops grouped together in this location, Sanfo is the place to come for outdoor wear, climbing and camping gear, as well as surfboards, mountain bikes and anything you might need if you're into adventure sports. It's something of a nexus for Běijīng's hikers and climbers – Sanfo organises weekend trips – and is a good place to pick up information, as well as the supplies you'll need if you're thinking of walking the Great Wall for a few days. There's a smaller, easier-to-get-to branch about 200m south of Fuchengmen subway station.

BĚIJĪNG BOOKS BUILDING   BOOKS
Map p278 (北京图书大厦; Běijīng Túshū Dàshà; ☏010 6607 8477; 17 Xichang'an Jie; 西长安街 17号; ⏰9am-9pm; Ⓢ Lines 1, 4 to Xīdān, exit C) Massive emporium crammed with tomes of all descriptions. The ones in English, and some other foreign languages too, are in the basement. There's a decent range of Lonely Planet guides as well, plus plenty of children's books.

Dashilar & Xīchéng South

Neighbourhood Top Five

1 Dashilar (p126) Peruse the historic, pedestrianised shopping street, still home to some of the oldest and most prestigious emporiums in the city. Whether it's silk or ancient aphrodisiacs, you'll find it here.

2 *Hútòng* (p129) Wind your way through the fascinating *hútòng* west of

Meishi Jie, which retain a local neighbourhood character in the face of rapid-fire development.

3 Niújiē Mosque (p126) Check out the capital's largest Muslim neighbourhood.

4 Běijīng Ancient Architecture Museum (p126) Visit this informative mu-

seum to discover how imperial Běijīng was built.

5 Fǎyuán Temple (p126) Pop into this little-visited Buddhist shrine, one of the city's oldest and most peaceful.

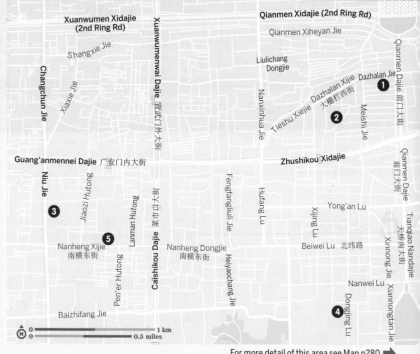

For more detail of this area see Map p280.

Explore Dashilar & Xīchéng South

Divided from neighbouring Dōngchéng by Qianmen Dajie, Dashilar (大栅栏) and Xīchéng South (南西城) take in the former district of Xuānwǔ. Its major sights are concentrated in two distinct areas: Dashilar and the Muslim district around Niu Jie, with nearby *hútòng* to explore as well.

Spend a morning visiting Dashilar's shops (p126), before lunch at one of the small restaurants on Dazhalan Xijie. The *hútòng* off Dazhalan Xijie were once the red-light district of old Peking and are well worth diving into.

From the western end of Dazhalan Xijie, it's a short stroll to Liulichang, the capital's premier shopping street for antiques, calligraphy and traditional Chinese art and a must for curio-hunters. In the evening, catch a show at one of the acrobatics or Peking opera theatres in the neighbourhood.

Begin a second day in the area with a trip to the Běijīng Ancient Architecture Museum (p126). Then, hop in a taxi to Niu Jie, the main drag of Běijīng's Muslim Huí neighbourhood. Visit the mosque, a blend of Chinese and Arabic styles, and eat at a local Muslim restaurant. Nearby Fǎyuán Temple (p126) is a serene shrine surrounded by intriguing *hútòng*.

Local Life

→ **Táoránting Park** North of Běijīng South Railway Station, this is the lungs of the neighbourhood and a great escape from the surrounding urban madness.

→ **Hútòng** Visit the alleyways sandwiched between Dazhalan Xijie and Qianmen Xidajie; they see far fewer foreigners than others in the area.

→ **Market** Locals head to the streets around Mǎliándào Tea Market (p131) for both tea and reasonably priced tea sets.

Getting There & Away

→ **Subway** For Dashilar, get off at the Qianmen stop on Line 2. Go to Hepingmen on the same line for Liulichang. Line 4 runs north–south through the neighbourhood towards Běijīng South Railway Station, with the stop at Caishikou walking distance from both Nui Jie and Fǎyuán Temple.

Lonely Planet's Top Tip

Avoid the restaurants off the south end of Dashilar; many still try to charge foreigners more than locals by offering them a special English menu. Instead, head down Dazhalan Xijie for cheaper options. Look for the places that have plenty of locals eating in them. Be wary of anyone in the Dashilar area offering to take you to a tea ceremony; it's a very expensive scam.

DASHILAR & XĪCHÉNG SOUTH

Best Places to Eat

→ Gǒubùlǐ (p128)
→ Turpan Restaurant (p128)
→ Liú Family Noodles (p126)

For reviews, see p126.➡

Best Entertainment

→ Tiānqiáo Acrobatics Theatre (p129)
→ Húguǎng Guild Hall (p129)
→ Lao She Teahouse (p129)

For reviews, see p129.➡

Best Places to Shop

→ Ruìfúxiáng (p130)
→ Xían Yàn Tāng (p130)
→ Mǎliándào Tea Market (p131)

For reviews, see p130.➡

⊙ SIGHTS

XIĀNNÓNG ALTAR & BĚIJĪNG ANCIENT ARCHITECTURE MUSEUM   MUSEUM

Map p280 (先农坛、北京古代建筑博物馆; Xiānnóngtán & Běijīng Gǔdài Jiànzhú Bówùguǎn; ☑010 6304 5608; 21 Dongjing Lu; 东经路21号; admission ¥15, audio guide ¥10; ◎9am-4pm Tue-Sun; Ⓢ Line 4 to Taoranting) This altar – to the west of the Temple of Heaven (p106) – was the site of solemn imperial ceremonies and sacrificial offerings. Here you'll find the excellent Běijīng Ancient Architecture Museum, which informatively narrates the elements of traditional Chinese building techniques. The museum is spread over the four 15th-century halls which face one another across the large courtyard. Each features different exhibits, but the centrepiece is the magnificent **Jupiter Hall** (太岁殿; Tàisuì Diàn), with exquisite detail in its ceiling.

The museum offers the chance to brush up on your *dǒugǒng* (brackets) and *sǔnmǎo* (joints), and get the low-down on Běijīng's courtyard houses, while eyeballing detailed models of stand-out temple halls and pagodas from across the land. There's a great scale model of the old walled city and English captions throughout. On Wednesdays, the first 200 visitors get in free.

Glance at any pre-1949 map of Běijīng and you can gauge the massive scale of the altar, which was built in 1420. Today, many of the altar's original structures survive and make up a tranquil and little-visited constellation of relics.

It's a fair walk from the subway station so tacking on a short cab ride isn't a bad idea.

DASHILAR   AREA

Map p280 (大栅栏; Dàzhàlan; Dazhalan Jie; Ⓢ Line 2 to Qianmen, exit B or C) This centuries-old pedestrianised shopping street, also known as Dazhalan Jie, is just west of Qianmen Dajie. While a misjudged makeover has sadly robbed it of much of its charm, many of the shops have been in business here for hundreds of years and still draw many Chinese tourists. Some specialise in esoteric goods – ancient herbal remedies, handmade cloth shoes – and most make for intriguing window shopping.

FǍYUÁN TEMPLE   BUDDHIST TEMPLE

Map p280 (法源寺; Fǎyuán Sì; 7 Fayuansi Qianjie; 法源寺前街7号; adult ¥5; ◎8.30-4pm; Ⓢ Lines 4, 7 to Caishikou, exit D) Infused with an air of reverence and devotion, this lovely temple dates back to the 7th century. The temple follows the typical Buddhist layout, with drum and bell towers. Do hunt out the unusual **copper-cast Buddha**, seated atop four further Buddhas ensconced on a huge bulb of myriad effigies in the Pilu Hall (the fourth hall).

Within the Guanyin Hall is a Ming dynasty **Thousand Hand and Thousand Eye Guanyin**, while a huge supine Buddha reclines in the rear hall. Originally built to honour Tang dynasty soldiers who had fallen during combat against the northern tribes, Fǎyuán is still a working temple, as well as home to the **China Buddhism College**, and you'll see plenty of monks about. To find it from the entrance of Niújiē Mosque, walk left 100m and then turn left into the first *hútòng*. Follow the *hútòng* for about 10 minutes and you'll arrive at the temple.

NIÚJIĒ MOSQUE   MOSQUE

(牛街礼拜寺; Niújiē Lǐbài Sì; ☑010 6353 2564; 18 Niu Jie; 牛街18号; adult ¥10, Muslims free; ◎8.30am-sunset; Ⓢ Lines 4, 7 to Caishikou, exit D) Dating back to the 10th century, this unique mosque blends traditional Chinese temple design with Middle Eastern flourishes. It's Běijīng's largest mosque and centre for its community of 10,000 or so Huí Chinese Muslims who live nearby. Look out for the **Building for Observing the Moon** (望月楼; Wàngyuèlóu), from where the lunar calendar was calculated. Also note the spirit wall on Nui Jie that guards the entrance, a feature of all Chinese temples regardless of denomination.

✕ EATING

LIÚ FAMILY NOODLES   NOODLES $

Map p280 (刘家人刀削面; Liú Jiārén Dāoxiāomiàn; 6 Tieshuxie Jie; 铁树斜街6号; noodles from ¥12; ◎11am-3pm & 5-10pm; Ⓢ Line 7 to Hufangqiao, or Line 2 to Qianmen, exit B or C) A rarity in this area: a restaurant that welcomes foreigners without trying to overcharge them. On the contrary, the prices couldn't be much lower, while the friendly owner is keen to practise her (limited) English. Choose from a selection of tasty noodle and cold dishes. To find it, look for the black sign with 'Best Noodles in China' written in English.

LONG TABLE   INTERNATIONAL $

Map p280 (长桌, Chángzhuō; ☑010 6302 8699; 55 Dazhalan Xijie, 大栅栏西街55号; dishes

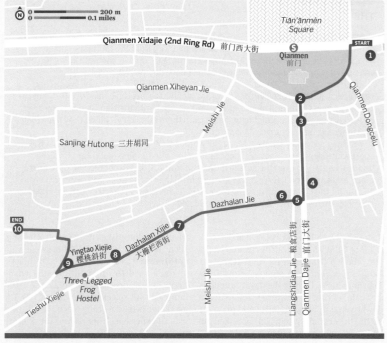

🏃 Neighbourhood Walk
Qianmen To Liulichang

START BĚIJĪNG RAILWAY MUSEUM
END LIULICHANG DONGJIE
LENGTH 2.5KM; ONE HOUR

Start at the **1** **Běijīng Railway Museum**, housed in the historic Qiánmén Railway Station building. Walk south to the **2** **Qiánmén Decorative Arch**, a rebuilt Five-Bay Decorative Arch (Wǔpáilóu) that was originally felled in the 1950s and reconstructed prior to the 2008 Olympics. The arch stands at the head of **3** **Qianmen Dajie**, a street completely revamped in the style of old Peking.

Look at some of the **4** **restored old shop buildings** along Qianmen Dajie, then turn right onto the historic shopping street of **5** **Dashilar** (p126), aka Dazhalan Jie. Down the first alley on the left is Liubiju, a traditional Běijīng lǎozìhào (old, established shop) famous for its pickled condiments.

Push on through the crowds on Dazhalan Jie. On your right at No 5 is **6** **Ruìfúxiáng** (p130), a famous old Běijīng silk store dat-

ing to 1893. Pop in and view the grey brickwork and carved decorative flourishes of the entrance hall.

Cross Meishi Jie and enter **7** **Dazhalan Xijie**, once known as Guanyin Temple Street. If you're peckish, stop at any of the many food vendors here; the *jianbing* stall (煎饼; savoury pancakes) opposite the Three Legged Frog hostel will hit the spot. Turn right at the fork with Yingtao Xiejie (樱桃斜街) to see the **8** **plaque** marking the site of the former Guanyin Temple (Nos 6 to 8 Yingtao Xiejie) that stood here; plans were in place to restore it to its former glory by 2019.

Continue along Yingtao Xiejie past the narrow and pinched Taitou Xiang (抬头巷; Raise Head Alley) for around 100m and examine the house at **9** **27 Yingtao Xiejie**. Look out for the faded characters painted on the wall 'Long Live the Revolution' (革命万岁), a legacy of a Cultural Revolution slogan.

Loop round to the right and at the end of Yingtao Xiejie, turn sharp left and the road will bend round to **10** **Liulichang Dongjie**, Běijīng's premier antique street.

LOCAL KNOWLEDGE

THE HUÍ

China's 25-million-odd Muslims are divided into two distinct groups. One is comprised of the Uighurs, a rebellious, Turkic-speaking minority from the far west of China whose roots lie in Central Asia. The other are the Huí. You can find both in the Niu Jie area, but it is predominantly a district associated with the Huí.

The descendants of Arab traders who came down the Silk Road well over a thousand years ago, the 10 million or so Huí are technically an ethnic minority. But they are spread all over China and have intermarried so much with the Han Chinese over the centuries that they are indistinguishable from them ethnically. Nor do they have their own language, speaking only Mandarin.

Yet, they are easily spotted. Many Huí women wear a headscarf, while the men sport white skullcaps. They are most associated with running restaurants; you can find a Huí eatery in even the smallest Chinese towns. Don't expect to find pork on the menu and some don't serve alcohol. Apart from the Niu Jie area, you're most likely to encounter the Huí serving up *yáng'ròu chuàn* (lamb skewers) from streetside stalls and hole-in-the-wall restaurants all over Běijīng.

from ¥29; ⏲8am-1am; 📶; [S]Line 2 to Qianmen, exit B or C) With its graffiti-covered walls and wooden benches, this is a backpacker hang out a (long-ish) stone's throw from Tiān'ānmén Sq. During the day it functions as a cafe serving up Western standards: all-day breakfasts, burgers, pasta and pizza. At night, the sound system gets cranked up and it all gets more raucous as the cheap beers (¥10) are downed at pace.

Upstairs is *365* Inn hostel.

GǑUBÙLǏ DUMPLING $$

Map p280 (狗不理; ☎010 6353 3338; 31 Dazhalan Jie; 大栅栏街31号; dumplings from ¥58; ⏲7.30am-10pm; [S]Line 2 to Qianmen, exit B or C) Decent, reasonably priced eats are hard to find in this area, so this outpost of the renowned Tiānjīn restaurant will delight dumpling devotees. True, they are more pricey here than at your average hole-in-the-wall joint, but there are eight different types to choose from, including meat, prawn, crab and veggie options, and each serving includes eight dumplings.

There's a picture menu in English and plenty of cold dishes to accompany your dumplings.

TURPAN RESTAURANT XINJIANG $$

(吐鲁番餐厅, Tǔlǔfān Cāntīng; ☎010 8316 4691; 6 Niu Jie, 牛街6号; kebabs from ¥12, dishes from ¥35; ⏲5am-9am, 10.30am-2.30pm & 4.30-9pm; [S]Lines 4, 7 to Caishikou, exit D) This huge place attracts the local Huí hordes, who flock here for the big, juicy and succulent lamb kebabs (nothing like the tiny skewers sold on the streets). Then there's the array of authentic Uighur dishes from far-off Xīnjiāng, such as salted beef rolls with sweet yam (¥46), as well as a selection of Halal choices.

You'll need to order the roasted whole lamb in advance, but we think the roast lamb leg with spices is a bargain at ¥58. Try and come here in a group; it's by far the best way to experience this restaurant. Picture menu.

🍷 DRINKING & NIGHTLIFE

BEERS89 BAR

Map p280 (89 Dazhalan Xijie; 大栅栏西街 89号; beers from ¥20; ⏲2pm-1am; [S]Line 7 to Hufangqiao, or Line 2 to Qianmen, exit B or C) A point of difference along this mainstream ultra-touristy strip is this tiny craft-beer bar with shelves lined with bottled beers and a couple more on tap. There's also its 'Ocean Monster' shots (¥10), *báijiǔ* infused in a jar of seahorses, starfish and snakes – so horrendous it's worth trying.

SOLOIST COFFEE CAFE

Map p280 (www.soloistcoffee.com; 39 Yangmeizhu Xiejie; 杨梅竹斜街39号; coffee from ¥30; ⏲noon-8pm; [S]Line 2 to Qianmen, exit B or C) Down a *hútòng* that's fast gaining recognition for its boutiques is this classy coffee roaster. It has an industrial-chic decor with exposed brick and vintage furniture. and if the sun's out head upstairs for its roof terrace. There's a good selection of single origin coffees, nitro lattes and cold brew.

★ ENTERTAINMENT

TIĀNQIÁO ACROBATICS THEATRE ACROBATICS

Map p280 (天桥杂技剧场, Tiānqiáo Zájì Jùchǎng; ☎010 6303 7449; 95 Tianqiao Shichang Lu Jie; 天桥市场街95号; tickets ¥180-380; ⏲performances 5.30pm; [S]Line 7 to Zhushikou) West of the Temple of Heaven Park, this 100-year-old theatre offers one of Běijīng's best acrobatic displays, a one-hour show performed by the Běijīng Acrobatic Troupe. Less touristy than the other venues, the theatre's small size means you can get very close to the action. The high-wire display is awesome. The entrance is on Beiwei Lu, along the eastern side of the building.

HÚGUǍNG GUILD HALL PEKING OPERA

Map p280 (湖广会馆, Húguǎng Huìguǎn; ☎010 6351 8284; 3 Hufang Lu; 虎坊桥路3号; tickets ¥180-680, opera museum ¥10; ⏲performances 8pm, opera museum 9am-5.30pm; [S]Line 7 to Hufangqiao, exit C) The most historic and atmospheric place in town for a night of Peking opera. The interior is magnificent, coloured in red, green and gold, and decked out with tables and a stone floor, while balconies surround the canopied stage. Opposite the theatre, there's a very small opera **museum** displaying operatic scores, old catalogues and other paraphernalia.

There are also colour illustrations of the *liǎnpǔ* (types of Peking opera facial makeup) – examples include the *hóu liǎnpǔ* (monkey face) and the *chǒujué liǎnpǔ* (clown face). The theatre dates back to 1807 and, in 1912, was where the Kuomintang (KMT), led by Dr Sun Yatsen, was founded. Shows here attract a lot of domestic tour groups. There are few English captions, but it's not hard to follow what's going on.

The restaurant here is also very good, and inexpensive, making for a nice pre- or post-theatre meal.

LAO SHE TEAHOUSE PERFORMING ARTS

Map p280 (老舍茶馆; Lǎoshě Cháguǎn; ☎010 6303 6830; www.laosheteahouse.com; 3rd fl, 3 Qianmen Xidajie; 前门西大街3号3层; evening tickets ¥180-580; ⏲performances 7.50pm; [S]Line 2 to Qianmen, exit C) Lao She Teahouse, named after the celebrated writer, has daily and nightly shows, mostly in Chinese, which blend any number of traditional Chinese performing arts. The evening performances of Peking opera, folk art and music, acrobatics and magic (7.50pm to 9.20pm) are the most popular. But there are also tea ceremonies, frequent folk-music performances and daily shadow-puppet shows.

Prices depend on the type of show and your seat. Phone ahead or check the schedule

LOCAL KNOWLEDGE

RED-LIGHT PEKING

These days, Dazhalan Xijie and the surrounding *hútòng* are Běijīng's backpacker central. But for hundreds of years, these innocuous-looking alleys were infamous for being old Peking's red-light district (红灯区; *hóngdēngqū*).

Centered on Bada Hutong, a collection of eight alleys, the area had already acquired a raunchy reputation in the 18th century. By the time of the fall of the Qing dynasty in 1912, there were more than 300 brothels lining the lanes. The working girls ranged from cultivated courtesans who could recite poetry and dance gracefully and whose clients were aristocrats and court officials, to more mundane types who served the masses. It was very much an area for the locals; the small foreign community had its own little zone of brothels, dive bars and opium dens in still-surviving Chuanban Hutong, close to the Chongwenmen subway stop.

Bada Hutong owed its dubious fame to the fact that it was outside the city walls (the emperors didn't want houses of ill repute near the royal palace), yet close enough to the Imperial City for customers to get there easily. But the fall of the emperors signalled the beginning of the end for Bada Hutong. Just over a month after the founding of the PRC in October 1949, soldiers marched into the area, closed down the brothels and 'liberated' the prostitutes working there.

Many of the eight alleys that made up Bada Hutong have been demolished and/or rebuilt. Shanxi Xiang, though, is still standing and the historic building that is now the hostel Leo Courtyard (p188) was once one of the most upmarket knocking shops in the capital. But it didn't do dorm beds back then.

online. Look for two stone lions guarding the front of the building.

LÍYUÁN THEATRE   PEKING OPERA

Map p280 (梨园剧场, Líyuán Jùchǎng; ☑010 6301 6688; Qianmen Jianguo Hotel, 175 Yong'an Lu; 永安路175号前门建国饭店; tickets ¥280-480, with tea ¥580; ☺performances 7.30pm; 🚇Line 7 to Hufangqiao, exit C) This touristy theatre, in the lobby of the **Qiánmén Jiànguó Hotel** (前门建国饭店, Qiánmén Jiànguó Fàndiàn; Map p280; www.hotelsjianguo.com/qianmenhotel), has daily performances for Peking opera newbies. If you want to, you can enjoy an overpriced tea ceremony while watching. The setting isn't traditional: it resembles a cinema auditorium (the stage facade is the only authentic touch), but it's a gentle introduction to the art form.

TIĀNQIÁO PERFORMING ARTS CENTRE   THEATRE

Map p280 (天桥艺术中心; Tiānqiáo Yìshù Zhōngxīn; ☑400 635 3355; www.tartscenter.com; 9 Tianqiao Nandajie; 天桥南大街9号; ☺box office 9.30am-8.30pm; 🚇Line 7 to Zhushikou) Officially opened in late 2015, Beijing's new modern performing arts centre comprises four theatres that host both foreign (*My Fair Lady, Phantom of the Opera*) and Chinese musicals and productions.

DÀGUĀNLÓU CINEMA   CINEMA

Map p280 (大观楼影城, Dàguānlóu Yìngchéng; 36 Dazhalan Jie; 大栅栏街36号; tickets ¥40-50; ☺8.30am-9.30pm; 🚇Line 2 to Qianmen, exit B or C) China's oldest cinema has been screening movies, including a few Western releases, since 1903.

The **Old Cinema Cafe** on the ground floor has a small exhibition on the cinema's history, alongside photos of old-time Chinese movie stars and a few ancient cameras and projectors. It makes a good pit stop for a coffee (¥25) or tea (from ¥20), if you need a break from shopping in Dashilar. And the cinema, despite its illustrious past, remains one of the cheapest places in town to catch a flick.

🔒 SHOPPING

Dashilar and Xīchéng South are among the capital's finest neighbourhoods for shopping. Apart from Dashilar (p126) itself, Liulichang (meaning 'glazed-tile factory') is Běijīng's best-known antiques street, even if the goods on sale are largely fake. The street is something of an oasis in the area and worth delving into for its quaint, albeit dressed-up, village-like atmosphere. At the western end of Liulichang Xijie, a collection of more informal shops flog bric-a-brac. For boutiques, keep an eye on the *hútòng* around Yangmeizhu Byway with this street emerging as a bit of a hot spot for art and design.**

XÍAN YÀN TĀNG   ARTS & CRAFTS

Map p280 (贤燕堂; ☑150 0107 6618; 102 Liliuchang Dongjie; 琉璃厂东街102号; ☺9am-6.30pm; 🚇Line 2 to Hepingmen, exit C2) Tucked down a tiny alley lined with examples of its handmade wares, this cubbyhole of a shop turns out traditional shadow puppets (¥25 to ¥150). They come in all shapes and sizes, and you can get them framed (they make good gifts) if you don't fancy using them to put on your own shadow play back home.

RUÌFÚXIÁNG   SILK, CLOTHING

Map p280 (瑞蚨祥丝绸店; Ruìfúxiáng Sīchóudiàn; ☑010 6303 5313; 5 Dazhalan Jie; 大栅栏街5号; ☺9.30am-8pm; 🚇Line 2 to Qianmen, exit B) Housed in a historic building on Dashilar, Ruìfúxiáng has been trading here since 1893 and is still one of the best places in town to browse for silk. There's an incredible selection of Shāndōng silk, brocade and satin-silk. The silk starts at ¥168 a metre, although most of the fabric is more expensive. Ready-made, traditional Chinese clothing is sold on the 2nd floor.

Ruìfúxiáng also has an outlet at Dianmenwai Dajie (p102).

NÈILIÁNSHĒNG SHOE SHOP   SHOES

Map p280 (内联升鞋店; Nèiliánshēng Xiédiàn; ☑010 6301 4863; 34 Dazhalan Jie; 大栅栏街34号; ☺9am-8.30pm; 🚇Line 2 to Qianmen, exit B or C) They say this is the oldest existing cloth-shoe shop in China (opened in 1853) and Mao Zedong and other luminaries had their footwear made here. You too can pick up ornately embroidered shoes, or the simply styled cloth slippers frequently modelled by Běijīng's senior citizens (from ¥226). It does cute, patterned kids' slippers (from ¥48) too.

BĚIJĪNG FCZ STAMPS   GIFTS & SOUVENIRS

Map p280 (18 Dazhalan Jie; 大栅栏街18号; ☺9am-6pm; 🚇Line 2 to Qianmen, exit B) Head

QING DYNASTY SHOPPING MALL

Shops were barred from the city centre in imperial Běijīng, so the *hútòng* south of Qiánmén served as early versions of the modern-day malls now spread across the capital. Dashilar (p126) was one of the most popular and known especially for silk, although its name refers to a wicket gate that was closed at night to keep prowlers out.

Bustling markets plying specialised products thronged the surrounding alleys – lace in one, lanterns in the other, jade in the next. Now, many of the *hútòng* have been demolished and you're more likely to find someone selling fake watches than anything of real value.

For some years there have been persistent rumours that the western end of Dashilar, Dazhalan Xijie, is next in line for a similar overhaul, one that would have a potentially dire effect on this still-*hútòng*-rich neighbourhood. At the time of writing, work was ongoing but it appeared to be more of a street upgrade than the beginning of an attempt to transform it into something like Nanluogu Xiang. But expect some changes when you visit.

downstairs to browse the catalogues from their collection of old Chinese stamps with classic Communist propaganda images from 1949 through to the 1980s. Prices generally aren't cheap, but there are some affordable souvenirs to snap up.

RÓNGBǍOZHĀI ART

Map p280 (荣宝斋; ☎010 6303 6090; 19 Liulichang Xijie; 琉璃厂西街19号; ☺9am-5.30pm; ⓈLine 2 to Hepingmen, exit D2) Spread over two floors and sprawling down a length of the road, the scroll paintings, woodblock prints, paper, ink and brushes here are presented in a rather flat, uninspired way by bored staff – a consequence of it being state-run – and not much English is spoken. Prices are generally fixed, although you can usually get 10% off.

The ground floor has ceramics and art and calligraphy supplies. Head to the 2nd floor for traditional Chinese ink and scroll paintings.

TÓNGRÉNTÁNG CHINESE MEDICINE

Map p280 (同仁堂; ☎010 6303 1155; 24 Dazhalan Jie; 大栅栏街24号; ☺8am-8pm; ⓈLine 2 to Qianmen, exit B or C) This famous, now international, herbal medicine shop has been peddling pills and potions since 1669. It was a royal dispensary in the Qing dynasty and its medicines are based on secret prescriptions used by China's imperial household. You can be cured of anything from fright to encephalitis, or so the shop claims. Traditional doctors are available on the spot for consultations. Look for the pair of *qílín* (hybrid animals that appear on Earth in times of harmony) standing guard outside.

MǍLIÁNDÀO TEA MARKET TEA

(马连道茶城, Mǎliándào Cháchéng; ☎010 6343 8550; www.mldteamall.com; 11 Maliandao Lu; 马连道路11号; ☺8.30am-6pm; ⓈLines 7 to Wanzi) Mǎliándào is the largest tea market in northern China and home to if not all the tea in China, then an awful lot of it. There are brews from all over the country here, including *pǔ'ěr* and oolong, while Maliandao Lu has hundreds of tea shops, where prices for tea and tea sets are lower than in tourist areas.

Although it's mostly for wholesalers, the market is a great place to wander for anyone interested in tea, and the vendors will happily invite you in to sample some. They also sell tea sets here, with prices ranging dramatically depending on the design, glaze and porcelain used. A single tea cup can cost upwards of ¥150, or you can pick up a basic tea set in the market and the nearby shops for ¥450. Maliandao Lu is south of Běijīng West Train Station. To find the tea market, look for the statue of Lu Yu, the 8th-century sage who wrote the first book on growing, preparing and drinking tea, which stands outside it.

CATHAY BOOKSHOP BOOKS, ARTS

Map p280 (中国书店, Zhōngguó Shūdiàn; ☎010 6303 2104; 34 Liulichang Xijie, 琉璃厂西街34号; ☺9am-6pm; ⓈLine 2 to Hepingmen, exit D2) This is the larger of the two branches of the Cathay Bookshop on the south side of Liulichang Xijie and is worth checking out for its wide variety of colour books on Chinese painting, ceramics and furniture, as well as tomes on religion (most are in Chinese). Upstairs has more art books, stone rubbings and antiquarian books.

Sānlǐtún & Cháoyáng

Neighbourhood Top Five

❶ 798 Art District (p134) Discover China's vibrant contemporary art scene at this unique, industrial complex.

❷ Pānjiāyuán Market (p147) Hunt for arts, crafts and antique treasures at this wonderfully chaotic market.

❸ Craft Beer (p145) Drink some seriously good beer at Sānlǐtún's many tap houses that brew their own craft beer.

❹ Duck de Chine (p142) Enjoy the best of Běijīng's fine dining at restaurants like this Peking duck specialist.

❺ Dōngyuè Temple (p136) Muse on life's finalities at the fascinatingly morbid Taoist shrine.

For more detail of this area see Map p282.

Explore Sānlǐtún & Cháoyáng

The only sights of real interest in the spread-out district of Cháoyáng (朝阳) are Dōngyuè Temple and the oasis that is Rìtán Park, although spending at least half a day at the 798 Arts District is more or less essential. Modern-architecture lovers will also want to visit the Olympic site. Once your sightseeing is done, it's time to focus on Cháoyáng's more hedonistic pleasures: shopping, eating and partying.

You'll find many of Běijīng's best and most eye-catching shopping malls here, as well as some of the city's finest markets. You could easily put aside a day for shopping, including a lazy brunch or lunch stop.

Come evening, the choice of restaurants is staggering. Whether you fancy keeping it real with dumplings, dressing up for posh nosh or sampling international cuisine from African to Thai, you can find it in Cháoyáng.

Once you've satisfied your hunger cravings, hop in a cab to one of the many bars in the area, where you can discuss where best to dance the night away over a cocktail or three.

Local Life

➡ **Food** If you want to sidestep the expats and moneyed out-of-towners and eat like a real Beijinger, head for Bàodǔ Huáng (p139).

➡ **Art** 798 Art District is well worth a trip, but true art-lovers should also head slightly further northeast, to the less-touristy galleries at Cǎochǎngdì.

➡ **Parklife** Rìtán Park (p136) is a favourite spot for locals who come here to fly kites, play cards and do their daily exercises. Other outdoor spaces include Cháoyáng and Tuánjiéhú Parks, which both have popular swimming complexes.

Getting There & Away

➡ **Subway** The main bar, restaurant and clubbing areas in Sānlǐtún are between Dongsi Shitiao and Tuanjiehu stations. Whichever way you're heading, you're faced with a 10- to 15-minute walk.

➡ **Dōngzhímén Transport Hub** The Airport Express terminates here, two subway lines meet here, and there are buses to every corner of the city, including ones to the Great Wall.

➡ **Bus** Bus 113 runs past Sānlǐtún and the Workers Stadium before turning north up Jiaodaokou Nandajie (for Nanluogu Xiang). Bus 120 goes from the east gate of the Workers Stadium to Wángfǔjīng and Qiánmén. Bus 701 runs the length of Gongrentiyuchang Beilu and continues west to Běihǎi Park.

Lonely Planet's Top Tip

The vendors at the markets in this area are very accustomed to foreign tourists, so prepare yourself for some seriously hard bargaining. There are no hard and fast rules as to how much to cut the starting price by. The best way to gauge how low vendors are prepared to go is simply to walk away, hopefully prompting a genuine 'last price'.

✕ Best Places to Eat

➡ Jīngzūn Peking Duck (p140)

➡ Bǎoyuán Dumpling Restaurant (p139)

➡ Home Plate BBQ (p139)

➡ In & Out (p137)

➡ Duck de Chine (p142)

For reviews, see p137. ➡

🍺 Best Places to Drink

➡ Great Leap Brewing (p143)

➡ Janes + Hooch (p144)

➡ Jing A Brewing (p143)

➡ Slow Boat Brewery (p143)

➡ Parlor (p143)

➡ Revolution (p144)

For reviews, see p142. ➡

🔒 Best Places to Shop

➡ Pānjiāyuán Market (p147)

➡ Shard Box Store (p147)

➡ Sānlǐtún Village (p147)

➡ Silk Market (p148)

➡ UCCA Design Store (p147)

For reviews, see p146. ➡

TOP SIGHT
798 ART DISTRICT

A vast area of disused factories built by the East Germans, 798 Art District, also known as Dà Shānzi (大山子), is Běijīng's main concentration of contemporary art galleries. The industrial Bahaus-style complex celebrates its proletarian roots in the communist heyday of the 1950s via retouched red Maoist slogans decorating gallery interiors and statues of burly, lantern-jawed workers dotting the lanes. The giant former factory workshops (with a few still operational) are ideally suited to multimedia installations and other ambitious projects.

While an increase in mainstream interest has seen 798 lose some of its edge, with a more commercialised feel, it nevertheless remains one of the world's coolest art precincts.

A further extensive colony of art galleries can be found 3km northeast of 798 Art District at Cǎochǎngdì (草场地). It's an inexpensive taxi ride away, or you can catch bus 909 here.

There are buses, but the subway is the easiest way to get here, taking Line 14 to Jiangtai from where it's a 15-minute walk or short cab ride.

DON'T MISS

➡ 798 Art Factory

➡ Faurschou Foundation Beijing

➡ Mansudae Art Studio

PRACTICALITIES

➡ 798 艺术新区; Qī Jiǔ Bā Yìshù Qū

➡ cnr Jiuxianqiao Lu & Jiuxianqiao Beilu; 酒仙桥路

➡ ⊙galleries 10am-6pm, most closed Mon

➡ 🚌403, 909, S Line 14 to Jiangtai, exit A

Galleries

One of the most iconic spaces is the **798 Art Factory** (798艺术工厂; 798 Yìshù Gōngchǎng; ☎186 1132 2248; 4 Jiuxianqiao Lu, 798 Art District; 酒仙桥路4号大山子艺术区; ⊙10am-6pm) FREE, a Bauhaus-designed hangar-like space decorated in 1950s Maoist slogans, with original machinery scattered among changing art exhibitions by Chinese and foreign artists.

For big names, head to the Danish gallery **Faurschou Foundation Běijīng** (林冠基金会北京; Línguān Jījīn Huì Běijīng; www.faurschou.com; 2 Jiuxuanqiao Lu, 798 Art District; 酒仙桥路2号798艺术区; ⊙10am-6pm), which has hosted shows by Lucien Freud, Ai Wei Wei, Andy Warhol and Yoko Ono. **Springs Centre of the Arts** (泉空间; Quán Kōngjiān; ☑010 5762 6373; www.springsart.com; 2 Jiuxianqiao Lu, 798 Art District; 酒仙桥路2号大山子艺术区; ¥10; ⊙10am-6pm Tue-Sun) also exhibits headliner artists from China and abroad, while **UCCA** (Ullens Center for Contemporary Art; 尤伦斯当代艺术中心, Yóulúnsī Dāngdài Yìshù Zhōngxīn; ☑010 5780 0200; http://ucca.org.cn/en/; 4 Jiuxianqiao Lu, 798 Art District; 酒仙桥路4号大山子艺术区; ¥10-60; ⊙10am-7pm Tue-Sun) is a big-money gallery with multiple exhibition halls and the attached cool UCCA Design Store (p147).

Other highlights include the **Xin Dong Cheng Space for Contemporary Art** (程昕东国际当代艺术空间; Chéngxīndōng Guójì Dāngdài Yìshù Kōngjiān; 4 Jiuxianqiao Lu, 798 Art District; 酒仙桥路4号大山子艺术区; ⊙10am-6.30pm Tue-Sun) FREE which showcases young avant-garde Chinese artists in an atmospheric space. **Zhu Bingren Art Museum** (朱炳仁美术博物馆; Zhūbǐngrén Měishù Bówùguǎn; www.cu100.com; 798 Art District; 大山子艺术区; ⊙10am-6pm) FREE features the work of renowned Shandong sculptor Zhu Bingren who produces interesting copper and bronze pieces. Also check out the Pyongyang-based **Mansudae Art Studio** (万寿台创作社; Wànshòutái Chuàngzuò Shè; ☑010 5978 9317; www.mansudaeartstudio.com; 2 Jiuxianqiao Lu, 798 Art District; 酒仙桥路2号大山子艺术区; ⊙10am-6pm Tue-Sun) FREE, which exhibits North Korean artists and sells DPRK collectibles.

Public Art

Inside the galleries isn't the only place to see art at 798, with plenty of quirky open-air sculptures scattered about the site. The caged dinosaurs out front of 798 Factory are popular, while original socialist-realism sculptures in the southwest of the complex include a headless Chairman Mao statue. Near to here are shipping containers splattered by graffiti artists. The area around 798 Live House is the best for stencils, murals and other street art.

TOP TIPS

Avoid visiting on Mondays, when the vast majority of galleries are closed. Weekends also get busy, so visit midweek if you don't like crowds. Allow at *least* half a day, as there's a lot to get through.

The 798 Art District has plenty of places to eat and drink. Timezone 8 (现代书店 北京艺术书屋; Xiàndài Shūdiàn Běijīng Yìshù Shūwū; ☑010 5978 9917; 4 Jiuxianqiao Lu, 798 Art District; 酒仙桥路4号大山子艺术区; mains from ¥55, sushi from ¥32; ⊙8.30am-2am; ☎) **is rightfully popular for its Japanese and Western dishes, plus sake and quality beers on tap. Cafe Flat White** (p140) **does fantastic burgers and white coffees, while Voyage Coffee** (798 Art District; coffee ¥25-50; ⊙9am-6pm; ☎) **is all about pour-overs – and one for aficionados. The industrial 798 Live House** (p146) **is worth popping by to see if there's any music going on.**

SIGHTS

798 ART DISTRICT GALLERY

See p134.

BIRD'S NEST ARCHITECTURE

(Beijing National Stadium; 北京国家体育场; Běijīng Guójiā Tǐyùchǎng; http://cyvu.org/english/; Beijing Olympic Park; 奥林匹克公园; entry ¥50; ⏲9am-5pm Nov-Mar, 9am-6.30pm Apr-Oct; [S]Line 8 to Olympic Sports Center, exit B2) The centerpiece from the 2008 Olympics is the National Stadium, known colloquially as the Bird's Nest (鸟巢; Niǎocháo). It's one primarily for lovers of contemporary architecture, or those interested in sporting history. Otherwise walking around the desolate Olympic Sports Centre midweek is rather like being stuck in one of those zombie movies where humans have all but been wiped out. Nevertheless, it remains an iconic piece of architecture designed by Swiss firm Herzog & de Meuron in consultancy with controversial Běijīng-born artist Ai Wei Wei.

CCTV HEADQUARTERS ARCHITECTURE

Map p282 (央视大楼; Yāngshì Dàlóu; 32 Dongsanhuan Zhonglu; 东三环中路32号; [S]Line 10 to Jintaixizhao, exit C) Shaped like an enormous pair of trousers, and known locally as Dà Kùchǎ (大裤衩), or Big Pants, the astonishing CCTV Tower is an architectural fantasy that appears to defy gravity. It's made possible by an unusual engineering design that creates a three-dimensional cranked loop, supported by an irregular grid on its surface. Designed by Rem Koolhaas and Ole Scheeren, the building is an audacious statement of modernity (despite its nickname) and a unique addition to the Běijīng skyline.

DŌNGYUÈ TEMPLE TAOIST TEMPLE

Map p282 (东岳庙; Dōngyuè Miào; 141 Chaoyangmenwai Dajie; adult ¥10, with guide ¥40; ⏲8.30am-4.30pm Tue-Sun, last entry 4pm; [S]Lines 2, 6 to Chaoyangmen, exit A, or Line 6 to Dongdaqiao, exit A) Dedicated to the Eastern Peak (Tài Shān) of China's five Taoist mountains, the morbid Taoist shrine of Dōngyuè Temple is an unsettling, albeit fascinating, experience and one of the capital's most unusual temples. An active place of worship tended by topknotted Taoist monks, the temple's roots go all the way back to the Yuan dynasty. Its most notable for its long corridor exhibiting a series of comically macabre displays of statues representing different 'departments' from the Taoist underworld.

Before going in, note the temple's fabulous **Páifāng** (memorial archway) lying to the south, divorced from its shrine by the intervention of the busy main road, Chaoyangmenwai Dajie.

Stepping through the entrance pops you into a Taoist Hades, where tormented spirits reflect on their wrongdoing and elusive atonement. You can muse on life's finalities in the **Life and Death Department** or the **Final Indictment Department.** Otherwise get spooked at the **Department for Wandering Ghosts** or the **Department for Implementing 15 Kinds of Violent Death**.

It's not all doom and gloom: the luckless can check in at the **Department for Increasing Good Fortune & Longevity**. Ornithologists will be birds of a feather with the **Flying Birds Department**, while the infirm can seek cures at the **Deep-Rooted Disease Department**. The **Animal Department** has colourful and lively fauna. English explanations detail department functions.

Other halls are no less fascinating. The huge **Dàiyuè Hall** (Dàiyuè Diàn) is consecrated to the God of Tàishān, who manages the 18 layers of hell. Visit during festival time, especially during the Chinese New Year and the Mid-Autumn Festival, and you'll see the temple at its most vibrant.

Just outside the complex, in a small car park to the east, stands the handsome, but rather lonely **Jiǔtiān Pǔhuā Gōng** (九天普化宫; Map p282; Chaoyangmenwai Dajie; [S]Lines 2, 6 to Chaoyangmen, exit A, or Line 6 to Dongdaqiao, exit A), a small temple hall which is the only remaining structure of two other Taoist temples that once also stood in this area. Built in 1647, the hall, which we think is now empty, once contained more than 70 clay and wooden statues dedicated to Léizǔ (雷祖), Taoism's God of Thunder. Unfortunately, it's not open to the public. Note the two impressive stone tablets that rise up from the platform at the front.

RÌTÁN PARK PARK

Map p282 (日坛公园; Rìtán Gōngyuán; 6 Ritan Beilu; 日坛北路6号; ⏲6am-9pm; [S]Lines 2, 6 to Chaoyangmen, exit A or Lines 1, 2 to Jianguomen, exit B) [FREE] Meaning 'Altar of the Sun', Rìtán (pronounced 'rer-tan') is a real oasis in the heart of Běijīng's business district. It's a nice place to stroll and take in the atmosphere of this beautifully landscaped park where you'll see locals dancing, singing, flying kites, playing table tennis and hanging out. It dates back to 1530 and was one of a set of

LOCAL KNOWLEDGE

TAICHI TIPS

Characterised by its lithe and graceful movements, *tàijíquán* (literally 'Fist of the Supreme Ultimate'), also known as taichi, is an ancient Chinese physical discipline practised by legions of Chinese throughout the land.

Considerable confusion exists about taichi – is it a martial art, a form of meditation, a *qìgōng* (exercise that helps channel *qì*, or energy) style or an exercise? In fact, taichi can be each and all of these, depending on what you seek from the art and how deep you dig into its mysteries.

In terms of health benefits, taichi strengthens the leg muscles, exercises the joints, gives the cardiovascular system a good workout and promotes flexibility. It also relaxes the body, dissolving stress, loosening the joints and helping to circulate *qì*.

As a system of meditation, taichi leaves practitioners feeling both centred and focused. Taichi introduces you to Taoist meditation techniques, as the art is closely allied to the philosophy of Taoism. And if you're adept at taichi, it is far easier to learn other martial arts, as you'll have learnt a way of moving that is common to all of the fighting arts.

Where to Learn

Mílún Kungfu School (p82)

Jīnghuá Wǔshù Association (p148)

The Hutong (p103)

imperial parks that covered each compass point – others include the Temple of Heaven and Temple of Earth (Dìtán Park).

CHINA SCIENCE & TECHNOLOGY MUSEUM MUSEUM

(中国科技馆; Zhōngguó Kējìguǎn; www.cstm.org.cn; 5 Beichendong Lu; 北辰东路5号; admission ¥30, 1 child free; 🕘9.30am-5pm Tue-Sun; [S]Line 8 to South Gate of Forest Park, exit C) About 8km north of the city centre and a big favourite with kids, this imposing facility has an array of hands-on scientific exhibitions, a kids' science playground and state-of-the-art 3D and '4D' cinemas. Walk east from South Gate of Forest Park subway station, then take the second right (10 minutes).

TUÁNJIÉHÚ PARK PARK

(团结湖公园; Tuánjiéhú Gōngyuán; 16 Tuanjiehunanli Lu; 团结湖南里16号; 🕘6am-10pm; [S]Lines 6, 10 to Hujialou, exit B) This pleasant park with a picturesque artificial lake and island is a good spot to stroll and observe local life among kitsch, such as paddleboats and a children's theme park. Its outdoor swimming area (weekday/weekend ¥40/50) is popular in the warmer months.

🍴 EATING

The presence of embassies and many foreign companies, as well as the Sānlǐtún bar and entertainment district, means Cháoyáng has the greatest concentration of international restaurants, foreign-friendly Chinese restaurants and fine-dining options in all Běijīng.

★IN & OUT YUNNAN $

Map p282 (一坐一忘; Yī Zuò Yī Wàng; ☎010 8454 0086; 1 Sanlitun Beixiaojie; 三里屯北小街1号; mains ¥28-60; 🕘11am-10pm; [S]Line 2 to Agricultural Exhibition Centre) This fashionable, but laid-back and friendly restaurant specialises in the many cuisines of the ethnic minority groups in southwestern Yúnnán province. The flavours are authentic and, given its popularity, the prices are surprisingly reasonable, unless you go for the mushroom dishes (Yúnnán mushrooms are prized across Asia). Try the classic Over the Bridge Noodles (¥45), the excellent Dongba beef ribs (¥56) or golden roast tiliapia glistening with chilli and lemongrass (¥58).

There's a good choice of Yúnnán beers and local rice wines. It's worth booking ahead, especially if you're in a group.

MORNING NOODLES $

Map p282 (过早; Guò Zǎo; 10 Chunxiu Lu; 春秀路10号; mains from ¥20; 🕘11am-2.30pm & 5-9.30pm; [S]Line 2 to Dongzhimen, exit C, or Dongsi Shitiao, exit B) A slick, modern space with blonde wood and designer furniture seems incongruous for a restaurant that specialises in cheap, old-school Húběi noodles, and it serves to make Morning all the cooler. Come for the traditional dry noodles, topped with pork mince and thick sesame paste that you'll need to stir through vigorously before you slurp it down.

YÀN LÁN LÓU GANSU $

Map p282 (燕兰楼; ☎010 6599 1668; 4th fl, 12 Chaoyangmenwai Dajie; 朝阳门外大街12号昆泰商厦4楼; noodles from ¥18; ⏲10.30am-2pm & 5.30-10pm; [S]Line 6 to Dongdaqiao, exit D) Famous for its hand-pulled noodles, a speciality of Gānsù Province in China's northwest, Yàn Lán Lóu is especially popular with Běijīng's Huí community (Muslims originally from the northwest). Don't expect to find any pork here – folks come for the delectable mutton. It's on the 4th floor of a building across from the Băinăohuì Computer Mall (p147). Little English is spoken, but there is a picture menu.

Noodle options aside, the other dishes on the menu reveal the influence of the Muslim cuisine of Níngxià and Xīnjiāng. They're more expensive than the noodle choices, but the charcoal roasted lamb leg (¥58) is definitely worth trying. This is also one of the few places in the capital where you'll find yak meat.

UIGHUR WILLOW XINJIANG $

Map p282 (新疆红柳餐厅; Xīnjiāng Hónglĭu Cāntīng; ☎010 5622 1508; 39 Shenlu Jie; 神路街39号日坛国际贸易中心; mains from ¥22,

LOCAL KNOWLEDGE

EMBASSY BITES

Reflecting the multicultural makeup of Sānlĭtún's Diplomatic Residential Compound (DRC), home to Běijīng's embassies and consulates, here you can dine at a range of international restaurants you're less likely to find elsewhere. They cater to local embassy workers, so you know it's going to be authentic.

Georgia's Feast (格鲁秀色; Gélŭ Xiùsè; Map p282; ☎010 8448 6886; 2 Sanlitun Beixiaojie; 三里屯北小街2号; dishes from ¥42; ⏲11am-11pm; [S]Line 10 to Agricultural Exhibition Center, exit D2) Head upstairs for Georgian home-style cooking in a space with traditional red-brick alcoves and decorative pieces. Expect a carb- and cheese-heavy menu of dumplings, *adjaruli khachapuri* (cheese and egg-filled bread), plus Georgian wines and homemade cheeses.

Indian Kitchen (北京印度小厨餐厅; Běijīng Yìndù Xiăo Chú Cāntīng; Map p282; ☎010 6462 7255; 2nd fl, 2 Sanlitun Beixiaojie; 三里屯北小街2号二楼; mains ¥45-100; ⏲11am-2.30pm & 5.30-10.30pm; [S]Line 10 to Agricultural Exhibition Center) Still the most reliable place in town for Indian food, attracting diplomats, expats and locals in equal numbers. There's an all-Indian cooking staff to ensure authenticity with its tikka and masala dishes and a good choice of dosas. There's a good-value weekday buffet (¥68) from 11am to 2.30pm.

Pinotage (品乐塔吉; Pĭnlètăjí; Map p282; 12 Dongzhimenwai Dajie; 东直门外大街12号; dishes ¥58-200; ⏲10.30am-1am; [S]Line 10 to Agricultural Exhibition Center, exit D2) Unsurprisingly this is Běijīng's only South African restaurant, and it has a leafy terrace and an authentic menu of braii, boerewors, bunny chow, mealie pap and ostrich burgers. It makes its own biltong too. There's an excellent selection of South African wines and home-brew beer to enjoy on the leafy terrace.

Schindler's Docking Station (申德勒码头餐厅; Shēndélēi Mătóu Cāntīng; Map p282; www.schindlers.com.cn/anlegestelle-dockingstation.html; 10 Sanlitun Beixiaojie; 三里屯北小街10号; mains from ¥50; ⏲10am-midnight; [S]Line 10 to Agricultural Exhibition Center) Cleverly positioned close to the German embassy, this authentic feeling Deutsch restaurant has mustard-coloured tablecloths, dark woods and an outdoor terrace. It has multiple German beers on tap to go with house-made wurst, pretzels and hearty mains. It also does schnapps and inexpensive German house wines.

Turkish Mum (土耳其妈妈; Map p282; 1-2 Gongrentiyuchang Beilu; 工体北路1-2号; dishes from ¥40; ⏲9am-midnight; [S]Line 10 to Tuanjiehu, exit A) In a precinct known for its Middle Eastern cuisine, this Turkish restaurant is well regarded for its stuffed meatballs, borek and meze dishes. Dine outdoors on its streetside terrace or in the smart interior with polished floorboards. It's also one of Běijīng's best spots to smoke shisha (¥80).

kebabs ¥10; ⏲10am-11pm; [S]Lines 2, 6 to Chaoyangmen, exit A) Down a lane of restaurants, almost directly opposite the north gate of Rìtán Park, that come alive at night, this is a friendly and comfortable establishment catering almost exclusively to Uighurs, the people native to Xīnjiāng in China's far west. It's alcohol-free and offers Uighur classics such as polo, *laghman* noodles and the obligatory kebabs.

MÉIZHŌU DŌNGPŌ JIǓLÓU SICHUAN $

Map p282 (眉州东坡酒楼; ☎010 5968 3370; Chunxiu Lu; 春秀路; mains from ¥27; ⏲6.30am-2am; [S]Line 2 to Dongsi Shitiao, exit B) Recognisable by its traditional Chinese-style frontage, this branch of the popular Sìchuán chain opens up to a modern interior that does good-quality, typically mouth-numbing dishes. The menu is in English and has photos as well as very handy chilli-logo spice indicators. Beer is ¥8 a bottle.

BǍOYUÁN DUMPLING RESTAURANT DUMPLING $

Map p282 (宝源饺子屋; Bǎoyuán Jiǎozi Wū; ☎010 6586 4967; 6 Maizidian Jie; 麦子店街6号; dumplings from ¥13, mains from ¥30; ⏲11.15am-10.15pm; [S]Line 10 to Liangmaqiao, exit C, or Agricultural Exhibition Centre, exit A) Fun for the kids – but also tasty enough for parents – this excellent dumpling restaurant dazzles diners with a huge selection of multicoloured *jiǎozi* (饺子; boiled dumplings), including many vegetarian options. The dough dyes are all natural (carrots make the orange; spinach the green) and only add to the flavour of the fillings; as good as any in Běijīng.

Dumplings are ordered and priced by the *liǎng* (about 50g). One *liǎng* gets you six dumplings. Not much English spoken, but there's an English sign and menu, and it's nonsmoking. Cash only.

BÀODǓ HUÁNG BEIJING $

Map p282 (爆肚皇; 15 Dongzhimenwai Dajie; 东直门外大街15号; mains ¥18-35; ⏲11am-2pm & 5-9pm; [S]Line 2 to Dongzhimen, exit E) Be prepared to queue at this no-nonsense apartment-block restaurant (look for the green sign with four yellow characters), where locals gobble and slurp their way through the authentic Běijīng-grub menu. The speciality is *bàodǔ* (爆肚; boiled lamb tripe; ¥20 or ¥38 depending on portion size). If you can't stomach that, then plump instead for a delicious *niúròu dàcóng ròubǐng* (牛肉大葱肉饼; beef and onion fried patty; ¥9).

The blanched vegetables are popular side dishes; choose from *chāo báicài* (焯白菜; blanched cabbage; ¥7), *chāo fěnsī* (焯粉丝; blanched glass noodles; ¥6) or *chāo dòng dòufu* (焯冻豆腐; blanched tofu; ¥7). And if you haven't ordered a meat patty, grab a *zhīma shāobing* (芝麻烧饼; roasted sesame-seed bun; ¥2) instead. True Beijingers will also nibble on *jiāo quān* (焦圈; deep-fried dough rings; ¥1), washed down with gulps of *dòu zhī* (豆汁; sour soy milk; ¥4). But you may prefer to go for a bottle of *píjiǔ* (啤酒; local beer; ¥6). No English spoken, no English menu, no English sign.

JÍXIÁNGNIĂO XIĀNGCÀI HUNAN $

Map p282 (吉祥鸟湘菜; ☎010 6552 2856; Jishikou Donglu; 吉市口东路; dishes from ¥29; ⏲11am-9.30pm; [S]Lines 2, 6 to Chaoyangmen, exit A) Not enough places in Běijīng serve *xiāng cài* (湘菜), the notoriously spicy cuisine of Húnán province, but this large, fiery restaurant is arguably the best of them. The pork belly braised in soy sauce and spices (¥48), known in China as *hóngshāo ròu* (红烧肉), is the house speciality: it was the favourite dish of Mao Zedong, who hailed from Húnán.

But the fish head with chopped chillis (¥78) and the ribs (¥128) are not be missed, while the dry pot dishes are also popular. You won't hear much English spoken, but there's a picture menu in English. It gets busy at lunchtimes especially. No English sign; look for the red Chinese characters on top of the roof.

BOCATA CAFE $

Map p282 (☎010 6417 5291; 3 Sanlitun Beilu; 三里屯北路3号; sandwiches from ¥32, coffee from ¥25; ⏲11.30am-midnight; 📶; [S]Line 10 to Tuanjiehu, exit A) Great spot for lunch, especially in summer, located slap-bang in the middle of Sānlǐtún's bar street and opposite Běijīng's trendiest shopping area. As the name suggests, there's a Spanish/Mediterranean theme to the food, with Iberian ham and cheeses and decent salads, as well as great chips, but most punters go for the fine baguettes.

The coffee, juices and smoothies go down a treat, too, and the large, tree-shaded terrace is very popular when the sun is out.

★HOME PLATE BBQ BARBECUE $$

Map p282 (本垒美式烤肉; Běnlěi Měishì Kǎoròu; ☎400 096 7670; www.homeplatebbq.com; Lot 10, Courtyard 4, off Gongrentiyuchang Beilu; 三里屯机电院10号; burgers from ¥45; ⏲11am-1am; [S]Line 10 to Tuanjiehu, exit A or D) Serving up some of the finest southern American barbecue in town is this Texas-owned restaurant-bar that's all about slow-cooked meats, burgers and craft beer. Its charcoal-wood smoker sits proudly on display, loaded with fruit wood to cook bone-lickin' ribs, plates of barbecued pulled pork, smoky chicken and beef brisket cooked for 12 hours.

Mains come with a choice of two sides from southern greens, grits, slaw etc. Wash it down with a draft craft beer or a jar of Home Plate's moonshine. Happy hour (11am to 7pm) is ¥10 off drinks.

★JĪNGZŪN PEKING DUCK PEKING DUCK $$

Map p282 (京尊烤鸭; Jīngzūn Kǎoyā; ☎010 6417 4075; 6 Chunxiu Lu; 春秀路6号; mains ¥26-98; ⏲11am-10pm; [S]Line 2 to Dongsi Shitiao, exit B) Very popular place to sample Běijīng's signature dish. Not only is the Peking duck here extremely good value at ¥138/79 for a whole/half bird, but you can also sit outside on its atmospheric wooden-decked terrace decorated with red lanterns. Otherwise, head upstairs to its booth seating overlooking the leafy street. It has its own draft beer too.

There's also a big choice of dishes from across China. During the summer, book ahead if you want a spot on the terrace.

TACO BAR MEXICAN $$

Map p282 (塔科酒吧; Tǎkē Jiǔbā; www.tacobarchina.com; Lot 10, Courtyard 4, off Gongrentiyuchang Beilu; 北京机电院内4号院; 3 tacos ¥45; ⏲5pm-midnight Tue-Fri, noon-midnight Sat & Sun; 📶; [S]Line 10 to Tuanjiehu, exit A or D) It's only appropriate that the city's coolest *taquería* be located within this happening Sānlǐtún precinct. The place is normally packed out with locals and expats feasting on Mexican street-style tacos such as *al pastor* (pork belly) or *carne asada* (steak) soft corn masa tacos, with a selection of homemade hot sauces. There's a mushroom taco for vegetarians, and authentic seafood varieties too.

You get a free taco with any alcoholic drink purchased Tuesday to Thursday, and after 7pm on weekends.

If you're not up for tacos, there's also a great range of *botanas* (appetisers) and *tortas* (sandwiches), plus the usual Tex Mex dishes. Brunch is popular on weekends, with Mexican breakfasts featuring spicy chorizo and eggy dishes.

BOOKWORM CAFE $$

Map p282 (书虫; Shūchóng; ☎010 6586 9507; www.beijingbookworm.com; Bldg 4, Nansanlitun Lu; 南三里屯路4号楼; mains from ¥60; ⏲9am-midnight; 📶; [S]Line 10 to Tuanjiehu, exit A or D) A combination of a bar, cafe, restaurant, library and bookshop, the Bookworm is a Běijīng institution and one of the epicentres of the capital's cultural life. Much more than just an upmarket cafe, there are 16,000-plus books here you can browse while sipping your coffee. For freelancers, it's one of the city's best workspaces. The food is reasonably priced, if uninspired, but there's a decent wine list.

The Bookworm also hosts lectures, poetry readings, a Monday-night quiz and a very well-regarded annual book festival. Any author of note passing through town gives a talk here. Check the website for upcoming events. There's a roof terrace with bar and hammocks in summer and a nonsmoking area.

DIN TAI FUNG DUMPLING $$

Map p282 (鼎泰丰; Dǐng Tài Fēng; ☎010 6553 1536; www.dintaifung.com.cn; 6f, Block D, SKP Mall, 87 Jianguo Lu; 建国路87号新光天地店6楼; 5/10 dumplings from ¥25/49; ⏲11.30am-9.30pm Sun-Thu, to 10pm Fri & Sat; [S]Lines 1, 14 to Dawanglu, exit A) The *New York Times* once picked the original Taipei branch of this upmarket dumplings chain as one of the 10 best restaurants in the world. That's no longer true, but the dumplings here are certainly special. The *xiǎolóngbāo* – thin-skinned packages with meat or veggie fillings that are surrounded by a superb, scalding soup – are especially fine.

Din Tai Fung also does Shànghǎi hairy crabmeat *jiǎozi* (stuffed dumplings) and *shāomài*, as well as excellent soups and noodle dishes. It's on the top floor of the posh SKP Mall, along with a host of other restaurants.

CAFE FLAT WHITE CAFE $$

(☎010 5978 9067; www.cafeflatwhite.com; 4 Jiuxianqiao Lu, 798 Art District; 朝阳区 酒仙桥路4号大山子艺术区; coffee ¥28, burgers from ¥65; ⏲9am-9pm; ❄📶; [S]Line 14 to Jiangtai, exit A) Set up by a New Zealander, this trendy cafe roasts its own coffee and does single origins as well as its eponymous flat white. There's an excellent breakfast menu, and lunches including juicy burgers, meat pies, lamb chops and salads. It now has six cafes across Běijīng, including another cafe within the 798 Art District.

HÓNG LÚ BEIJING $$

Map p282 (红炉; ☎010 6595 9872; 60 Sanlitun Nanlu; 三里屯南路6号楼南侧60米; dishes from

¥28; ⏰11.30am-10pm; Ⓢ Line 10 to Tuanjiehu, exit D) A great place to sample authentic Běijīng dishes in a clean environment (it's non-smoking). The braised beef (¥58) is wonderfully tender, the Manchu Bannerman lamb (¥58) is packed with flavour, while you can get half a duck here for ¥58 (but it's not Peking style). The plum juice makes a healthy accompaniment to the meal. There's no English sign, but it's next door to Slow Boat Brewery: look for the bright red door.

BIG SMOKE
GASTROPUB $$

Map p282 (⏰010 6416 5195; 1/F Lee World Bldg, Xingfucun Zhong Lu; 幸福村中路57号利世商务楼一层; dishes from ¥36; ⏰11am-midnight Mon-Thu, to 1am Fri & Sat, to 10pm Sun; Ⓢ Line 2 to Dongsi Shitiao, exit B) Just off the main street down an alley is this popular red brick brew pub specialising in American dude food. Expect the likes of apple-wood smoked pork sliders, southern fried chicken, jalapeno mac 'n' cheese, truffle oil french fries etc. It goes beautifully with a range of beers from Jing A Brewing (p143), that brews six beers on-site.

There are three areas to sit to suit your mood: a casual front bar with long wooden communal tables; an atmospheric dining room for larger groups; or a speakeasy-style bar that mixes top-notch cocktails. Happy hour is 4pm to 7pm.

DESERT ROSE
TURKISH $$

Map p282 (沙漠玫瑰; Shāmò Méiguī; ⏰010 8569 3576; 1-07, 39 Shenlu Jie; 神路街39号院1号楼 1-07; mains from ¥30; ⏰9am-1am; Ⓢ Lines 2, 6 to Chaoyangmen, exit A) Down an eating precinct that specialises in Central Asian restaurants is this Turkish–Azerbaijan-run place with a huge range of superb kebabs (from ¥50), as well as different varieties of pilaf.

Tobacco fiends can head to the outside terrace, although you are allowed to smoke a shisha inside. Make sure to try the different teas and sweet pastries.

NÀJIĀ XIǍOGUǍN
CHINESE $$

Map p282 (那家小馆; ⏰010 6567 3663; 10 Yong'an Xili, off Jianguomenwai Dajie, Chunxiu Lu; 建国门外大街永安西里10号; mains ¥40-90; ⏰11.30am-9pm; Ⓢ Line 1 to Yonganli, exit A2) There's a touch of the traditional Chinese teahouse to this excellent restaurant, housed in a reconstructed two-storey interior courtyard, and bubbling with old-Peking atmosphere. The menu is based on an old imperial recipe book known as the *Golden Soup Bible*, and the dishes are consistently good (and fairly priced considering the quality).

The imperial Manchu theme could be tacky, but it's carried off in a fun but tasteful way that doesn't give you the feeling you're in a tourist-only restaurant. You don't need to book (in fact, at peak times you can't), but be prepared to hang around for at least half an hour for a table. It's worth the wait. No English sign and not much English spoken, but the menu is in English.

XIǍO WÁNG'S HOME RESTAURANT
CHINESE $$

Map p282 (小王府; Xiǎo Wángfǔ; ⏰010 6591 3255; 2 Guanghua Dongli; 光华东里2号; mains ¥28-98; ⏰11am-10.30pm; Ⓢ Line 10 to Jintaixizhao, exit A) This clean and well-run restaurant has been serving customers for almost 20 years and has grown over time to occupy part of three floors of an atmospheric, old-fashioned, low-rise housing block. The menu is a medley of Chinese cuisine, but make sure to try the deservedly famous pork ribs with pepper and salt. The Peking duck (half/whole ¥88/158) is good value here.

The restaurant has some balcony seating and an English sign, but is tucked away down an alley and can be hard to find. It's best accessed from Guanghua Lu.

PURPLE ISLE
THAI $$

Map p282 (⏰010 6413 0899; 55 Xingfu Yicun, off Gongrentiyuchang Beilu; 工人体育场北路幸福一村55号; mains from ¥46; ⏰11.30am-10.30pm; 📶; Ⓢ Line 2 to Dongsi Shitiao, exit B) The restaurant formerly known as Purple Haze has undergone a refit but it remains one of the most popular and authentic Thai restaurants in town. Dishes can get spicy, but you can soothe your tongue on its ¥30 cocktails.

BELLAGIO
TAIWANESE $$

Map p282 (鹿港小镇; Lùgǎng Xiǎozhèn; ⏰010 6551 3533; 6 Gongrentiyuchang Xilu; 工体西路6号; mains ¥30-85; ⏰11am-5am; Ⓢ Lines 2, 6 to Chaoyangmen, exit A) This is a slick, late-opening Taiwanese restaurant conveniently located next to the strip of nightclubs on Gongrentiyuchang Xilu (Gongti Xilu). The large menu includes Taiwanese favourites such as three cup chicken (¥54), as well as a wide range of vegetarian options. But the real reason to come here is for the renowned shaved-ice puddings.

Try the red beans with condensed milk on shaved ice (¥27) and the fresh mango cubes on shaved ice (¥36). Top-notch coffee too. During the day and the evening, it attracts cashed-up locals and foreigners. After midnight, the club crowd moves in.

PANGU 7 STAR HOTEL BUFFET $$$

(Auspicious Garden Restaurant; 盘古七星酒店; Pángǔ Qīxīng Jiǔdiàn; ☎010 5906 7777; 27 North Fourth Ring Rd; 北四环中路27号; buffet incl beer ¥521; 🕒11.30am-2.30pm; [S]Line 8 to Olympic Sports Center, exit B2) Putting on one of Beijing's best spreads, the lunch buffet on the 2nd floor of the Auspicious Garden Restaurant at the Pangu 7 Star Hotel is famed for its 'lobster mountain' – a stacked mound of all-you-can-eat Boston lobsters. Grab your plate to browse the myriad choices, from different cuts of steak, Peking duck, crab claws, and sushi bar among an overwhelming selection of dishes and desserts. Champagne is extra, but beer and soft drink are included.

Otherwise, if you're not up for such a feast, head up to its rooftop Happiness Lounge for a drink with fantastic views overlooking the Olympic venues, a real spectacle when they're illuminated at night.

DUCK DE CHINE PEKING DUCK $$$

Map p282 (全鸭季; Quányājì; ☎010 6521 2221; Courtyard 4, 1949 Hidden City, off Gongrentiyuchang Beilu; 工体北路4号; mains ¥78-488; 🕒11am-2pm & 5.30-10pm; [S]Line 10 to Tuanjiehu, exit A or D) Housed in a reconstructed industrial-style courtyard complex known as 1949, this very slick and stylish operation incorporates both Chinese and French duck-roasting methods to produce some stand-out duck dishes, including a leaner version of the classic Peking roast duck (¥268); no half serving available. The mix of expats and moneyed locals who flock here argue it's the best bird in town.

The service is as good as it gets in Běijīng, while the wine list is lengthy and expensive. Alternatively, the pumpkin infused with sour plums makes a delicious accompaniment. Book ahead.

O'STEAK FRENCH $$$

Map p282 (欧牛排法式餐厅, Ōu Niúpái Fàshì Cāntīng; ☎010 8448 8250; 55-7 Xingfucun Zhonglu; 幸福村中路55-7杰座大厦底层; steaks from ¥98; 🕒11.30am-11pm; [S]Line 2 to Dongsi Shitiao, exit B) Superior cuts in a relaxed atmosphere at this French-run steakhouse that will delight meat-lovers searching for a decently priced chunk of beef. There's a selection of sauces to accompany the steak of your choice, as well as salads and starters such as snails in a Burgundy style, and some very tempting puddings if you can find room for one.

There's popular outdoor seating streetside in the summer. Unsurprisingly, considering its popularity with Běijīng's French community, the wine list is extensive.

OKRA JAPANESE $$$

Map p282 (☎010 6593 5087; www.okra1949.com; Courtyard 4, 1949 Hidden City, off Gongrentiyuchang Beilu; 工人体育场北路4号院1949内（盈科中心南面）; mains from ¥120, sushi per piece from ¥25, 6-course menu ¥318; 🕒6-10pm; [S]Line 10 to Tuanjiehu, exit A or D) The minimalist design and customer service can feel a little cold, but legendary Běijīng chef Max Levy knows his fish, and the sushi and sashimi are as fresh as you'll find in the capital. You can watch him at work while you sip a cocktail or some sake. Reservations recommended.

MOSTO EUROPEAN $$$

Map p282 (摸石头; Mō Shítou; ☎010 5208 6030; www.mostobj.com; 3rd fl, Nali Patio, 81 Sanlitun Lu; 三里屯路81号D308 那里花园3F; mains ¥98-298, 5-course tasting menu ¥298; 🕒11.30am-3pm & 5.30-10pm; [S]Line 10 to Tuanjiehu, exit A) Consistently popular, especially at lunchtimes thanks to its attractive set lunch deal (two courses for ¥95), Mosto serves up solid, well-presented dishes with a vaguely Mediterranean theme. You can sit outside on the terrace, or inside around the open kitchen. There's a good wine list, excellent desserts and attentive service. Reserve on weekends.

APRIL GOURMET DELI

Map p282 (绿叶子食品店; Lûyèzi Shípǐn Diàn; 1st fl, Lianbao Mansion, Xingfucun Zhonglu; 三里屯幸福村中路联保公寓1层; 🕒8am-midnight; [S]Line 2 to Dongsi Shitiao, exit B) April Gourmet caters for Westerners craving a taste of home. Cheese, fresh bread, butter, wine, sauces, Western soups, coffee, milk, meats and frozen food are all available. This branch stays open till midnight.

DRINKING & NIGHTLIFE

The days when Sānlǐtún was the be-all and end-all of Běijīng nightlife are long gone. These days, the main drag of Sanlitun Lu is rather tawdry – at night the

touts for massage parlours and hookers emerge – and the bars are strictly for the undiscerning. But head south of Workers Stadium Rd, beyond 'Sānlǐtún's Bar Strip', and you'll find a compound home to some of Běijīng's coolest restaurants and drinking spots. And for those wanting to hit the clubs, Courtyard 4 (just south of Gongrentiyuchang Beilu) and the Workers Stadium, are jumping areas which contain most of Běijīng's busiest nightclubs.

★JING A BREWING MICROBREWERY

Map p282 (京A Brewing Co.; www.jingabrewing.com; Courtyard 4, 1949 Hidden City, off Gongrentiyuchang Beilu; 工体北路4号院; beers ¥40-60; ⏲5pm-1am Mon-Thu, 4pm-2am Fri, 11am-2am Sat, 11am-midnight Sun; 📶; [S]Line 10 to Tuanjiehu, exit A or D) Though Jing A has been brewing in Běijīng at Big Smoke (p141) for some time, now it's finally opened its own taproom. Set within the classy red-brick 1949 precinct, the bar has earned its reputation as a producer of some of Běijīng's best (and most experimental) beers, with a fantastic selection of ales using local ingredients.

There are 15 beers on tap, featuring a mix of core and seasonal ales, and a few guest breweries. Signature beers include the Flying Fist IPA and Worker's Pale Ale, but keep an eye out for the Airpocalypse IPA, whose price fluctuates in accordance to the air pollution index – the more polluted, the cheaper it is! Happy hour is ¥10 off beers to 7pm.

There's good food too, from kimchi Ruben sandwiches to pan-fried Yunnan cheese and air-dried Sichuan pork.

★GREAT LEAP BREWING BREWERY

Map p282 (GLB #12; 大跃啤酒; Dàyuè Píjiǔ; ☎010 5712 4376; www.greatleapbrewing.com; Ziming Mansion, Unit 101, 12 Xinzhong Jie; 新中街乙12号紫铭大厦101室; beers ¥25-50, burgers from ¥40; ⏲11am-1am Sun-Thu, 11am-2am Fri & Sat; 📶; [S]Line 2 to Dongsi Shitiao, exit B) An entirely different beast to its original *hútòng* bar (p97), Great Leap's flagship venue is more your classic North American brewpub. It's a hot spot for local expats, and anyone in search of a decent beer, and its wooden benches and long bar get rammed come lunch time and nights. There's 20 or so of its beers on tap, with a selection of IPAs, pale, blonde and white ales, and some inventive seasonals, all brewed on-site.

The burgers are another reason to visit, especially the cheeseburger; don't miss the weekday lunch specials where you get a free beer with every burger.

There's a third branch that does fantastic pizzas, but it's a tad out of the way.

★PARLOR COCKTAIL BAR

Map p282 (香; Xiāng; ☎010 8444 4135; 39-9 Xingfu'ercun, Xindong Lu; 新东路幸福二村39-9号; cocktails from ¥65; ⏲6pm-late; [S]Line 2 to Dongsi Shitiao, exit B) Discretely positioned away from Sānlǐtún's main strip, Parlor aims to recreate the atmosphere of an old-school Shànghǎi speakeasy. Here you'll get bartenders in bow ties mixing originals and classics, a solid wooden bar counter and the roaring 1920s decor. To find it, walk to the end of an alley leading into a car park just before the Bank of China on Xingfu'ercun and look for the wooden door and sign.

There's also upstairs seating, with jazz bands and swing classes on Sunday to Thursday nights.

ARROW FACTORY BREWING MICROBREWERY

Map p282 (箭厂啤酒; Jiàn Píjiǔchǎng; ☎010 8532 5335; www.arrowfactorybrewing.com; 1 Xindong Lu, on Liangmaqiao Lu; 新东路1号外交公寓亮马河南岸; ⏲11.30am-midnight Tue-Thu, to 2am Fri & Sat; 📶; [S]Line 10 to Agricultural Exhibition Center) The new flagship Arrow Factory taphouse is in a leafy residential riverside street with around 15 beers on tap. All are brewed on-site with a stellar selection of core and seasonal IPAs and pale ales being the standouts, as well as decent Belgian and German beers. All go beautifully with their selection of handmade sausages (German wurst, English bangers and Spanish chorizo; from ¥33), steak sandwiches and pies. There's a rooftop terrace come summer.

SLOW BOAT BREWERY BREWERY

Map p282 (www.slowboatbrewery.com; 6 Sanlitun Nanlu; [S]Line 10 to Tuanjiehu, exit A or D) Opened in 2016, this Slow Boat location is a wonderful addition to this popular pocket of Sānlǐtún. In comparison to its intimate *hútòng* bar (p78), this is a behemoth, with three levels of taprooms, a rooftop and streetside seating. All beers are brewed on-site and pulled fresh from the tank. Their signature awesome burgers are also here.

THE LOCAL PUB

Map p282 (☎010 6591 9525; www.beijing-local.com; Lot 10, Courtyard 4, off Gongrentiyuchang Beilu; 工体北路4号机电院; beers from ¥20, mixed drinks from ¥40; ⏲11am-2am; 📶; [S]Line 10 to Tuanjiehu, exit A or D) Living up to its name, this indeed is a local favourite with a quality selection of craft and local beers on tap, good mixed drinks, a busy pool table and seriously good food. Live sports are a big feature, and it's one of the most reliable places to catch AFL, Premier League and American sports. Happy hour is 4pm to 8pm.

JANES + HOOCH COCKTAIL BAR

Map p282 (☎010 6503 2757; www.janeshooch.com; Lot 10, Courtyard 4, off Gongrentiyuchang Beilu; 工体北路4号机电院; cocktails from ¥80; ⏲7pm-2am; [S]Line 10 to Tuanjiehu, exit A or D) Coming in at number 18 for the 2016 *Asia's 50 Best Bars*, Janes + Hooch is the bar of the moment, and as popular with locals as it is with Westerners. Sip your drink at the stylish, dark-lit long bar on the ground floor, or head upstairs and grab a table. The drinks are quality, with some good originals, and the service efficient. Happy hour runs 7pm to 9pm.

REVOLUTION BAR

Map p282 (革命酒吧; Gémìng Jiǔbā; ☎010 6415 8776; west side of Yashow Market, Gongti Beilu; 工体北路雅秀市场西侧; beers from ¥35, cocktails from ¥45; ⏲5pm-1am Sun & Mon, 5pm-2am Tue-Sat; [S]Line 10 to Tuanjiehu, exit A) Amenable and cute cubbyhole of a bar with a Cultural Revolution theme: photos of Mao adorn the walls and patriotic Chinese movies from the 1960s play on the TV. But the strong selection of cocktails and single-malt whiskies, all reasonably priced, are a bigger draw than the Chairman. Happy hour is 5pm to 8pm. Great pizzas too.

ANCHOR PUB

Map p282 (锚, Máo; 65 Xingfucun Zhonglu; 幸福村中路65 杰座大厦底层; ⏲5pm-late; [S]Line 2 to Dongsi Shitiao, exit B) Run by mad Arsenal supporter Sherry, this pint-sized English pub is named after her local in Bristol. It's popular mostly for live Premier League games, but it's a fun little pub anytime (¥20 pints before 10pm). Keep an eye out for her impressive collection of signed memorabilia.

SPARK CLUB

Map p282 (☎010 6587 1501; B108, The Place, Guanghua Lu; 光华路9号世贸天阶B108; entry ¥80-200; ⏲10pm-late Fri & Sat, 10pm-2.30am Sun-Tue, 10pm-3.30am Wed & Thu; [S]Line 6 to Dongdaqiao, exit D, or Line 1 to Yong'anli, exit B) Despite its incongruous location in the basement of a shopping mall, Spark is where the beautiful people come to groove to mainstream house and electro, often spun by overseas DJs. It's the Běijīng branch of the Taiwanese club chain. The entry fee drops during the week.

LANTERN CLUB

Map p282 (灯笼俱乐部; Dēnglóng Jùlèbù; Gongrentiyuchang Xilu; 工人体育场西门向北100米; entry ¥30-100; ⏲10am-6am Thu-Sun; [S]Line 2 to Dongsi Shitiao, exit C) This semi-underground dance club has a roster of the best local DJs (and occasional foreign guests) spinning a more eclectic mix of techno and house than you'll hear anywhere else. The ticket price varies depending on who's playing.

XIÙ BAR

Map p282 (秀酒吧; Xiù Jiǔbā; 6th fl, Park Hyatt, Yintai Centre, 2 Jianguomenwai Dajie; 建国门外大街2银泰中心柏悦酒店6层; cocktails from ¥80; ⏲6pm-3am; [S]Lines 1, 10 to Guomao, exit C) With its fantastic, open wood-decked terrace, traditional *hútòng*-courtyard architecture and luxurious water features, the Park Hyatt's 6th-floor drinking spot beats other swish hotel bars come summer. It would be a calm, almost serene, space were it not for the crowd of flush locals and expats who assemble here. The cocktails are decent without being Běijīng's best and there's live music and DJs.

MIX CLUB

Map p282 (密克斯; Mìkèsī; ☎010 6530 2889; www.clubmixchina.com; Workers Stadium, North Gate, Gongrentiyuchang Beilu; 工人体育场北路，工人体育场北门; entry free-¥50; ⏲8pm-6am; [S]Line 2 to Dongsi Shitiao, exit C) Mainstream hip-hop and R&B are the drawcards at this ever-popular nightclub with big-name DJs making occasional guest appearances and a packed dance floor. It attracts a younger clientele.

VICS CLUB

Map p282 (威克斯; Wēikèsī; ☎010 5293 0333; Workers Stadium, North Gate, Gongrentiyuchang Beilu; 工人体育场北路，工人体育场北门; entry Sun-Thu ¥50, Fri & Sat ¥100; ⏲8.30pm-5am; [S]Line 2 to Dongsi Shitiao, exit C, or Line 10 to Tuanjiehu, exit D) Not the most sophisticated nightclub, but a favourite with the young (and older and sleazy) crowd for many years now, which makes it some sort of an institution. The tunes are mostly standard R&B and hip-hop and there's an infamous ladies' night on Wednesdays (free drinks for women before midnight).

It's located inside the north gate of the Workers Stadium. The attached **V Sports Bar** (Map p282; 工人体育场北路，工人体育场北门; beer from ¥30, cocktails from ¥50; ⏲11.30am-2am) has pool and darts and is a good place to catch live football on one if its many screens.

STONE BOAT
BAR

Map p282 (石舫咖啡; Shífǎng Kāfēi; ☎010 6501 9986; Rìtán Park; beers & coffee from ¥20, cocktails from ¥40; ⏲10am-8pm; [S]Lines 1, 2 to Jianguomen, exit B) Overlooking a picturesque pond is this lovely, low-key bar, with mellow live music and an outside area where you can sip your drink beneath the trees. During the day, it's an equally pleasant cafe. To get here after the park shuts, tell the guards at the south gate where you're going and they'll let you in.

MIGAS BAR
BAR

Map p282 (米家思; Mǐ Jiā Sī; ☎010 5208 6061; www.migasbj.com; 6th fl, Nali Patio, 81 Sanlitunbei Lu; 三里屯北路81号那里花园6层; mains from ¥98; ⏲noon-2.30pm & 6-10.30pm, bar 6pm-late; 📶; [S]Line 10 to Tuanjiehu, exit A) A good-quality Spanish restaurant, cosy bar and enticing rooftop terrace are three reasons why Migas remains one of the most popular venues in the area. During summer, the terrace offers cocktails and city views and is jammed at weekends. There are DJs on Fridays and live music on Tuesdays, while the separate restaurant is almost as busy most evenings.

The tapas are excellent, and the three-course set lunch (¥95) is a solid deal, while its brunch buffet (¥268) is popular on weekends.

PADDY O'SHEA'S
SPORTS BAR

Map p282 (爱尔兰酒吧; Aì'érlán Jiǔbā; ☎010 6415 6389; www.paddyosheasbeijing.com; 28 Dongzhimenwai Dajie; 东直门外大街28号; beers from ¥25; ⏲11.30am-2am; 📶; [S]Line 2 to Dongzhimen, exit C) One of the top spots in Běijīng for watching sport on TV (Premiership football especially, but also American sports, AFL, rugby and Formula 1), Paddy's has a large number of screens, allowing for multi-channel viewing. Though be aware streams can drop out. It's about as Irish as a Guinness poster, but there's a proper bar to sit at, the service is warm and efficient and it does pub grub.

There's a good range of beers on tap, and a choice of spirits too. Happy hour is 2pm to 8pm Monday to Friday and till 6pm weekends. There's a handy Indian restaurant upstairs to order from too. It's a 15-minute walk from Dongzhimen station.

DESTINATION
GAY & LESBIAN

Map p282 (目的地; Mùdìdì; www.bjdestination.com; 7 Gongrentiyuchang Xilu; 工体西路7号; entry ¥60; ⏲8pm-late; [S]Lines 2, 6 to Chaoyangmen, exit A) A club for boys who like boys and girls who want a night off from them; check out the teddy bears behind the bar. The rough-hewn and concrete-walled interior doesn't stop Destination being packed on weekends. But then, as Běijīng's only genuine gay club, it doesn't have to worry about any competition.

SELL DRUNK SUPERMARKET
BAR

Map p282 (4 Ritan Beilu; 日坛北路4号; pint ¥20; ⏲noon-late; [S]Line 6 to Dongdaqiao, exit D) A muddled name that makes sense after a few drinks, this bar has a good choice of craft beers in the fridge and a few on tap, best enjoyed at tables on its streetside terrace.

LOCAL KNOWLEDGE

CRAFT BEERS & BARBEQUE

A revolution began in Běijīng in 2010. For once, it didn't concern politics. Instead, it was all about beer. When Great Leap Brewing (p143) and Slow Boat Brewery (p143) started making their own ales from 100% local ingredients, it marked the emergence of the capital's very own craft breweries. Now, at least five microbreweries are operating in Běijīng.

Great Leap, Slow Boat Brewery, Jing A Brewing (p143), and Arrow Factory Brewing (p143) are by far the best of the North American expat brewers, but Chinese microbreweries such as NBeer (p122) and Panda Brew (p98), among others, have risen to the challenge and produce equally impressive ales.

And with craft beers increasing popular with both locals and foreigners, there are more and more places around town where you can sample their ales.

CHOCOLATE
CLUB

Map p282 (巧克力; Qiǎokèlì; ☎010 8561 3988; 19 Ritan Beilu; 日坛北路19号; ⏲9pm-6am; [S]Lines 2, 6 to Chaoyangmen, exit A) In an area known as Little Moscow (just north of Rìtán Park) is this over-the-top club with gold-themed decor, cheesy dance shows (10pm and midnight) and party techno tunes. A shot of vodka starts at ¥20, beers at ¥30. It gets going after midnight. If you're in a group, do as as the Russians do and order a bottle of vodka (from ¥288).

TREE
BAR

Map p282 (树酒吧; Shù Jiǔbā; ☎010 6415 1954; www.treebeijing.com.cn; 43 Sanlitun Beijie; 三里屯北街43号; beers from ¥20; ⏲10am-2am; 📶; [S]Line 2 to Tuanjiehu, exit A) A low-key, long-term favourite, the Tree attracts a mix of locals, expats and tourists. There's a fine selection of Belgian beers (from ¥45) and the thin-crust pizzas (from ¥55), cooked in a wood-fired oven, have long been the best feature of the menu. Around the corner is its close relative **Nearby the Tree** (树旁边酒吧; Shù Pángbiān Jiǔbā; Map p282; Xingfu Sancun Yixiang, off Sanlitunbei Lu; 三里屯北路幸福三村一巷; beers from ¥20; ⏲noon-2am; 📶; [S]Line 10 to Tuanjiehu, exit A).

☆ ENTERTAINMENT

WORKERS' STADIUM
SPECTATOR SPORT

Map p282 (工人体育场; Gongren Tiyuchang; North Gate, Workers Stadium, Gongrentiyuchang Beilu; 工人体育场北路， 工人体育场北门; [S]Line 2 to Dongsi Shitiao, exit C or Line 10 to Tuanjiehu, exit D) Built in 1959, Běijīng's main soccer stadium is home to Běijīng Guó'ān (www.fcguoan.com), the capital's sole football (soccer) team. It also hosts concerts by touring big-name bands. Look for the socialist-realist sporting statues that surround the stadium.

CHÁOYÁNG THEATRE
ACROBATICS

Map p282 (朝阳剧场; Cháoyáng Jùchǎng; ☎010 6507 2421; www.bjcyjc.com/en; 36 Dongsanhuan Beilu; 东三环北路36号; tickets ¥200-880; ⏲performances 3.50pm, 5.30pm & 7pm; [S]Lines 6, 10 to Hujialou, exit C1) The Cháoyáng Theatre hosts visiting acrobatic troupes from around China who fill the stage with plate spinning and hoop jumping. It's an accessible place for foreign visitors, and tickets are available from its box office, but often bookable through your hotel.

POLY PLAZA INTERNATIONAL THEATRE
CLASSICAL MUSIC

Map p282 (保利大厦国际剧院; Bǎolì Dàshà Guójì Jùyuàn; ☎010 6506 5343; www.blpw.cn; 14 Dongzhimen Nandajie; 东直门南大街14号; tickets ¥80-1200; ⏲performances 7.30pm; [S]Line 2 to Dongsi Shitiao, exit B) Right by Dongsi Shitiao subway station, this venue hosts a range of performances, including ballet, classical music, opera and traditional Chinese folk music. It also puts on an increasing number of works by foreign playwrights.

798 LIVE HOUSE
LIVE MUSIC

(798剧场LiveHouse, 798 Jùchǎng Live House; 4 Jiuxianqiao Lu, 798 Art District; 朝阳区 酒仙桥路4号大山子艺术区; [S]Line 14 to Jiangtai, exit A) Within a former factory is this mid-sized venue that retains its industrial set-up while equipped with a start-of-the-art sound and lighting system. It hosts local bands most weekends.

MEGABOX
CINEMA

Map p282 (美嘉欢乐影城; Měijiā Huānlè Yǐngchéng; ☎010 6417 6118; B1 Fl Sanlitun Village South, 19 Sanlitun Lu; 三里屯路19号三里屯Village南区地下1层; tickets ¥80-120; ⏲performances noon-midnight; [S]Line 2 to Tuanjiehu, exit A) The most convenient place to catch English-language Hollywood blockbusters, MegaBox is a multiplex cinema in the basement of the trendy Sānlǐtún Village (p147) shopping mall. It always shows at least one or two English-language films and offers an experience almost identical to cinemas in the West (although don't expect much English from the attendants who work here).

🛍 SHOPPING

The Cháoyáng district has some of the swankiest malls in town, as well as many of the most popular markets for visitors, including the Silk Market and Alien's Street Market, two multifloor indoor clothes and souvenir markets that are heaving at weekends. Key areas for purchases are Sānlǐtún and Guómào, but there are shops of all descriptions spread across the district. Pānjiāyuán Market is on the edge of Cháoyáng and is the city's premier souvenir market. 798 Art District is home to some boutique art stores that have some good shopping.

★SHARD BOX STORE JEWELLERY

(慎德阁; Shèndégé; ☎010 5135 7638; shardboxs@hotmail.com; 2 Jiangtai Rd; 将台路2号; ⌚9am-7pm; [S]Line 14 to Jiangtai) Using porcelain fragments from Ming and Qing dynasty vases that were destroyed during the Cultural Revolution, this fascinating family-run store creates beautiful and unique shard boxes, bottles and jewellery. The boxes range from the tiny (¥50), for storing rings or cufflinks, to the large (¥780). It also repairs and sells jewellery, both handmade and sourced from Tibet and Mongolia. Check out the photos of the former US presidents who've visited here.

It's located behind the Holiday Inn Lido.

★PĀNJIĀYUÁN MARKET ANTIQUES, MARKET

(潘家园古玩市场; Pānjiāyuán Gǔwán Shìchǎng; west of Panjiayuan Qiao; 潘家园桥西侧; ⌚8.30am-6pm Mon-Fri, 4.30am-6pm Sat & Sun; [S]Line 10 to Panjiayuan, exit B) Hands down the best place in Běijīng to shop for *yìshù* (arts), *gōngyì* (crafts) and *gǔwán* (antiques). Some stalls open every day, but the market is at its biggest and most lively on weekends, when you can find everything from calligraphy and cigarette ad posters, to Buddha heads, ceramics, Qing dynasty–style furniture and Tibetan carpets. It's also one of the best places to pick up authentic Cultural Revolution propaganda posters.

Pānjiāyuán hosts around 3000 dealers and up to 50,000 visitors a day, all scoping for antiques. The serious collectors are early birds, swooping here at dawn to snare precious relics. If you want to join them, an early start is essential. You probably aren't going to find that rare Qianlong *dòucǎi* stem cup or late Yuan dynasty *qīnghuā* vase, but what's on view is still a compendium of post-1950 Chinese curios and an A to Z of Middle Kingdom knick-knacks. The market is chaotic and can be difficult if you find crowds or hard bargaining intimidating. Ignore the 'don't pay more than half' rule here – some vendors might start at 10 times the real price. Make a few rounds to compare prices and weigh it up before forking out for something.

To get here, come out of exit B at Panjiayuan subway station, then walk west for 200m to find the main entrance to the market.

SANLIPOP CLOTHING

Map p282 (☎010 8405 9225; http://sanlipop.net; 29 Sanlitun Beilu; 三里屯路北29号楼103室; ⌚11am-10pm; [S]Line 10 to Agricultural Exhibition Center, exit D2) Set up by a bunch of young Běijīngers who met in London, this tiny boutique stocks its favourite designers for both men's and women's clothing, and lifestyle accessories. Expect brands such as Maison Kitsuné, Saint James and other names you can't find in Běijīng.

UCCA DESIGN STORE CLOTHING, SOUVENIRS

(尤伦斯当代艺术中心; Yóulúnsī Dāngdài Yìshù Zhōngxīn; ☎010 5780 0224; http://ucca.org.cn/en/uccastore/; 4 Jiuxianqiao Lu, 798 Art District; 酒仙桥路4号798艺术区; ⌚10am-6pm Tue-Sun; [S]Line 14 to Jiangtai, exit A) A haven for style mavens, UCCA is the place to come for limited-edition prints and lithographs by famous local artists, as well as stylish clothes (including kidswear), jewellery, books on art and design, and all manner of quirky potential gifts and mementos. It's attached to the UCCA gallery (p135) in the 798 Art District.

ALIEN'S STREET MARKET CLOTHING

Map p282 (老番街市场; Lǎo Fān Jiē Shìchǎng; Chaowaishichang Jie; 朝外市场街; ⌚9am-7pm; [S]Lines 2, 6 to Chaoyangmen, exit A) Located just north of Rìtán Park – and part of Běijīng's 'Little Moscow' precinct – this market is packed with a huge variety of clothing, as well as heaps of accessories. You can find most things here and it's popular with visiting Russian traders, which means the clothes come in bigger sizes than usual and the vendors will greet you in Russian, and with generally less hassle. Haggling is essential.

BǍINǍOHUÌ COMPUTER MALL ELECTRONICS

Map p282 (Buy Now; 百脑汇电脑市场; Bǎinǎohuì Diànnǎo Shìchǎng; http://beijing.buynow.com.cn; 99 Chaoyangmenwai Dajie; 朝阳门外大街99号; ⌚9.30am-7.30pm; [S]Line 6 to Dongdaqiao, exit A) Three floors of gadgetry, including computers, iPods, MP3 players, blank CDs, DVDs, gaming gear, software and other accessories. The prices are fairly competitive and you can bargain here, but don't expect too much of a reduction. There are also a number of shops that are good places to pick up mobile phones and local SIM cards.

SĀNLǏTÚN VILLAGE MALL

Map p282 (三里屯太古里; 19 Sanlitun Lu; 三里屯路19号; ⌚10am-10pm; [S]Line 10 to Tuanjiehu, exit A) This eye-catching collection of mid-sized malls is a shopping and architectural highlight of this part of the city. The Village (known officially as Taikooli; Tàigǔlǐ;

太古里) looms over what was once a seedy strip of dive bars and has transformed the area into a hot spot for locals and foreigners alike. There are two parts to the complex: South Village and North Village.

The South Village was completed a few years back and is home to Běijīng's first Apple store, the world's largest Adidas shop and a number of midrange Western clothing stores, as well as cafes, restaurants and the multiplex cinema MegaBox. Nearby North Village is home to more high-end labels and local designer boutiques, and is set beside Běijīng's fancy-pants boutique hotel Opposite House.

SILK MARKET CLOTHING, SOUVENIRS

Map p282 (秀水市场; Xiùshuǐ Shìchǎng; 14 Dongdaqiao Lu; 东大桥路14号; ⏰9.30am-9pm; [S]Line 1 to Yonganli, exit A1) The six-storey Silk Market is wildly popular with package tourists here for fake clothing, bags, electronics and jewellery. It's more upmarket than it once was, namely because many vendors were being hit by lawsuits from top-name brands tired of being counterfeited on such a huge scale. The silk, which you'll find on the 3rd floor, is one of the few genuine items on sale here.

With coach loads of tourists descending on the market daily, effective bargaining is difficult. But this is a good place for cashmere, T-shirts, jeans, shirts, skirts and, of course, silk. There's a food court on the top floor.

3.3 SHOPPING CENTRE MALL

Map p282 (服饰大厦; Fúshì Dàshà; 33 Sanlitun Beijie; 三里屯北街33号; ⏰11am-11pm; [S]Lines 10 to Tuanjiehu or Agricultural Exhibition Center) With its collection of trendy boutiques and accessories stores, as well as massage and manicure salons, this mall, sandwiched between the North and South blocks of the even trendier Sānlǐtún Village, caters for Běijīng's bright young things. Prices are accordingly high. But with 300 shops here, it's good window-shopping territory.

SPORTS & ACTIVITIES

KORYO TOURS TRAVEL AGENCY

Map p282 (☎010 6416 7544; www.koryogroup.com; 27 Beisanlitun Nan; [S]Line 2 to Dongsi Shitiao, exit C, or Line 10 to Tuanjiehu, exit A) Long-established and reputable outfit that organises highly rated tours to North Korea.

DRAGONFLY THERAPEUTIC RETREAT MASSAGE

Map p282 (☎010 8529 6331; www.dragonfly.net.cn; Kerry Centre, 1 Guanghua Lu; 嘉里中心光华路1号; 1hr massage from ¥188; ⏰10am-11pm; [S]Line 10 to Jintaixizhao, exit A) Swish, professional operation located in the basement of the Kerry Centre.

BODHI THERAPEUTIC RETREAT MASSAGE

Map p282 (菩提会所; Pútí Huìsuǒ; ☎010 6417 9595; www.bodhi.com.cn; 17 Gongrentiyuchang Beilu; 工体北路17号; ⏰11am-12.30am; [S]Line 2 to Dongsi Shitiao, exit B) The serene setting, just moments away from the madness of Běijīng's traffic, helps you shift gears straightaway and that's before one of the many massage therapists here gets to work in a comfy, private room. Bodhi offers aromatherapy, Ayurvedic, Thai- and Chinese-style massage, as well as great foot reflexology massages and a wide range of facial treatments.

There's free snacks and drinks, and with TVs in all the rooms, you can lie back and watch a DVD while being pummelled into shape. Prices start at ¥198 for a basic full-body massage, although Thai and Ayurvedic massages cost ¥348. Massages are sometimes discounted during weekday afternoons.

HAPPY MAGIC WATER PARK SWIMMING

(水立方嬉水乐园; Shuǐlìfāng Xīshuǐ Lèyuán; ☎010 8437 8966; www.water-cube.com/en/sights/waterpark; 11 Tianchen Donglu, Olympic Park; 天辰东路11号[], Beijing National Aquatics Center, 国家游泳中心; water park adult/child from ¥200/160, swimming only ¥60; ⏰10am-8pm; [S]Line 8 to Olympic Sports Center, exit B2) Unlike most of the 2008 Olympics venues, Běijīng's National Aquatics Centre, aka the Water Cube, has found a new lease of life post-Olympics. The otherworldly, bubble-like structure now houses Běijīng's largest indoor water park. It's a fave with children, who can negotiate neon plastic slides, tunnels, water jets and pools, all set alongside elaborate, surreal underwater styling.

There's a lazy river, a 40ft free-fall drop inside a plastic tube, and a wave pool designed to mimic the ocean. The park is about 7km north of the city centre.

JĪNGHUÁ WŬSHÙ ASSOCIATION MARTIAL ARTS

Map p282 (京华武术协会; Jīnghuá Wǔshù Xiéhuì; ☎010 6410 4198; Basement, Pulse Club, Kempinski Hotel, Liangmaqiao Lu; 亮马桥路凯宾斯基地下一层脉搏俱乐部; ⏰3-4pm & 4.15-

"GUÓ'ĀN, GUÓ'ĀN, BĚIJĪNG GUÓ'ĀN!"

While you'll rarely see kids playing soccer on the streets of Běijīng (basketball being the main game of choice), watching soccer is far more popular. Until recently, Chinese football fans contented themselves with viewing the big European leagues on TV. Now, though, increasing numbers of people are going to see a live game in the Chinese Super League, China's premier competition. In Běijīng, that means following Běijīng Guó'ān (www.fcguoan.com), the capital's sole team. Although it lacks the cash and star names of Guǎngzhōu Evergrande and Shànghǎi Shēnhuā, it is still one of China's most successful teams. Best of all, it has a passionate fan base and draws large crowds for its home games at the Workers Stadium (p146). It's not unusual for over 30,000 spectators to attend big games. Going to see one before hitting the bars and clubs in the area makes a fun night out for footie fans, even if the standard of football isn't that high.

The season runs from March until November. Match days can be Thursday, Friday, Saturday or Sunday; kick-offs are usually 7.30pm. You can find Guó'ān's fixtures in English on www.worldfootball.net. Tickets are sold online through Chinese-language websites, or over the phone (Chinese only), but sell out very quickly through these official channels. Many people opt to just go to the stadium an hour or so before kick-off and buy tickets off ticket touts, who charge at least double or triple the face value of the ticket. This can run around ¥100 to ¥150 per ticket.

If you're interested in playing football while you're in Běijīng, contact the guys who run China Club Football (www.clubfootball.com.cn).

5.15pm Sat & Sun; Ⓢ Line 10 to Liangmaqiao, exit B) Run from the gym at Pulse Club in the basement of the building next to Kempinski Hotel, classes here are held in English and are given by teachers trained in traditional Shàolín forms. *Wǔshù, qìgōng* and taichi are all taught here. Ten classes costs ¥1500; a single class is ¥180. There are classes for kids (five years and over), too.

If you're not staying at the Kempinski, you can use the Pulse Health Club for ¥300 a day. Aerobics, yoga and belly-dancing classes are available, as are squash courts.

YOGA YARD   YOGA
Map p282 (瑜珈苑; Yújiā Yuàn; ☑010 6413 0774; www.yogayard.com; 6th fl, 17 Gongrentiyuchang Beilu; 工体北路17号6层; ⊘7am-7.45pm; Ⓢ Line 2 to Dongsi Shitiao, exit B) This friendly English-speaking centre has traditional hatha yoga classes, from beginners to advanced. Ninety-minute lessons are ¥150, but lunchtime classes are ¥100.

LE COOL ICE RINK   ICE SKATING
Map p282 (国贸溜冰场; Guómào Liūbīngchǎng; ☑010 6505 5776; Basement 2, China World Shopping Mall, 1 Jianguomenwai Dajie; 建国门外大街1号; per 90min ¥30-50; ⊘10am-10pm; Ⓢ Lines 1, 10 to Guomao, exit A) Like many of the rinks in Běijīng, Le Cool is not very big. But it's easily accessible and perfect for kids. Visit in the morning or evening if you want to avoid the crowds. Skate hire is included in the price, which varies depending on the time of day. Individual, 30-minute lessons are ¥180.

During winter there's also ice skating on the frozen Hòuhǎi Lakes.

BRIDGE SCHOOL   LANGUAGE
Map p282 (桥学校; Qiáo Xuéxiào; ☑010 6506 4409; www.bridgeschoolchina.com; Level 9, Room 903, e-Tower, Guanghua Lu; 光华路内12号楼01大厦9层; per 50min ¥110; ⊘8.30am-7pm; Ⓢ Line 10 to Jintaixizhao, exit A) Group and one-on-one classes. Has scheduled classes you can join at various language levels. Also offers a range of cultural courses from cooking to mahjong classes.

CHINA CULTURE CENTER   CULTURAL PROGRAMS
Map p282 (Kent Center; ☑weekdays 010 6432 9341, weekends 010 8420 0671; www.chinaculturecenter.org; Victoria Gardens D4, Chaoyang Gongyuan Xilu; 朝阳公园西路, 维多利亚花园 D4; Ⓢ Line 14 to Zaoying or Line 10 to Tuanjiehu, exit C) Offers a range of cultural programs taught in English and aimed squarely at foreign visitors and expats. The club also conducts popular tours around Běijīng and expeditions to other parts of China.

Summer Palace & Hǎidiàn

Neighbourhood Top Five

1 **Summer Palace** (p152) Enjoying a taste of imperial high life at this glorious former summer retreat of emperors.

2 **Fragrant Hills Park** (p158) Communing with nature and seeing the maple-leaf-covered hillsides.

3 **Wǔdàokǒu** (p159) Spending a night exploring the buzzing restaurants and clubs of Běijīng's student heartland.

4 **Běijīng Botanic Gardens** (p155) Pushing through the bamboo fronds at China's top collection of flora.

5 **Wǔtǎ Temple** (p155) Temple-hopping your way around this shrine-heavy district.

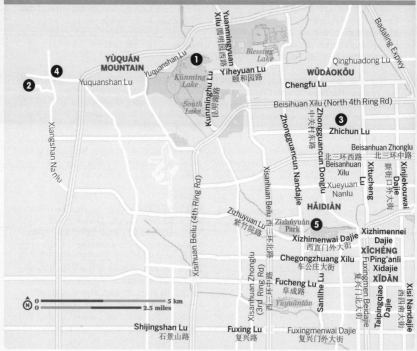

For more detail of this area see Map p281 and p286.

Explore Summer Palace & Hǎidiàn

Hǎidiàn sprawls across a huge mass of west and northwest Běijīng, so you'll need to attack it in chunks.

You could easily spend a day exploring the Summer Palace's sumptuous gardens, temples, pavilions and corridors. Don't miss climbing Longevity Hill for fine views over Běijīng. From the palace, it's a short bus or taxi ride to the Fragrant Hills Park, especially beautiful in the autumn. Nature buffs will also want to visit the nearby Botanic Gardens.

In the evening head to Wǔdàokǒu, one of Běijīng's most happening areas. Surrounded by universities, it's the capital's student heartland and home to many cafes and bars, as well as some of the most authentic Korean and Japanese restaurants in town.

Hǎidiàn is one of Běijīng's best neighbourhoods for temple-hopping. Begin at the Indian-inspired Wǔtǎ Temple. From there, walk due west to Wànshòu Temple and then northeast towards the Great Bell Temple. End the day in quiet contemplation at the superb Azure Clouds Temple inside Fragrant Hills Park.

Local Life

➡ **Hang-outs** Lush (p159) and the Bridge Café (p157) are busy around the clock.

➡ **Shopping** Wǔdàokǒu has stacks of quirky clothes shops for hipster students.

➡ **Parks** Hǎidiàn has many parks hidden beneath the tower blocks; retreat to them to avoid the urban sprawl, especially in the early evening.

Getting There & Away

➡ **Subway** Getting around Hǎidiàn is a breeze. Line 4 connects with Line 2 at Xizhimen, then runs north. When the Western Suburban Line is completed in the next few years, it will link the Summer Palace, Běijīng Botanic Gardens and Fragrant Hills Park to subway Line 10. For Wǔdàokǒu and Dazhongsi, take Line 13, which also connects with Line 2 at Xīzhímén. Line 10 runs east–west across the centre of Hǎidiàn, while Line 2 runs east–west across the south of the neighbourhood.

➡ **Bus** Useful buses include 331, which links Wǔdàokǒu with the Old Summer Palace and the Summer Palace, Běijīng Botanic Gardens, Sleeping Buddha Temple and Fragrant Hills Park. Bus 375 connects Wǔdàokǒu with Xīzhímén.

Lonely Planet's Top Tip

China has a special university (民族大学; Mínzú Dàxué) for its many ethnic minorities and the area around it is where you'll find some of the most authentic restaurants serving up their local cuisines. The hub is Weigong Jie, where you can find fantastic Dai (a minority from the far south of Yúnnán province) food, as well great Korean and Mongolian eateries. To get there, jump on Line 4 to Weigongcun and then walk south 400m.

✕ Best Places to Eat

➡ Xiǎodiàolitāng (p157)
➡ Golden Peacock (p157)
➡ Khan Baba (p157)
➡ Salang-Bang (p158)

For reviews, see p157.➡

🍷 Best Place to Drink

➡ Lush (p159)
➡ La Bamba (p157)
➡ Wǔ (p159)

For reviews, see p159.➡

◉ Best Temples

➡ Wànshòu Temple (p154)
➡ Wǔtǎ Temple (p155)
➡ Azure Clouds Temple (p158)
➡ Great Bell Temple (p156)

For reviews, see p152.➡

TOP SIGHT
SUMMER PALACE

The splendid regal encampment of the Summer Palace (颐和园; Yíhé Yuán) in the northwest of town is one of Běijīng's must-see sights. This former playground for the imperial court fleeing the insufferable summer torpor of the old Imperial City is a marvel of landscaping: a wonderful, over-the-top mix of temples, gardens, pavilions, lakes, bridges, gate towers and corridors. It's a fine place just to amble around in the sunshine, but is also packed with stunning individual sights.

It might sound like a contradiction visiting the Summer Palace in winter, but if you do so you'll get to see the splendid spectacle of a frozen Kūnmíng Lake. You'll also be surrounded by fewer people. But whenever you visit, try to avoid weekends and public holidays as the crowds are intense.

DON'T MISS

- Longevity Hill
- Long Corridor

PRACTICALITIES

- 颐和园; Yíhé Yuán
- Map p286, C1
- 19 Xinjian Gongmen; 新建宫门19号
- Apr-Oct ¥30, through ticket ¥60, Nov-Mar ¥20, through ticket ¥50, audio guide ¥40
- 🕐7am-7pm, sights 8am-5pm summer, 8.30am-4.30pm winter
- [S]Xiyuan or Beigongmen

Hall of Benevolence & Longevity

The main building at ground level, this **hall** (仁寿殿; Rénshòu Diàn; Map p286) sits by the east gate and houses a hardwood throne. Look for the bronze animals that decorate the courtyard in front, including the mythical *qílín* (a hybrid animal that appeared on Earth only at times of harmony).

Kūnmíng Lake

Three-quarters of the parkland in the palace is water, made up of Kūnmíng Lake (Kūnmíng Hú). Check out the extravagant **Marble Boat** (清晏舫; Qīngyuàn Chuán; Map p286) moored on the northwestern shore. First built in 1755, it was restored in 1893 on the orders of Empress Cixi (using money meant to go towards building ships for the Chinese Navy). Much of it is actually wood that has been painted to look like marble. Nearby are fine Qing dynasty boathouses and the **Gate Tower of the Cloud-Retaining Eaves** (宿云檐城关; Sùyúnyán Chéngguān; Map p286), which once housed an ancient silver statue of Guanyu (God of War).

Boats ply the lake (¥15) between April and October, running from the northern shore to South Lake Island, home to the **Dragon King Temple** (龙王庙; Lóngwáng Miào; Map p286), where royalty came to pray to the Dragon King's fearsome statue for rain in times of drought. But you can also hire your own pedalo (four/six people ¥80/100 per hour, ¥300 deposit) or electric-powered boat (¥120 per hour, ¥400 deposit) to sail around at your own pace.

The Long Corridor

Awesome in its conception and execution, the **Long Corridor** (长廊; Cháng Láng; Map p286) is absolutely unmissable. Open at the sides but covered with a roof to shield the emperors from the elements, and with four pavilions along the way, it stretches for more than 700m towards the foot of Longevity Hill. Its beams, the pavilion walls and some of the ceiling are decorated with 14,000 intricate paintings depicting scenes from Chinese history and myths, as well as classic literary texts. Your neck will ache from all that staring upwards, but the pain is worth it.

Longevity Hill

Rearing up by the side of Kūnmíng Lake and at the far end of the Long Corridor, the slopes of this 60m-high hill are covered in temples and pavilions, all arranged on a north–south axis. The most prominent and important are the **Buddhist Fragrance Pavilion** (佛香阁; Fóxiāng Gé; Map p286) and the **Cloud Dispelling Hall** (排云殿; Páiyún Diàn; Map p286), which are connected by corridors. Awaiting you at the peak of the hill is the **Buddhist Temple of the Sea of Wisdom** (智慧海; Zhìhuì Hǎi; Map p286), featuring glazed tiles (many sadly damaged) depicting Buddha. On a clear day there are splendid views of Běijīng from here.

West Causeway

A great way to escape the crowds who converge here is to strike out along the **West Causeway** (西堤; Xīdī; Map p286) and then do a circuit of the lake by returning along the east shore. The causeway is lined with delightful willow and mulberry trees, and along the way you'll come across the grey and white marble **Jade Belt Bridge** (玉带桥; Yùdài Qiáo; Map p286), which dates from the 18th century. There's also the graceful **17-Arch Bridge** (十七孔桥; Shíqīkǒng Qiáo; Map p286), which links the east shore to South Lake Island.

Wénchāng Gallery

South of the main entrance, come to the **Wénchāng Gallery** (文昌阁; Wénchāng Gé; Map p286) to take at look at Empress Cixi's handwriting (some of her calligraphy is on display), as well porcelain, bronzes and a jade gallery. Various other Qing-era artefacts are on show as well.

THE RISE & FALL & RISE OF THE SUMMER PALACE

Emperor Qianlong created the Summer Palace in 1749, on the site of what had long been a royal garden. About 100,000 workers enlarged the gardens and deepened Kūnmíng Lake, while Longevity Hill was named in honour of Qianlong's mother's 60th birthday. The palace was badly damaged by British and French soldiers at the end of the Second Opium War in 1860, and then restored by Empress Cixi, only for foreign soldiers to return in 1900 in the wake of the Boxer Rebellion. The palace was finally repaired after 1949 and the communist takeover.

The original name of the Summer Palace was the romantic, but not very regal, Garden of Clear Ripples. It was Empress Cixi who redubbed it in 1888.

SIGHTS

SUMMER PALACE HISTORIC SITE

See p152.

WÀNSHÒU TEMPLE BUDDHIST TEMPLE

Map p281 (万寿寺; Wànshòu Sì; ☎00 685 697; Xisanhuan Beilu; 西三环北路; adult ¥20; ⏰9am-4.30pm Tue-Sun; [S]National Library) Ringed by a red wall on the southeastern corner of Suzhou Jie (off the 3rd Ring Rd), the tranquil, little-visited Ming dynasty Wànshòu Temple, or Longevity Temple, was originally consecrated for the storage of Buddhist texts. Its name echoes the Summer Palace's Longevity Hill (Wànshòu Shān), and the imperial entourage would stop here to quaff tea en route to and from the palace.

The temple was one of almost 50 that once lined the canal route from the western edge of the Imperial City walls (at Xīzhímén) to the Summer Palace. Now it is pretty much the only one that remains (Wǔtǎ Temple (p155) being another notable survivor). The temple fell into disrepair after the fall of the Qing dynasty in 1912, with the Wànshòu Hall burning down. Things went from bad to worse, and during the Cultural Revolution the temple served as an army barracks.

There's an interesting introduction to the history of the temple in the small hall (once the temple's Drum Tower), immediately to your left as you enter the complex. And as you walk through the Hall of the Deva Kings, which leads to the second courtyard, notice the illustration on your right that shows all the temples that once lined the canal. The names are in Chinese only, but see if you can spot the temple you're in (万寿寺) as well as neighbouring Yánqìng Temple (延庆寺; Yánqìng Sì), nearby Dragon King Temple (龙王庙; Lóngwáng Sì) and the magnificent Wǔtǎ Temple (marked on the map with its former name, 真觉寺), all of which still stand, at least in part.

The highlight of a visit here, though, is to view the prized collection of bronze Buddhist statuary in the **Buddhist Art Exhibition of Ming & Qing Dynasties**, housed in two small halls on either side of the second courtyard. The displays guide you through the Buddhist pantheon with statues of Sakyamuni, Manjusri, Amitabha, Guanyin (in bronze and *déhuà*, or white-glazed porcelain) and exotic tantric pieces. Also look out for the *kapala* bowl made from a human skull, *dorje* and *purbhas* (Tibetan ritual daggers). Further halls contain museum exhibitions devoted to Ming and Qing porcelain and jade.

Also worth checking out are the Buddhist stone and clay sculptures housed in the large unnamed central hall at the back of the second courtyard. There are four magnificent central pieces, plus a dozen or so *arhats* (Buddhist disciples) lining the flanks.

As you exit the temple, see if you can track down the nearby remains of **Yánqìng Temple** (延庆寺; Yànqìng Si; Map p281; [S]National Library) [FREE] and **Dragon King Temple** (龙王寺; Lóngwáng Sì; Map p281; [S]National Library)

LOCAL KNOWLEDGE

BRAINY BĚIJĪNG

Hǎidiàn's residents are some of the cleverest in all China. Not only are there more than 60 universities in the district, but Hǎidiàn is also home to Zhōngguāncūn, the Chinese equivalent of California's Silicon Valley.

With so many tech heads, students and academics working and living in Hǎidiàn, it's no wonder that the area has long been associated with brain power. As far back as 1937, Lao She – the father of modern Chinese literature – described the neighbourhood as an 'academic village' in his classic novel *Rickshaw Boy*.

It was the founding of **Peking University** (北京大学; Běijīng Dàxué; Map p287; [S]East Gate of Peking University) and **Qīnghuá University** (清华大学; Qīnghuá Dàxué; Map p287; [S]Wudaokou) in 1908 and 1911 respectively that set Hǎidiàn on the road to academic stardom. Still China's two most prestigious colleges, they were joined in the area by newer universities who thought they could attract students by being in the same location as their more famous counterparts. After 1949 and the founding of the People's Republic of China, government institutions were established here too.

You'll find many of Běijīng's brightest young things (and a few old ones) in the cafes and restaurants of Wǔdàokǒu. Alternatively, follow a trip to the **Arthur M Sackler Museum of Art & Archaeology** (p155) with strolling the attractive Peking University campus, where the museum is located.

WORTH A DETOUR

BĚIJĪNG BOTANIC GARDENS

Exploding with blossom in spring, the well-tended **Běijīng Botanic Gardens** (北京植物园; Běijīng Zhíwùyuán; adult ¥5, through ticket ¥50; ⏲6am-8pm Apr-Oct, last entry 7pm, 7.30am-5pm Nov-Mar, last entry 4pm; 🚌331, [S]Xiyuan or Yuanmingyuan), set against the backdrop of the Western Hills and about 1km northeast of Fragrant Hills Park, makes for a pleasant outing among bamboo fronds, pines, orchids, lilacs and China's most extensive botanic collection. Containing a rainforest house, the standout **Běijīng Botanical Gardens Conservatory** (Běijīng Zhíwùyuán Wēnshì; with Běijīng Botanical Gardens through ticket ¥50; ⏲8am-4.30pm Apr-Oct, 8.30am-4pm Nov-Mar) bursts with 3000 different varieties of plants.

About a 15-minute walk from the front gate (follow the signs), but still within the grounds of the gardens, is **Sleeping Buddha Temple** (卧佛寺; Wòfó Sì; adult ¥5, or entry with through ticket; ⏲8am-4.30pm summer, 8.30am-4pm winter). The temple, first built during the Tang dynasty, houses a huge reclining effigy of Sakyamuni weighing 54 tonnes; it's said to have 'enslaved 7000 people' in its casting.

On the eastern side of the gardens is the **Cao Xueqin Memorial** (曹雪芹纪念馆; Cáo Xuěqín Jìniàn Guǎn; 39 Zhengbaiqi Cun; 正白旗村; ⏲8.30am-4.30pm Apr-Oct, 9am-4pm Nov-Mar; 👪) [FREE], where Cao Xueqin lived in his latter years. Cao (1715–63) is credited with penning the classic *Dream of the Red Mansions*, a vast and prolix family saga set in the Qing period. Making a small buzz in the west of the gardens is the little **China Honey Bee Museum** (中国蜜蜂博物馆; Zhōngguó Mìfēng Bówùguǎn), open 8.30am to 4.30pm March to October.

[FREE], further east along the canal. To walk from here to Wǔtǎ Temple takes around 20 minutes. Note that on Wednesdays the first 200 visitors get in for free.

WǓTǍ TEMPLE — BUDDHIST TEMPLE

Map p281 (五塔寺; Wǔtǎ Sì; 24 Wutasi Cun; 五塔寺村24号; adult ¥20, audio guide ¥10; ⏲9am-4pm Tue-Sun; [S]National Library) The distinctive Wǔtǎ Temple (Five Pagoda Temple) is a hugely rewarding place to visit. That's not just because of its unusual architectural style – the temple is topped by its five attractive namesake pagodas and appears at first to owe more to Indian temple design than Chinese – but also because of the magnificent collection of stone carvings contained within its grounds.

Previously known as Zhēnjué Temple (真觉寺; Zhēnjué Sì), the exterior of the main hall is decorated with *dorje*, hundreds of images of Buddha and legions of beasts, amid traces of red pigment. During Ming times the temple ranged to at least six halls, all later tiled in yellow during Qing times; the terrace where the Big Treasure Hall once stood can still be seen. The temple, dating from 1473, is highly unusual for Běijīng, and well worth a visit in itself, but the highlight here is the extraordinary collection of stone carvings, some housed carefully in buildings at the back of the complex but many just scattered around the temple grounds. Pieces you might stumble across include gravestones, animal statues, carved human figures, stone stele and some enormous *bìxì* (mythical tortoise-like dragons often seen in Confucian temples). The pieces were all recovered from various places in Běijīng and put here for their protection during the latter end of the last century. Most are Qing and Ming dynasty, but there are a number of Yuan, Tang, Jin and even Eastern Han dynasty pieces, some of which are almost 2000 years old. Many, although not all, have explanatory captions in English; those captioned in Chinese only do at least have the date of origin written in numerals.

On Wednesdays the first 200 visitors get in for free. Take exit C at the National Library subway stop and then take the first left to get here. Note, you can enter the north gate of Běijīng Zoo from here. Cross the canal over the decorative arched bridge.

ARTHUR M SACKLER MUSEUM OF ART & ARCHAEOLOGY — MUSEUM

Map p287 (赛克勒考古与艺术博物馆; Sàikèlè Kǎogǔ Yǔ Yìshù Bówùguǎn; Peking University; ⏲9am-4.30pm Tue-Sun; [S]East Gate of Peking University) [FREE] Excellent collection of relics brought together on the campus of Peking University (enter via the west gate), although some English captions would be nice given

WORTH A DETOUR

OLD SUMMER PALACE

Located northwest of the city centre, the **Old Summer Palace** (圆明园; Yuánmíng Yuán; ☎010 6261 6375; 28 Qinghua Xilu; 清华西路28号; adult ¥10, through ticket ¥25, map ¥6; ⏲7am-6pm Apr-Oct, 7am-5.30pm Nov-Mar; [S]Yuanmingyuan) was laid out in the 12th century. The ever-capable Jesuits were subsequently employed by Emperor Qianlong in the 18th century to fashion European-style palaces for the gardens, incorporating elaborate fountains and baroque statuary. In 1860, during the Second Opium War, British and French troops torched and looted the palace, an event forever inscribed in Chinese history books as a low point in China's humiliation by foreign powers. Most of the wooden palace buildings were burned down in the process and little remains, but the hardier Jesuit-designed European Palace buildings were made of stone, and a melancholic tangle of broken columns and marble chunks survives. Note: to see these remains, you need to buy the more expensive 'through ticket'.

The subdued marble ruins of the **Palace Buildings Scenic Area** (Xīyánglóu Jǐngqū) can be mulled over in the **Eternal Spring Garden** (Chángchūn Yuán) in the northeast of the park, near the east gate.

The **Great Fountain Ruins** (Dàshuǐfǎ) themselves are considered the best-preserved relics. Built in 1759, the main building was fronted by a lion-head fountain. Standing opposite is the **Guānshuǐfǎ**, five large stone screens embellished with European carvings of military flags, armour, swords and guns. The screens were discovered in the grounds of Peking University in the 1970s and later restored to their original positions. Just east of the Great Fountain Ruins stood a four-pillar archway, chunks of which remain.

West of the Great Fountain Ruins are the vestiges of the **Hǎiyàntáng Reservoir** (Hǎiyàntáng Xùshuǐchí Táijī), where the water for the impressive fountains was stored in a tower and huge water-lifting devices were employed. The metal reservoir was commonly called the Tin Sea (Xīhǎi). Also known as the Water Clock, the **Hǎiyàntáng**, where 12 bronze human statues with animal heads jetted water for two hours in a 12-hour sequence, was constructed in 1759. The 12 animal heads from this apparatus ended up in collections abroad, and Běijīng is attempting to retrieve them (four can now be seen at the Poly Art Museum). Just west of here is the **Fāngwàiguàn**, a building that was turned into a mosque for an imperial concubine. An artful reproduction of a former labyrinth called the **Garden of Yellow Flowers** is also nearby.

The palace gardens cover a huge area – 2.5km from east to west – so be prepared for some walking. Besides the ruins, there's the western section, the **Perfection & Brightness Garden** (Yuánmíng Yuán) and, in the southern compound, the **10,000 Springs Garden** (Wànchūn Yuán).

Bus 331 goes from the south gate (which is by exit B of Yuanmingyuan subway station) to the east gate of the Summer Palace before continuing to the Botanic Gardens and eventually terminating at Fragrant Hills Park.

the significance of this collection. Exhibits include the skeleton of the Jīnniúshān Man, thought to be more than 250,000 years old, bronze artefacts, jade pieces and a host of other relics from primordial China. Bring your passport for free entry.

Afterwards, make sure to wander the pleasant, historic campus, a great way to tune out Běijīng's frantic mayhem.

GREAT BELL TEMPLE BUDDHIST SITE

Map p287 (大钟寺; Dàzhōng Sì; ☎010 8213 9050; 31a Beisanhuan Xilu; 北三环西路31a号; ¥20; ⏲9am-4.30pm Tue-Sun; [S]Dazhongsi) Newly refurbished, this famous shrine (originally called Juéshēng Temple) was once a pit stop for Qing emperors who came here to pray for rain. Today the temple is named after its massive Ming dynasty bell (6.75m tall and weighing a hefty 46.5 tonnes), which is inscribed with Buddhist sutras, comprising more than 227,000 Chinese characters, and decorated with Sanskrit incantations.

The bell was cast during the reign of Emperor Yongle in 1406, with the tower built in 1733. To transport the bell from the foundry to the temple, a shallow canal was dug, and when it froze over in winter, the bell was shunted across the ice by sled. Nowadays, the bell is rung just once a year, on Lunar New Year's Eve. If you're bell crazy, you'll be spellbound by the exhibitions on bell casting, and the collection of bells from France, Russia, Japan, Korea and other nations. Also on view are copies of the bells and chimes of the Marquis of Zeng and a collection of Buddhist and Taoist bells, including *vajra* bells and the wind chimes hung from temple roofs and pagodas.

MILITARY MUSEUM MUSEUM

Map p281 (军事博物馆; Jūnshì Bówùguǎn; 9 Fuxing Lu; 复兴路9号; ¥20; ⏲9am-5pm Tue-Sun; [S]Military Museum) Military enthusiasts will get a rush at this hulking monolith of a building topped with a communist star. Cold War–era fighters, tanks and surface-to-air missiles muster below, while upstairs bristles with more weaponry. The Hall of Agrarian Revolutionary War and the Hall of the War to Resist US Aggression and Aid Korea are a truly revolutionary tour de force of communist spin.

At the time of research, the main building was closed as part of a massive, seemingly never-ending renovation project. It is scheduled to reopen August 2017. But a large collection of tanks, aircraft, boats and artillery are on view in the forecourt, which is free to enter (bring your passport).

YUÁN DYNASTY WALLS RELICS PARK PARK

Map p287 (元大都城垣遗址公园; Yuán Dàdū Chéngyuán Yízhǐ Gōngyuán; [S]Xitucheng) [FREE] The name is an ambitious misnomer as there are not many genuine Yuan dynasty relics here, but this slender strip of parkland, running alongside the Little Moon River (Xiǎoyuè Hé), commemorates a strip of the long-vanished Mongol city wall that it is built upon. At 9km in length, this is Běijīng's longest parkland and a relaxing place for a stroll.

🍴 EATING

BRIDGE CAFÉ CAFE $

Map p287 (桥咖啡; Qiáo Kāfēi; ☎010 8286 7026; 12-8 Huaqing Jiayuan; 华清嘉园12-8; dishes from ¥40; ⏲24hr; 📶; [S]Wudaokou) Friendly, lively and light-filled place that's a top spot for Western breakfasts and paninis, as well as homemade pasta and tasty pizzas, or coffee and drinks at any time of day or night. There's a popular open-mic night on Thursdays. It's on the 2nd floor; enter through the door to the side of a gift shop and climb the stairs.

LA BAMBA MEXICAN $

Map p287 (☎010 8286 6755; Wudaokou, Huaqing Jiayuan East Gate; 五道口华清嘉园东门北侧12-3; dishes from ¥25; ⏲10am-5am; 📶; [S]Wudaokou) Heaving on the weekend, and busy most nights thanks to the daily food and drink specials, La Bamba is a key student hangout. It's not the most authentic Mexican food you'll ever taste, but the cheap beer (from ¥20) and pool table are as big an attraction as the burritos. The menu also features a wide selection of Western classics.

★**GOLDEN PEACOCK** DAI $$

Map p281 (金孔雀德宏傣味餐厅; Jīn Kǒngquè Déhóng Dǎiwèi Cāntīng; ☎010 6893 2030; Weigongcun; 魏公村韦伯豪家园南门对面; dishes from ¥28; ⏲11am-10pm; [S]Weigongcun) Make sure you try the pineapple rice and the tangy dried beef at this unpretentious and popular restaurant (get here early or reserve). It specialises in the cuisine of the Dǎi people, an ethnic minority from southwest China, who use flavourings such as lemongrass, common to Southeast Asia. Thanks to its proximity to the Mínzú Dàxué (民族大学), China's university for its 55 official ethnic minorities, Weigoncun is a great place to try other minority cuisines, especially Korean, Mongolian and Uighur food.

XIǍODIÀOLÍTĀNG BEIJING $$

Map p287 (小吊梨汤; ☎010 6264 8616; 66 Baofusi; 保福寺66号; dishes from ¥22; ⏲11am-3pm & 5-9pm; [S]Zhichunli) This place specialises in *Guānfǔ Cài*, the cuisine associated with Qing dynasty mandarins. It's basically a more refined take on traditional Běijīng dishes. Unsurprisingly, given the restaurant's name, pear soup – *lítāng* – accompanies each meal and a lot of the dishes on the picture menu incorporate pears, such as shrimp and fried pears (¥38). It's popular: expect to queue at lunchtime. Everything here is MSG-free. The restaurant is tucked away to the side of the Zhongguancun Sports & Culture Centre.

KHAN BABA PAKISTANI $$

Map p287 (汗吧吧餐厅; Hàn Bābā Cāntīng; ☎010 5692 7068; www.khanbababeijing.com; 2/f Jixin Plaza, Zhanchunyuanxi Lu; 展春园西路蓟鑫大厦北侧2层; mains ¥42-58; ⏲11.30am-3pm & 5.30-10.30pm; [S]Wudaokou) Fine and friendly Pakistani-run restaurant with a loyal and ever-increasing following of both foreigners and locals. The weekday lunchtime buffet (¥55) is an excellent deal, allowing you to sample any number of dishes.

ISSHIN JAPANESE RESTAURANT
JAPANESE $$

Map p287 (日本料理一心; Rìběn Liàolǐ Yī Xīn; ☑010 6257 4849; www.isshin.info; Room 403, West Bldg, 35 Chengfu Lu; 成府路35号院内西楼403室; sushi from ¥10, dishes from ¥36; ⊙11am-10pm; Ⓢ Wudaokou) A long-time local favourite, Isshin is well worth tracking down if you're in the area. With its thoughtful design, laid-back atmosphere and reasonable prices, it's a place where business types, expat Japanese and students can all feel at home. The sushi bar is made for solo travellers, while the sushi bowls (¥48), including salad, are a great deal.

The extensive menu includes hotpots, udon noodles and teriyaki dishes. You'll find the restaurant set back from the road, about 50m north of the traffic lights at the intersection of Chengfu Lu and Wudaokou station.

LĂO CHĒ JÌ
SICHUAN $$

Map p287 (老车记; ☑010 6266 6180; 5th fl, Wŭdàokŏu U-Centre, 36 Chengfu Lu; 成府路36 号五道口购物中心5层; meals for 2 from ¥88; ⊙10am-10pm; Ⓢ Wudaokou) The speciality here is *málàxiāngguō* (麻辣香锅), a kind of dry hotpot where you add your own meat, fish and veggies, but it comes without the bubbling broth you get with standard hotpots. Choose from three different levels of spice; go for the lowest if you can't handle the heat. You can also pick up a bowl of noodles from ¥10. It has a picture menu.

SALANG-BANG
KOREAN $$

Map p287 (舍廊房; Shèláng Fáng; ☑010 8261 8201; 3rd fl, Dōngyuán Plaza, 35 Chengfu Lu; 成府路35号东源大厦3层; dishes from ¥30; ⊙11am-2.30am; Ⓢ Wudaokou) Always busy with expat-Korean students looking for a taste of home, this is one of the most popular of the many Korean eateries in Wŭdàokŏu. The various hotpots, including the classic *shíguō bànfàn* (rice, vegetables, meat and an egg served in a claypot), start at ¥30. Alternatively, grill your choice of seafood and meat at your table. Picture menu.

WORTH A DETOUR

FRAGRANT HILLS PARK

Easily within striking distance of the Summer Palace are Běijīng's Western Hills (西山; Xī Shān), another former villa-resort of the emperors. The part of Xī Shān closest to Běijīng is known as **Fragrant Hills Park** (香山公园; Xiāng Shān Gōngyuán; Apr-Oct ¥10, Nov-Mar ¥5; ⊙6am-6.30pm Apr-Oct, to 6pm Nov-Mar; ☐331, Ⓢ Xiyuan or Yuanmingyuan, then). Beijingers flock here in autumn when the maple leaves saturate the hillsides in great splashes of red.

Scramble up the slopes to the top of **Incense-Burner Peak** (Xiānglú Fēng), or take the **chairlift** (one way/return ¥80/160, 9am to 4pm). From the peak, you get an all-embracing view of the countryside, and you can leave the crowds behind by hiking further into the Western Hills.

Near the north gate of Fragrant Hills Park, but still within the park, is the excellent **Azure Clouds Temple** (碧云寺; Bìyún Sì; Xiāngshān Gōngyuán; 香山公园; adult ¥10; ⊙9am-4.30pm; ☐331, Ⓢ Xiyuan or Yuanmingyuan), which dates back to the Yuan dynasty. The **Mountain Gate Hall** (Shānmén) contains two vast protective deities, Heng and Ha, beyond which is a small courtyard and the drum and bell towers, leading to a hall with a wonderful statue of Mílèfó – it's bronze, but coal-black with age. Only his big toe shines from numerous inquisitive fingers.

The **Sun Yatsen Memorial Hall** (Sūn Zhōngshān Jìniàn Táng) contains a statue and a glass coffin donated by the USSR on the death of Mr Sun (the Republic of China's first president) in 1925. At the very back is the marble **Vajra Throne Pagoda** (Jīngāng Bǎozuò Tǎ), where Sun Yatsen was interred after he died, before his body was moved to its final resting place in Nánjīng. The **Hall of Arhats** (Luóhàn Táng) is well worth visiting; it contains 500 statues of *luóhàn* (those freed from the cycle of rebirth), each crafted with an individual personality.

Southwest of the Azure Clouds Temple is the Tibetan-style **Temple of Brilliance** (Zhāo Miào), and not far away is a glazed-tile pagoda. Both survived visits by foreign troops intent on sacking the area in 1860, and then in 1900.

There are dozens of restaurants and snack stalls on the approach road to the north gate of the park, making this your best bet for lunch out of any of the sights in this part of the city. At the time of writing, it was expected that sometime in the future the subway will extend here via the Summer Palace and Botanic Gardens.

DRINKING & NIGHTLIFE

LUSH BAR

Map p287 (☎010 8286 3566; www.lushbeijing.com; 1 Huaqing Jiayuan, Chengfu Lu; 华清嘉园1号楼2层; beers from ¥20, cocktails from ¥30; ⏲10am-3am Mon-Thu, 8am-4am Fri-Sun; 📶; [S]Wudaokou) For the hordes of students in Wǔdàokǒu, both foreign and local, all roads lead to Lush. During the day it's a cafe with a Western menu, including breakfast (from ¥35) and sandwiches and salads (from ¥35). After dark, it offers something different every night, including live music, a pub quiz and an open-mic night for aspiring poets and singers. There's a daily happy hour from 8pm to 10pm and Monday is martini night. It's above the Meet Fresh Café.

WǓ CLUB

Map p287 (五; ☎130 2118 4769, 130 2118 4769; 1/f, NW Corner, Wudaokou U-Centre, Chengfu Lu; 成府路36号五道口购物中心一层西北角; cover ¥20, beers from ¥10; ⏲8.30pm-5am; [S]Wudaokou) Firmly aimed at the college crowd, with daily drink specials and party tunes, Wǔ is nevertheless slightly more upmarket than other clubs in the area. It's located on the ground floor of the U-Centre shopping mall, very close to the subway station. On Sundays, holders of international student cards get free entry and drinks.

WǓDÀOKǑU BEER GARDEN BAR

Map p287 (Huaqing Jiayuan; 华清嘉园; beers ¥10; ⏲5pm-midnight; [S]Wudaokou) When Běijīng emerges from the deep freeze of its winter, so do its residents. Come summer in Wǔdàokǒu, the area just west of the subway stop turns into a popular open-air beer garden. Locals congregate at the tables, sipping draught beers and snacking on *shāokǎo* (barbecue) from the food stalls surrounding them. The party starts in the late afternoon and continues late, getting louder and louder as those ¥10 beers disappear down thirsty throats.

PROPAGANDA CLUB

Map p287 (☎010 8286 3991; Huaqing Jiayuan; 华清嘉园; ⏲8pm-5.30am; [S]Wudaokou) Wǔdàokǒu's student crew are drawn to this unprepossessing but long-running club for its suspiciously cheap drinks, hip-hop sounds and the chance for cultural exchange with the locals. Entry is free. It's 100m north of the east gate of Huaqing Jiayuan.

ENTERTAINMENT

NATIONAL LIBRARY ARTS CENTRE CLASSICAL MUSIC, DANCE

Map p281 (国图艺术中心; Guó Túshūguǎn Zhōngxīn; ☎010 8854 4777; 33 Zhongguangcun Nandajie; 中关村南大街33号; tickets ¥50-300; ⏲performances 7.30pm; [S]National Library) Newly refurbished, this impressive venue doesn't just put on recitals and concerts (many by overseas musicians); it's also a good place to catch Chinese classical dance, which blends martial-arts styles with traditional dance performances.

13 CLUB LIVE MUSIC

Map p287 (13俱乐部; 13 Jùlèbù; ☎010 8261 9267; china13club@gmail.com; 161 Chengfu Lu; 成府路161号; cover from ¥30; ⏲5pm-midnight; [S]Wudaokou) A dark and forbidding venue down a suitably grimy alley. A lot of metal acts play here, so if you're a fan of guitar solos and making the sign of the horns, this is the place for you. Look for the red sign.

UME INTERNATIONAL CINEPLEX CINEMA

Map p287 (☎010 8211 5566; 44 Kexueyuan Nanlu; 科学院南路44号; tickets ¥50-85; [S]Renmin University) Posh multiplex that shows the latest Western movie releases (the ones that pass muster with the Chinese censors), but check they haven't been dubbed into Chinese.

SHOPPING

CENTERGATE COMO ELECTRONICS

Map p287 (科贸电子城; Kēmào Diànzǐchéng; 18 Zhongguancun Dajie; 中关村大街18号; ⏲9am-7pm; [S]Zhongguancun) Zhōngguāncūn is China's Silicon Valley, and this mall is one of the biggest in the area, an eight-floor space full of vendors selling reasonably priced electronics. Not all of it is the genuine article, but you can bargain. Go to the 2nd floor for laptop repairs. There's a food court on the 8th floor.

SPORTS & ACTIVITIES

FRIENDSHIP HOTEL SWIMMING, TENNIS

Map p287 (☎6849 8888 ext 32; 1 Zhongguancun Nandajie; 友谊宾馆 中关村南大街1号; ⏲7am-10.30pm; [S]Renmin University) This hotel has a great Olympic-sized pool, costing ¥150 for a day or however long you stay. There are also tennis courts for hire (¥400 per hour) and a gym (¥100 per hour) and sauna (¥268).

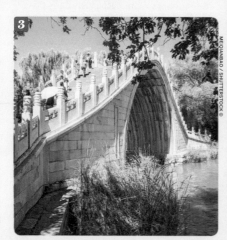

1. Hall of Benevolence & Longevity (p152)
The main building in the Summer Palace

2. Summer Palace (p152)
View of the splendid Summer Palace over Kūnmíng Lake

3. Jade Belt Bridge (153)
Dating from the 18th century, this grey and white marble bridge links the tree-lined causeway

The Great Wall

Mùtiányù 慕田峪 **p164**
Tobogganing down this elegantly restored strip of the Wall that is also short enough to walk.

Gǔběikǒu 古北口 **p165**
Basing yourself in this historic village, which offers two great hikes along a less dangerous stretch of Wild Wall.

Jiànkòu 箭扣 **p166**
Watching your step as you hike the Wild Wall at its most raw and untamed, with fantastic views of the ramparts hugging the mountain ridges.

Huánghuā Chéng 黄花城 **p167**
Hiking in either direction along one of the least-visited, but very steep sections of the Wall.

Zhuàngdàokǒu 撞道口 **p167**
Two options: a short restored stretch with fabulous views, or a highly challenging off-the-beaten-track hike.

Jīnshānlǐng 金山岭 **p168**
Walking the most remote part of the Wall from Běijīng, free from the crowds.

Bādálǐng 八达岭 **p169**
The most famous and crowded, but picturesque, stretch of the Wall.

Hiking the Great Wall p170
Seven of our favourite hikes along the Great Wall.

History

The Great Wall (长城; Chángchéng), one of the most iconic monuments on earth, stands as an awe-inspiring symbol of the grandeur of China's ancient history. Dating back 2000-odd years, the Wall snakes its way through 17 provinces, principalities and autonomous regions. But nowhere is better than Běijīng for mounting your assault on this most famous of bastions.

Official Chinese history likes to stress the unity of the Wall through the ages. In fact, there are at least four distinct Walls. Work on the 'original' was begun during the Qin dynasty (221–207 BC), when China was unified for the first time under Emperor Qin Shihuang. Hundreds of thousands of workers, many of them political prisoners, laboured for 10 years to construct it. An estimated 180-million cu metres of rammed earth was used to form the core of this Wall, and legend has it that the bones of dead workers were used as building materials, too.

After the Qin fell, work on the Wall continued during the Han dynasty (206 BC–AD 220). Little more was done until almost 1000 years later, during the Jin dynasty (1115–1234), when the impending threat of Genghis Khan spurred further construction. The Wall's final incarnation, and the one most visitors see today, came during the Ming dynasty (1368–1644), when it was reinforced with stone, brick and battlements over a period of 100 years and at great human cost to the two to three million people who toiled on it. During this period it was home to around one million soldiers.

The great irony of the Wall is that it rarely stopped China's enemies from invading. It was never one continuous structure; there were inevitable gaps and it was through those that Genghis Khan rode in to take Běijīng in 1215. While the Wall was less than effective militarily, it was very useful as a kind of elevated highway for transporting people and equipment across mountainous terrain. Its beacon tower system, using smoke signals generated by burning wolves' dung, quickly transmitted news of enemy movements back to the capital. But with the Manchus installed in Běijīng as the Qing dynasty (1644–1911) and the Mongol threat long gone, there was little need to maintain the Wall, and it fell into disrepair.

Ruin & Restoration

The Wall's decline accelerated during the war with Japan and then the civil war that preceded the founding of the new China in 1949. Compounding the problem, the communists didn't initially have much interest in the Wall. In fact, Mao Zedong encouraged people living near it to use it as a source of free building materials, something that still goes on unofficially today. It wasn't until 1984 that Mao's successor Deng Xiaoping ordered that the Wall be restored in places and placed under government protection.

But classic postcard images of the Wall – flawlessly clad in bricks and stoutly undulating over hills into the distance – do not reflect the truth of the bastion today. While the sections closest to Běijīng and a few elsewhere have been restored to something approaching their former glory, huge parts of the Wall are either rubble or, especially in the west, simply mounds of earth that could be anything.

Visiting the Wall

The heavily reconstructed section at Bādálǐng is the most touristy part of the Wall. Mùtiányù and Jīnshānlǐng are also restored sections. These can feel less than authentic, but have the advantage of being much more accessible (with cable cars, handrails etc). Huánghuā Chéng and Zhuàngdàokǒu are part-restored, part-'wild' and offer some short but challenging hikes. Unrestored sections of 'Wild Wall' include Gǔběikǒu and Jiànkòu, but there are many others. All of these can be reached using public transport (you can even get to

THE GREAT WALL

JUST HOW GREAT IS IT?

The Chinese call the Great Wall the '10,000 Lǐ Wall' (万里长城; Wànlǐ Chángchéng). With one 'Lǐ' equivalent to around 500m, this makes the Wall around 5000km long. More modern calculations, though, reveal the Wall to be much longer. A report by China's State Administration of Cultural Heritage in April 2009 estimated the noncontinuous length of the Ming dynasty wall at 8851km. But the Ming dynasty was just one of 13 dynasties to have contributed to the Wall over the course of history. A 2012 Chinese government survey calculated the total length of all fragments of the Great Wall that have ever stood, including sections that run parallel with others to be 21,196km.

The Great Wall

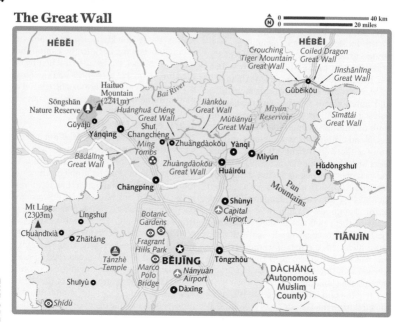

N

0 ————————— 40 km
0 ————————— 20 miles

Bādálǐng by train), although some people choose to hire a car to speed things up. Staying overnight by the Wall is recommended.

Tours run by hostels, or by specialist tour companies, are far preferable to those run by ordinary hotels or general travel companies. Not only do they cater to the needs of adventurous Western travellers, they don't come with any hidden extras, such as a side trip to the Ming Tombs (a common add-on) or a tiresome diversion to a gem factory or traditional Chinese medicine centre. The following reputable companies and associations run trips to the Wall that we like.

Bespoke Běijīng (☑010 6400 0133; www.bespoketravelcompany.com) High-end trips and tours.

Great Wall Hiking (www.greatwallhiking.com) Locally run hiking trips.

China Hiking (☑156 5220 0950; www.chinahiking.cn) Affordable hiking and camping trips run by a Chinese-Belgian couple.

Běijīng Hikers (☑010 6432 2786; www.beijinghikers.com) Organises some breathtaking outings out of town.

Bike Běijīng (☑010 6526 5857; www.bikebeijing.com) For cycling trips.

Běijīng Sideways (☑139 1133 4947; www.beijingsideways.com) For trips in a motorbike sidecar.

Mùtiányù

Explore

Famed for its 26 Ming-era guard towers and excellent views, the 3km-long section of Wall at Mùtiányù (慕田峪) is an impressive, largely recently restored Ming dynasty structure that was built upon an earlier Northern Qi dynasty edifice.

From the ticket office at Mùtiányù, shuttle buses (¥15 return, 7.20am to 7pm April to October, 8.20am to 6pm November to December) run the 3km to the Wall, where there are three or four stepped pathways leading up to the Wall itself, plus a **cable car** (缆车; Lǎn Chē; one way/return ¥80/100, kids half-price), a **chairlift** (索道; Suǒdào; combined ticket with toboggan ¥80), called a 'ropeway' on the signs here, and a **toboggan ride** (滑道; Huá Dào; one way ¥80), making this ideal for those who can't manage too many steps, or who have kids in tow.

Top Tip

If taking bus 916快 to Huáiróu, ignore the tout who often gets on this bus at Nánhuá Shìchǎng bus stop and tries to lure foreign tourists onto an expensive minibus tour to the Great Wall. He sometimes wears a bus-driver shirt to aid the scam.

Getting There & Away

Bus From Dōngzhímén Wai bus stand, bus 867 makes a special detour to Mùtiányù twice every morning (¥16, 2½ hours, 7am and 8.30am, 15 March to 15 November only) and returns from Mùtiányù twice each afternoon (2pm and 4pm). Otherwise, go via Huáiróu: from Dōngzhímén Transport Hub (Dōngzhímén Shūniǔzhàn) take bus 916快 (the character is 'kuài', and means 'fast') to Huáiróu (¥11, one hour, 6.30am to 7.30pm). Get off at Míngzhū Guǎngchǎng (明珠广场) bus stop, where private taxis and minivans wait to take passengers to Mùtiányù (per person ¥20, 30 minutes). Note that after around 1pm, you'll probably have to charter your own car or van (¥60 one way). Return minivans start drying up at around 6pm. The last 916快 back to Běijīng leaves Huáiróu at around 7pm. If you miss that, catch a taxi from Huáiróu to Shùnyì subway station (顺义地铁站; Shùnyì Dìtiě Zhàn; about ¥100) on Line 15, or all the way back to Dōngzhímén (¥220).

Taxi A taxi costs around ¥600 to ¥700 for a return day trip from Běijīng.

Need to Know

➡ **Location** 70km from Běijīng
➡ **Price** adult ¥45
➡ **Hours** 7am to 7pm April to October, 7.30am to 6.30pm November to March

✗ EATING & SLEEPING

YÌ SŌNG LÓU RESTAURANT   CHINESE $$
(翼松楼餐厅; Yì Sōng Lóu Cāntīng; mains ¥22-80; ⏰8.30am-5pm) Restaurant up by the main entrance to Mùtiányù Great Wall. It does OK Chinese food.

BRICKYARD ECO RETREAT   GUESTHOUSE $$$
(瓦厂; Wǎ Chǎng; ☑010 6162 6506; www.brick yardatmutianyu.com; Běigōu Village, Huáiróu District; 怀柔区渤海镇北沟村; r ¥1040-4746; ❋☎) 🍴 A 1960s glazed-tile factory renovated into a beautiful guesthouse, sporting lovingly restored rooms, each with views of the Great Wall. Rates include breakfast, use of a spa, and shuttle services to the Wall and surrounding villages. Brickyard is in Běigōu village (北沟村; Běigōu Cūn), about 2km from the Mùtiányù Great Wall. Reservations are essential.

Gǔběikǒu

Explore

The historic, far-flung town of Gǔběikǒu (古北口) is just a village these days, but was once an important, heavily guarded gateway into Běijīng from northeast China. There are two main sections of Wall here: the Coiled Dragon (蟠龙; Pán Lóng), which runs along the ridge that cuts Gǔběikǒu village in two and which eventually leads to Jīnshānlǐng Great Wall, and Crouching Tiger Mountain (卧虎山; Wò Hǔ Shān), on the other side of the Cháo Hé River. Both make for fabulous hiking, although Crouching Tiger is extraordinarily steep.

Getting There & Away

Bus Take bus 980快 from Dōngzhímén Transport Hub (Dōngzhímén Shūniǔzhàn) to its terminus at Mìyún bus station (密云汽车站; Mìyún qìchēzhàn; ¥17, 100 minutes, 6am to 8pm). The 快 (kuài) means fast. Then, turn right out of the bus station, cross the main road and turn right and walk for 200m to find the stop for bus 25, which runs to Gǔběikǒu (¥10, 70 minutes). To catch the bus back to Mìyún from Gǔběikǒu, walk through the tunnel by the entrance to the village, cross the road and the bus stop is 400m ahead of you. The last bus 25 back to Mìyún leaves at 4.35pm. The last bus 980 back to Dōngzhímén is at 6.30pm.

Taxi Taxis cost ¥1000 to ¥1200 return for a day trip from Běijīng.

Need to Know

➡ **Location** 130km from Běijīng
➡ **Price** admission ¥45 through ticket (Great Wall and town), ¥20 town only

✗ EATING & SLEEPING

There are dozens of *nóngjiāyuàn* (农家院; village guesthouses), so there's no need to book. There's English signage, but little English is spoken. Expect to pay ¥150 to ¥280 for a room with a bathroom. All the guesthouses double as restaurants.

★ **GREAT WALL BOX HOUSE**   GUESTHOUSE $
(团园客栈; Tuán Yuán Kèzhàn; ☑010 8105 1123; http://en.greatwallbox.com; No 18 Dongguan,

ℹ️ WHEN TO GO

➜ Spring and autumn are good times to hike the Wall, when it's not too hot or cold.

➜ Summers can see the Wall overwhelmed by visitors. Go for one of the less-visited sections such as Jīnshānlǐng or Mùtiányù.

➜ In winter, it gets frigid at the Wall – it's always colder than in Běijīng – but you'll likely have many parts of it all to yourself, especially during the week.

➜ Do not hike the sections of the Wild Wall in the rain: it's too easy to slip and fall.

➜ Avoid visiting the Wall at weekends or public holidays, if at all possible.

Gǔběikǒu Village; 古北口镇东关甲18号; weekday/weekend incl dinner 6-bed dm ¥180/200, 4-bed room ¥180/200, deluxe d ¥1200/1350; ⊙mid-Mar–mid-Nov; ⊜🛜) Run by the friendly, English-speaking Joe, this wonderful place is housed in a 100-year-old courtyard building that was an abandoned chessboard factory before being lovingly renovated. Rooms surround a long, well-tended garden-courtyard, and are large (the dorm is enormous), bright, comfortable and spotlessly clean. Incredibly, a small, overgrown section of the Great Wall runs along one side of the property.

The shared bathroom is modern (with sit-down toilets), there's a small kitchen-dining area and a number of cats. Joe dishes out reliable hiking advice and offers free mountain-bike hire. It also does tasty vegetarian meals. Get off the bus just before the Gǔběikǒu Tunnel and, instead of walking through the archway, walk along the lane to the south of the village stream. You'll see the Box House sign after about 500m.

Jiànkòu

Explore

For stupefying hikes along perhaps Běijīng's most incomparable section of 'Wild Wall', head to the rear section of the Jiànkòu Great Wall (后箭扣长城; Hòu Jiànkòu Cháng-chéng), accessible from Xīzhàzi village (西栅子村; Xīzhàzi Cūn), via the town of Huáiróu. The Wall here meanders dramatically along a mountain ridge in both directions and the setting is truly sublime. One favourite route is to turn left when you hit the Wall and hike for 90 minutes to Mùtiányù. But remember this is completely unrestored wall and dangerous to hike. Footwear with very good grip is required, and never attempt to traverse this section in the rain.

Top Tip

If you don't plan on staying the night or aren't hiking to another section of the Wall, make sure you get your taxi driver to wait for you (don't pay until afterwards) because it's tough to find taxis at Xīzhàzi village.

Getting There & Away

Bus Take bus 916快 from the Dōngzhímén Transport Hub (Dōngzhímén Shūniǔzhàn) to its terminus at Huáiróu bus station (怀柔汽车站; Huáiróu qìchēzhàn, ¥12, 90 minutes, 6.30am to 7.30pm). Turn left out of the station, right at the crossroads and take bus 862 from the first bus stop to Yújiāyuán (于家园; ¥2, five stops), then take the H25 to Xīzhàzi (西栅子; 70 minutes, ¥8). Note, the H25 only runs twice a day; at 11.30am and 4.30pm. The return H25 bus leaves Xīzhàzi at 6.30am and 1.15pm, so you can't do this in a day trip on public transport alone.

Taxi It costs around ¥700 to ¥900 for a return day trip from Běijīng. From Huáiróu to Xīzhàzi village, expect to pay at least ¥120 one way.

Need to Know

➜ **Location** 100km from Běijīng

➜ **Price** admission ¥25

➜ **Hours** no official opening hours

EATING & SLEEPING

There are an ever-increasing number of guesthouses in Xīzhàzi village, but Jiànkòu is now a very popular destination for local visitors, so book ahead at weekends, especially in summer. Expect to pay ¥120 and up for a room with a bathroom. All guesthouses in the area double as restaurants; some have picture menus.

YÁNG ÈR   GUESTHOUSE $

(杨二; ☑136 9307 0117, 6161 1794; Xīzhàzi Village No 1; 西栅子村一队; r ¥120; ❄ 🛜) This is the first *nóngjiāyuàn* (农家院; village guesthouse) you come to as you enter Hamlet No 1 of Xīzhàzi village. Rooms are set around a vegetable-patch courtyard, and are simple, but have private bathrooms. The food menu (mains ¥25 to ¥50) includes some photos. No English.

ZHÀO SHÌ SHĀN JŪ   GUESTHOUSE $

(赵氏山居; ☑135 2054 9638, 6161 1762; www.jk wall.com; r ¥120-420; ❄ 🛜) The last property in the valley (Hamlet No 5 of Xīzhàzi village), this is a favourite for Chinese hikers (not much English is spoken here and the website is in Chinese only). There is a large shaded terrace dining area with fine Great Wall views. Rooms are neat and clean, and sleep two to seven people. Most have attached bathrooms. Keep walking along the main road beyond where the bus terminates, and you'll see it up on your right. The food menu (mains ¥20 to ¥60) has photos.

Huánghuā Chéng

Explore

Strikingly free of both visitors and hawkers, Huánghuā Chéng (黄花城) is an extremely rewarding, partially restored section of the Wall. From the road, you can go either west (left) towards Zhuàngdàokǒu or east (right) up the stupidly steep section, which eventually leads to Jiànkòu (after about two days). For the eastern route, cross the small dam, pay the enterprising local who sells unofficial ¥3 entrance tickets, and follow the path beside the reservoir until you reach a metal ladder which is used to access the Wall. To head west, climb the path that leads up to the Wall from behind Ténglóng Hotel and which ends at a watchtower that leads onto the Wall itself. You can continue from here to Zhuàngdàokǒu village (45 minutes); turn left off the Wall at its lowest point.

Getting There & Away

Bus From Dōngzhímén Transport Hub (Dōngzhímén Shūniǔzhàn) take bus 916 快 to Huáiróu (¥12, one hour, 6.30am to 7.30pm). Get off at Nánhuáyuán Sānqū (南花园三区) bus stop, then walk straight ahead about 200m (crossing one road), until you get to the next bus stop, called Nánhuáyuán Sìqū (南花园四区). From here take the H14 bound for Èr Dào Guān (二道关) and get off at Huánghuā Chéng (¥8, one hour, until 6.30pm). It only runs about once an hour; taxi drivers hover by the bus stop to test your patience (¥100 one way). Returning from Huánghuā Chéng, you can catch either the H14 or the H21, which passes the bus station in Huáiróu, where the 916快 originates. The last 916快 from Huáiróu back to Běijīng leaves Huáiróu at around 7pm.

Taxi A taxi is around ¥700 to ¥800 return for a day trip from Běijīng.

Need to Know

➡ **Location** 77km from Běijīng

➡ **Price** ¥3 (unofficial)

➡ **Hours** no official opening hours

 **EATING & SLEEPING**

TÉNGLÓNG HOTEL   GUESTHOUSE $

(滕龙饭店; Ténglóng Fàndiàn; ☑010 6165 1929; r with/without bathroom ¥120/60; 🛜) One of a number of small guesthouses in Huánghuā Chéng. Most are on the river side of the road, but this friendly place, accessed via steps on your left just before the Wall, clings to the hillside on the other side and offers fine views of the Wall. Rooms are basic, but clean and sleep three to four people.

No English is spoken, but the restaurant, with terrace seating, has an English menu (mains ¥20 to ¥60).

Zhuàngdàokǒu

Explore

Zhuàngdàokǒu (撞道口), a small village just over the hill to the east of Huánghuā Chéng, has access to a rarely visited and completely unrestored section of 'Wild Wall'. It's also possible to hike over to Huánghuā Chéng on a restored and very steep section from here. The bus will drop you at the far end of Zhuàngdàokǒu village. Walk uphill until you reach a rocky pathway that leads to the Wall. Once at the Wall, turn right for the one-hour walk to Huánghuā Chéng, from where you can catch the H14 or H21 back to Huáiróu. Alternatively, turn left for a two-hour hike along a crumbling stretch of Wall towards the **Huánghuāchéng Great Wall Lakeside Reserve** (黄花城水长城旅游区; Huánghuāchéng Shuǐchángchéng Lǚyóuqū; ¥45; ☺8am-5pm Apr-Oct, to 4.30pm Nov-Mar). From here you can catch the H21 bus back to Huáiróu. The latter route is extremely tough underfoot. Take care.

Getting There & Away

Bus From Dōngzhímén Transport Hub (Dōngzhímén Shūniǔzhàn) take bus 916快 to Huáiróu (¥12, one hour, 6.30am to 7.30pm). Get off at Nánhuáyuán Sānqū (南花园三区) bus stop, then walk straight ahead about 200m (crossing one road), until you get to the next bus stop, which is called Nánhuáyuán Sìqū (南花园四区). Note that the bus you need, the H21, is not listed on the bus stop. Catch the H21 to Shuǐ Chángchéng (水长城), which stops at Zhuàngdàokǒu (¥8, one hour, every 30 minutes until 6.30pm). The last 916快 bus from Huáiróu back to Běijīng leaves Huáiróu at around 7pm. A taxi from Huáiróu to Zhuàngdàokǒu will cost ¥100.

Taxi A taxi costs around ¥700 to ¥800 for a return day trip from Běijīng.

Need to Know

➡ **Location** 80km from Běijīng
➡ **Price** no entrance fee
➡ **Hours** no official opening hours

✗ EATING & SLEEPING

ZǍOXIĀNG YARD   GUESTHOUSE **$**
(枣香庭院; Zǎoxiāng Tíngyuàn; ☎135 2208 3605; r ¥80-150; ☞) This modest but comfortable-enough guesthouse is housed in a 70-year-old courtyard building, which has some traditional features such as wooden window frames and paper windowpanes, as well as a terrace to eat on. There are 12 rooms, eight with private bathrooms. The owners are pleasant and their food is decent (mains ¥20 to ¥65; English menu). It's on your right on the main road, just before where the bus drops you off.

Jīnshānlǐng

Explore

The Jīnshānlǐng (金山岭) section of the Great Wall is a completely restored and, in places, very steep stretch, but it sees far fewer tourists than other fully restored sections. Hiking (in either direction) on the Wall here is straightforward. There's an east gate and a west gate (about 2km apart), although at the time of writing the east gate was closed, so you can only get onto the Wall from the west gate. There's a cable car by the west-gate ticket office. If you want to find some unrestored sections, turn right when you hit the Wall and just keep going. This stretch eventually leads to Gǔběikǒu (6½ hours), although you have to leave the Wall for an hour or two in order to walk around the boundary of a small military camp.

Getting There & Away

Bus From April to November, direct buses run from Wàngjīng West subway station (Line 13) to the Jīnshānlǐng ticket office. Come out of Exit C of the subway station and look over your right shoulder to see the red sign for the 'Tourist Bus to Jīnshānlǐng Great Wall' (金山岭长城旅游班车; Jīnshānlǐng Chángchéng lǚyóu bānchē) on the other side of the road. The bus leaves at 8am and returns to Běijīng at 3pm (¥32, 100 minutes). Otherwise, catch a bus to Luánpíng (滦平; ¥32, 90 minutes, 7.30am to 4pm) from the forecourt behind the red sign for the tourist bus, which will drop you at a service station on the highway close to Jīnshānlǐng. Taxis wait at the bus drop-off to drive the 9km to the west gate (¥100). If you want them to wait, expect to pay ¥200. Buses

GUIDED TOURS

A number of hostels in Běijīng run recommended trips by minibus to Jīnshānlǐng for the four-hour hike to Sīmǎtái. Buses usually leave at around 6am or 7am. They drop you at Jīnshānlǐng, then pick you up four hours later in Sīmǎtái. The entire journey from Běijīng and back takes up to 12 hours. Expect to pay around ¥300 per person.

return to Běijīng from the service station. The last bus back leaves at 4.20pm.

Taxi A taxi costs around ¥1000 to ¥1200 for a return day trip from Běijīng.

Need to Know

- **Location** 142km from Běijīng
- **Price** summer/winter ¥65/55
- **Hours** 8am to 5pm

🍴 EATING

JĪNSHĀN FÀNGUǍN CHINESE $$

(金山饭馆; West Gate of Jīnshānlǐng Great Wall; 金山岭长城内; dishes ¥20-80; ⌚9am-8pm Apr-Oct, to 4pm Nov-Mar) One of the few restaurants by the west gate of Jīnshānlǐng Great Wall that stays open in winter. It has an English menu.

Bādálǐng

Explore

The mere mention of Bādálǐng (八达岭) sends a shudder down the spine of hardcore Wall walkers, but this is the easiest part of the Wall to get to and, if you are really pushed for time, this may be your only option. You'll have to put up with huge crowds of domestic tourists and a lot of souvenir hawkers, while the Wall itself was completely renovated in the 1980s and so lacks a true sense of historical authenticity. On the plus side, the facilities are good, the scenery is raw and striking, and the Wall, which dates back to Ming times (1368–1644) and snakes off in classic fashion across the hills, is extremely photogenic. There is a **cable car** (缆车; Lǎn Chē; 1 way/return ¥80/100; ⌚8am-4.30pm) from the bottom of the west car park, and a toboggan ride (¥80/100 one way/return; called a 'sliding car' on the signs here), which descends to the east car park.

Top Tip

Give the despicable Bear Park a wide berth.

Getting There & Away

Bus The 877 (¥12, one hour, 6am to 5pm) leaves for Bādálǐng from the northern side of the Déshèngmén Gateway (p120), about 400m east of Jīshuǐtán subway station. It goes to the east car park at Bādálǐng. From there, walk uphill a little, turn left through a covered souvenir-shop strip, then left again at the end and uphill to the ticket office, which is between two large fortified archways. Buses return to Běijīng from just south of where they drop you: you'll see the queue of people waiting for them. The last bus back leaves at 5pm (4.30pm November to March).

Train Getting here by train is the cheapest and most enjoyable option. Bādálǐng train station is a short walk downhill from the west car park; come out of the train station and turn left for the Wall (about 1km). Trains (¥6, 70 to 80 minutes) leave from **Běijīng north train station** (北京北站; Běijīng Běizhàn; Map p278; ☎010 5186 6223; [S]Lines 2, 4, 13 to Xizhimen, exit A1), which is connected to Xīzhímén subway station, at the following times: Tuesday to Thursday 6.12am, 8.34am, 10.57am and 12.42pm; Friday to Monday 6.12am, 7.58am, 9.02am, 10.57am, 1.14pm and 1.35pm. On your return, trains leave from Bādálǐng train station at: Tuesday to Thursday 1.40pm, 3.08pm, 5.30pm, 7.34pm and 9.33pm; Friday to Monday 1.33pm, 3.43pm, 4.14pm, 5.30pm, 7.55pm and 9.31pm.

Taxi Expect to pay around ¥600 to ¥700 for a round trip from Běijīng.

Need to Know

- **Location** 70km from Běijīng
- **Price** ¥40 April to October, ¥35 November to March
- **Hours** summer 6am to 7pm, winter 7am to 6pm

👁 SIGHTS

CHINA GREAT WALL MUSEUM MUSEUM

(中国长城博物馆; Zhōngguó Chángchéng Bówùguǎn; included with ticket to Bādálǐng section of Wall; ⌚9am-4pm Tue-Sun; 🚌877) This museum offers a comprehensive history of the Wall, from its origins as an earthen embankment in the far-off Qin dynasty (221–207 BC) to the Ming-era battlements you see today. There are decent English captions and it's a good way to get a sense of just how astonishing and extensive a structure the Wall is. The museum is just south of the east car park.

EATING

ĀTÀI BĀOZI   CHINESE $

(阿泰包子; ¥20-32; ⊙7am-4pm) Just up from the east car park at Bādálǐng, this place does OK dumplings, as well as rice and noodle dishes. It has a picture menu, so you can point and pick.

Hiking the Great Wall

Explore

Běijīng is within striking distance of a number of stretches of the Great Wall and that means there are plenty of excellent hiking opportunities for would-be adventurers. Following is a list of some of our favourite Great Wall hikes near the capital. Don't take any of these lightly, though. The Wall is incredibly steep in places, crumbling away in parts, often very exposed to the elements and at the unrestored sections it usually has no sides. Wear shoes with good grip and take a rucksack so you have both hands free for clambering. And bring plenty of water.

Jīnshānlǐng West Gate to Jīnshānlǐng East Gate

➡ 90 minutes

Turn right when you hit the Wall, then climb down to your left once you reach East Tower with Five Holes (东五眼楼; Dōngwǔyán Lóu). At the time of writing, the east gate was shut, so until it opens again, you'll have to retrace your steps back to the west gate.

Jiànkòu to Mùtiányù

➡ Two hours (plus an hour climb to the Wall)

Unrivalled for pure Wild Wall scenery, the Wall at Jiànkòu is very tough to negotiate. This short stretch, which passes through the 180-degree u-turn known as the Ox Horn, is equally hairy, but it soon links to an easier, restored section at Mùtiányù. Access the Wall from hamlet No 1 in Xīzhàzi village (西栅子村一队; Xīzhàzi Cūn Yīduì). It takes an hour to reach the Wall from the village; from the sign that says 'this section of the Great Wall is not open to the public', follow a narrow dirt path uphill and through a lovely pine forest. When you reach a small clearing,

go straight on (and down slightly), rather than up to the right. Later, when you hit the Wall, turn left. You'll climb/clamber up to, and round, the Ox Horn before descending (it's very slippery here) all the way to Mùtiányù, where cable cars, toboggan rides and transport back to Běijīng await.

Huánghuā Chéng to Zhuàngdàokǒu

➡ 45 minutes

This is a short hop rather than a hike, and on a mostly restored part of the Wall. It comes with stunning views of the Wall by a reservoir and can be extended to take in the crumbling sections beyond Zhuàngdàokǒu. At Huánghuā Chéng, climb up the Wall to the west (left) of the road. Having scaled the Wall's high point, walk down to the lowest part of the Wall (above an archway), then climb down to your left and follow the path to Zhuàngdàokǒu village, from where you can pick up a bus back to Huáiróu.

Zhuàngdàokǒu to Huánghuā Chéng

➡ One hour (plus 20-minutes to the Wall)

It's a mostly restored part of the Wall, and comes with stunning views of the Wall by a reservoir once you reach the summit of your climb. Access the Wall from Zhuàngdàokǒu village; turn right at the end of the village, by the small river, then follow the river (keeping it on your left) before turning right, up the hill between the houses, to climb a stony pathway. When you reach the Wall, turn right and keep going until you reach the last watchtower, where a path to the right leads down to the main road by the reservoir. Don't attempt to descend to the road via the last stretch of Wall here, as it is suicidally steep. You can pick up buses, such as the H14, to Huáiróu from here (until 6pm).

Zhuàngdàokǒu to Shuǐ Chángchéng

➡ Two hours (plus 20-minutes to the Wall)

Climb up to the Wall from Zhuàngdàokǒu village, and turn left at the Wall to be rewarded with this dangerous but fabulous stretch of crumbling bastion. The Wall eventually splits at a corner tower: turn left. Then, soon after you reach another tower from where you can see the reservoir far below you, the Wall crumbles down the mountain, and is impassable. Instead of risking

CAMPING ON THE WALL

Although, strictly speaking, camping on the Great Wall is not allowed, many people do it; some of the watchtowers make excellent bases for pitching tents, or just laying down a sleeping bag. Remember, though; don't light fires and don't leave anything behind. You'll find fun places to camp at Zhuàngdàokǒu, Jiànkòu and Gǔběikǒu.

There are plenty of places to buy camping equipment in Běijīng, but one of the best in terms of quality and choice is Sanfo (p123). There are branches across the city, but this location on a side road of the middle section of the North 3rd Ring Rd stands out because it has three outlets side by side, as well as a few smaller cheaper camping shops next door. Turn right out of Exit D of Jiandemen subway station (Line 10) and walk south for about 800m, then cross under the 3rd Ring Rd and the camping shops will be on your right.

There's a smaller, easier-to-get-to **branch** (Map p278; www.sanfo.com; 9-4 Fuchengmen Dajie; 阜城门大街9—4号; ⏰10am-8.30pm; [S] Line 2 to Fuchengmen, exit C), about 200m south of Fuchengmen subway station.

your life, take the path that leads down to your left, just before the tower. This path eventually links up with the Wall again, but you may as well follow it all the way down to the road from here, where you'll be able to catch the H21 bus back to Huáiróu from the lower one of the two large car parks.

The Coiled Dragon Loop

➡ 2½ hours

This scenic but manageable hike starts and finishes in the town of Gǔběikǒu and follows a curling stretch of the Wall known as the Coiled Dragon. From the Folk Customs Village (the southern half of Gǔběikǒu), walk up to the newly reconstructed **Gǔběikǒu Gate** (古北口关; Gǔběikǒu Guǎn) but turn right up a dirt track just before the gateway. You should start seeing yellow-painted blobs, left over from an old marathon that was run here: follow them. The first section of Wall you reach is a very rare stony stretch of **Northern Qi Dynasty Wall** (1500 years old). It soon joins up with the Ming dynasty bricked version, which you should continue to walk along (although at one stage, you need to follow yellow arrows down off the Wall to the left, before rejoining it later). Around 90 minutes after you set off, you should reach a big sweeping right-hand bend in the Wall (the coil), with three towers on top. The first and third of these towers are quite well preserved, with walls, windows and part of a roof (great for camping in). At the third tower (called **Jiangjun Tower**), turn left, skirting right around it, then walk down the steps before turning right at a point marked with a yellow 'X' (the marathon went straight on here). Follow this pathway all the way back to Gǔběikǒu (30 minutes), turning right when you reach the road.

Gǔběikǒu to Jīnshānlǐng

➡ 6½ hours

This day-long adventure takes in some ancient stone Wall, some crumbling unrestored brick Wall and some picture-perfect, recently renovated Wall, as well as a 90-minute detour through the countryside. Bring plenty of water and enough food for lunch. Follow the first part of our Coiled Dragon Loop hike, but instead of leaving the Wall just after **Jiangjun Tower**, continue along the Wall for another hour until you reach the impressive **24-Window Tower** (there are only 15 windows left these days). Here, follow the yellow arrows off the Wall, to avoid a military zone up ahead, and walk down through the fields for about 25 minutes. Take the first right, at another yellow arrow, beside a vegetable plot, and climb the path back towards the Wall. After about half an hour you'll pass **Qing Yun Farmhouse**, where you may be able to buy food and drinks (but don't bank on it). It's a 25-minute climb up to the Wall from here (at the fork, the left path is easier). At the Wall, walk through the cute doorway to get up around the other side of the tower, then continue along the Wall to the restored section at Jīnshānlǐng. You'll have to buy a ticket off a lady at **Xiliang Zhuandao Tower**, from where it's about 30 minutes to **Little Jinshan Tower** (for the path, or cable car, down to the west gate), or about 90 minutes to **East Tower with Five Holes** (for the path down to the east gate, from where it's a 30-minute walk to the bus back to Běijīng).

1

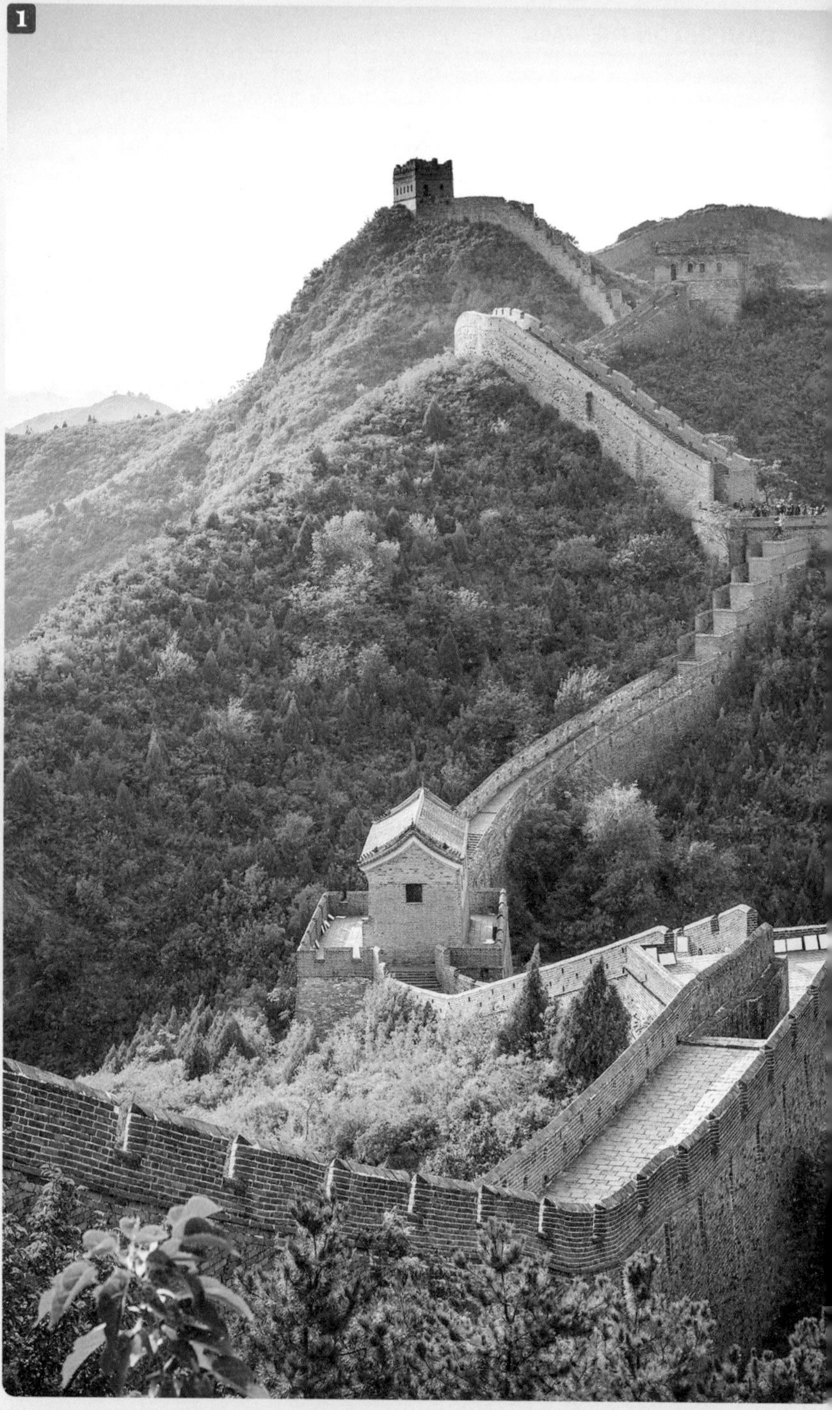

HUNG CHUNG CHIH / SHUTTERSTOCK ©

3

BERNARD TAN / GETTY IMAGES ©

. Jīnshānlǐng (p168)
sit one of the most remote sections of
e Wall

2. Hiking the Great Wall (p170)
Set out on an adventure along one of the
many sections of the wall close to Běijīng

3. Mùtiányù (p164)
Take in the excellent views along this 3km
restored section of the Wall

Day Trips from Běijīng

Ming Tombs p175

Unesco-protected burial site for 13 of China's emperors.

Chuāndǐxià p176

Gorgeous, well-preserved Ming dynasty village, nestled in a remote valley.

Shídù p177

Picnic and play by the Jùmǎ River in this picturesque valley.

Wǎnpíng Town p180

A unique Ming dynasty walled town with a 900-year-old stone bridge beside it.

Ming Tombs

Explore

The Unesco-protected **Ming Tombs** (十三陵; Shísān Líng; ☎010 6076 1643; Changchi Lu, Chāngpíng; 昌平区昌赤路; per site ¥20-60, through ticket ¥100 Nov-Mar, ¥135 Apr-Oct; 🕒8am-5.30pm; 🚌872, [S]Ming Tombs) are the final resting place for 13 of the 16 Ming dynasty emperors and make for a fascinating half-day trip. The scattered tombs, each a huge temple-like complex guarding an enormous burial mound at its rear, back onto the southern slopes of Tiānshòu Mountain. Only three of the 13 tombs are open to the public, and only one has had its underground burial chambers excavated, but what you are able to see is impressive enough and leaves you wondering just how many priceless treasures must still be buried here.

Getting There & Away

The Ming Tombs are now on the subway, although the station is almost at the end of the Chángpíng Line – a long haul from central Běijīng – and is inconveniently located 3km from the entrance to the Spirit Way, requiring you either to take a taxi (¥13) there, or a bus (¥2) and then walk another 1km.

If you're catching the bus, take exit C out of the station, turn right and then turn right again at Nanjian Lu; the bus stop for the 昌53 is around 100m ahead on the right. The 昌 character stands for Cháng, as in Chángpíng. Get off at Jiàntǒu Lùkǒu (涧头路口), walk ahead for 200m and then turn left at Changchi Lu – the entrance to the Spirit Way is 10 minutes ahead.

A more direct way to get there is on bus 872 (¥9, one hour, 7.10am to 7.10pm) from the north side of Déshèngmén Gateway (p120). It passes all the sights, apart from Zhāo Líng, before terminating at Cháng Líng. Last bus back is at 6pm.

Getting Around

It's easy to bus-hop around the Ming Tombs. Get off the 872 at Dà Gōng Mén bus stop (大宫门), and walk through the triple-arched Great Palace Gate (大宫门) that leads to the Spirit Way. After walking the length of the Spirit Way, catch bus 67 from Hú Zhuāng bus stop (胡庄), the first bus stop on your right, to its terminus at Zhāo Líng (¥2); walk straight through the village to find the tombs. Then, coming back the way you came, catch another 67 (¥2), or walk (1.5km; left at the end of the road, then left again) to Dìng Líng, from where you can catch bus 314 to Cháng Líng (¥2).

Need to Know

- **Location** 50km from Běijīng
- **Price** ¥20 to ¥60, combined ticket ¥135 April to October/¥100 November to March
- **Hours** 8am to 5.30pm

SIGHTS

CHÁNG LÍNG TOMB

(长陵; ¥45 Apr-Oct/¥30 Nov-Mar, audio guide ¥50; 🚌872) The resting place of the first of the 13 emperors to be buried at the Ming Tombs, Cháng Líng contains the body of Emperor Yongle (1402–24), his wife and 16 concubines. It's the largest, most impressive and most important of the tombs. Like all the tombs it follows a standard imperial layout, with a main gate (祾恩门; *lín'ēn mén*) leading to the first of a series of courtyards and the main hall (祾恩殿; *líng'ēn diàn*). Beyond this lie gates leading to the **Soul Tower** (明楼; Míng Lóu), behind which

Ming Tombs

rises the burial mound surrounded by a fortified wall (宝成; *bǎo chéng*). Seated upon a three-tiered marble terrace, the standout structure in this complex is the **Hall of Eminent Favours** (灵恩殿; Líng'ēn Diàn), containing a recent statue of Yongle, various artefacts excavated from Dìng Líng, and a breathtaking interior with vast *nánmù* (cedar wood) columns. As with all three tombs here, you can climb the Soul Tower at the back of the complex for fine views of the surrounding hills.

DÌNG LÍNG TOMB

(定陵; ¥60 Apr-Oct, ¥40 Nov-Mar, audio guide ¥50) Dìng Líng, the resting place of Emperor Wanli (1572–1620) and his wife and concubines, is at first sight less impressive than Cháng Líng (p175) because many of the halls and gateways have been destroyed. Many of the priceless artefacts were ruined after being left in a huge, unsealed storage room that leaked water. What treasures that were left – including the bodies of Emperor Wanli and his entourage – were looted and burned by Red Guards during the Cultural Revolution. The small **Museum of the Ming Tombs** (明十三陵博物馆; Míng Shísānlíng Bówùguǎn; admission with Dìng Líng ticket), just inside the complex, contains a few precious remaining artefacts, plus replicas of destroyed originals.

ZHĀO LÍNG TOMB

(昭陵; ¥30 Apr-Oct, ¥20 Nov-Mar) Zhāo Líng is the smallest of the main three Ming Tombs (p175), and many of its buildings are recent rebuilds. It's much less visited than the others, though, so is more peaceful, and the **fortified wall** (宝成; *bǎo chéng*) surrounding the burial mound is unusual in both its size and form. The tomb, which is the resting place of Emperor Longqing (1537–72), is at the end of the small village of Zhāolíng (昭陵村; Zhāolíng Cūn).

SPIRIT WAY AREA

(神道; Shéndào; ¥30 Apr-Oct, ¥20 Nov-Mar; 🚌872) The road leading to the Ming Tombs (p175) is a 7km stretch called the Spirit Way. Commencing from the south with a triumphal triple archway, known as the **Great Palace Gate** (大宫门; Dàgōng Mén), the path passes through the **Stele Pavilion** (碑亭; Bēi Tíng; admission with Ming Tombs through ticket ¥100 Nov-Mar, ¥135 Apr-Oct; ♿), which contains a giant *bìxì* (mythical tortoise-like dragon) bearing the largest stele in China. A guard of 12 sets of giant stone animals and officials ensues.

EATING

NÓNGJIĀFÀN KUÀICĀN CHINESE $

(农家饭快餐; mains ¥18-68; ⊗8.30am-5.30pm) Nóngjiāfàn Kuàicān is a small restaurant in the car park at Dìng Líng (no English sign or menu). Dishes include *xīhóngshì jīdàn miàn* (西红柿鸡蛋面; egg and tomato noodles; ¥18), *zhájiàng miàn* (炸酱面; Běijīng-style pork noodles; ¥20), *huíguō ròu* (回锅肉; spicy cured pork; ¥32), *gōngbào jīdīng* (宫爆鸡丁; spicy chicken with peanuts; ¥24) and *yúxiāng ròusī* (鱼香肉丝; sweet and spicy shredded pork; ¥24).

MÍNG CHÁNG LÍNG RESTAURANT CHINESE $

(明长陵餐厅; Míng Cháng Líng Cāntīng; Cháng Líng Ming Tomb; dishes from ¥18; ⊗8.30am-4.30pm) Simple but clean restaurant, with an English menu, just beside the Cháng Líng (p175) ticket office.

Chuāndǐxià

Explore

Nestled in a valley 90km west of Běijīng and overlooked by towering peaks, the Ming dynasty village of Chuāndǐxià (爨底下) is a gorgeous cluster of historic courtyard homes with old-world charm. The backdrop is lovely: terraced orchards and fields with ancient houses and alleyways rising up the hillside and temples in the surrounding area. Two hours is more than enough to wander around the village because it's not big, but staying the night allows you to soak up its historic charms without the distraction of all those day trippers.

Top Tip

Bear in mind that almost all inns and restaurants in Chuāndǐxià shut down between November and April, when the village becomes a freezing ghost town.

Getting There & Away

Bus 892 leaves frequently from a bus stop 400m west of Pínggyuǒyuán subway station (use Exit D and turn right; the bus stop is just past the first big set of traffic lights under the highway) and goes to Zhāitáng (斋堂; ¥15, two hours, 6.30am to 5.50pm), from where you'll have to take a taxi (¥20) for the last

6km to Chuāndǐxià. There's one direct bus to Chuāndǐxià which leaves Píngguǒyuán at 7am. The direct bus back to Píngguǒyuán leaves Chuāndǐxià at 6.50am. There are also two buses from Chuāndǐxià to Zhāitáng (9.30am and 3.30pm; ¥2). The last bus from Zhāitáng back to Píngguǒyuán leaves at 5pm. If you miss that, it's around ¥200 for a taxi.

Need to Know
➡ **Location** 90km from Běijīng
➡ **Price** ¥35
➡ **Hours** No official opening hours

SIGHTS

The main attractions in Chuāndǐxià are the **courtyard homes** and the cobbled steps and alleyways that link them up. Great fun can be had from just wandering the village and poking your head into whichever ancient doorways take your fancy. Most of the homes date from the Qing dynasty, although a few remain from Ming times. Many have been turned into small restaurants or guesthouses, meaning you can eat, drink tea or even stay the night in a 500-year-old Chinese courtyard. Chuāndǐxià is also a museum of **Maoist slogans**, especially up the incline among the better-preserved houses. Look for the very clear, red-painted slogan just past the Landlord's Courtyard (the village's principal courtyard), which reads: 用毛泽东思想武装我们的头脑 (*yòng Máozédōng sīxiǎng wǔzhuāng wǒmen de tóunǎo*; use Mao Zedong thought to arm our minds).

EATING & SLEEPING

CUÀNYÙN INN CHINESE **$$**
(爨韵客栈; Cuànyùn Kèzhàn; 23 Chuāndǐxià Village; 爨低下村23号; mains ¥20-60; ⊙6.30am-8.30pm, closed Nov-Mar; 🌐) The best place to sample roast leg of lamb (烤羊腿; *kǎo yáng tuǐ*; ¥200). On the right of the main road as you enter the village. It has a photo menu.

GǓCHÉNGBǍO INN INN **$**
(古城堡客栈; Gǔchéngbǎo Kèzhàn; 📱136 9135 9255; Mon-Thu r ¥100, with bathroom ¥120, Fri-Sun ¥180; mains ¥20-60; ⊙closed Nov-Mar; 🌐) This 400-year-old building is perched high above much of the village and enjoys fine views from its terrace restaurant. Rooms are in the back courtyard and are basic but charming. Each room has a traditional stone *kàng* bed, which sleeps up to four people and can be fire-heated in winter.

Shídù

Explore

Best visited during the summer rainy season, Shídù (十渡) is a scenic valley containing pinnacle-shaped rock formations, which tower over the Jùmǎ River. There is, potentially, some great hiking to be done here, but most people come for some good honest family fun: boating, kids' rides, bungee jumping and riverside barbecues. Shídù means '10 crossings': before the new road and bridges were built, you had to cross the Jùmǎ River 10 times while travelling along the gorge from Zhāngfāng (张坊) to Shídù.

Getting There & Away

To visit Shídù, take bus 836 from Liuliqiao East subway station (come out of Exit E then walk back to a bus stop 200m away). Shídù (¥20, two hours, 6am to 5pm) should be the last stop, but check with the bus conductor as some 836 buses don't go that far.

Need to Know
➡ **Location** 80km from Běijīng
➡ **Price** Free
➡ **Hours** No official opening hours

 SIGHTS

A couple of kilometres before Shídù, at Zhāngfāng Village, you can visit the **Zhāngfāng Ancient Battle Tunnel** (张坊古战道; Zhāngfāng Gǔ Zhàndào; 📞010 6133 1451; ¥20; ⊙9am-5pm), a 1000-year-old underground military facility that was discovered by chance in 1991. Bus 836 stops here before it reaches Shídù; the entrance to the tunnels is inside the rebuilt ancient gateway, 200m ahead of the bus stop.

EATING & SLEEPING

There are restaurants – none very cheap – and snack stalls at each of the crossings, as

SINO IMAGES / GETTY IMAGES ©

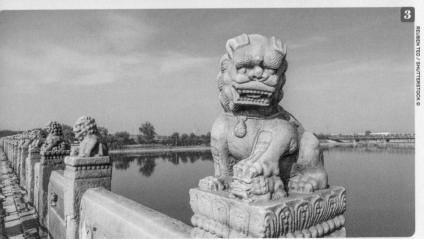

REUBEN TEO / SHUTTERSTOCK ©

1. Ming Tombs (p175)
Stone statue of a Chinese Emperor at the Unesco-protected Ming Tombs

2. Chuāndǐxià (p176)
Nestled in a scenic valley, this Ming-dynasty village offers a gorgeous mix of charm and history

3. Wǎnpíng Town (p180)
Individually carved stone lions on the 900-year-old Marco Polo Bridge

well as a few shops where you can pick up supplies. Or do what many people do and bring your own picnic.

JIĀYÙN NÓNGJIĀYUÀN GUESTHOUSE $
(佳运农家院; ☎134 3686 0728; r ¥80-100) Modest guesthouse set around a small courtyard.

ACTIVITIES

Each river crossing, or *dù*, is like a small village. Most of the action takes place at the ninth crossing (九渡; *jiŭ dù*), where you'll find the **Juma Happy Garden** amusement park, a cable car, a bungee jump, a zip line, boat rides and loads of restaurants. Other crossings have more low-key attractions: bamboo rafts, dinghy rides etc. You can walk the valley along the river, or bus-hop from crossing to crossing.

Wǎnpíng Town

Explore

The star attraction here is the famous 900-year-old Marco Polo Bridge (卢沟桥; Lúgōu Qiáo), but the unexpected bonus is the chance to see, at one end of the bridge, the enormous, war-torn, Ming dynasty walls of the once heavily guarded Wǎnpíng Town (宛平城; Wǎnpíng Chéng). Then there's also the well-presented, if clumsily named, Museum of the War of Chinese People's Resistance Against Japanese Aggression.

Getting There & Away

Bus Bus 662 comes here from Chángchūnjiē subway station (Line 2). Come out of Exit A1 and the bus stop is in front of you on the right. Get off the bus at Lú Gōu Xīn Qiáo (卢沟新桥) bus stop (¥2, 40 minutes) then turn right, beside a petrol station, and bear left to follow the road to the Marco Polo Bridge and the West Gate (400m).

Train Dāwǎyáo subway station (Line 14) is about a 1km walk from the East Gate of Wǎnpíng Town. Come out of Exit A, turn left at the junction and walk alongside the highway for about 600m before turning right down Chengnei Jie (城内街), which leads to the walls.

Need to Know

- **Location** 15km from central Běijīng
- **Price** ¥20
- **Hours** No official opening hours

SIGHTS

MARCO POLO BRIDGE BRIDGE
(卢沟桥; Lúgōu Qiáo; ¥20; ⏰7am-8pm Apr-Oct, to 6pm Nov-Mar; [S]Changchunjie then bus 662) Described by the great traveller himself, this 266m-long, multiarched granite bridge is the oldest bridge in Běijīng and is decorated beautifully with 485 individually carved stone lions, each one different. Dating from 1189, although widened in 1969, it spans the Yǒngdìng River, and was once the main route into the city from the southwest.

WǍNPÍNG OLD TOWN CITY WALLS
(宛平城; Wǎnpíng Chéng; [S]Dawayao or Changchunjie, then bus 662) [FREE] An astonishing sight, this double-gated, Ming dynasty walled town is still lived in today. Although few of its original buildings still stand (residents live in newish brick bungalows these days), its 2km-long, 6m-high, battle-scarred town walls date from 1640.

MUSEUM OF THE WAR OF CHINESE PEOPLE'S RESISTANCE AGAINST JAPANESE AGGRESSION MUSEUM
(中国人民抗日战争纪念馆; Zhōngguó Rénmín Kàng Rì Zhànzhēng Jìniànguǎn; ☎010 6377 7088; Chengnei Jie; 城内街; entry free with passport, audio guide ¥120; ⏰9am-4.30pm Tue-Sun; [S]Dawayao) [FREE] This modern museum, on the north side of the main road in Wǎnpíng Town, is dedicated to the July 7th Incident (as it's called here) and the ensuing war with Japan. It's obviously biased but some thought has gone into the presentation and there are tons of exhibits and good English captions.

EATING

CHUĀN XIĀNG CHUĀN QÍNG SHÍFǓ SICHUAN $$
(川香川情食府; ☎010 8389 3301; 1 Chengnei Jie; 城内街1号; dishes ¥22-68; ⏰10am-10pm) Reliable and reasonably priced Sìchuān restaurant just inside the east gate of Wǎnpíng Town. It gets busy at lunchtime. No English is spoken, but there is a picture menu.

🛏 Sleeping

Běijīng's increasingly impressive hotel scene has something for everyone: a huge range of youth hostels, loads of business hotels and all the international five-star hotel brands you'd expect of a city this size. The jewel in the crown, though, is its charming courtyard hotels, which offer a wonderful opportunity to experience life in Běijīng's unique hútòng (alleyways).

Hostels

Youth hostels offer much more than just dorm beds and budget prices. Many are hidden away in historic buildings down Běijīng's *hútòng*, with comfortable single and double rooms, and staff tuned into foreign travellers' needs. Travel advice is often honest, impartial and knowledgeable, and staff members usually speak excellent English. They have free wi-fi, often rent bicycles and tend to run worthwhile day trips and tours to places such as the Great Wall.

Courtyard Hotels

If you want history, look no further than Běijīng's courtyard hotels, which allow you to enjoy the city's *hútòng* ambience and inimitable courtyard residences. The downside, considering the relatively high prices, is the smallish size of the rooms, but courtyard hotels come with an atmosphere that is uniquely Běijīng and a charm that other hotels cannot imitate.

Luxury Hotels

The top-end bracket is crammed with options in most parts of town (apart from in the Dōngchéng North neighbourhood). All the major players in the world of international five-star hotels are represented – Hyatt, Hilton, St Regis etc – and some have multiple locations around the city.

Standard Hotels

Run-of-the-mill midrange Chinese hotels lack character but can be good value as they often come with generous discounts. Expect clean rooms (although some may be smoky) with TV, wi-fi, kettle, fridge and small attached bathrooms. Staff at these types of places rarely speak much English.

Many of the city's cheapest guesthouses, often known as *zhāodàisuǒ* (招待所), still refuse to take foreigners because of the rigmarole involved with registering foreign guests with the local police.

Homestays & Long-Term Rentals

Homestays are a great way to experience Chinese culture (and improve your Chinese language skills). Běijīng also has a large and fast-expanding couch-surfing community and short-term room rentals can be found at www.airbnb.com.

The rental market in Běijīng is good value, considering how much homes cost here now. Prices start at around ¥4000 per month for a two-bed apartment, although that won't be in the centre of town. If you speak Chinese, just make enquiries at any estate agent in the part of town you wish to live in. If you don't, your easiest option is to check the accommodation pages of the websites of Běijīng's expat magazines.

NEED TO KNOW

Price Ranges

The following price ranges represent a standard double room per night.

$ less than ¥400

$$ ¥400–¥1000

$$$ more than ¥1000

Discounts

Discounts of 20% to 40% are the norm in ordinary, midrange, Chinese-run hotels. Hostels, courytard hotels and boutique hotels tend to be more transparent, and will just charge the rack rates. Whatever the hotel, booking online and in advance – especially through large, well-established booking sites such as www.ctrip.com or www.booking.com – will often help you secure the best discounts.

Reservations

Hotel rooms are easy to find, although it's worth booking ahead during public holidays. It's always advisable to prebook courtyard hotels, as they often have only four or five rooms in total.

Checking In

When checking into a hotel, you will need to complete a registration form, a copy of which will be sent to the local Public Security Bureau (PSB; Gōng'ānjú), and your passport will be scanned or photocopied.

Service Charge & Tips

A 15% service charge is levied at midrange and top-end hotels. Tipping is only expected in top-end hotels.

Lonely Planet's Top Choices

Temple Hotel (p184) Class and serenity in a beautifully restored, 250-year-old Buddhist temple complex.

Great Wall Box House (p165) Lovingly renovated village hostel, with Great Wall remains running alongside it.

City Walls Courtyard (p184) Fabulous location and a traditional courtyard to laze in.

Courtyard 7 (p187) Ravishing courtyard hotel, oozing Qing dynasty charm.

Opposite House Hotel (p189) So trendy it hurts; the city's swankiest boutique hotel.

Best by Budget

$

Beijing Drum Tower International Youth Hostel (p186) Superb views from the roof terrace.

Běijīng Downtown Backpackers (p186) Great location. Great staff.

Three-Legged Frog Hostel (p188) Good, honest cheapie with a friendly welcome.

Nostalgia Hotel (p186) Trendy alternative to the youth hostels.

Běijīng Feel Inn (p184) Understated hostel, hidden away in an imperial *hútòng*.

$$

Great Wall Box House (p165) Fabulous guesthouse right beside the Great Wall.

Emperor (p187) Rooftop pool overlooking Tiān'ānmén Sq.

Orchid (p186) The hipsters' *hútòng* hotel of choice.

Jǐngshān Garden Hotel (p184) Calm courtyard in a quieter part of central Běijīng.

Graceland Yard (p188) A 500-year-old abandoned

temple converted into a serene courtyard hotel.

$$$

Temple Hotel (p184) Utterly unique, Unesco-acclaimed temple conversion.

Opposite House (p189) Hotels don't come cooler than this.

Courtyard 7 (p187) Bags of history. Plenty of class.

Aman at Summer Palace (p190) Pure indulgence on the outskirts of the city.

Côté Cour (p185) Exquisite rooms off a magnolia-filled courtyard.

Best Courtyard Hotels

Courtyard 7 (p187) Qing dynasty residence transformed into one of the city's most charming hotels.

Temple Hotel (p184) Luxury lodgings off a series of 250-year-old Buddhist-temple courtyards.

Graceland Yard (p188) Smaller, more modest temple conversion with 500 years of history.

Jǐngshān Garden Hotel (p184) Simple, pleasant courtyard in a quieter part of town.

Hulu Hotel (p184) Trendy new addition to the courtyard-hotel scene.

Best Hútòng Hostels

Dragon King Hostel (p184) Historic building and central location.

Běijīng Downtown Backpackers (p186) Nanluogu Xiang's first hostel...and still its best.

Pagoda Light (p187) Stylish, laid-back hostel in a serene setting.

Běijīng Feel Inn (p184) Tucked away discreetly; a stone's throw from the Forbidden City.

Where to Stay

NEIGHBOURHOOD	FOR	AGAINST
FORBIDDEN CITY & DŌNGCHÉNG CENTRAL	Hugely historic. Highest concentration of sights. Good mix of ordinary hotels and *hútòng* accommodation.	Some parts are less residential than other neighbourhoods, and so can be eerily quiet in the evenings. Slim pickings on the nightlife front.
DRUM TOWER & DŌNGCHÉNG NORTH	Běijīng's most desirable neighbourhood. Perfect for delving deep into the *hútòng*. Plenty of courtyard hotels. Cafes, bars and live music on your doorstep.	Budget backpackers may be priced out. No five-star hotels.
BĚIHǍI PARK & XĪCHÉNG NORTH	Plenty of *hútòng* action, and the area by the lakes sees little motorised traffic, and so can be peaceful. Less touristy than Dōngchéng District.	Evening karaoke bars can ruin the lakeside ambience. Choice of accommodation, restaurants and bars is more limited.
DASHILAR & XĪCHÉNG SOUTH	Backpacker Central. Great choice of hostels; some historic. *Hútòng* vibe is still strong around Dashilar.	Extensive reconstruction has stolen some of the character from the area (particularly around Qiánmén) and seen restaurant prices rise, although hostel rooms are still cheap.
SĀNLǏTÚN & CHÁOYÁNG	Great for shopping, eating and nightlife, and excellent choice of mid- and high-range places to stay.	Area lacks character and any historical narrative.
SUMMER PALACE & HǍIDIÀN	Less touristy than more central areas, while the presence of lots of students means there's nightlife.	A trek from the centre of town and the choice of accommodation is limited.

SLEEPING WHERE TO STAY

🛏 Forbidden City & Dōngchéng Central

★**CITY WALLS COURTYARD** HOSTEL $

Map p270 (城墙旅舍; Chéngqiáng Lǚshè; ☑010 6402 7805; www.beijingcitywalls.com; 57 Nianzi Hutong; 碾子胡同57号; dm/s/tw ¥100/260/420; ❄@🛜; ⓢLines 6, 8 to Nanluoguxiang, exit A) Hidden among a maze of *hútòng* is this attractive choice within a fabulous location. Private rooms and dorms all have private bathrooms; spacious four-bed dorms are especially great value. The main selling point is its traditional courtyard decorated with eclectic knick-knacks, plants and couches to enjoy cheap large beers (¥4), ground coffee (¥10) and meals. To get here, from Jingshan Houjie, look for the *hútòng* opening just east of Jǐngshān Table Tennis Park. Walk up the *hútòng* and follow it around to the right and then left; the hostel is on the left-hand side.

DRAGON KING HOSTEL HOSTEL $

Map p270 (万里路青年酒店东四九条店; Wànlǐlù Qīngnián Jiǔdiàn Dōngsì Jiǔtiáo Diàn; ☑010 8400 2660; www.9dragons.hostel.com; 78 Dongsi Jiutiao; 东四九条78号; dm¥80-100, d¥300; ❄🛜; ⓢLine 5 to Zhangzizhonglu, exit C) Down a *hútòng* featuring some rowdy local restaurants, Dragon King is classic Běijīng with its historic building festooned with Chinese lanterns. There are rough edges, but its central location is close to all the action. Dorm beds have curtains for privacy, while private rooms have plenty of space. Its cosy backpacker-style pub does cheap beer and food.

BĚIJĪNG FEEL INN HOSTEL $

Map p268 (非凡客栈; Fēifán Kèzhàn; ☑010 6528 7418, 139 1040 9166; www.beijingfeelinn.com; 2 Ciqiku Hutong, off Nanheyan Dajie; 南河沿大街,磁器库胡同2号; dm ¥50-60, r from ¥268; ❄@🛜; ⓢLine 1 to Tian'anmen East, exit A) A small, understated hostel with a hidden, backstreet location, Feel Inn is tucked away among the *hútòng* containing the little-known Pǔdù Temple. Has simple, clean rooms, a small bar-restaurant and wi-fi throughout. It rents bikes for ¥30 per day.

★**JĪNGSHĀN GARDEN HOTEL** HUTONG HOTEL $$

Map p270 (景山花园酒店; Jīngshān Huāyuán Jiǔdiàn; ☑010 8404 7979; www.jingshangarden-hotel.com; 68 Sanyanjing Hutong, off Jingshan Dongjie; 景山东街,三眼井胡同68号; r incl breakfast ¥550-650; ❄@🛜; ⓢLines 6, 8 to Nan-luoguxiang, exit A) This delightful, unfussy, two-storey guesthouse has bright, spacious rooms surrounding a large, peaceful, flower-filled courtyard. First-floor rooms are pricier, but larger and brighter than the ground-floor ones, and some have *slight* views of Jǐngshān Park from their bathrooms. It also has an upstairs Sìchuān restaurant. Walking down Sanyuanjing Hutong from the direction of Jīngshān Park, turn right down the first alleyway, and the hotel is at the end.

HÚLÚ HOTEL HUTONG HOTEL $$

Map p270 (壶庐宾馆; Húlú Bīnguǎn; ☑010 6543 9229; www.thehuluhotel.com; 91 Yanyue Hutong, off Dongsi Nandajie; 东四南大街,演水胡同91号; r¥718-900; ⓢLine 5 to Dengshikou, exit A, or Lines 5, 6 to Dongsi, exit C) Hulu's converted *hútòng* space is minimalist throughout, with cool grey-painted wood beams, slate-tiled bathrooms and a cleverly renovated courtyard that combines its old-Běijīng roots with a modern, comfortable design. The atmosphere is laid-back, and the young staff speak excellent English. There are three grades of room (size increases with price), all of which have large double beds – no twins. There's a homely cafe at reception that does breakfast, coffee and bar drinks. The small, leafy rooftop terrace is just the place to relax.

HOME INN PLUS HOTEL $$

Map p270 (如家快捷酒店加; Rújiā Kuàijié Jiǔdiàn Jiā; ☑010 6559 5900; www.homeinns.com; 212 Dongsi Beidajie; 东四北大街212号; r incl breakfast ¥500; ❄🛜; ⓢLine 5 to Zhangzizhonglu, exit C) Centrally located, and right by the subway, this excellent-value business hotel offers an alternative to those not wanting to stay in *hútòng* hotels. Rooms are modern, comfortable and come with filtered water taps in the bathroom. Perks include free buffet breakfast, a full-sized billiard table, complimentary coffee and free laundry – a space which bizarrely doubles as a small gym.

★**TEMPLE HOTEL** HUTONG HOTEL $$$

Map p270 (东景缘; Dōngjǐng Yuán; ☑010 8401 5680; www.thetemplehotel.com; 23 Shatan Beijie, off Wusi Dajie; 五四大街,沙滩北街23号; d/ste from ¥2000/4500; ❄🛜; ⓢLines 6, 8 to Nan-luoguxiang, exit B, or Lines 5, 6 to Dongsi, exit E) Unrivalled by anything else on the Běijīng hotel scene, this unique heritage hotel forms part of a renovation project that was recognised by Unesco for its conservation efforts. A team spent five years renovating what was left of Zhīzhù Sì (智珠寺; Temple of Wisdom), a part-abandoned, 250-year-old Buddhist temple, and slowly transformed it into one of the most alluring places to stay in the capital.

There are eight rooms, each with its own story to tell. Some once formed part of the monks' dormitories during the Qing dynasty. Others are industrial in style, as befits their former incarnation as a television factory in the 1960s. The two-storey suites, meanwhile, have close-up views of the fabulous main temple hall, now used for film screenings. The rooms are huge, and the atmosphere within the courtyard complex is serene. There's also a classy gallery (p70) here.

★CÔTÉ COUR   HUTONG HOTEL $$$

Map p270 (北京演乐酒店; Běijīng Yǎnyuè Jiǔdiàn; ☑010 6523 3958; www.hotelcotecourbj.com; 70 Yanyue Hutong; 演乐胡同70号; d/ste incl breakfast ¥1166/1995; ❄@🛜; Ⓢ Line 5 to Dengshikou, exit A, or Lines 5, 6 to Dongsi, exit C) With a calm, serene atmosphere and a lovely magnolia-filled courtyard, this atmospheric *hútòng* hotel makes a charming place to rest your head. The decor is exquisite and there's plenty of space to relax in the 500-year-old courtyard or on the extensive rooftop. Staff are sweet and friendly, and bicycles are available for rent (¥50). Nonguests can eat at the stylish rooftop restaurant, which is open every evening from 6.30pm to 10pm.

★W BĚIJĪNG   BOUTIQUE HOTEL $$$

Map p282 (北京长安街 W 酒店; ☑010 6515 8855; www.whotels.com/beijing; 2 Jianguomennan Jie; 建国门南大街2号; r from ¥2000; Ⓢ Lines 1, 2 to Jianguomen, exit B) The W is all about flashy installations that feel more nightclub than hotel. Rooms are full of gadgetry, from remote-control rotating sofas and touchscreen colour-adjustment wheels to spotlight projectors and automatic sliding curtains. A major downside, though, is its out-of-the-way location beside a big highway.

There's a mosaic-floored swimming pool and gym with personal trainers. The **X25** cocktail bar has regular DJs and live music. There's a choice of several restaurants, including the **Kitchen Table** with outdoor patio, open kitchen and herb garden, or **Yen**, which specialises in Peking duck.

★RED CAPITAL RESIDENCE   HUTONG HOTEL $$$

Map p270 (新红资客栈; Xīnhóngzī Kèzhàn; ☑010 8401 8886, 010 8403 5308; 9 Dongsi Liutiao; 东四六条9号; r incl breakfast ¥1050; ❄@🛜; Ⓢ Line 5 to Zhangzizhonglu, exit C) Dressed up with

Liberation-era artefacts and established in a gorgeous Qing dynasty courtyard, this tiny but unique guesthouse offers a heady dose of nostalgia for a vanished age. Make your choice from rooms decked out with paraphernalia that wouldn't look out of place in a museum. Though standards have slipped, it remains one of Běijīng's most unique hotels.

Rooms and bathrooms are small, but beautifully decorated. What makes this place even *more* unique, though, is the 'wine shelter' housed below the courtyard in an underground bomb shelter! There's also an atmospheric cigar lounge at reception, packed with Communist decorative pieces.

LEGENDALE HOTEL   HOTEL $$$

Map p270 (励骏酒店; Lìjùn Jiǔdiàn; ☑010 8511 3388; www.legendalehotel.com; 90-92 Jinbao Jie; 金宝街90-92号; r from ¥1500; ❄@🛜; Ⓢ Line 5 to Dengshikou, exit C) Resembling an opulent scene from a 19th-century oil painting, this ritzy neoclassical hotel is a replica of a Versailles palace. Though it's all faux elegance (it's a new building commissioned by a Macau casino-owner), it's an impressive reproduction nevertheless. Rooms are decorated with period-style furnishings.

There are four restaurants here, including a recommended Portuguese eatery.

RAFFLES BĚIJĪNG   HOTEL $$$

Map p270 (北京饭店莱佛士酒店; Běijīng Fàndiàn Láifóshì Jiǔdiàn; ☑010 6526 3388; www.raffles.com/beijing; 33 Dongchang'an Jie; 东长安街33号; r from ¥1800; ➤❄@🛜; Ⓢ Line 1 to Wangfujing, exit C1) Sandwiched between two drab edifices, the seven-storey Raffles oozes cachet and grandeur. The heritage building dates to 1900 when it was the Grand Hotel de Pekin, and it stays true to its historic roots.

Illuminated in a chandelier glow, the elegant lobby yields to a graceful staircase leading to immaculate standard doubles that are spacious and well proportioned, decked out with period-style furniture and large bathrooms. The ground floor contains the hotel's most historic feature: the Writers Bar, once a common meeting place for Communist Party cadres, including Mao Zedong, and now a splendid spot for high tea (2.30pm to 5.30pm, one/two people ¥258/328) or a cocktail.

RED WALL GARDEN   HUTONG HOTEL $$$

Map p270 (红墙花园酒店; Hóngqiáng Huāyuán Jiǔdiàn; ☑010 5169 2222; www.rwghotel.com; 41 Shijia Hutong; 史家胡同41号; r incl breakfast ¥1000-1600; ❄@🛜; Ⓢ Line 5 to Dengshikou, exit C)

Despite its old *hútòng* location, there's nothing historic about this reconstructed courtyard hotel popular with tour groups. However, it offers top-end rooms, complete with very comfortable beds and some beautiful pieces of traditional Chinese wood furniture in its two-storey complex, and it surrounds two sides of a huge, nicely landscaped central courtyard. It has a small, atmospheric bar and a decent restaurant. There's free bicycle rental and cultural performances Tuesday and Friday evenings at 7pm.

🛏 Drum Tower & Dōngchéng North

⭐**BĚIJĪNG DRUM TOWER**
INTERNATIONAL YOUTH HOSTEL   HOSTEL $
Map p274 (鼓韵青年旅舍; Gǔyùn Qīngnián Lǚshè; ☑010 801 6565; www.24hostel.com; 51 Jiugulou Dajie; 旧鼓楼大街 51号; dm/d from ¥88/288; ✳@🛜; Ⓢ Lines 2, 8 to Guloudajie, exit G) A large, dependable hostel, the Drum's point of difference is its capsule bunk beds, which are equipped with lockable doors. They offer complete privacy so it's a step up from the usual dorms, but their cramped interior won't suit claustrophobics. Private rooms, on the other hand, are massive and have plenty of natural light. There's a peaceful rooftop terrace with magnificent views over the Drum Tower, and a cool cafe downstairs.

NOSTALGIA HOTEL   HOTEL $
Map p274 (时光漫步怀旧主题酒店; Shíguāng Mànbù Huáijiù Zhǔtí Jiǔdiàn; ☑010 6403 2288; www.nostalgiahotelbeijing.com; 46 Fangjia Hutong; 安定门内大街·方家胡同46号; r from ¥428; ✳@🛜; Ⓢ Line 5 to Beixinqiao, exit A) A good-value option if you don't fancy staying in a youth hostel, this large, funky hotel is housed in a small arts zone on trendy Fangjia Hutong. Rooms are decorated with a Chinese retro theme and knick-knacks throughout. Staff on reception speak English, and there's lift access. There's a breakfast room, but no restaurant. To find it, enter the small arts zone named after its address (46 Fangjia Hutong) and walk to the far left corner of the complex.

BĚIJĪNG DOWNTOWN
BACKPACKERS   HOSTEL $
Map p274 (东堂客栈; Dōngtáng Kèzhàn; ☑010 8400 2429; www.backpackingchina.com; 85 Nanluogu Xiang; 南锣鼓巷85号; dm incl breakfast ¥70-100, r ¥180-320; ✳@🛜; Ⓢ Lines 6, 8 to Nanluoguxiang, exit E) Downtown Backpackers is

Nanluogu Xiang's original youth hostel and it hasn't forgotten its roots. Rooms are basic, therefore cheap, but are kept clean and tidy, and staff members are fully plugged in to the needs of Western travellers. Dorms have curtains for added privacy, along with power sockets and lamps. There's a rooftop terrace (complete with bench press and dumbbells) and a basement lounge to hang out in.

The hostel rents bikes (per day ¥40) and runs recommended hiking trips to the Great Wall (¥280), plus a range of other city trips.

PEKING YOUTH HOSTEL   HOSTEL $
Map p274 (北平国际青年旅社; Běipíng Guójì Qīngnián Lǚshè; ☑010 8403 9098, 010 6401 3961; www.peking.hostel.com; 113 Nanluogu Xiang; 南锣鼓巷113号; dm/tw from ¥180/500; ✳@🛜; Ⓢ Lines 6, 8 to Nanluoguxiang, exit E) Slick, colourful, but rather cramped rooms are located round the back of the flower-filled Peking Cafe, which opens out onto Nanluogu Xiang. Prices reflect the sought-after location rather than the size or quality of the rooms. All the usual youth-hostel services are dished up, including bike hire and trips to the Great Wall. Enter via Yu'er Hutong.

⭐**ORCHID**   COURTYARD HOTEL $$
Map p274 (兰花宾馆; Lánhuā Bīnguǎn; ☑010 5799 0806; www.theorchidbeijing.com; 65 Baochao Hutong; 鼓楼东大街宝钞胡同65号; d ¥805-1800; ✳@🛜; Ⓢ Lines 2, 8 to Guloudajie, exit F, or Line 8 to Shichahai, exit A2) This place may lack the history of other courtyard hotels, but it's been renovated into a beautiful space, with a peaceful courtyard and some rooftop seating with distant views of the Drum and Bell Towers. Rooms are doubles only, and are small, but are tastefully decorated and come with Apple TV home entertainment systems, complimentary loan of mobile phones and bike rental. There are also self-contained apartments with cooking facilities, and it has the well-regarded Toast (p94) restaurant. It does Great Wall tours (from ¥1100 including lunch, admission and transport), and can organise taxis for city tours. Hard to spot, the Orchid is down an unnamed, shoulder-width alleyway opposite Mr Shi's Dumplings.

161 LAMA TEMPLE
COURTYARD HOTEL   HUTONG HOTEL $$
Map p274 (北京161酒店–雍和宫四合院店; ☑010 8401 5027; www.161hotel.com; 46 Beixinqiao Santiao; 北新桥三条46号; r ¥500-600; Ⓢ Line 5 to Beixinqiao, exit B) This hotel-cum-hostel, located on a *hútòng* which comes alive with

restaurants in the evening, has 11 rooms, each themed on a different tourist sight in Běijīng. Rooms have a huge photo-mural to match their theme, and are small but spotless; the bathrooms likewise. The higher-category rooms come with a traditional wooden tea-drinking table, which can double up as an extra single bed. There's a charming little cafe in reception and some cute courtyard seating. Bike hire is ¥50 per day.

OLD BĚIJĪNG SQUARE HOTEL HUTONG HOTEL $$

Map p274 (未名精品酒店; Wèimíng Jīngpǐn Jiǔdiàn; ☎010 8402 5337; weimingjiudian@163.com; 38 Baochao Hutong; 宝抄胡同38号; d/tr/q incl breakfast ¥580/880/1280; ❄📶; [S]Lines 2, 8 to Guloudajie, exit G) This well-reconstructed courtyard hotel has been done with taste and charm, with plenty of natural light seeping through the glass roof into the central courtyard. Rooms are small (bathrooms tiny) but furnished well, and staff are sweet. It's hidden down an unmarked alley off Baochao Hutong, next to a cheap hotel which doesn't accept foreigners. There's free bike rental, complimentary coffee and tea, and an opportunity to practise your calligraphy.

COURTYARD 7 HUTONG HOTEL $$$

Map p274 (四合院酒店; Sìhéyuàn Jiǔdiàn; ☎010 6406 0777; www.courtyard7.com; 7 Qiangulouyuan Hutong, off Nanluogu Xiang; 鼓楼东大街南锣鼓巷前鼓楼苑胡同7号; r incl breakfast ¥900-1200; ❄📶; [S]Lines 6, 8 to Nanluoguxiang, exit E) Immaculate rooms, decorated in traditional Chinese furniture, face onto a series of different-sized, 400-year-old courtyards. Rooms come with modern comforts such as underfloor heating, wi-fi and cable TV. Standard rooms are less atmospheric so upgrade to the superior rooms surrounding the courtyard. The *hútòng* location is also a winner.

Temple of Heaven Park & Dōngchéng South

EMPEROR HOTEL $$

Map p276 (皇家驿站; Huángjiā Yìzhàn; ☎010 6701 7790; www.theemperor.com.cn; 87 Xianyukou St, Qianmen Commercial Centre; 前门商业区鲜鱼口街87号; r ¥700; ❄📶🏊; [S]Qianmen) Brand new, this modernist hotel comes with a spa and a rooftop pool that enables you to laze in the sun while enjoying fine views over nearby Tiān'ānmén Sq. The cool, all-white rooms aren't huge, but the price is reasonable for a hotel of this quality and the location is perfect. Service is attentive and the atmosphere laid-back.

Běihǎi Park & Xīchéng North

PAGODA LIGHT HOSTEL $

Map p278 (宝塔灯; Bǎotǎ dēng; ☎010 6655 2188; 185 Fuchengmennei Dajie; 阜成门内大街185号; dm/d ¥138/448; ❄📶; [S]Line 2 to Fuchengmen, exit B, or Line 4 to Xisi, exit A) Within a beautifully converted light-filled *hútòng* courtyard building is this stylish new hostel that mixes boutique design with traditional decor. It has a relaxed low-key vibe in keeping with its location next door to the Miàoyīng Temple White Dagoba (p117). For dorms, go for the more spacious bunk beds over the cramped tatami rooms. Private rooms are smallish, but modern with comfortable touches.

There's a small lounge at the front, but the Lotus Cafe & Bar (p122) upstairs is the place to hang out. There's 24-hour reception and multilingual staff.

SIHEJU COURTYARD HOSTEL HOSTEL $

Map p278 (☎186 1145 8911; 12 Xisi Beiertiao; 西四北二条12号; dm ¥130, r ¥450-700; [S]Line 4 to Xisi, Exit A) Down an atmospheric *hútòng*, you'll definitely feel like you're in Běijīng at this wonderful little hostel full of traditional charm and character. Rooms are clean, beds are comfortable and dorms have their own bathrooms. Staff are super friendly and speak good English. To find it, walk north on Xisi Beidajie from Xisi metro; it's two *hútòng* up on the left.

RED LANTERN HOUSE HOSTEL $

Map p278 (仿古园; Fǎnggǔ Yuán; ☎010 8328 5771; www.redlanternhouse.com; 5 Zhengjue Hutong; 正觉胡同 5号; dm ¥80-85, s/d without bathroom ¥180/220, d/tw/tr/family with bathroom from ¥260/290/390/580; ❄@📶; [S]Line 2 to Jishuitan, exit C) Clean and simple rooms around a pleasant, covered courtyard, and a fantastic, nontouristy *hútòng* location make this welcoming hostel a sound choice. All rooms come with shared bathrooms. If you want private bathrooms, or if this place is full, ask to see its laid-back, but less charming sibling, Red Lantern House East Yard. It's a couple of minutes' walk away in an alley off Zhengjue Hutong. Bike rental costs ¥15/30 for a half/full day.

★ GRACELAND YARD   COURTYARD HOTEL $$
Map p278 (觉心酒店; Juepin Jiudian; ☎010 8328 8366; www.graceland-yardhotel.com; 9 Zhengjue Hutong; 正觉胡同9号; s/d/ste ¥666/799/999; @🛜; 🚇Line 2 to Jishuitan, exit C) Graceland is an exquisitely renovated courtyard hotel, housed within the grounds of the abandoned, 500-year-old Zhèngjué Temple. Each of the eight rooms is slightly different but each is decorated with style, using traditional Buddhist-themed furnishings. There's no restaurant – not even breakfast – but you're not short of eateries in the surrounding *hútòng*.

SHÍCHÀHǍI SHADOW ART HOTEL   HÚTÒNG HOTEL $$
Map p278 (什刹海皮影酒店; Shíchàhǎi Píyǐng Jiǔdiàn; ☎136 8303 2251, 010 8328 7847; www.shichahaitour.com; 24 Songshu Jie; 松树街24号; tw & d incl breakfast ¥630-994; 🚇Line 6 to Beihai North, exit A) This modern hotel offers a very comfortable stay in an interesting, mostly residential section of the Hòuhǎi Lakes area. Rooms are individually themed and mix modern design with touches of traditional China. There's a small stage in the teahouse-lookalike lobby, where shadow-puppet shows are performed every Tuesday, Thursday and Saturday evening (nonguests ¥120).

There are larger, more expensive rooms in its equally natty sister hotel, **Shíchàhǎi Sandalwood Boutique Hotel** (什刹海紫檀酒店; Shíchàhǎi Zǐtán Jiǔdiàn; Map p278; ☎010 8322 6686; www.sch-hotel.com; 42 Xinghua Hutong; 兴华胡同42号; r¥600-1300; 🌸🛜; 🚇Line 6 to Beihai North, exit A), located a five-minute walk away, in Xinghua Hutong.

🛏 Dashilar & Xīchéng South

365 INN   HOSTEL $
Map p280 (☎010 6308 5956; 55 Dazhalan Xijie; 大栅栏西街 55号; dm ¥55-100, d ¥200-250; 🌸@🛜; 🚇Line 2 to Qianmen, exit B or C) An old-school backpackers, 365 Inn has a social atmosphere with a downstairs pub that makes it one of Běijīng's best for meeting fellow travellers. It also scores points for its prime location that brings you walking distance to most sights. Reception's often understaffed, but the team are friendly and helpful.

LEO HOSTEL   HOSTEL $
Map p280 (广聚园宾馆; Guǎngjùyuán Bīnguǎn; ☎010 6303 3318, 010 6303 1595; www.leohostel.com; 52 Dazhalan Xijie; 大栅栏西街 52号; dm

¥50-90, r¥300-380; 🌸@🛜; 🚇Line 2 to Qianmen, exit B or C) More atmospheric than its once-venerable cousin Leo Courtyard, the dorms and rooms are also more modern. There's a fair-sized communal area with big-screen TV, bar and food. It's in a central location on this touristy pedestrianised strip and close to Tiān'ānmén Sq and the surrounding sights. It's always busy, so it's worth booking ahead.

LEO COURTYARD   HOSTEL $
Map p280 (上林宾馆; Shànglín Bīnguǎn; ☎010 8316 6568; leocourtyard2015@outlook.com; 22 Shanxi Xiang; 陕西巷胡同 22号; dm/d/tr from ¥60/200/300; 🌸🛜; 🚇Line 7 to Hufangqiao, or Line 2 to Qianmen, exit B or C) It's a superb, historic warren of a building with a racy past featuring courtesans and the imperial elite, but like most courtyard hotels, the rooms are a little old-fashioned and the dorms on the small side. The attached bar-restaurant next door is a good place for a libation come sundown. It's down an alley off Dazhalan Xijie.

QIÁNMÉN HOSTEL   HOSTEL $
Map p280 (前门客栈; Qiánmén Kèzhàn; ☎010 6313 2370, 010 6313 2369; www.qianmenhostel.net; 33 Meishi Jie; 煤市街 33号; dm ¥60-80, r with/without bathroom ¥280/200; 🌸@🛜; 🚇Line 2 to Qianmen, exit B or C) A five-minute trot southwest of Tiān'ānmén Sq, this heritage hostel with a cool courtyard offers a relaxing environment with able staff. The rooms are clean and simple but not big. Despite the busy location, this is an easy place to switch off and appreciate the high ceilings, original woodwork and charming antique buildings. An affable old-hand, hostel owner Genghis Kane does his best to keep his standards high. Great Wall tours can be arranged.

THREE-LEGGED FROG HOSTEL   HOSTEL $
Map p280 (京一食青年旅舍; Jīngyī Shí Qīngnián Lǚshè; ☎010 6304 0749; 3legs@threelegged froghostel.com; 27 Tieshu Xiejie; 铁树斜街 27号; dm/d/tr/f ¥75/380/450/600; 🌸🛜; 🚇Line 7 to Hufangqiao, or Line 2 to Qianmen, exit B or C) The name is a mystery but the decent-sized six-

---

ENGLISH-LANGUAGE SKILLS

While more hotel staff have OK English-language skills, there are still plenty who can't speak English. Youth hostels typically have excellent English speakers, as do five-star hotels – it's the ones in between that may not.

bed dorms with bathrooms are an excellent deal, while the private rooms are compact but clean. All are set around a cute courtyard that's pleasant in the summer, and has a communal area out front that does Western breakfasts and evening beers.

🛏 Sānlǐtún & Cháoyáng

SĀNLǏTÚN YOUTH HOSTEL
HOSTEL $

Map p282 (三里屯青年旅馆; Sānlǐtún Qīngnián Lǚguǎn; ☎010 5190 9288; www.sanlitun.hostel. com; Chunxiu Lu; 春秀路南口往北250米路东; 4-/6-/8-bed dm ¥90/88/70, d/tw with/without bathroom ¥280/230; ❋@🛜; 🚇Line B to Dongsi Shitiao, exit B) Sānlǐtún's only decent youth hostel, this place has efficient, amiable staff and is always busy. Rooms and dorms are functional and clean, although the shared bathrooms are a little pungent. Great Wall tours are available, as is bike hire (¥30 per day). There's an outdoor terrace for the summer and a good-value bar-restaurant area with a pool table.

HOTEL IBIS
HOTEL $

Map p282 (宜必思酒店; Yíbìsī Jiǔdiàn; ☎010 6508 8100; www.ibis.cn-accorhotels.com; 30 Zhongfang Jie (Sanlitun Nanlu); 中纺街30号 (三里屯南路); r ¥349; ❋@🛜; 🚇Line 6 to Dongdaqiao, exit B) Compact, modern and minimalist rooms at this chain hotel outpost within walking distance of Sānlǐtún's main restaurant, bar and shopping zones and a subway stop. Its location alone makes it a decent deal.

YOYO HOTEL
HOTEL $

Map p282 (优优客酒店; Yōuyōu Kèjiǔdiàn; ☎010 6417 3388; www.yoyohotel.cn; Bldg 10 Dongsanjie Erjie; 三里屯北路东三街二街中10楼; r ¥369-399; ❋@🛜; 🚇Line 10 to Tuanjiehu, exit A) There's a boutique feel here, but the rooms, especially bathrooms, are tiny. Nevertheless, they are excellent value for the location and fine if you're not planning on spending too much time in the hotel. Staff members speak some English and are friendly considering how rushed off their feet they usually are.

HOLIDAY INN EXPRESS
HOTEL $$

Map p282 (智选假日酒店; Zhìxuǎn Jiàrì Jiǔdiàn; ☎010 6416 9999; www.holidayinnexpress. cn; 1 Chunxiu Lu; 春秀路1号; r incl breakfast from ¥606; ❋@🛜; 🚇Line 2 to Dongsi Shitiao, exit B) There are 350 comfortable rooms at this well-located place with more personality than most chain hotels. Bright, pastel-coloured,

clean rooms come with excellent beds and big puffy pillows. All are equipped with widescreen TVs, free wi-fi and cable internet access. The lobby has Apple computers for the use of guests. Staff members are friendly and speak English. There's an outdoor sculpture garden, a small gym, an open-plan cafe with lunch-time buffet (¥88) and a games room featuring a PlayStation and foosball table.

★OPPOSITE HOUSE HOTEL
BOUTIQUE HOTEL $$$

Map p282 (瑜舍; Yúshè; ☎010 6417 6688; www. theoppositehouse.com; Bldg 1, Village, 11 Sanlitun Lu; 三里屯11号院1号楼; r from ¥2500; 🏊❋@🛜❄; 🚇Lines 10 to Tuanjiehu, exit A, or Agricultural Exhibition Center, exit D2) With see-all open-plan bathrooms, American oak bathtubs, lovely mood lighting, underfloor heating, sliding doors, complimentary beers, TVs on extendable arms and a metal basin swimming pool, this trendy Swire-owned boutique hotel is top-drawer chic. The location is ideal for shopping, restaurants and drinking. No obvious sign. Just walk into the striking green glass cube of a building and ask.

It's not the sort of place to take the kids, but couples can splash out or sip drinks in trendy **Mesh** (网孔; Wǎng Kǒng; Map p282; cocktails from ¥70; ⏱5pm-2am; 🚇Lines 10 to Tuanjiehu or Agricultural Exhibition Center). It also has the Chinese restaurant **Jing Yaa Tang**, known for Peking duck and dim sum, and **Sureño** for wood-fired pizzas. Its lobby features contemporary artwork from Red Gate Gallery.

★ROSEWOOD BĚIJĪNG
BOUTIQUE HOTEL $$$

Map p282 (北京瑰丽酒店; Běijīng Guīlì Jiǔdiàn; ☎010 6597 8888; www.rosewoodhotels.com/en/ beijing; Jing Guang Centre, East 3rd Middle Ring Rd; 呼家楼京广中心; r from ¥2000; ❋🛜❄; 🚇Line 10 to Jintaixizhao, exit A, or Lines 6, 10 to Hujialou, exit D) The elegant Rosewood fits modern luxury within a traditional Chinese design that incorporates decorative arts and a subtle yin-and-yang theme throughout. Its entry gate leaves a striking first impression with two large Jiao Tu (Sons of Dragon) sculptures that guard the hotel. The art-filled rooms are massive with designer furniture, TV mirrors and automatic blinds that open to views of the iconic CCTV building.

As well as the **Mei Bar** (魅酒吧; Mèi Jiǔbā; Map p282; http://mei-bar.com; 5th Fl, Rosewood Beijing, Jing Guang Centre; 朝阳区 呼家楼京广中心北京瑰丽酒店5层; ⏱6pm-2am Mon-Sat, 5pm-midnight Sun; 🛇; ⓢ Line 10 to Jintaixizhao, exit A or Lines 6, 10 to Hujialou, exit D), its classy **Country Kitchen** restaurant is acclaimed for its Peking duck. There's also its elegant **Sense Spa**, and a glassed-roof swimming pool, candlelit at night and surrounded by lush plants.

CONRAD
LUXURY HOTEL $$$

Map p282 (康莱德酒店; Kānglàidé Jiǔdiàn; ☎010 6584 6000; http://conradhotels3.hilton.com; 29 Dongsanhuan Bei; 东三环北路29号; r ¥2000; ⊛⊛@🛜🛇; ⓢLines 6, 10 to Hujialou, exit A) Its all-white, Swiss-cheeselike facade of different-shaped windows ensures you can't miss the striking Conrad. Rooms are equally slick and very big, and include smart features such as mirror TVs, double-headed showers and coffee makers. The terrace of the Vivid Bar (open from 7pm) on the 5th floor is a hot spot for Běijīng's beautiful people. Staff are very helpful. The only drawback is the outrageous ¥120 per day charge for wi-fi. It also has the **Chapter** restaurant on its ground floor, which has an antique library–themed decor and serves international cuisine.

PARK HYATT
LUXURY HOTEL $$$

Map p282 (柏悦酒店; Bóyuè Jiǔdiàn; ☎010 8567 1234; www.beijing.park.hyatt.com; 2 Jianguomenwai Dajie; 建国门外大街2号; r ¥2500-6500; ⊛⊛@🛜🛇; ⓢLines 1, 10 to Guomao, exit C) Almost too cool for school, the beautiful Park Hyatt draws business types and cashed-up hipsters. Ride the ear-popping lift to reception on the 63rd floor to be greeted by a fantastic, panoramic view of the surrounding area. Big, light-filled rooms with stylish bathrooms and great views, as well as top-notch service and all the facilities that come with a hotel of this standing. Its gym overlooks the CCTV Tower and has a deluxe infinity lap pool. For even more dramatic views, head to the 65th-floor China Bar for evening drinks (cocktails from ¥70; open 6pm to 2am).

ST REGIS
LUXURY HOTEL $$$

Map p282 (北京国际俱乐部饭店; Běijīng Guójì Jùlèbù Fàndiàn; ☎010 6460 6688; www.stregis.com/beijing; 21 Jianguomenwai Dajie; 建国门外大街21号; r from ¥2000; ⊛⊛@🛜🛇; ⓢLines 1, 2 to Jianguomen, exit B) An extravagant foyer, thorough professionalism and good location make the St Regis a good, if costly, five-star choice. Though getting on a bit, rooms are sumptuous and soothing with 24-hour butlers at hand to fine-tune your stay. Chinese and Italian restaurants offer some of Běijīng's finest dining experiences.

🛏 Summer Palace & Hǎidiàn

LTH HOTEL
HOTEL $

Map p287 (兰亭汇快捷酒店; Lántínghuì Kuàijié Jiùdiàn; ☎010 6261 8596, 010 6261 9226; www.lth hotel.com; 35-5 Chengfu Lu; 成府路 35-5号; d & tw ¥268-358, tr ¥498; ⊛@🛜; ⓢWudaokou) Newish, modern hotel, unlike many in the area, with bright rooms (the ones with windows, anyway) and compact bathrooms. It has a prime location close to the subway and the bar-, cafe- and club-zone of Wǔdàokǒu. It's just to the side of the Dongyuan Plaza.

PEKING UNI INTERNATIONAL HOSTEL
HOSTEL $

Map p287 (未名国际青年旅舍; Wèimíng Guójì Qīngnián Lǔshè; ☎010 6254 9667, 010 8287 1309; www.weiminghotel.com; 150 Chengfu Lu; 成府路; 4-/6-/8-bed dm ¥80/70/60, d & tw ¥278-298, tw without bathroom ¥218; ⊛⊛@🛜; ⓢWudaokou) This busy hostel is located in an office building and so lacks the character of many other hostels around town. But the dorms and rooms, while a little cramped, are clean and sound enough, as are the shared bathrooms, and there's a big communal area. Be sure to check the rooms before you decide as some don't have windows. It caters far more for domestic travellers than it does for foreigners, making it a good place to meet the locals. The staff are amenable, even if you won't hear too much English spoken.

⭐ AMAN AT SUMMER PALACE
HERITAGE HOTEL $$$

Map p286 (颐和安缦; Yíhé Ānmàn; ☎010 5987 9999; www.amanresorts.com; 1 Gongmen Qianjie; 宫门前街 1号; r ¥3000, courtyard r ¥4800, ste ¥5600-8400; ⊛⊛@🛜🛇; ⓢXiyuan) Hard to fault this exquisite hotel, a candidate for best in Běijīng. It's located around the corner from the Summer Palace (p152). The big rooms are superbly appointed, and contained in a series of picture-perfect pavilions set around courtyards. Stepping through the imposing red gates here is to enter a very different, very hushed and very privileged world. Choice restaurants, a spa, a library, a cinema, a pool, squash courts and, of course, silky-smooth service round off the refined picture. Try the daily afternoon tea (2pm to 5pm; ¥268) if you can't afford to stay here. Expect 20% discounts in winter, but everything here comes with a 15% service charge.

Understand Běijīng

Běijīng Today

Běijīng has been transformed over the past 20 years. Unprecedented investment and massive population growth have fuelled breakneck development. In terms of wealth and opportunities, Beijingers have never had it so good, but rapid change has come at a cost. Transport systems are full to bursting, pollution levels are at an all-time high, and the very fabric of traditional society is being threatened as age-old *hútòng* (narrow alleyway) districts continue to make way for more modern alternatives.

Best on Film

In the Heat of the Sun (1994) Dreamlike, evocative tale of Běijīng youth running wild during the Cultural Revolution in the 1970s.
Lost in Beijing (2007) Raw and explicit, modern-day tale of a ménage à quatre involving a young woman, her boss, her husband and her boss's wife. Banned in China.
The Last Emperor (1987) Bernardo Bertolucci's multi-Oscar-winning epic, charting the life of Puyi during his accession and the ensuing disintegration of dynastic China.
Mr Six (2015) An ageing gangster struggles to adapt to modern Běijīng as he settles his son's debts.

Best in Print

The People's Republic of Amnesia: Tiananmen Revisited (Louisa Lim; 2014) The social impact of the Tiān'ānmén crackdown, told through eyewitness accounts.
Midnight in Peking (Paul French; 2012) Gripping account of the mystery surrounding the brutal 1937 murder of Englishwoman Pamela Werner.
Rickshaw Boy (Lao She, translated by Shi Xiaoqing; 1981) Masterpiece by one of Běijīng's most-beloved writers about a rickshaw-puller in early-20th-century Běijīng.

Maintaining Harmony

Inevitably, nonstop development brings increased pollution. The condition of the region's soil and water causes much concern to locals (Beijingers never drink their tap water), but perhaps most depressing is the sustained levels of the city's now infamous smog.

Air pollution counts hit record levels in January 2013, a month dubbed 'Airpocalypse' by the world's media. Expatriates began leaving in droves, but Beijingers are equally unimpressed with the often dire situation – it is a major topic of conversation, as well as complaints to local authorities. Any repeat visitor to the city will notice a marked rise in the number of people wearing face masks.

The smog isn't continual – Běijīng still experiences days of wonderfully clear blue skies – but worryingly, the smog seems to be increasing rather than diminishing.

Continued Economic Growth

The authorities can be commended for their continued investment in an increasingly impressive public transport system. Běijīng has an extensive fleet of natural-gas-powered and electric-powered buses, and its subway system is now the world's second-largest (behind Shànghǎi) and is still expanding, with another 12 lines set to open by 2021. Plans for a monorail system in the eastern outskirts of the city have also been mooted, although protests from local residents have seen the scheme shelved for now; a rare case of people power triumphing over the state in China.

Demolition & Gentrification

Běijīng – the last of China's imperial capitals – functioned as the moral and spiritual centre of the entire country; a cosmic focal point where the 'Son of Heaven' (the emperor) mediated between earthly and heavenly realms. Due to the city's divine nature, Chinese leaders throughout history paid special attention to the design of their capital. Even the slightest change to the configuration of the imperial city was regarded as an affront to tradition and thus to the established world order.

How times have changed. Today, shimmering superstructures, designed as freestanding landmarks, spring up around the city like individual monuments of modernity, jeopardising the forces of architectural yin and yang that once harmonised the whole structure of the city. Often making way for them are the older, more run-down neighbourhoods made up of ancient *hútòng*. The most recent high-profile example is the *hútòng* housing that was demolished to make way for the dazzling Soho Galaxy building.

Historic buildings, including *sìhéyuàn* (四合院; traditional courtyard houses), are often protected, but it's the *dàzáyuàn* (大杂院; high-density courtyard compounds with many families living together) which continue to be threatened, either by being demolished to make way for modern superstructures, or by having their essence as residential communities squeezed out of them by large-scale gentrification projects.

Qianmen, until recently the largest uninterrupted *hútòng* block in Běijīng, was demolished and rebuilt as a Qing-style shopping and residential district, just before the 2008 Olympics. And in 2014, part of the charming residential *hútòng* district surrounding the historic Drum Tower and Bell Tower was demolished, as the square between the towers was blocked off and turned into a soulless zone.

if Běijīng were 100 people

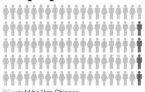

96 would be Han Chinese
4 would be Chinese ethnic minorities

Belief systems
(% of the population)

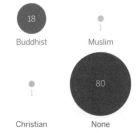

Buddhist 18
Muslim 1
Christian 1
None 80

population per sq km

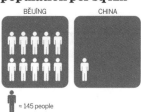

BĚIJĪNG   CHINA

≈ 145 people

History

Běijīng's long and colourful history goes back some 3000 years, but the city didn't become the centre of Chinese rule until 1272 when Kublai Khan made it the capital of the Mongol-led Yuan dynasty. From that time on, with the exception of two brief interludes (1368–1421 and 1928–49), Běijīng has served as the seat of power for all of China.

From the Beginning

The Great Capital of the Mongols

The place we now call Běijīng first rose to true prominence when it was turned into a capital city by Kublai Khan (1215-94), the founder of the Mongol-ruled Yuan dynasty. The Mongols called the city Khanbalik, and it was from here that the descendants of Genghis Khan (Kublai Khan was his grandson) ruled over the largest land empire in world history. This is where Marco Polo, one of many thousands of foreigners drafted to help the Mongols govern China, came to serve as an official. Běijīng was really only the winter capital for Kublai Khan, who chose to spend the summer at Běijīng's sister city, Xanadu, which lay to the north, 1800m up on the steppes. That city was called the 'Upper Capital', or 'Shàngdū' in Chinese, while Běijīng was 'Dàdū' or 'Great Capital'.

Běijīng was a curious place to have been selected as capital of the Yuan empire, or indeed any empire. It lacks a river or access to the sea. It's on the very outer edge of the great northern plain, and very far indeed from the rich rice granaries in the south and the source of China's lucrative exports of tea, silk and porcelain. Throughout history the Han Chinese considered this barbarian territory, home to a series of hostile predatory dynasties such as the Liao (916-1125) and the Jin (1115-1234), who also both made Běijīng their capital. To this day Chinese historians describe these peoples as primitive 'tribes' rather than nations, perhaps a prejudice from the ancient antipathy between nomadic pastoralist peoples and the sedentary farmers who are the Chinese.

The Mongols became the first 'barbarian' tribe to attempt to rule China. They ruled from Běijīng for just short of a century, from 1272 to 1368.

TIMELINE	500,000 BC	pre–11th century BC	c 600 BC
	Peking man (*Sinanthropus pekinensis*), an example of *Homo erectus*, inhabits the Běijīng region; Peking man fossils are excavated at Zhōukǒudiàn in Běijīng municipality between 1923–27.	The first settlements in the Běijīng area are recorded (evidence suggests Paleolithic cultures living in the central areas of Běijīng).	Laotzu (Laozi), founder of Taoism, is supposedly born. The folk religion of Taoism goes on to coexist with later introductions such as Buddhism.

Běijīng's First City Walls

Běijīng had first become a walled settlement back in AD 938 when the Khitans, one of the nomadic 'barbarian tribes', established it as an auxiliary southern capital of their Liao dynasty. When they were overthrown by Jurchens from Manchuria, the progenitors of the Manchus, it became Zhōngdū or 'Middle Capital'. Each of these three successive barbarian dynasties enlarged the walled city and built palaces and temples, especially Buddhist temples. They secured a supply of water by channelling streams from the otherwise dry limestone hills around Běijīng, and stored it in the lakes that still lie at the heart of the city.

During the time of the Khitans, Běijīng was sometimes called Yānjīng, or the 'City of Swallows'. This is still the name of a beer produced by a local brewery.

The Lifeline of the Grand Canal

The Khitans relied on the Grand Canal to ship goods such as silk, porcelain, tea and grain from the Yangzi River delta. Each successive dynasty shortened the Grand Canal. It was originally 2500km long when it was built in the 5th century by the Chinese Sui dynasty to facilitate the military conquest of northeast China and Korea. From the 10th century it was used for a different purpose: to enable these northern peoples to extract the wealth of central China. Běijīng's role was to be the terminus.

Remaining Traces

For 1000 years, half a million peasants spent six months a year hauling huge barges from Hángzhōu up the Grand Canal to Běijīng. You can still see the canal after it enters the city from Tōngzhōu, now a suburb of Běijīng, and then winds around the 2nd Ring Rd. The tax or tribute from central China was then stored in huge warehouses, a few of which remain. From Běijīng, the goods were carried out of the West Gate or Xīzhímén (where Xīzhímén subway station is today), and taken up the Tánqín Gorge to Bādálǐng, which once marked the limits of the Chinese world. Beyond this pass, the caravans took the road to Zhāngjiākǒu, 6000ft above sea level where the grasslands of inner Asia begin.

End of 'Barbarian' Rule

The ultimate aim of the Khitans, Jurchens, Mongols and Manchus was to control the lucrative international trade in Chinese-made luxuries. Chinese dynasties such as the Song faced the choice of paying them off or staging a bloody resistance. The Southern Song did attack and destroy Běijīng, but when it failed to defeat the Liao dynasty of the Khitans it resorted to a strategy of 'using the barbarian to defeat the barbarian'. It made a pact with the Jurchens, and together they captured Běijīng in 1125. But instead of just helping to defeat the Khitans, the Jurchens carried on south and took the Song capital at Kāifēng. The

The Mongols referred to Zhāngjiākǒu as Kalgan, 'the Gate'. This trading route, leading to inner Asia's grasslands, was also the favourite route chosen by invaders, such as Genghis Khan.

551 BC	5th–3rd century BC	214 BC	AD 938
The birth of Confucius. Collected in the *Analects*, his ideas of an ethical, ordered society would dominate Chinese culture until the early 20th century.	The state of Yan conquer the state of Ji and form a larger walled city called Yānjīng – which is still the name of the local beer here.	Emperor Qin indentures thousands of labourers to link existing city walls into one Great Wall, made of tamped earth. The later stone-clad bastion dates from the Ming dynasty.	Běijīng is established as auxiliary capital of the Liao dynasty. Běijīng's oldest street – Sanmiao Jie, or Three Temples St – dates to this time, when it was known as Tanzhou Jie.

Jurchens, however, chose not to try to govern China by themselves and instead opted to milk the Southern Song dynasty.

Ming Dynasty Běijīng

A True Chinese City

Běijīng can properly be said to have been a Chinese city only during the Ming dynasty (1368–1644), when Emperor Yongle used more than 200,000 prisoners of war to rebuild the city and imperial palace, construct its massive battlements, and establish the magnificent Ming Tombs. He forced tens of thousands of leading Chinese families to relocate from Nánjīng, the capital founded by his father, and unwillingly settle in what they considered an alien land at the extremity of the Chinese world. Throughout the Ming dynasty, Běijīng was constantly under attack by the Mongols, and on many occasions their horsemen reached the very gates of the city. Mongol bandits roamed the countryside or hid out in the marshes south of the city, threatening communications with the empire.

Beefing up the Great Wall

Everything needed for the gigantic enterprise of rebuilding the city – even tiles, bricks and timber – had to be shipped up the Grand Canal, but in time Běijīng grew into a city of nearly a million residents. Although farms and greenhouses sprang up around the city, it always depended on the Grand Canal as a lifeline. Most of the canal was required to ship the huge amounts of food needed to supply the garrison of more than a million men that Yongle press-ganged into building and manning the new Great Wall. The emperor was fearful of a resurgent Mongol threat. The Mongols had been pushed out of China as the Ming came to power in 1368, but they were still formidable, and by the dawn of the 15th century they were itching to reconquer the rich lands to the south of the Great Wall. This Wall, unlike earlier walls, was clad in brick and stone, not pounded earth, and the Ming emperors kept enlarging it for the next 250 years, adding loops, spurs and watchtowers. For long stretches, the fortifications ran in two parallel bands.

The Forbidden City

Běijīng grew from a forward defence military headquarters into an administrative centre staffed by an elite corps of mandarins. They had to pass gruelling examinations that tested candidates' understanding of classical and Confucian literature. Then they were either assigned to the provinces or selected to work in the central government ministries, situated in what is now Tiān'ānmén Sq, south of the Meridian Gate and

1153	1215	1272	1286
Běijīng becomes capital of the Jin dynasty and becomes known as Zhōngdū or 'Middle Capital'; the city walls are expanded and paper currency enters circulation.	The Mongols, under Genghis Khan, break through the Great Wall at several points and sack Zhōngdū, razing it to the ground and slaughtering its inhabitants.	Kublai Khan renames the city Dàdū, or 'Great Capital', and officially unveils it as the capital of the Yuan dynasty. Běijīng is, for the first time, the capital of China.	The Grand Canal is extended to Běijīng, becoming a major artery for the transport of grain, salt and other important commodities between north and south China.

the entrance to the Forbidden City. Each day the mandarins and the generals entered the 'Great Within' and kowtowed before the emperor, who lived inside, like a male version of a queen bee, served by thousands of women and eunuchs. Ming emperors were the only males permitted to live in the palace. Yongle established rigid rules and dreary rituals, and many of his successors rebelled against the constrictions.

Power of the Eunuchs

Under later Ming emperors, the eunuchs came to be more trusted and more powerful than the mandarins. There were 100,000 by the end of the Ming dynasty, more than in any other civilisation in history. A few became so powerful they virtually ruled the empire, but many died poor and destitute. Some used their wealth to build grandiose residences and tombs, or to patronise temples and monasteries located in the hills outside the walls.

Eunuchs tended to be Buddhists (while mandarins honoured Confucius), as it gave them hope they would return as whole men in a future reincarnation.

A Centre for Arts & Science

Over time Běijīng became the most important religious centre in Asia, graced by more than 2000 temples and shrines. Daoists and Buddhists vied for the favour of the emperor who, as a divine being, was automatically the patron of every approved religious institution in the empire. As the residence of the emperor, Běijīng was regarded by the Chinese as the centre of the universe. The best poets and painters also flocked to Běijīng to seek court patronage. The Forbidden City required the finest porcelain, furniture and silverware, and its workshops grew in skill and design. Literature, drama, music, medicine, map-making, astrology and astronomy flourished, too, so the imperial city became a centre for arts and sciences.

Although early visitors complained about the dust and the beggars, most were awed and inspired by the city's size, magnificence and wealth. Ming culture was influential in Japan, Korea, Vietnam and in other neighbouring countries. By the close of the 15th century the Ming capital, which had started out as a remote and isolated military outpost, had become a wealthy and sophisticated Chinese city.

The Fall of the Ming

Despite the Great Wall, the threat from the north intensified. The Manchus (formerly the Jurchens) established a new and powerful state based in Shěnyáng (currently the capital of Liáoníng province) and watched as the Ming empire decayed. The Ming had one of the most elaborate tax codes in history, but corrupt eunuchs abused their growing power. Excessive taxation sparked a series of peasant revolts. Silver,

1368	1368–1644	1403–21	1420
Zhu Yuanzhang takes Dàdū and proceeds to level its palaces, renaming the city Běipíng ('Northern Peace') and establishing the Ming dynasty.	The Great Wall is rebuilt and clad with bricks, and the basic layout of modern Běijīng is established. Běijīng becomes the world's largest city.	Emperor Yongle moves the capital south to Nánjīng ('Southern Capital'). Běijīng is reinstated as capital in 1421 when the Forbidden City is completed (1406–20).	The Temple of Heaven is constructed at the same time as the Forbidden City. The Gate of Heavenly Peace is completed and is called Chengtianmen, only to be destroyed by lightning in 1457.

the main form of exchange, was devalued by imported silver from the new world, leading to inflation.

One peasant rebel army, led by Li Zicheng (1606–45), actually captured Běijīng. The last Ming emperor, Chongzhen (1611–44), called on the Manchus for help and after crossing the Great Wall at Shānhǎiguān, in current-day Héběi province, they helped rout Li Zicheng's army. The Manchus then marched on Běijīng, where Emperor Chongzhen hanged himself on a tree on Coal Hill, the hill in Jīngshān Park, which overlooks the Forbidden City.

Qing Dynasty Běijīng

The Manchus Move In

The Han Chinese were forced to wear their hair in a queue (pigtail) as a symbol of their subjugation to the ruling Manchus.

The Manchus established the Qing dynasty in 1644, although it took several decades before they completed the conquest of the Ming empire. As a foreign dynasty, they took great pains to present themselves as legitimate successors to the Chinese Ming dynasty. For this reason they kept Běijīng as their capital and changed very little, effectively preserving Yongle's city. The Manchu imperial family, the Aisin Gioro Clan, moved into the Forbidden City, and imperial princes took large courtyard palaces.

Summer Palaces

The Aisin Gioro family felt that living inside the confines of the Forbidden City was claustrophobic. The great Emperor Kangxi (1654–1722) effectively moved the court to what is now called the Old Summer Palace, a vast parkland of lakes, canals and palaces linked to the city by the Jade Canal. The Manchus, like the Mongols, enjoyed hunting, riding, hawking, skating and archery. In summer, when Běijīng became hot and steamy, the court moved to Chéngdé, a week's ride to the north. At Chéngdé, the court spent three months living in felt tents (or yurts) in a walled parkland.

Bannermen

The Manchu army was divided into regiments called banners, so the troops were called Bannermen (Qírén). Each banner had a separate colour by which it was known and its troops settled in a particular residential area in Běijīng. The Embroidered Yellow Bannermen, for example, lived near the Confucius Temple, and some of their descendants remain there today. Only a minority were actually ethnic Manchus – the rest were Mongols or Han Chinese.

Policing a Divided City

Běijīng at this stage was a Manchu city and foreigners called it the 'Tartar City' ('Tartars' being the label given to any nomadic race from

1465	1644	1850–68	1898
The Gate of Heavenly Peace is rebuilt but is torched by peasant rebels in 1644 prior to the arrival of Manchu soldiers. The reconstruction of the gate is completed in 1651.	Manchu troops impose the Qing dynasty on China; Emperor Chongzhen hangs himself from a tree in Jīngshān Park. Běijīng is known in Manchu as Gemun Hecen.	The quasi-Christian Taiping Rebellion blazes across China from Guǎngxī province, killing an estimated 20 million people. Rebels establish their 'Heavenly Capital' in Nánjīng.	Emperor Guangxu permits major reforms, including new rights for women, but is thwarted by the Dowager Empress Cixi, who has many reformers arrested and executed.

CHINA'S DYNASTIES

DYNASTY	CHINESE NAME	PERIOD OF RULE
Xià	夏	2070–1600 BC
Shāng	商	1600–1046 BC
Western Zhou	西周 (Xī Zhōu)	1046–771 BC
Eastern Zhou	东周 (Dōng Zhōu)	770–256 BC
Spring & Autumn	春秋 (Chūn Qiū)	771–476 BC
Warring States	战国 (Zhàn Guó)	476–221 BC
Qín	秦	221–206 BC
Western Han	西汉 (Xī Hàn)	206 BC–AD 9 & AD 23–25
Xīn	新	AD 9–23
Eastern Han	东汉 (Dōng Hàn)	AD 25–220
Three Kingdoms	三国 (Sān Guó)	220–65
Western Jin	西晋 (Xī Jìn)	265–317
Eastern Jin	东晋 (Dōng Jìn)	317–420
Southern & Northern	南北朝 (Nán Běi Cháo)	420–589
Suí	隋	581–618
Táng	唐	618–907
Five Dynasties & Ten Kingdoms	五代十国 (Wǔ Dài Shí Guó)	907–60
Kingdom of Dali	大理国 (Dà Lǐ Guó)	937–1253
Northern Song	北宋 (Běi Sòng)	960–1127
Southern Song	南宋 (Nán Sòng)	1127–1279
Liáo	/辽	916–1125
Jīn	金	1115–1234
Western Xia	西夏 (Xī Xià)	1038–1227
Yuán	元	1271–1368
Míng	明	1368–1644
Qīng	清	1644–1911

inner Asia). The Han Chinese lived in the 'Chinese city' to the south of Tiān'ānmén Sq. This was the liveliest, most densely populated area, packed with markets, shops, theatres, brothels and hostels for provincial visitors. If Chinese people wanted to get to north Běijīng, they had to go all the way round the outside walls. The Bannermen posted at the

1900	1905	1908	1911
Boxer rebels commence the long siege of the Foreign Legation Quarter. The Hànlín Academy is accidentally burned down by rebels trying to flush out foreigners in the British Legation.	Major reforms in the late Qing, including the abolition of the 1000-year-long tradition of examinations in the Confucian classics to enter the Chinese bureaucracy.	Two-year-old Puyi ascends the throne as China's last emperor. Local elites and new classes such as businessmen no longer support the dynasty, leading to its ultimate downfall.	The Qing dynasty collapses and the modernisation of China begins in earnest; Sun Yatsen (fundraising in America at the time) is declared president of the Republic of China.

gates prevented anyone from entering without permission. Up to 1900, the state provided all Bannermen families with clothing and free food that was shipped up the Grand Canal and stored in grain warehouses.

Fashioning Běijīng Culture

It was the Manchu Bannermen who really created a Běijīng culture. They promoted Peking opera, and the city at one time had more than 40 opera houses and many training schools. The sleeveless *qípáo* dress is essentially a Manchu dress. The Bannermen, who loved animals, raised songbirds and pigeons and bred exotic-looking goldfish and miniature dogs such as the Pekinese. After the downfall of the Qing empire, they kept up traditional arts such as painting and calligraphy.

Language, Politics & Religion

Through the centuries of Qing rule, the Manchus tried to keep themselves culturally separate from the Chinese, speaking a different language, wearing different clothes and following different customs. For instance, Manchu women did not bind their feet, wore raised platform *patens* (shoes), and coiled their hair in distinctive and elaborate styles. All court documents were composed in the Manchu script; Manchu, Chinese and Mongolian script were used to write name signs in such places as the Forbidden City.

At the same time, the Qing copied the Ming's religious and bureaucratic institutions. The eight key ministries (Board of Works, Board of Revenue, Board of State Ceremonies, Board of War, Board of Rites, Board of Astronomy, Board of Medicines and Prefecture of Imperial Clan Affairs) continued to operate from the same buildings in what is now Tiān'ānmén Sq. The Qing dynasty worshipped their ancestors at rites held in a temple, which is now in the Workers Cultural Palace, a park immediately southeast of the Forbidden City. They also built a second ancestral temple devoted to the spirits of every Chinese emperor that ever ruled. For some time it was a girls' school, but it has since reopened as the Temple of Ancient Monarchs (p118).

Buddhist Ties

The study of Confucius was encouraged in order to strengthen the loyalty of the mandarins employed by the state bureaucracy. The Manchus carried out the customary rituals at the great state temples. By inclination, however, many of the Manchu emperors were either Shamanists or followers of Tibetan Buddhism. The Shamanist shrines have disappeared, but Běijīng is full of temples and stupas connected with Tibetan Buddhism. Emperor Qianlong considered himself the incar-

1912	1916	4 May 1919	1927
Yuan Shikai, leader of China's most powerful regional army, goes to the Qing court to announce that the game is up: on 12 February the last emperor, six-year-old Puyi, abdicates.	Yuan Shikai dies less than a year after attempting to establish himself emperor. Yuan's monarchical claims prompt widespread resistance from Republicans.	Students demonstrate in Běijīng against foreign occupation of territories in China and the terms that conclude WWI. The date of the protests leads to the name of the movement.	The first shots of the Chinese Civil War are fired between the Kuomintang (KMT) and the communists. The war continues on and off until 1949.

EMPRESS DOWAGER CIXI

The Empress Dowager Cixi (1835–1908), a daughter of a Bordered Blue Bannermen, was a young concubine when the Old Summer Palace was burned down by foreign troops in 1860. Cixi allowed the palace to fall into decay, associating it with a humiliation, and instead built herself the new Summer Palace (Yíhé Yuán). She was left with a profound hatred and distrust of the Western barbarians and their ways.

Over the four decades in which Cixi ruled China 'from behind the curtain' through a series of proxy emperors, she resisted pressure to change and reform. After a naval defeat at the hands of the Japanese in 1895, young Chinese officials put forward a modernisation program. She had some of them executed outside Běijīng's walls, and imprisoned their patron and her nephew, Emperor Guangxu (1871–1908).

She encouraged the Boxers to attack Westerners, especially foreign missionaries in northern China, and when Boxers besieged the Foreign Legation Quarter in 1900, Cixi stood by. When the allied forces marched into Běijīng to end the siege, she fled in disguise, an ignominious retreat that marked the final humiliation that doomed the Qing dynasty. When Cixi returned in disgrace a year later, China's modernisation had begun in earnest, but it was too late to save the Qing dynasty – it fell in 1911.

nation of the Bodhisattva Manjusri and cultivated strong links with various Dalai Lamas and Panchen Lamas. Many visited – a round trip usually lasted three years – and special palaces were built for them. The Manchus deliberately fostered the spread of Tibetan Buddhism among the warlike Mongols in the hope of pacifying them. Běijīng therefore developed into a holy city attracting pilgrims of all kinds.

The Jesuits

The arrival of the first Jesuits and other Christians made Běijīng an important centre of Christianity in China. Emperor Qianlong employed many Jesuits to build the baroque palaces that can still be seen in the ruins of the Old Summer Palace, which was burned down in 1860 during the Second Opium War, by a combined force of British and French troops.

Foreign Powers & the Fall of the Qing

Foreign Legation Quarter

After the military defeats of the Opium Wars, the Western nations forced the Qing emperors to allow them to open formal embassies or legations in the capital. Hitherto, the emperor had had no equal in the world – foreign powers could only send embassies to deliver tribute, and they were housed in tributary hostels.

1928	7 July 1937	1946	1 October 1949
The nationalists move the capital to Nánjīng, and Běijīng is again renamed Běipíng. This is the first time the capital of the entire nation has been in Nánjīng for almost 500 years.	The Marco Polo Bridge Incident signals the beginning of the Japanese occupation of Běijīng and the start of the Second Sino-Japanese War, which lasts until September 1945.	Communists and the KMT fail to form a coalition government, plunging China back into civil war.	With the communist victory over the KMT, Mao Zedong announces the founding of the People's Republic of China from the Gate of Heavenly Peace.

Boxer Rebellion

The British legation was the first to open after 1860. It lay on the east side of Tiān'ānmén Sq and stayed there until the 1950s when its grounds were taken over by the Ministry of State Security. By 1900 there were a dozen legations in an odd foreign ghetto with an eclectic mixture of European architecture. The Foreign Legation Quarter never became a foreign concession like those in Shànghǎi or Tiānjīn, but it had banks, schools, shops, post offices, hospitals and military parade grounds. Much of it was reduced to rubble when the army of Boxers (a quasi-religious cult) besieged it in the summer of 1900. It was later rebuilt.

Republican China

After 1900 the last tribute barges arrived in Běijīng and a railway line ran along the traditional invasion route through the Jūyōng Pass to Bādálǐng. You can see the handsome clock tower and sheds of Běijīng's first railway station (Qiánmén Railway Station), now restored as the Běijīng Railway Museum, on the southeast corner of Tiān'ānmén Sq. Běijīng never became an industrial or commercial centre – that role went to nearby Tiānjīn on the coast. Yet it remained the political and intellectual centre of China until the late 1920s.

Hotbed of Student Activity

In the settlement imposed after the Boxer Rebellion, China had to pay the victors heavy indemnities. Some of this money was returned to China and used to build the first modern universities, including what are now the Oxford and Cambridge of China – Qīnghuá and Peking universities. Běijīng's university quarter was established in the Hǎidiàn district, near the Old Summer Palace (some campuses are actually in the imperial parkland). Intellectuals from all over China continued to gravitate to Běijīng, including the young Mao Zedong, who arrived to work as a librarian in 1921.

For an insight into the sinful under-world of 1930's Běijīng, read Paul French's excellent 2012 crime thriller *Midnight in Peking*; a gripping account of the investigation behind the brutal, 1937 murder of Englishwoman Pamela Werner.

1919 May Fourth Movement

Běijīng students and professors were at the forefront of the 1919 May Fourth Movement. This was at once a student protest against the Versailles Treaty, which had awarded Germany's concessions in China to Japan, and an intellectual movement to jettison the Confucian feudal heritage and Westernise China. Mao himself declared that to modernise China it was first necessary to destroy it. China's intellectuals looked around the world for models to copy. Some went to Japan, others to the USA, Britain, Germany or, like Deng Xiaoping and Zhou Enlai, France. Many went to study Marxism in Moscow.

1956–57	1958	16 May 1966	1972
The Hundred Flowers Movement promises an era of intellectual freedom, but instead leads to a purge of intellectuals, artists and thinkers who are labelled rightists and persecuted.	The Great Leap Forward commences but plans to rapidly industrialise China result in a disastrous famine that kills millions of Chinese.	The Great Proletarian Cultural Revolution is launched by Mao Zedong in Běijīng. In August millions of Red Guards pack into Tiān'ānmén Sq. From August to September, 1772 Beijingers are killed.	US President Richard Nixon meets with Mao Zedong in Běijīng, marking a major rapprochement during the Cold War, and the start of full diplomatic relations between the two countries.

HISTORY REPUBLICAN CHINA

Modernising the City

As the warlords marched armies in and out of Běijīng, the almost-medieval city began to change. Temples were closed down and turned into schools. The last emperor, Puyi, left the Forbidden City in 1924 with his eunuchs and concubines. As the Manchus adapted to the changes, they tried to assimilate and their presence faded. Western-style brick houses, shops and restaurants were built. City gates were widened and new ones added, including one at Jiànguóménwài to make way for the motorcar. Běijīng acquired nightclubs, cinemas, racecourses and a stock exchange; brothels and theatres flourished. Despite political and diplomatic crises, this was a period when people had fun and enjoyed a unique period of individual freedom.

Generalissimo Chiang Kaishek united most of the country under Chinese National Party (KMT, or Kuomintang in Chinese) rule and in 1928 he moved the capital to Nánjīng. Even so, Běijīng's romantic air of decaying grandeur attracted Chinese and Western writers and painters trying to fuse Western and Chinese artistic traditions.

Some of 20th-century China's best literature was written in Běijīng in the 1920s and '30s by the likes of Lao She, Lin Huiyin, Xu Zhimou and Shen Congwen.

Japanese Occupation

It all came to end when Japan's Kwantung Army moved down from Manchuria and occupied Běijīng in 1937. By then, most people who could had fled, some to Chóngqìng in Sìchuān province, which served as Chiang Kaishek's wartime capital. Others joined Mao Zedong in his communist base at Yán'ān, in Shaanxi province. Many universities established campuses in exile in Yúnnán province.

The Japanese stayed in Běijīng for eight years and, before their WWII defeat in 1945, had drawn up plans to build a new administrative capital in an area to the west of the city walls near Gōngzhǔfén. It was a miserable time for Běijīng, but the architecture was left largely untouched by the war. When the Japanese surrendered in August 1945, Běijīng was 'liberated' by US marines. The city once again became a merry place famous for its parties – the serious events took place elsewhere in China. When the civil war broke out in earnest between nationalists and communists in 1947, the worst fighting took place in the cities of Manchuria.

During the Japanese invasion, a large proportion of the collection of imperial treasures was secretly removed, eventually ending up in Taiwan where they can still be seen in Taipei's National Palace Museum.

Communist Takeover

In 1948 the Communist Eighth Route Army moved south and encircled Běijīng. General Fu Zuoyi, commander-in-chief of the Nationalists' Northern China Bandit Suppression Headquarters, prepared the city for a prolonged siege. He razed private houses and built gun emplacements and dugouts along the Ming battlements. Nationalist planes dropped bags of rice and flour to relieve the shortages, some

'Communism is not love. Communism is a hammer which we use to crush the enemy.' Mao Zedong, quoted in Time (New York, 18 December 1950).

1976	1977–79	1980	1987
The death of Premier Zhou Enlai sparks spontaneous protests known as the Tiān'ānmén Incident; the mighty Tángshān earthquake is blamed on a cosmic correction after the death of Mao Zedong in September.	The 'Běijīng Spring' sees the first shoots of nascent political freedom. Deng Xiaoping's reformist agenda commences in 1979.	The one-child policy is enforced. The state adopts it as a means of reducing the population, but at the same time imposes unprecedented control over the personal liberty of women.	The Last Emperor, filmed in the Forbidden City, collects an Oscar for Best Picture, and marks a new openness in China towards the outside world.

hitting skaters on frozen Běihǎi Lake. Both sides seemed reluctant to fight it out and destroy the ancient capital. The rich tried to flee on the few planes that took off from a runway constructed at Dongdan on Chang'an Dajie (Chang'an means 'Avenue of Eternal Peace'). Another airstrip was opened at Temple of Heaven Park by cutting down 20,000 trees, including 400 ancient cypresses.

On 22 January 1949 General Fu signed a surrender agreement, and on 31 January his KMT troops marched out and the People's Liberation Army (PLA) entered. A truck drove up Morrison St (now Wangfujing Dajie) blasting a continuous refrain to the residents of Běijīng (or Pěipíng as it was known then): 'Welcome to the Liberation Army on its arrival in Pěipíng! Congratulations to the people of Pěipíng on their liberation!' Behind it marched 300 soldiers in battle gear. A grand victory parade took place on 3 February with 250 assorted military vehicles, virtually all US-made and captured from the KMT over the previous two years.

Mao's Běijīng

> Mao worked as a library assistant at the former Peking University campus known as Hóng Lóu (the Red Building), now a small museum.

The People Stand Up

On 1 October 1949 Mao ascended the Gate of Heavenly Peace and declared the founding of the People's Republic of China, saying the Chinese people had stood up. He spoke only a few words in one of the very few public speeches he ever made.

Mao then moved into Zhōngnánhǎi, part of the chain of lakes and gardens immediately west of the Forbidden City and dating back to Kublai Khan. Marshal Yuan Shikai (1859–1916) had lived there too during his short-lived attempt to establish his own dynasty after 1911. Nobody is quite sure why Mao chose Běijīng as his capital, or why he failed to carry out his intention to raze the Forbidden City.

After 1949 many of China's new top leaders followed Mao's cue and moved their homes and offices into the old princely palaces *(wángfǔ)*, thus inadvertently preserving much of the old architecture.

Industrialising

> The last of the Foreign Legation Quarter's embassies left in 1967. Now most embassies are located east of the centre, in Cháoyáng District.

Mao wished to turn Běijīng into a city of production. Speaking to China's premier architectural historian, Liang Sicheng, as they stood on the Gate of Heavenly Peace looking south, Peng Zhen, the first Party Secretary of Běijīng, said that Chairman Mao wanted to make Běijīng into a large, modern city with lots of heavy industry.

Factories Galore

Thousands of factories sprang up in Běijīng and quite a few were built in old temples. In time, Běijīng developed into a centre for steel, chemi-

June 1989	1997	25 April 1999	22 July 1999
Democracy protestors fill Tiān'ānmén Sq as parallel protests are held across the land. Běijīng imposes martial law and on the evening of 3 June soldiers clear the streets, killing hundreds in the process.	Deng Xiaoping dies before having the chance to see Hong Kong returned to Chinese rule that same year. The reconstruction of Běijīng is launched.	In the largest protest since Tiān'ānmén Sq, 10,000 practitioners of the quasi-religious movement Falun Gong protest against escalating harassment by state media.	Two days after security forces abduct and detain thousands of Falun Gong practitioners, the government declares the movement an illegal organisation.

cals, machine tools, engines, electricity, vinegar, beer, concrete, textiles, weapons – in fact, everything that would make it an economically self-sufficient 'production base' in case of war. By the 1970s, Běijīng had become one of the most heavily polluted cities in the world.

The Great Leap Forward

The move to tear down the city's walls, widen the roads and demolish the distinctive *páilóu* (ceremonial arches) started immediately after 1949, but was fiercely contested by some intellectuals, including Liang Sicheng, who ran the architecture department of Qīnghuá University. So in the midst of the demolition of many famous landmarks, the municipal authorities earmarked numerous buildings and even old trees for conservation. However, it was all to no avail – Mao's brutal political purges silenced all opposition.

The Cultural Revolution

Those intellectuals who escaped persecution in the 1950s were savagely dealt with during the Cultural Revolution (1966–76). Qīnghuá University became the birthplace of the Red Guards (a mass movement of young radicals, mobilised by Mao). In the 'bloody August' of 1966, Běijīng's middle-school students turned on their teachers, brutally murdering some of them. Some reports estimate almost 2000 people were killed in Běijīng at this time. The number excludes those beaten to death as they tried to escape Běijīng on trains – their registration as residents of Běijīng was suddenly cancelled.

End of the Mao Era

In Mao's time the geomantic symmetry of Běijīng was radically changed. The north–south axis of the Ming city was ruined by widening Chang'an Dajie into a 10-lane, east–west highway. This was used for huge annual military parades or when visiting dignitaries arrived and the population was turned out to cheer them. In the 1950s, the centre was redesigned by Soviet architects and modelled on Moscow's Red Sq. Three major gates and many other Ming buildings, including the former government ministries, were demolished, leaving the concrete expanse of Tiān'ānmén Sq you see today.

Mao used the square to receive the adulation of the millions of Red Guards who flocked to Běijīng from 1966 to 1969, but after 1969 Mao exiled the Red Guards, along with 20 million 'educated youth', to the countryside. From 1976, the square became the scene of massive anti-government protests – when Premier Zhou Enlai died in 1976 the large and apparently spontaneous protest in the square was quelled by the police. Mao himself died in the same year.

In the 1958 Great Leap Forward, the last qualms about preserving old Běijīng were abandoned. A new plan was approved to destroy 80% of the old capital. The walls were pulled down, but the series of ring roads planned at the time were never built.

HISTORY MAO'S BĚIJĪNG

Designs to demolish the Forbidden City and erect new party headquarters on the site were drawn up in the late 1960s but never implemented. The palace was closed for nearly 10 years and became overgrown with weeds.

2001	2001	2002	1 August 2008
Work commences on the National Centre for the Performing Arts, Běijīng's futuristic answer to the Shànghǎi Grand Theatre. The building is not completed for a further seven years.	After winning the bid to host the 2008 Olympic Games, Běijīng embarks on a massive public-transport development project, expanding the subway system from two lines to 17.	Hu Jintao becomes China's new political leader when he is appointed general secretary of the Communist Party. He governs China for the next 10 years.	The Běijīng to Tiānjīn 'bullet train' opens for operation, reaching a top speed of 330km/h during its 29-minute journey, and setting the record for the fastest conventional train service in the world.

Reform & Protest

Calls for Democracy

In August and September of 1966, a total of 1772 people were killed in the capital, according to a report published by the *Beijing Daily* after 1979.

Deng Xiaoping (1904–97), backed by a group of veteran generals, seized power in a coup d'état and threw Mao's widow, Jiang Qing (1914–91), and her ultraleftist cronies into the notorious Qínchéng prison outside the city, where Mao had incarcerated so many senior party veterans. The prison still exists not far from the Ming Tombs.

The Democracy Wall

At the third plenum of the 11th Party Congress, Deng consolidated his grip on power and launched economic reforms. At the same time thousands of people began putting up posters along a wall west of Zhōngnánhǎi, complaining of injustices under the 'Gang of Four' (Jiang Qing and her three associates) and demanding democracy. Deng initially appeared to back political reforms, but soon the activists were thrown into jail, some in the Běijīng No 1 Municipal Prison (demolished in the mid-1990s).

Rising Discontent

Many of the activists were former Red Guards or exiled educated youth. After 1976 they drifted back to the city, but could only find jobs in the new private sector running small market stalls, tailor shops or restaurants. After the universities opened, conditions remained poor and the intelligentsia continued to be treated with suspicion. Frustrations with the slow pace of reforms prompted fresh student protests in the winter of 1986. Peasants did well out of the first wave of reforms, but in the cities many people felt frustrated. Urban life revolved around 'work units' to which nearly everyone was assigned. The work unit distributed food, housing, bicycles, travel permits and almost everything else. Běijīng was still a rather drab, dispiriting place in the 1980s; there was much more to eat but everything else was in a lamentable state. For 30 years there had been little investment in housing or transport.

Contrary to popular belief, much of the violence that shook the city – and the watching world – on 4 June 1989 didn't take place in Tiān'ānmén Sq itself, but in the surrounding streets.

1989 Tiān'ānmén Square Protests

In January 1987 the party's conservative gerontocrats ousted the prore-form party chief Hu Yaobang and, when he suddenly died in the spring of 1989, Běijīng students began assembling on Tiān'ānmén Sq. Officially, they were mourning his passing but they began to raise slogans for political reform and against corruption. The protests snowballed as the Communist Party leadership split into rival factions, causing a rare paralysis. The police stood by as the protests spread across the country and workers, officials and ordinary citizens took to the streets. When

8 August 2008	2011	June 2011	2012
Běijīng hosts the Olympic Games; restrictions on international media are temporarily lifted.	Artist and political activist Ai Weiwei is seized at Běijīng Airport and placed under house arrest for almost three months.	The high-speed rail link between Běijīng and Shànghǎi opens to the public, slashing train journey times between the two cities from 10 hours to just five.	Blind civil-rights activist Chen Guang-cheng takes refuge in the US embassy in Běijīng. After weeks of high-level negotiations between Běijīng and US officials, China agrees to him leaving for America.

the military tried to intervene, Beijingers surrounded the tanks. The students set up tents on Tiān'ānmén Sq and went on a hunger strike. When the premier Li Peng held a dialogue with the students that was aired live on TV, student leaders sarcastically upbraided him.

The students created the first independent student union since 1919 and celebrated the anniversary of the May Fourth Movement with a demonstration in which more than a million people took to the streets. For the first time since 1949, the press threw off the shackles of state censorship and became independent. When Soviet leader Mikhail Gorbachev entered on a state visit, and was enthusiastically welcomed as a symbol of political reform, it seemed as if the Chinese Communist Party (CCP), too, would embrace political change. Party General Secretary Zhao Ziyang led the reformist faction, but the older-generation leaders, led by Deng Xiaoping, decided to arrest Zhao and retake the city with a military assault. On the night of 3 June, tens of thousands of troops backed by tanks and armoured personnel carriers entered the city from four directions, bulldozing aside the hastily erected barricades.

Many people died – some say hundreds, some thousands – and by the early hours of 4 June the troops were in control of the square. In the crackdown that followed across the country, student leaders escaped abroad while the Communist Party arrested thousands of students and their supporters. In the purge of party members that followed, China's reforms seemed to be going into reverse.

Louisa Lim's 2014 book *The People's Republic of Amnesia: Tiananmen Revisited* is an excellent analysis of the impact the Tiān'ānmén Square crackdown has had on China.

HISTORY RAPID DEVELOPMENT

Rapid Development

Economic Reform

Things began to change when Deng Xiaoping emerged from the shadows and set off in 1992 on a so-called 'southern tour', visiting his special economic zones in the south and calling for more and faster reform. Despite opposition in the party, he won the day. China began a wave of economic reforms, which transformed urban China and brought new wealth and opportunities to most urban residents, though the political system remained unchanged and some 40 million workers in state-owned factories lost their jobs. Deng's reforms pulled in a tide of foreign investment, creating two economic booms, after 1992 and 1998. Stock markets reopened, state companies were privatised and private enterprise began to flourish, especially in the service sector, which created millions of new jobs. More than 100 million peasants left the countryside to work on construction sites or in export-processing factories. The factories were moved out of Běijīng and the city once again became a 'centre of consumption'.

Běijīng boasted more than 3679 historic *hútòng* (narrow alleyways) in the 1980s, but by 2006 only 430 were left, according to a field survey by the Běijīng Institute of Civil Engineering and Architecture.

July 2012	November 2012	January 2013	October 2013
Seventy-seven people die and more than 65,000 are evacuated from their homes after Běijīng is hit by its worst floods in 60 years.	Xi Jinping is appointed as China's new president as part of the nation's once-in-a-decade transfer of power.	Běijīng's notoriously toxic air pollution reaches record levels. The month is dubbed 'Airpocalypse'.	A car crashes beside Tiān'ānmén Sq in what police describe as a terrorist suicide attack. Five people die: the three inside the vehicle, plus two tourists.

The Dalai Lama's former Běijīng palace is now rented out by the government of the Tibet Autonomous Region.

Losing the Heritage Protection Battle

The economy was given a huge impetus by decisions to rebuild all major cities virtually from scratch, privatise housing and sell 50- or 70-year land leases to developers. There was resistance by Party Secretary Chen Xitong to the destruction of Běijīng's centre. During the 1980s and early 1990s, Chen approved redevelopment plans that aimed to preserve and restore Běijīng's historic centre and characteristic architecture. Chen had earlier helped persuade many army and civilian work units to vacate historical sites they'd occupied during the 1970s. However, in 1995, he was ousted by Jiang Zemin, and imprisoned on corruption charges.

Rebuild & Relocate

Once the Party apparatus was under his direct control, President Jiang approved plans to completely rebuild Běijīng and relocate its inhabitants. New shopping malls, office blocks, hotels and luxury housing developments were thrown up at astonishing speed. Only a dictatorship with the vast human and industrial resources of China at its command could ever have achieved this.

Jiang wanted to turn Běijīng into another Hong Kong, with a forest of glass-and-steel skyscrapers. The new municipal leadership threw out the old zoning laws, which limited the height of buildings within the 2nd Ring Rd. It revoked existing land deeds by declaring old buildings to be dilapidated slums. Such regulations enabled the state to force residents to abandon their homes and move to new housing in satellite cities. Under the plan, only a fraction of the 67 sq km Ming city was preserved.

Looking Forward Only

Some see the rebuilding as a collective punishment on Běijīng for its 1989 rebellion, but others see it as the continuing legacy of Mao's Cultural Revolution and the late Qing dynasty reformers. Many of China's recent leaders have been engineers and ex–Red Guards, including former President Hu Jintao, who graduated from Qīnghuá University during the Cultural Revolution. Běijīng's state-of-the-art new architecture – the Bird's Nest, the CCTV Building, Soho Galaxy – seems designed to embody their aspiration to create a new, forward-looking, hi-tech society, and mark the realisation of the goal of a new modern China. Meanwhile the older parts of the city, such as its historic *hútòng* neighbourhoods, are hanging on by a thread.

March 2014	June 2015	August 2015	February 2016
Malaysia Airlines flight MH370 from Kuala Lumpur to Běijīng is declared missing, sparking the largest and most-expensive multinational search and rescue effort in history.	Běijīng introduces the toughest antismoking law in Chinese history, in a bid to make the capital much more smoke-free.	Běijīng hosts the World Athletic Championships, the first major sporting event held at the iconic 'Birds Nest' stadium since the 2008 Olympics.	China's State Council bans 'bizarre' and 'odd-shaped' buildings, signalling an end to the wave of wacky buildings that have popped up in Běijīng over the last decade.

Historic Hútòng

The essence of Běijīng are its *hútòng* (胡同), the distinctive alleyways that cut across the centre of town. These enchanting passageways offer a very real glimpse of what Běijīng was like before the bulldozers and construction crews got to work, and are still home to almost 20% of the residents of inner Běijīng. Immersing yourself in the *hútòng* is an essential part of any visit to the capital and by far the best way to experience Běijīng street life in all its frenetic and fascinating glory.

Origins

Hútòng first appeared in Běijīng in the Yuan dynasty (1271–1368), in the wake of Genghis Khan's army. With the city, then known as Zhōngdū, reduced to rubble in typical Mongol style, it was redesigned with *hútòng* running east–west. At first, their numbers were comparatively small – there were no more than 380 by the end of the Mongol reign over Běijīng – but they began to increase during the Ming dynasty. By the Qing dynasty more than 2000 *hútòng* riddled Běijīng, giving rise to the Chinese saying, 'There are 360 *hútòng* with names and as many nameless *hútòng* as there are hairs on a cow'.

The number of alleyways peaked in the 1950s, when there were reckoned to be more than 6000. In recent decades the construction of office buildings and apartment blocks, as well as the widening of roads, has resulted in the demolition of many of them. However, it's likely that somewhere between 1000 and 2000 of these beguiling lanes have avoided the wrecking balls.

Venerable alleys include Zhuanta Hutong (砖塔胡同; Brick Pagoda Alley), dating from Mongol times and found west off Xisi Nandajie; and Nanluogu Xiang, which dates back 800 years and is now the best-known alley in town thanks to its emergence as a nightlife hub. Other *hútòng* survive in name only, like 900-year-old Sanmiao Jie (三庙街; Three Temple St) in Xuānwǔ District, which dates back to the Liao dynasty (916–1125). Long cited as the oldest *hútòng* of them all, little is left of the ancient alley as its courtyard houses were demolished in 2009.

Most *hútòng* lie within the loop of the 2nd Ring Rd. The most *hútòng*-rich neighbourhoods are in the centre and north of Dōngchéng District, closely followed by the northern part of Xīchéng District, especially the area around and to the west of Hòuhǎi Lakes. The *hútòng* here were the closest to the Forbidden City, and the nearer you lived to the imperial palace, the higher your status. For that reason, the *hútòng* immediately east and west of the Forbidden City were reserved for aristocrats and the city elite. It's in these *hútòng* that you'll find the oldest and most prestigious *sìhéyuàn* (traditional courtyard houses), many of which are now government offices. Most date from the Qing dynasty, though many of the actual lanes are older.

The alleys around or close to the Forbidden City have been largely protected from the ravages of redevelopment. The houses further away were the homes of merchants and artisans, featuring more functional design with little or no ornamentation. It is these *hútòng,* especially the ones southeast and southwest of Tiān'ānmén Sq, that have suffered the most from the wrecking ball.

Walk through the once vibrant neighbourhood directly due east of Qianmen Dajie, near where Lìqún Roast Duck Restaurant (p111) is located, and you'll get a vivid impression of how many *hútòng* are clinging on for dear life in the face of property development. Nevertheless, the area around Dazahlan Xijie, itself a *hútòng,* still has many alleys left, although they lack the aesthetic value of their posher counterparts to the north.

But you can find *hútòng* of one sort or another in all Běijīng's neighbourhoods, even if some are relatively recent creations and are basically low-level housing rather than anything worthy of preservation. Wherever you choose to plunge into *hútòng* land, you'll be treading streets that have hundreds of years of history behind them.

Imperial City Hútòng

The Imperial City failed to survive the convulsions of the 20th century, but the *hútòng* that threaded through the imperial enclave remain. Many bore names denoting their former function during imperial days. Zhonggu Hutong (钟鼓胡同; Bell and Drum Alley) was responsible for the provision of bells and drums to the imperial household. Jinmaoju Hutong (巾帽局胡同; Cloth and Cap Department Alley) handled the caps and boots used by the court, while Zhiranju Hutong (织染局胡同; Weaving and Dyeing Department Alley) supplied its satin and silk. Jiucuju Hutong (酒醋局胡同; Wine and Vinegar Department Alley) managed the stock of spirits, vinegar, sugar, flour and other culinary articles.

Candles were vital items during Ming and Qing times. Supply was handled by the Làkù, which operated from Laku Hutong (蜡库胡同; Candle Storehouse). The Jade Garden Hotel sits on the former site of the Cíqìkù (Porcelain Storehouse), which kept the Forbidden City stocked with porcelain bowls, plates, wine cups and other utensils.

West of Běihǎi Park, the large road of Xishiku Dajie (西什库大街; West Ten Storehouse St) gets its name from the various storehouses scattered along its length during Ming times. Among items supplied to the Imperial City from warehouses here were paper, lacquer, oil, copper, leather and weapons, including bows, arrows and swords.

There are also *hútòng* named after the craftworkers who supplied the Forbidden City with its raw materials, such as Dashizuo Hutong (大石作胡同; Big Stonemason's Alley), where stonemasons fashioned the stone lions, terraces, imperial carriageways and bridges of the Imperial City.

Now-vanished temples are also recalled in *hútòng* names, such as the Guangming Hutong (光明胡同), south of Xi'anmen Dajie, named after the huge Guāngmíng Diàn (Guāngmíng Temple) that is no more.

Hútòng Today

Hútòng land is now a hotchpotch of the old and the new, where Qing dynasty courtyards come complete with recently added brick outhouses and stand beneath grim apartment blocks. Adding to the lack of uniformity is the fact that many *sìhéyuàn* were subdivided in the 1960s so that they could house more people.

The shortage of space, as well as the paucity of modern facilities such as heating, proper plumbing, private bathrooms and air-conditioning, is the main reason many *hútòng* dwellers have been happy to leave the alleyways for newly built high-rise flats. Older residents are more reluctant to abandon the *hútòng,* preferring the sense of living in a community, as opposed to a more isolated existence in the suburbs.

Foreigners long ago cottoned on to the charm of courtyard life and breached this conservative bastion, although many are repelled by poor

The origins of the word '*hútòng*' are hazy. Originally a Mongolian term, it could have referred to a passageway between *gers* or 'yurts', the traditional Mongol tents; or it might come from the word '*hottog*' (a well) – wherever there was water in the dry plain around Běijīng, there were inhabitants.

heating, and neighbours who can be too close for comfort by Western standards. In addition, some *hútòng* homes still lack their own toilets, explaining the malodorous public loos strung along many alleyways. But other homes have been thoroughly modernised and sport such features as varnished wooden floors, fully fitted kitchens, split-level bedrooms and numerous bathrooms. Converted courtyards are prized and are much more expensive to buy or rent than even the swishest apartments.

While large numbers of old courtyard houses have been divided into smaller units, many of their historical features remain, especially their roofs. Courtyard communities are served by small shops and restaurants spread throughout the *hútòng,* making them very much their own self-contained worlds.

An Uncertain Future

A few years ago, it seemed that Běijīng's government had finally realised the aesthetic value of preserving the historic heart of the capital. Now, though, the future of the *hútòng* appears less certain. People are still being evicted from homes their families have occupied for generations, as local authorities continue to demolish whole alleys in the name of what they regard as progress.

The latest assault took place in the Drum and Bell Tower area, with some of the surrounding *hútòng* levelled as part of the authorities' misguided attempt to develop the area. The result is a sanitised, wholly fake version of an 18th-century Qing dynasty neighbourhood. To the distress of many Beijingers, local officials still seem to have a vision of a gleaming, new Běijīng that purposefully excludes the *hútòng*.

Despite laws that are supposed to protect them, it is telling that perhaps the best guarantee for the survival of a *hútòng* is whether it has commercial value. The successful remodelling of Nanluogu Xiang into a nightlife hot spot and tourist hub has been replicated elsewhere: some of the alleys off Gulou Dongdajie and Andingmen Dajie have also sprouted shops, bars, cafes and restaurants and have become almost as popular. As long as a *hútòng* is generating significant tax revenue for the local authority, officials appear willing to shield them from redevelopment.

Old Walled Courtyards

Sìhéyuàn (四合院) are the building blocks of the *hútòng* world. Some old courtyards, such as the Lǎo Shě Museum, have been quaintly mothballed as museums, but many remain inhabited and hum with domestic activity inside and out. Doors to communal courtyards are typically left open, while from spring to autumn men collect outside their gates, drinking beer, smoking and chewing the fat. Inside, trees soar aloft, providing shade and a nesting place for birds.

Prestigious courtyards are entered by a number of gates, but the majority have just a single door. Venerable courtyards are fronted by large, thick red doors, outside of which perch either a pair of Chinese lions or drum stones (*bǎogǔshí;* two circular stones resembling drums, each on a small plinth and occasionally topped by a miniature lion or a small dragon head). A set of square *méndāng* (wooden ornaments) above the gateway is a common sight. You may even see a set of stepping-on stones *(shàngmǎ shí)* that the owner would use for mounting his steed. The more historic courtyard gates are accessed by a set of steps, both topped with and flanked by ornate brick carvings – the generosity of detail indicates the social clout of the courtyard's original inhabitants.

Many of these impressive courtyards were the residences of Běijīng's officials, wealthy families and even princes; Prince Gong's Residence on Dingfu Jie is perhaps the most celebrated example. In more recent times,

The rectangular waffle-grid pattern of the *hútòng* stamps the points of the compass on the Běijīng psyche. You can still hear older locals exclaiming, *'wǒ gāoxìng de wǒ bù zhī běi le,'* meaning 'I was so happy, I didn't know which way was north' (an extremely disorientating state of joy).

Many of the grandest *sìhéyuàn* are occupied by high-ranking CCP cadres or are government offices. A number of senior officials live in the *hútòng* off Nanluogu Xiang, while former Premier Zhao Ziyang spent the last 15 years of his life under house arrest in a courtyard once occupied by Empress Cixi's hairdresser.

HISTORIC HÚTÒNG AN UNCERTAIN FUTURE

many were appropriated by work units to provide housing for their workforce. Others still belong to private owners, or are used by the government or universities, but the state ultimately owns all property in China, which leaves the fate of the *hútòng* in the hands of local authorities.

Wind-Water Lanes

By far the majority of *hútòng* run east–west, ensuring that the main gate faces south, so satisfying feng shui (geomancy, literally 'wind and water') requirements. This south-facing aspect guarantees maximum sunshine and protection from negative forces prevailing from the north. This positioning mirrors the layout of all Chinese temples, which nourishes the yang (the male and light aspect) while checking the yin (the female and dark aspect). Less significant north–south running alleyways link the main lanes.

Some courtyards used to be further protected by rectangular stones bearing the Chinese characters for Tài Shān (Mt Tài) to vanquish bad omens. Other courtyards preserve their screen walls or spirit walls (*yǐngbì*) – feng shui devices erected in front of the main gate to deflect roaming spirits. Běijīng's two most impressive spirit walls are the Nine Dragon Screens at the Forbidden City and in Běihǎi Park.

Trees provide *qì* (life energy) and much-needed shade in summer, and most old courtyards have a locust tree at the front, which would have been planted when the *sìhéyuàn* was constructed.

Names

Some *hútòng* are christened after families, such as Zhaotangzi Hutong (赵堂子胡同; Alley of the Zhao Family). Other *hútòng* simply took their names from historical figures, temples or local features, while a few have more mysterious associations, such as Dragon Whiskers Ditch Alley (Lóngxūgōu; 龙须沟胡同). Many reflect the merchandise that was for sale at local markets, such as Ganmian Hutong (干面胡同; Dry Flour Alley), while some *hútòng*, such as Gongbei Hutong (弓背胡同; Bow Back Hutong), have names derived from their shape.

Other names reflect some of the rather unusual industries that coalesced around the Forbidden City. Young Girl Lane was home to future concubines and Wet Nurse Lane was full of young mothers who breastfed the imperial offspring; they were selected from around China on scouting trips four times a year. Clothes Washing Lane was the residence of the women who did the imperial laundry. The maids, having grown old in the service of the court, were subsequently packed off to faraway places until their intimate knowledge of royal undergarments was out of date and no longer newsworthy.

Some *hútòng* names conceal their original monikers, which were considered either too unsavoury or unlucky, in homophones or similarly sounding words, or are euphemisms for what actually went on there. Guancai Hutong (棺材胡同), or 'Coffin Alley', was dropped for Guangcai Hutong (光彩胡同), which means 'Splendour Hutong'. Muzhu Hutong (母猪胡同), 'Mother Pig Hutong' or 'Sow Hutong', was elevated to the much more poetic Meizhu Hutong (梅竹胡同), or 'Plum Bamboo Hutong'. Rouge Hutong (胭脂胡同; Yanzhi Hutong) earned its name because it was the haunt of prostitutes, 'rouge' being old Běijīng slang for a working girl.

Dimensions

Despite an attempt at standardisation, Běijīng's alleys have their own personalities and proportions. The longest is Dongjiaomin Xiang (东交民巷), which extends for 3km, while the shortest – unsurprisingly called Yichi Dajie (一尺大街; One Foot St) – is a brief 25m. Some people contest

You can experience these delightful lanes to the full by spending a night in a *hútòng* courtyard hotel. There are also restaurants, such as Dali Courtyard or Source, where you can dine inside a *sìhéyuàn*, as well as a growing number of cafes and bars located within former courtyard homes.

For a bird's-eye panorama of Běijīng's *hútòng* universe, view the diorama of the modern city at the Běijīng Planning Exhibition Hall. The excellent NGO Běijīng Cultural Heritage Protection Centre (www.bjchp.org) is a great source on efforts to preserve the city's remaining *hútòng*.

THE CHANGING FACE OF HÚTÒNG LAND

One by-product of the commercialisation of some *hútòng* is that they cease to be the fascinating microcosms of local life they once were. Ten years ago, Nanluogu Xiang was still full of families who had lived there for generations and was lined with *xiǎomàibù* (small general stores) and greengrocers rather than bars.

Now, virtually none of those residents remain. The vast majority have leased their courtyard homes as shops, restaurants, bars and cafes and used the sky-high rents to relocate to comfy new apartment blocks in the suburbs. Whereas once kids played in the street on summer nights, while the adults sat fanning themselves or playing Chinese chess, now young Beijingers and domestic tourists stroll up and down, shopping, eating and drinking.

This transition from living, breathing communities into something far less organic is being mimicked elsewhere; for example, at Wudaoying Hutong near the Lama Temple and at the nearby Fangjia Alley, where hipsters mingle with the remaining original residents.

The *hútòng* dwellers aren't complaining too much, though. On the contrary, it is now near impossible to buy a *sìhéyuàn* in such areas because their residents know they can guarantee their long-term future by renting them out instead. But if you're looking for a taste of truly authentic alley life, you'll need to plunge into the *hútòng* that haven't been touched by the hand of Mammon.

that Guantong Xiang (贯通巷; Guantong Alley), near Yangmeizhu Xijie, which is east of Liulichang Dongjie, is even shorter, at 20m.

Some *hútòng* are wide and leafy boulevards, whereas others are narrow, claustrophobic corridors. Běijīng's broadest alley is Lingjing Hutong (灵境胡同; Fairyland Alley), with a width of 32m, but the aptly named Xiaolaba Hutong (小喇叭胡同; Little Trumpet Alley), the city's smallest, is a squeeze at 50cm.

Chubby wayfarers would struggle even more in Qianshi Hutong (钱市胡同), situated not far from Qiánmén and Dàzhàlan – its narrowest reach is a mere 44cm, although it's a pathway rather than a genuine *hútòng*. Nor do all the lanes run straight: Jiuwan Hutong (九湾胡同; Nine Bend Alley) has no fewer than 13 turns in it.

Tours

Exploring Běijīng's *hútòng* is an unmissable experience. Go on a walking or cycling tour and delve deep into this alternately ramshackle and genteel, but always magical, world. Best of all, just wander off the main roads in the centre of Běijīng into the alleyways that riddle the town within the 2nd Ring Rd. Getting lost is part of the fun of exploring the *hútòng,* and you don't have to worry about finding your way back because you'll never be far from a main road.

Good places to plunge into are the alleys to the west of Hòuhǎi Lakes, the area around Nanluogu Xiang, the roads branching west off Chaoyangmen Beixiaojie and Chaoyangmen Nanxiaojie, east of Wangfujing Dajie, and the lanes southwest of Tiān'ānmén Sq.

Hiring a bike is by far the best way to explore this historic world. But if you want to join a tour, the China Culture Center (p238) runs regular tours, or can arrange personalised tours. Call for further details, or check the website. Bike Běijīng (p236) also does guided *hútòng* tours. Many hotels run tours of the *hútòng,* or will point you in the direction of someone who does. Alternatively, any number of pedicab touts infest the roads around Hòuhǎi Lakes, offering 45-minute or one-hour tours. Such tours typically cost ¥60 to ¥120 per person. If you want an English-speaking rickshaw rider, the Běijīng Tourist Information Centre opposite the north gate of Běihǎi Park can find you one.

During the Cultural Revolution, selected *hútòng* were rechristened to reflect the political fervour of the times. Nanxiawa Hutong was renamed Xuemaozhu Hutong, literally 'Study Mao's Writings Hutong', while Doujiao'er Hutong became Hongdaodi Hutong, or 'Red to the End Hutong'.

Arts

Běijīng's arts scene has flourished in recent decades, fuelled by China opening up to the world and the subsequent influx of ideas from overseas. Lobotomised during the Cultural Revolution, the capital's creative faculties have since sparked into life and found space. Visual arts have prospered. From humble beginnings in the 798 Art District, Chinese contemporary art has achieved global recognition. But Běijīng is also China's unofficial film-industry capital, the home of its finest bands and the best place to catch traditional Chinese performing arts. Whatever your tastes, you'll find it in Běijīng.

Literature

The eternal Běijīng versus Shànghǎi argument occurs in the arts too. The capital is grittier and edgier than its southern counterpart, and slightly less obsessed with making money. For those reasons, and despite its authoritarian reputation as the centre of power for the Chinese Communist Party (CCP), Běijīng attracts far more creative talent than Shànghǎi.

In keeping with its well-read and creative reputation among ordinary and educated Chinese, Běijīng has been home to some of China's towering modern writers. The literary landscapes of Lao She, Lu Xun, Mao Dun and Guo Moruo are all forever associated with the capital. Venue of the inspirational May Fourth Movement, the first stirrings of the Red Guards and the democracy protests of 1989, Běijīng's revolutionary blood has naturally seeped into its literature. Over the past century, local writers have penned their stories of sorrow, fears and aspirations amid a context of ever-changing trends and political upheaval.

The Birth of Modern Chinese Literature

The publication of Lu Xun's short story 'Diary of a Madman' in 1918 had the same type of effect on Chinese literature as the leather-clad Elvis Presley had on the American music scene in the early 1950s. Until Lu Xun, novels had been composed in classical Chinese *(gǔwén),* a kind of Shakespearean language far removed from colloquial speech *(báihuà).* That maintained the huge gulf between educated and uneducated Chinese, putting literature beyond the reach of the common person and fashioning a cliquey *lingua franca* for officials and scholars.

The opening paragraph of Lu's seminal story uses that classical language. The stultifying introduction – peppered with archaic character use and the excruciatingly pared-down grammar of classical Chinese – continues as one solid block of text, without any new paragraphs or indentation. Then suddenly the passage concludes and the reader is confronted with the appearance of fluent colloquial – *spoken* – Chinese.

For Lu Xun to write his short story – itself a radical fable of palpable terror – in the vernacular was dynamite. Chinese people were at last able to read language as it was spoken and the short story's influence on creative expression was electric. Lu Xun's tale records the diary entries of a man descending into paranoia and despair. Fearful that those around him are engaging in cannibalism, the man's terrifying suspicions are seen as a critique of the self-consuming nature of feudal society. It is a haunting and powerful work, which instils doubts as to the madness of the narrator and concludes with lines that offer a glimmer of hope. From this moment on, mainstream Chinese literature would be written as it was thought and spoken: Chinese writing had arrived in the modern age.

Pre-1989 Literature

Contemporary Chinese literature is commonly grouped into two stages: pre-1989 and post-1989. The 1949 ascendancy saw literature gradually become a tool of state control and mere propaganda. Publishing was nationalised and most work in this period echoed the Communist Party line, with dull, formulaic language and cardboard characters in a socialist-realist framework.

The Hundred Flowers Movement (1956–57) promised a period of open criticism and debate, but instead resulted in a widespread crackdown on intellectuals, including writers. During the Cultural Revolution (1966–76), writers either toed the line or were mercilessly purged. The much-loved Běijīng writer Lao She (1899–1966) was badly beaten and humiliated by Red Guards at the Confucius Temple in August 1966 and committed suicide the next day.

After Mao's death in 1976, Chinese artists and writers threw off political constraints and began to explore new modes of literary expression.

The text of 'Diary of a Madman' (aka 'A Madman's Diary') can be downloaded for free at www.marxists.org, as can many of Lu Xun's other works. His novels can be picked up in translation at the Lu Xun Museum and are widely available in the West.

ARTS LITERATURE

BĚIJĪNG BOOKSHELF

➡ *Beijing Coma* (Ma Jian; 2008) Novel revolving around protagonist Dai Wei's involvement with the prodemocracy protests of 1989 and the political coma that ensues.

➡ *Diary of a Madman and Other Stories* (Lu Xun, translated by William Lyell; 1990) Classic tale of mental disintegration and paranoia, and a critique of Confucianism in prerevolutionary China from the father of modern Chinese literature. China's first story published in *báihuà* (colloquial speech), save the first paragraph.

➡ *Rickshaw Boy* (Lao She, translated by Shi Xiaoqing; 1981) A masterpiece by one of Běijīng's most beloved authors and playwrights about a rickshaw-puller living in early-20th-century China.

➡ *Blades of Grass: The Stories of Lao She* (translated by William Lyell; 2000) This collection contains 14 stories by Lao She – poignant descriptions of people living through times of political upheaval and uncertainty.

➡ *Kinder than Solitude* (Yiyun Li; 2014) Haunting novel in English by native Beijinger Yiyun Li that moves between 1990s Běijīng and the present-day US as it explores the complex relationship between three childhood friends.

➡ *The Maker of Heavenly Trousers* (Daniele Vare; 1935) Republished tale of old Běijīng with a splendid cast of dubious foreigners and plenty of insights into Chinese life in the capital in the chaotic pre-WWII days.

➡ *The Noodle Maker* (Ma Jian, translated by Flora Drew; 2004) A collection of interconnected stories as told by a state-employed writer during the aftermath of the Tiān'ānmén Square protests. Bleak, comical and unforgettable.

➡ *Midnight in Peking* (Paul French; 2012) True-life mystery of a brutal murder of an English girl in the Legation era, with lots of juicy detail about the sinful underworld of pre-1949 Běijīng.

➡ *Black Snow* (Liu Heng, translated by Howard Goldblatt; 1993) Compelling novel about workers in Běijīng. Superbly written – a fine translation.

➡ *Peking Story: The Last Days of Old China* (David Kidd; 2003) A true story of a young man who marries the daughter of an aristocratic Chinese family in Běijīng two years before the 1949 Communist Revolution. The writing is simple, yet immersive.

➡ *Empress Orchid* (Anchee Min; 2004) Historical novel about Empress Cixi and her rise to Empress of China during the last days of the Qing dynasty. Good historical background of Běijīng and entertaining to read.

➡ *Beijing: A Novel* (Philip Gambone; 2003) A well-written account of an American working in a medical clinic in Běijīng who falls in love with a local artist. One of the few books out there to explore in-depth the intricacies of Běijīng gay subculture.

'Scar Literature' – novels exploring the traumatic impact of the Cultural Revolution on Chinese society – was the most significant of all the literary movements that flowered during the late 1970s and 1980s. It still flourishes today, with authors like Yu Hua, Jiang Rong and Ha Jin delving into those dark days.

Western books began to appear in translation for the first time, exposing Chinese authors to a wide array of literary techniques and styles.

One important writer to emerge during this period was Zhang Jie, who first drew the attention of literary critics with the publication of her daring novella *Love Must Not Be Forgotten* (1979). With its intimate portrayal of a middle-aged woman and her love of a married man, the book challenged the traditional mores of marriage. The authorities disparaged the work, calling it morally corrupt, but the book was extremely popular with readers and won a national book award.

Zhang went on to write the novels *Heavy Wings* (1980) and *The Ark* (1981). *The Ark,* about three women separated from their husbands, established Zhang as China's 'first feminist author'. Shen Rong was another talented female author. Her novella *At Middle Age* (1980) tells the plight of a Chinese intellectual during the Cultural Revolution who must balance her family life with her career as a doctor.

Post-1989 Literature

The tragic events of 1989 inspired a more 'realist' style of literature pioneered by writers such as Wang Shuo and Yu Hua. Wang, a sailor-turned-fiction-writer, is famous for his satirical stories about China's underworld and political corruption. Wang's stories – dark, sometimes fantastic and taking jabs at just about every aspect of contemporary Chinese society – are notable for their inventive use of Běijīng slang; his style is similar to the way the Scottish author Irvine Welsh uses the Edinburgh vernacular in novels such as *Trainspotting*.

One of Wang's most contentious novels is *Please Don't Call Me Human*. Written after the Tiān'ānmén Square democracy protests, it provides a mocking look at the failures of China's state security system. Wang's works appeal to a broad spectrum of Chinese society, despite being banned. He has written more than 20 books as well as screenplays for TV and film. Books available in English include *Playing for Thrills* (2000) and *Please Don't Call Me Human* (1998).

Like Wang, Yu Hua grew up during the Cultural Revolution and that experience is filtered through all his work. Yu, too, uses extreme situations

EXILES

Chinese authors living overseas, either through choice or because of their political views, have been responsible for some of the most effective writing about China in recent years. London-based Ma Jian left China after the Tiān'ānmén Square protests. His novel *Beijing Coma* (2008), which recounts the events of June 1989 from the perspective of a student left in a coma after being shot during the crackdown on the protestors, is the finest piece of fiction dealing with that momentous time.

Ma's masterpiece, though, is the remarkable *Red Dust* (2001), a memoir of the three years in the early 1980s Ma spent travelling around the remote edges of China, including Tibet, on the lam. Its opening chapters provide a fascinating snapshot of the then tiny community of bohemians in Běijīng and the suspicions they aroused among the authorities.

Native Beijinger Yiyun Li, who now lives in California, writes exquisite short stories. Both *A Thousand Years of Good Prayers* (2005) and *Gold Boy, Emerald Girl* (2010) reveal the lives of ordinary Chinese caught up in the sweeping cultural changes of the past 20 years and are told in memorable prose.

Another US-based author who writes in English is Ha Jin. His novel *Waiting* (1999) is a love story that spans two decades as its hero hangs on 18 years for official permission to get divorced so he can remarry. The harsher, more satirical *War Trash* (2004) examines the complicated web of loyalties – to family, country and political party – many Chinese struggled to reconcile in the wake of the communist takeover of China in 1949.

and humour, and often violence, to illustrate his essentially absurd vision of modern-day China. But unlike Wang, Yu's novels are vast, sweeping affairs that cover decades. *To Live* (1992) follows the tribulations of one family from the founding of the new China through the Cultural Revolution. Its impact overseas helped turn Yu into a global name. His subsequent novels – *Chronicle of a Blood Merchant* (1995), which moves from the 1950s to the 1980s; *Brothers* (2005), a vicious, dark satire on the rush for riches that has characterised the last two decades in China; and the more reflective *The Seventh Day* (2015) – are all available in English translation.

Mo Yan (real name Guan Moye: 'Mo Yan' is a pen-name that means 'don't speak' in Mandarin) has become a worldwide literary star since winning the Nobel Prize for Literature in 2012. His short stories and novels are less pitiless and abrasive than those of Yu Hua and Wang Shuo and, like the great Lu Xun, are essentially social commentary. Most of his work is available in English. The short story collection *Shifu: You'll Do Anything for a Laugh* (2002) provides a great introduction to his writing.

By far the biggest literary hit of recent years has been Jiang Rong's *Wolf Totem* (2004), which received widespread exposure in the West after being published in English in 2008. Set in the grasslands of Inner Mongolia, it's a lyrical, semi-autobiographical tale of a young Běijīng student 'sent down' to live among Mongolian nomads during the Cultural Revolution and the contrasts between their lives and the one he has left behind.

The advent of the internet has spawned a whole new generation of young writers who have sprung to fame by first publishing their work online. Now, legions of wannabe authors are posting their short stories, novels and poetry on websites. At the same time, the first writers from the one-child generation (born post-1980) to attract national attention have emerged. The work of Han Han and Guo Jingming will never win any literary prizes (indeed, both authors have been accused of plagiarism, or of merely being the front for teams of ghost writers), but their tales of urban youth have made them media icons and the bestselling authors in China.

Visual Arts

The founding of the new China in 1949 saw the individual artistic temperament suborned to the service of the state. Art was now for the masses and the socialist-realist style emerged dominant, with all human activity in paintings expressing the glory of the communist revolution.

Traditional precepts of Chinese classical painting were sidelined and foreign artistic techniques were imported wholesale. Washes on silk were replaced with oil on canvas while a realist attention to detail supplanted China's traditional obsession with the mysterious and ineffable. Landscapes were replaced with harder-edged panoramas in which humans occupied a central, commanding position. The entire course of Chinese painting – which had evolved in glacial increments over the centuries – was redirected virtually overnight.

It was only with the death of Mao Zedong in September 1976 that the individual artistic temperament was once again allowed more freedom and painters such as Luo Zhongli employed the realist techniques they learned in China's art academies to portray the harsh suffering etched in the faces of contemporary peasants. Others escaped the suffocating confines of socialist realism to explore new horizons, experimenting with a variety of contemporary forms.

A voracious appetite for Western art put further distance between traditional Chinese aesthetics and artistic endeavour. One group of artists, the Stars, found retrospective inspiration in Picasso and German expressionism. The ephemeral group had a lasting impact on the development of Chinese art in the 1980s and 1990s, leading the way for the New Wave movement that emerged in 1985.

In late February and March there are two literary festivals you can attend. The Bookworm stages the International Literary Festival, while the Capital M Literary Festival is held at the Capital M restaurant. Both attract local and international authors – another sign of Běijīng's emergence as a true world city.

ARTS VISUAL ARTS

Běijīng's Best Galleries & Art Neighbourhoods
....
798 Art District
....
Cǎochǎngdì
....
Red Gate Gallery
....
National Art Museum

Yue Minjun's grotesque 'laughing' portraits of himself and friends, which are designed to convey a sense of boredom and mock joviality, have become perhaps the most recognisable images of Chinese contemporary art. Yue is now a globally known artist whose individual paintings sell for more than US$1 million.

New Wave artists were greatly influenced by Western art, especially the iconoclastic Marcel Duchamp, and further challenged traditional Chinese artistic norms. The New Wave artist Huang Yongping destroyed his works at exhibitions, in an effort to escape from the notion of 'art'. Some New Wave artists adapted Chinese characters into abstract symbols, while others employed graphic images in a bid to shock viewers. Political realities became instant subject matter with performance artists wrapping themselves in plastic or tape to symbolise the repressive realities of modern-day China.

Post-Tiān'ānmén

The disturbing events during and after June 1989 created artistic disillusionment with the political situation in China and hope soured into cynicism. This attitude was reflected through the 1990s in artworks permeated with feelings of loss, loneliness and social isolation. Two of the most important Běijīng artists during this period of 'Cynical Realism' were Yue Minjun and Fang Lijun.

Experiments with American-style pop art were another reaction to the events of 1989. Inspired by Warhol, some artists took symbols of socialist realism and transformed them into kitschy visual commentary. Images of Mao appeared against floral backgrounds and paintings of rosy-cheeked peasants and soldiers were interspersed with ads for Canon cameras and Coca-Cola. Artists were not only responding to the tragedies of the Tiān'ānmén protests but also to the rampant consumerism that was sweeping the country. Indeed, reaction to the rapid modernisation of China has been a consistent theme of much Běijīng art from the 1990s to the present day.

Throughout the 1990s, artists who felt marginalised from the cultural mainstream found escape from political scrutiny by living together in ad hoc communes and setting up their own exhibitions in nonofficial spaces outside state-run institutions. Most artists relied on the financial support of foreign buyers to continue working. Despite political

SCISSOR-HAPPY

A walk through the thought-provoking, sometimes controversial galleries of the 798 Art District, or its less-commercial counterpart at Cǎochǎngdì, might make any visitor wonder why the fuss about freedom of expression and censorship in China? On the surface at least, artists appear to be enjoying more freedom than they have since 1949 and the beginning of communist rule.

But appearances, like art itself, can be deceptive. Painters may be enjoying a relative lack of scrutiny, with the Chinese Communist Party (CCP) having sensibly decided that no picture ever inspired a revolution (and it's no coincidence that freedom has made the visual arts by far the most vibrant of China's creative industries), but that isn't the case for other mediums. Cinema, TV and literature in particular remain tightly controlled and there are serious limits to what can and can't be said. To overstep them no longer results in a prison sentence, as it does for political dissidents, but it still leads to a ban on making movies or publishing books that can last for a number of years.

Even worse than official censorship is the way 60-plus years of being constrained by the knowledge that art needs to satisfy the CCP's censors has created a culture of self-censorship. Many artists consciously, or unconsciously, hold back from doing anything that might antagonise the government.

This self-suppression is in part due to the fact that children are taught the CCP's vision of the world in school and that the Chinese education system remains dominated by rote-learning. That is not well suited to nurturing creativity, out-of-the-box thinking and inventive criticism. Until this changes, the artistic ceiling in China will remain far lower than it should.

pressure from authorities, some artists began to receive international attention for their art, sparking the beginning of a worldwide interest in and appetite for Chinese contemporary art. A defining moment for artists was in 1999, when 20 Chinese artists were invited to participate in the Venice Biennale for the first time.

Chinese art's obsessive focus on contemporary socio-economic realities makes much creativity from this period parochial and predictable, but more universal themes have become apparent over recent years and the art climate in Běijīng has changed dramatically. Many artists who left China in the 1990s have returned, setting up private studios and galleries. Government censorship remains, but artists are branching out into other areas and moving away from overtly political content and China-specific concerns.

With scores of private and state-run galleries, Běijīng is a fantastic city to witness the changing face of contemporary Chinese art. While traditional Chinese art is still practised in the capital, Běijīng has fully surrendered to the artistic currents that sweep the international sphere. And whereas once it was foreign buyers who drove the booming art market, increasingly it is now the new local rich who are acquiring art.

Today, Běijīng is home to a vibrant community of artists practising a diverse mix of art forms, from performance art, photography, installations and video art to film, although painting remains the most popular visual-arts medium. Běijīng artists compete internationally in art events, and joint exhibitions with European and North American artists are frequent. At the same time, numerous Western artists have flocked to Běijīng in an aesthetic *entente cordiale*.

The capital hosts several art festivals, including the Dàshānzi International Arts Festival (every spring), SURGE Art Běijīng in May and the Běijīng Biennale, held every two years in September/October, which attract artists, dealers and critics from around the world.

Music

China was a definite latecomer to pop and rock music. By the time Elvis and John Lennon were dead and punk had given way to floppy-fringed '80s new wave, Beijingers were still tapping their feet to 'The East is Red'. Like all of the arts, music was tranquillised during the Cultural Revolution as China's self-imposed isolation severed creative ties with the outside world.

It was a young, classically trained trumpet player named Cui Jian who changed all that. Cui swapped his horn for a guitar in the mid-'80s, founded a band, and by 1989 was already a name to be reckoned with. But it was when his song 'Nothing to My Name' ('yī wú suǒ yǒu'), with its abrasive vocal style and lyrics describing feelings of loneliness and alienation, became the anthem of the 1989 Tiān'ānmén protests that he really kick-started the Chinese music scene.

Since those early days, Běijīng has always been China's rock-music mecca. The masses may still prefer the saccharine confections of mainstream Cantopop and Mandopop, but the capital is home to a medley of different bands who take their sonic inspiration from punk and indie, to blues, heavy metal, jazz and electronica.

Mostly, they labour in the twilight. Few local bands have record deals, or are able to make any money by making music available for download. Indeed, the Chinese music industry in general suffers from widespread piracy – hardly any young Chinese would ever consider actually buying music. The upside for visitors is that bands have to rely on gigging to make a living, which means there's someone playing somewhere in Běijīng almost every night of the week.

One of the most talented contemporary Chinese artists is Ai Wei Wei. A former member of the 1980s Stars group of avant-garde artists, he's now more known for his political activism than his multimedia art and has been detained by the authorities on a number of occasions.

ARTS MUSIC

Music festivals are catching on in a big way in China, despite the authorities' automatic suspicion of any large-scale gathering of young people. In and around Běijīng, the Midi Music Festival and Strawberry are two of the best organised events and showcase both local and international acts.

Traditional Chinese musical instruments include the two-stringed fiddle (*èrhú*), famed for its desolate wail; two-stringed viola (*húqín*); vertical flute (*dòngxiāo*); horizontal flute (*dízi*); four-stringed lute (*pípa*); and Chinese zither (*zhēng*). You can catch traditional music performances at the Lao She Teahouse, near Tiān'ānmén Sq in the south of Xīchéng.

There's an incestuous flavour to the scene, with frequent collaborations and musicians rotating between different groups. Some of the most popular and enduring bands are the postpunk/new wave–influenced Carsick Cars and Re-TROS, and the noise-pop trios Hedgehog and Snapline. Also worth checking out are the psychedelic-tinged Chui Wan, the New Order–inspired The Big Wave and indie kids Steely Heart. But there are also bands riffing on reggae, rockabilly, ska, '70s-style hard rock and any number of indigenous folk styles. Jazz, too, has always been popular in China, a legacy of the foreign influence on pre-1949 Shànghǎi.

Hip-hop is in its infancy, but China has embraced electronic music in all its different glories. Club-goers can get a groove on to house, drum and bass, techno and trance most weekends. The local DJ hero is Mickey Zhang; you'll see his name on flyers all over town. Check the local listings magazines for details of upcoming gigs and club nights.

For classical-music and opera lovers, as well as fans of classical Chinese dance, the National Centre for the Performing Arts is the hub of all activity, but there are other venues around the city too. The Běijīng Music Festival (www.bmf.org.cn), held for around 30 days during October and November, features music performances by opera, jazz and classical artists from around the world, while an increasing number of orchestras and opera groups pass through town on a regular basis.

Peking Opera

Peking opera (aka Běijīng opera) is still regarded as the crème de la crème of all the opera styles in China and has traditionally been the opera of the masses. Intrigues, disasters or rebellions are common themes, and many opera narratives have their source in the fairy tales, stock characters and legends of classical literature.

The style of music, singing and costumes in Peking opera are products of their origins. In the past opera was performed on open-air stages in markets, streets, teahouses or temple courtyards. The orchestra had to play loudly and the performers had to develop a piercing style of singing, which could be heard over the throng. The costumes were a garish collection of sharply contrasting colours because the stages were originally lit by oil lamps.

Dance styles as far back as the Tang dynasty (618–907) employed similar movements and techniques to those used in today's opera. Provincial opera companies were characterised by their dialect and style of singing, but when these companies converged on Běijīng they started a style of musical drama called *kunqu*. This developed during the Ming dynasty, along with a more popular variety of play-acting pieces based on legends, historical events and popular novels. These styles gradually merged by the late 18th and early 19th centuries into the opera we see today.

The undisputed king of Peking opera was Mei Lanfang. Mei, who died in 1961, made his name playing female roles and introduced the world to China's most famous art form via overseas tours. Now, his name adorns one of Běijīng's top theatres and his former courtyard home is a museum.

Musicians usually sit on the stage in plain clothes and play without written scores. The *èrhú*, a two-stringed fiddle that is tuned to a low register and has a soft tone, generally supports the *húqín*, a two-stringed viola tuned to a high register. The *yuèqín*, a sort of moon-shaped four-stringed guitar, has a soft tone and is used to support the *èrhú*. Other instruments are the *shēng* (a reed flute) and the *pípa* (lute), as well as drums, bells and cymbals. Last but not least is the *ban*, a time-clapper that virtually directs the band, beats time for the actors and gives them their cues.

Apart from the singing and the music, the opera also incorporates acrobatics and mime. Language is often archaic Chinese, and the music is ear-splitting (bring some cotton wool), but the costumes and make-up are magnificent. Look out for a swift battle sequence – the female warriors especially are trained acrobats who leap, twirl, twist and somersault in attack.

If you get bored after the first hour or so, check out the audience antics – spitting, eating apples, plugging into a transistor radio (important sports match perhaps?) or loud tea slurping. It is lively audience entertainment fit for an emperor. Many theatres around town stage performances of Peking opera.

Cinema

Cinema in China dates to 1896, when a Spaniard with a film projector blew the socks off a crowd in a Shànghǎi teahouse garden. Although Shànghǎi's cosmopolitan gusto would help make the city the capital of China's film industry pre-1949, China's first movie – *Conquering Jun Mountain* (an excerpt from a piece of Peking opera) – was actually filmed in Běijīng in 1905.

Like all the arts, China's film business went into a steep decline after 1949; the dark days of the Cultural Revolution (1966–76) were particularly devoid of creative output. While Taiwan's and Hong Kong's movie industries flourished, China's cinema business was satisfying political agendas with output focused on the glorification of the Communist Party. The film industry in China has yet to recover: taboo subjects still have directors walking on eggshells and criticism of the authorities remains hazardous. Contemporary Chinese TV shows are mostly wooden and artificial, and are often costume dramas set in far-off, and politically safe, dynasties.

Western audiences awoke to a new golden age of Chinese cinema in the 1980s and 1990s when the lush palettes and lavish tragedies of the Fifth Generation directors such as Chen Kaige and Zhang Yimou stimulated the right aesthetic nerves. Garlanded with praise and rewarded with several major film awards, rich works such as *Raise the Red Lantern* (Zhang Yimou; 1991) and *Farewell My Concubine* (Chen Kaige; 1993) redefined Chinese cinema, radiating a beauty that entranced Western cinema-goers and made their directors the darlings of Cannes and other film festivals. But with many of the early Fifth Generation films banned in their home country, few Chinese cinema-goers got to admire their artistry.

Sixth Generation film directors collectively shunned the exquisite beauty of the Fifth Generation, taking the opposite tack to render the angst and grimness of modern urban Chinese life. Their independent, low-budget works, often made without official permission, put an entirely different spin on mainland Chinese filmmaking. Zhang Yuan set the tone with *Mama* (1990), a beautiful but disturbing film about a mother and her autistic child. This low-key film, created without government sponsorship, had a huge influence on Zhang's peers.

Other notable Sixth Generation directors include Wang Xiaoshuai, whose *Beijing Bicycle* (2001) is a tale of a Běijīng youth seeking to recover the stolen bike that he needs for his job, and Guan Hu, whose gritty *Dirt* (1994) chronicled the emerging Běijīng rock scene. In contrast, Lou Ye shoots his films, such as *Suzhou River* (2000), *Summer Palace* (2006) and *Mystery* (2012), in a dreamy, neo-noir style that marks him out from his contemporaries.

But it is Jia Zhangke who is the most talented of the filmmakers who emerged in the 1990s. His debut *Pickpocket* (1997) is a remarkable portrait of a small-time criminal in a bleak provincial town, while its follow-up *Platform* (2000) was a highly ambitious tale of a changing China told through the story of a musical group who transform from being a state-run troupe performing patriotic songs into a pop band. Subsequent movies such as *Still Life* (2006), *24 City* (2008), *A Touch of Sin* (2013) and the futurist drama *Mountains May Depart* (2015) have

Few props are used in Peking opera; instead the performers substitute for them with each move, gesture or facial expression having a symbolic meaning. A whip with silk tassels indicates an actor riding a horse, while lifting a foot means going through a doorway.

ARTS CINEMA

China is a nation in thrall to hierarchies, a legacy of Confucianism, hence filmmakers are ranked by generation. The most famous of them all is the Fifth, the first generation to attend the Běijīng Film Academy after the end of the Cultural Revolution. The current generation is the Seventh.

BEST FILMS ABOUT BĚIJĪNG

➡ *In the Heat of the Sun* (1994) Adapted from a Wang Shuo novel, a fantastic tale of Běijīng youth during the latter days of the Cultural Revolution.

➡ *The Last Emperor* (1987) Bernardo Bertolucci's celebrated (seven Oscars including best director, best costume design and best cinematography) and extravagant epic.

➡ *Summer Palace* (2006) Unusually explicit account of two students' intense love affair set against the backdrop of the Tiān'ānmén Square protests that got its director Lou Ye banned from making films for five years.

➡ *Farewell My Concubine* (1993) Charting a dramatic course through 20th-century Chinese history from the 1920s to the Cultural Revolution, Chen Kaige's film is a sumptuous and stunning narrative of two friends from Peking opera school whose lives are framed against social and political turmoil.

➡ *Cell Phone* (2003) Feng Xiaogang's funniest movie, a delicious satire of Běijīng's emerging middle classes centred on two men's extramarital affairs.

➡ *Lost in Beijing* (2007) Directed by Lu Yi, China's leading female director, this banned production examines the ménage à quatre between a young female worker in a massage parlour, her boss and his wife against the backdrop of a rapidly changing Běijīng.

➡ *Beijing Bicycle* (2001) Eschewing the lavish colour of Fifth Generation directors and viewing Běijīng through a Realist lens, Wang Xiaoshuai's film follows young and hapless courier Guo on the trail of his stolen mountain bike.

➡ *The Gate of Heavenly Peace* (1995) Using original footage from the six weeks preceding the ending of the Tiān'ānmén Square protests, Richard Gordon and Carma Hinton's moving three-hour tribute to the spirit of the student movement and its demise is a must-see.

➡ *The World* (2005) Jia Zhangke's social commentary on the effects of globalisation is set in a Běijīng theme park called 'World Park', where workers and visitors play out their lives among replicas of the world's monuments.

➡ *Cala, My Dog!* (2003) Sly and subtle comedy about a Běijīng factory worker and avid gambler trying to raise money for a licence for the beloved family dog, while coping with his jealous wife and wayward teenage son.

➡ *Mr Six* (2015) An ageing and ailing gangster discovers that the Běijīng underworld is changing just as fast as the rest of the city.

shown an increasing maturity that bodes well for the future, although like many Sixth Generation filmmakers much of his work has never been seen in Chinese cinemas.

While the Sixth Generation were focusing on China's underbelly, an increasing number of directors have gone in the opposite direction by making unashamedly commercial movies. Native Beijinger Feng Xiaogang is the best of them and his clever comedies such as *Cell Phone* (2003), *If You Were the One* (2008) and *Personal Tailor* (2013) have made him China's most bankable director. Following in his footsteps is Ning Hao, who came to prominence with the fun crime capers *Crazy Stone* (2006) and *Crazy Racer* (2009). His most recent movies, the Chinese-style western *No Man's Land* (2013) and the romantic comedy *Breakup Buddies* (2014), both stormed the domestic box office.

Architecture

Whether it's the Hall of Prayer for Good Harvests at Temple of Heaven Park or the CCTV Building, Běijīng's shape-shifting architecture wows. Amble from an ancient *hútòng* (narrow alleyway) past the classical Forbidden City, then alongside the Stalinist bulk of the Great Hall of the People to the sci-fi-style National Centre for the Performing Arts – you'll have seen an architectural narrative at least six centuries long. Běijīng's buildings are as unique to the capital as the aroma of Peking duck.

Traditional Architecture

The oldest standing structure in the Běijīng municipality is the Great Wall. Although the wall dates from the 3rd century BC, most of what you will see is the work of Ming dynasty (1368–1644) engineers, while the tourist sections have largely been rebuilt over the past 30 years or so.

In fact, while Běijīng as we know it today dates to the Yuan dynasty (1271–1368), nearly all traditional architecture in the capital is a legacy of the Ming and Qing dynasties (1368–1911), although most Ming-era buildings were rebuilt during the Qing dynasty. A few fitful fragments have somehow struggled through from the Mongol era, but they are rare.

Standout structures from early dynasties include the magnificent Forbidden City (the largest architectural complex in China at 72 hectares), the Summer Palace, and the remaining *hútòng* and courtyard-style homes in the centre of the city. There are also fine examples of older temple architecture at places such as Temple of Heaven Park, Běihǎi Park and, further afield, at Tánzhè Temple.

To see how the Ming and Qing dynasties built Běijīng, visit the Běijīng Ancient Architecture Museum, which has a great scale model of the old imperial city and shows how the courtyard houses of the *hútòng* were constructed.

BĚIJĪNG'S MOST NOTABLE BUILDINGS

CCTV Building Designed by Rem Koolhaas and Ole Scheeren, this fantastic continuous loop of a building appears to defy gravity.

National Centre for the Performing Arts Běijīng's most loved/hated building – Paul Andreu's creation is either a masterpiece or a blot on the landscape. You decide.

Forbidden City China's incomparably majestic imperial palace.

Hall of Prayer for Good Harvests The *ne plus ultra* of Ming dynasty design and a feast for the eyes.

Capital Museum Cutting-edge example of modern Chinese museum design.

Legation Quarter A too-rare example of thoughtful and tasteful restoration.

Great Hall of the People This monster of Soviet-inspired socialist-realist design, erected during the Great Leap Forward, would look right at home in Pyongyang.

National Stadium The 2008 Olympics may be a distant memory, but this intricate mesh of steel, still known to Beijingers as the 'Bird's Nest', remains iconic.

Galaxy Soho Curvacious and controversial, this space-station-lookalike business and retail complex makes an incongruous neighbour to the next-door 15th-century Buddhist temple.

NO MORE BIZARRE BUILDINGS

The frenzied wave of construction in Běijīng over the last decade has resulted in some truly eye-catching buildings popping up on the capital's skyline. Not all have been embraced by the sometimes bemused locals. The National Centre for the Performing Arts (p69) was swiftly dubbed 'The Alien Egg' by Beijingers, while the astonishing CCTV Headquarters (p136) is known locally as 'The Big Underpants'.

Those extravagant buildings are likely to be some of the last to cause such controversy. In February 2016, China's State Council announced new guidelines on urban planning and they include a ban on so-called 'bizarre' and 'odd-shaped' buildings. Instead, new architecture in China must be 'economic, green and beautiful'.

The new regulations were likely prompted by an October 2014 speech given by China's president Xi Jinping, in which he called for morally inspiring architecture that serves the people. The ban on bizarre buildings will undoubtedly devastate avant-garde architects around the world, who have come to regard China as a place where they can design outlandish structures that other countries won't tolerate. But many locals will be disappointed as well. After all, wacky buildings give everyone something to laugh and gossip about.

Most historic buildings, however, date from the Qing dynasty (1664–1911) or later. Little survives from the Ming dynasty, although the conceptual plan of the city dates from Ming times. Old buildings were constructed with wood and paper, so fire was a perennial hazard (spot the huge bronze water vats dotted around the Forbidden City for extinguishing flames that could rapidly reduce halls to smoking mounds). Because buildings were not durable, even those that escaped fire were not expected to last long.

Home Sweet Home

Most residences in old Běijīng were once *sìhéyuàn,* houses situated on four sides of a courtyard. The houses were aligned exactly – the northern house was directly opposite the southern, the eastern directly across from the western. *Sìhéyuàn* can still be found within the 2nd Ring Rd, and although many have disappeared, an increasing number have been transformed into hotels.

Traditionally, the Chinese followed a basic ground plan when they built their homes. In upper-class homes as well as in palaces and temples, buildings were surrounded by an exterior wall and designed on a north–south axis, with an entrance gate and a gate to block spirits that might try to enter the building. Behind the entry gates in palaces and residential buildings was a public hall and behind this were private living quarters built around a central court with a garden. The garden area of upper-class gentry and imperial families spawned an entire subgenre of 'recreational architecture', which included gardens, pavilions, pagodas, ponds and bridges.

Many temples have been restored to their original purpose, but others are still occupied by residents or, as with Dàgàoxuán Temple, by the military. Some have been converted to offices (Bǎilín Temple), while the ancient Sōngzhùyuàn Temple is now one of the city's trendiest restaurants.

Religious Architecture

With today's religious renaissance drawing more and more Chinese people to prayer, Běijīng's temples and shrines are increasingly busy places of worship (although don't expect to be swept off your feet with religious fervour – atheism still rules over here). What isn't in doubt, though, is that temples are some of the finest structures in the city.

Buddhist, Taoist and Confucian temples may appear complex, but their layout and sequence of deities tend to follow quite strict schematic patterns. Temples are virtually all arranged on a north–south axis in a series of halls, with the main door of each hall facing south, as is done in courtyard houses and the halls of the Forbidden City.

Chinese temples are strikingly different from Christian churches because of their open plan and succession of halls; buildings follow a hierarchy and are interspersed with breezy open-air courtyards. This allows the weather to permeate the empty spaces, changing the mood of the temple depending on the climate. The open-air layout also allows the *qì* (flow of vital or universal energy) to circulate, dispersing stale air and allowing incense to be liberally burned.

Large numbers of Běijīng's temples, such as the Big Buddha Temple, whose memory is commemorated in the street name Dafosi Dongjie, have vanished since the Qing dynasty. Others are in the process of disappearing, such as the small Guānyīn Temple just off Dazhalan Xijie, or remain shut, such as Guǎngfúguàn Taoist Temple.

Buddhist Temples

Although there are notable exceptions, most Buddhist temples tend to follow a predictable layout. The first hall is frequently the Hall of Heavenly Kings (Tiānwáng Diàn), where a sedentary statue of the smiling and podgy Bodhisattva Maitreya (Mílèfó), also known as the Monk with the Bag or the Laughing Buddha, is flanked by the ferocious Four Heavenly Kings. Behind is the first courtyard, where the drum and bell towers often stand, if the temple is large enough, and smoking braziers for the burning of incense may be positioned. The largest hall is usually named the Great Treasure Hall (Dàxióng Bǎodiàn), where you will often discover a golden trinity of statues, representing the historic, contemporary and future Buddhas. You can often find two rows of nine *luóhàn* (Buddhists, especially monks, who have achieved enlightenment and passed to nirvana at death) on either wall to the side. In other temples the *luóhàn* appear in a crowd of 500, housed in a separate hall; the Azure Clouds Temple in Fragrant Hills Park has an example.

A statue of Guanyin (the Goddess of Mercy) often stands at the rear of the main hall, facing north, atop a fish's head or a rocky outcrop. The goddess may also be venerated in her own hall and often has a multitude of arms. The rear hall may house sutras (Buddhist scriptures) in a building called the Scripture Storing Hall (Cángjīnglóu).

Sometimes a pagoda *(tǎ)* may rise above the main halls or may be the last vestige of a vanished temple. These were originally built to house the remains of Buddha, and later other Buddhist relics, and were also used for storing sutras, religious artefacts and documents. Some pagodas can still be climbed for excellent views, but many are too fragile and are out of bounds. The most astonishing collection of pagodas in Běijīng can be found at Tánzhè Temple.

Taoist Temples

As Taoism predates Buddhism and connects to a more primitive and distant era, Taoist shrines are more netherworld-like and project more of an atmosphere of superstition and magic. Nonetheless, in the arrangement of their halls, Taoist temples appear very similar to Buddhist temples.

You will almost certainly see the shape of the circular *bāguà* (a circular figure made up of eight possible combinations of three parallel lines) reflected in eight-sided pavilions and diagrams. The yin–yang Taiji diagram is also a common motif. Effigies of Laotzu (the Jade Emperor), and other characters popularly associated with Taoist myths, such as the Eight Immortals and the God of Wealth, are customary.

Taoist temple entrances are often guarded by Taoist door gods, similar to those in Buddhist temples, and the main hall is usually called the Hall of the Three Clear Ones (Sānqīng Diàn) and devoted to a triumvirate of Taoist deities.

China's most legendary figure has endured a roller-coaster ride throughout Chinese history. These days, Confucius is enjoying an upswing with his 'harmonious society' vision now endorsed by the Chinese Communist Party (CCP). That's in marked contrast to the Cultural Revolution, when Red Guards savaged his teachings as one of the 'Four Olds'.

ARCHITECTURE RELIGIOUS ARCHITECTURE

GOING, GOING, GONE

Although Běijīng has been radically altered in every decade since 1949, the current building mania really picked up pace in the 1990s, with a housing renovation policy that resulted in thousands of old-style homes and Stalinist concrete structures from the 1950s being torn down and replaced by modern apartment buildings. In the following decade, office blocks began to mushroom across the city, prompting yet more demolition.

So much of Běijīng's architectural heritage perished in the 1990s that the capital was denied a World Heritage listing in 2000 and 2001. That led the government to establish 40 protection zones throughout the older parts of the city to protect the remaining heritage buildings. But according to Unesco, more than a third of the 62 sq km area that made up the central part of the old city has been destroyed since 2003, displacing close to 580,000 people.

One of the hardest-hit areas was the central neighbourhood of Qiánmén, once the home of scholars and opera singers. Preservationists and residents have petitioned for government protection. However, a resolution passed in 2005 to protect Běijīng's historic districts did not include many places, including Qiánmén, which had been approved for demolition before the order was passed. Road widening has bulldozed its way through the area; Qianmen Dajie itself has been restored in a mock historic style, and the Dashilar area next door is thought to be next in line for redevelopment.

Confucian Temples

Běijīng's Confucius Temple is China's second largest after the temple in Qūfù in Shāndōng, the birthplace of the sage.

Confucian temples bristle with steles celebrating local scholars, some supported on the backs of *bìxì* (mythical tortoise-like dragons). A statue of Kongzi (Confucius) usually resides in the main hall, overseeing rows of musical instruments and flanked by disciples. A mythical animal, the *qílín* (a statue exists at the Summer Palace), is commonly seen. The *qílín* was a hybrid animal that appeared on earth only in times of harmony.

Rebuilding Běijīng

For first-time visitors to Běijīng, the city can be an energising and inspiring synthesis of East and West, old and new. Yet after 1949 the characteristics of the old city of Běijīng – formidable and dwarfing city walls, vast and intimidating gates, unbroken architectural narrative and commanding sense of symmetry – were flung out the window.

Many argue (such as author Wang Jun in *Story of a City*) that the historic soul of Běijīng has been extirpated, never to return. It's a dismal irony that in its bid to resemble a Western city, Běijīng has lost a far larger proportion of historic architecture than have London, Paris or Rome.

In with the New

Since 1949, replacing what has gone and integrating new architecture seem to have been done without much thought. The vast Legendale Hotel on Jinbao Lu is a kitsch interpretation of a Parisian apartment block curiously plonked in central Běijīng, while the glass grill exterior of the hip Hotel Kapok on Donghuamen Dajie is a jab in the eye of the staid Jade Garden Hotel next door. But it is the futuristic, domelike National Centre for the Performing Arts that is perhaps Běijīng's most controversial building, thanks to its location so close to the Forbidden City.

More recently, the spaceship-lookalike Galaxy Soho complex drew complaints from heritage-preservation campaigners when it 'touched down' in an old *hútòng* neighbourhood, one block north of the 15th-century Zhìhuà Temple.

In 1949 Mao Zedong declared that 'Forests of factory chimneys should mushroom in Běijīng'. He didn't let ancient architecture stand in the way. When the mighty Xīzhí Mén was being levelled in 1969, the Yuan dynasty gate of Héyì Mén was discovered within the later brickwork; it disappeared too.

Religion & Belief

Spiritual ideas have always possessed a certain volatility in China, and things have often come to a head in Běijīng: the Boxer Rebellion (1898–1900); the Tiān'ānmén Square protests (1989); the outlawing of the Falun Gong movement (1999). Nevertheless, today's Chinese are increasingly returning to religion after decades of state-orchestrated atheism.

Buddhism

Although not an indigenous faith, Buddhism (佛教; *Fójiào*) is the religion most associated with China. Many Chinese may not be regular temple-goers, but they possess an interest in Buddhism.

Chinese Buddhism is not the same as the Buddhism which arrived from India around AD 50. The individualist nature of the dominant Theravada school of Buddhism didn't appeal to the group-oriented, ancestor-worshipping Chinese, so the relatively unimportant Mahayana School came to dominate in China. This school is partly characterised by worship of Bodhisattvas (菩萨; *púsà;* enlightened beings that postpone their entry into nirvana in order to help others).

Ethnic Tibetans and Mongols in China practise a unique form of Mahayana Buddhism, known as Tibetan Buddhism or Lamaism (喇嘛教; *Lǎmajiào*), where priests, called lamas, are believed to be reincarnations of highly evolved beings, the Dalai Lama being the supreme patriarch.

Taoism

A home-grown philosophy-religion, Taoism (道教; *Dàojiào*) – perhaps the hardest of Chinese religions to grasp – is a natural counterpoint to Confucian order and correctness.

Taoism predates Buddhism in China and much of its religious culture connects to a distant animism and shamanism. In its earliest and simplest form, Taoism draws from the *Tao Te Ching* (道德经; *Dàodé Jīng, The Classic of the Way and its Power*), written in around 500 BC by the philosopher Laotzu (老子; *Lǎozi*). Devoid of a godlike being or deity, Laotzu's writings instead endeavour to address the unknowable and ineffable principle of the universe, which he calls Tao (道; *Dào*), or 'the way'.

Confucianism

Confucianism (儒教; *Rújiào*) is based upon the teachings of Confucius (孔子; *Kǒngzǐ*), a 6th-century BC philosopher. The central emphasis is on five basic hierarchical relationships: father-son, ruler-subject, husband-wife, elder-younger, friend-friend. Confucius believed that if each individual carried out his or her proper role in society, social order would be achieved.

Christianity

Christianity (基督教; *Jīdūjiào*) didn't really take a foothold in Běijīng until the arrival of the Jesuits in the 16th century. They made few converts, but they became popular figures in the imperial court, and helped

Falun Gong is a quasi-religious lifestyle philosophy that gained so much traction in the 1990s that it was labelled a cult by Chinese authorities, and subsequently outlawed. Its followers at the time numbered between 60 and 70 million.

KNOW YOUR TEMPLES

All Chinese temples follow the same basic pattern. Built with careful respect for feng shui, they face southwards and are symmetrical along a north–south axis. Each temple consists of a series of halls, with the most important at the rear. Entrance is from the south, through imposing gateways which open onto a courtyard protected by a spirit wall. It is by the interior that you can tell the various types of Chinese temples apart.

Confucian Temples

Confucian temples are devoted to the memory of Confucius and the philosophers of Confucianism, and are the least noisy, colourful and lively of Chinese temples. Their courtyards are usually filled with stelae (stone tablets) dedicated to local scholars. Běijīng's only Confucius temple is the second largest in China.

Buddhist Temples

Buddhist temples often contain the same combination of deities. First is a hall containing huge, multicoloured statues of the angry-looking Four Heavenly Kings. Next is often a chubby 'laughing Buddha' (Maitreya). There may be other halls with other deities, but the main hall usually contains three enormous Buddhas, side by side; the Buddhas of past, present and future. Around the back you will often find the multiarmed Guanyin, a popular cross-religious figure, believed to lend a hand during childbirth. At the sides of the main hall you will often find several dozen *arhats*, caricaturish statues of Buddhist saints. Central Běijīng's largest and most significant Buddhist temple is the Lama Temple (p85), although ancient Tánzhè Temple, nestled in the hills outside the city centre, is also hugely impressive.

Taoist Temples

Taoist temples tend to be the most colourful and gaudy. The main gates are painted with fierce-looking mythical heroes to scare off evil spirits. The halls can contain any number of different deities, the many-armed Guanyin among them. Other likely deities include the Eight Immortals and the Three Purities, believed to be the founders of civilisation.

Two of Běijīng's largest and most impressive Taoist temples are White Cloud Temple (p118) and Dōngyuè Temple (p136), both of which hold fascinating, traditional temple fairs (庙会; miàohuì) during Lunar New Year.

design the astronomical instruments you can still see at the Ancient Observatory (p71). Běijīng's first church, South Cathedral (p120; 1605), was built on the site of the house of the Jesuit priest Matteo Ricci.

The so-called 'Unequal Treaties' that followed the Opium Wars (1839–42 and 1856–60) gave foreign missionaries the legal right to proselytise in China, but their new beliefs, and the general treatment of Chinese people by foreign powers at this time, were not well received. Hostilities culminated in the Boxer Rebellion (1898–1900), a violent anti-Christian, antiforeign movement, which was crushed by Allied troops. Christianity has seen a revival in recent years. Most Chinese Christians belong to illicit house churches, rather than the state-recognised Protestant or Catholic churches, so the precise number of Christians is hard to fathom.

During the Cultural Revolution, many temples and churches in Běijīng served as warehouses or factories. Zhīzhù Temple, for example, was a television factory in the 1960s. It's now a heritage hotel.

Islam

Islam (伊斯兰教; *Yīsīlán Jiào*) in China dates to the 7th century, when it was brought by Arab and Persian traders along the Silk Road. The descendants of these groups, now scattered across the country, gradually integrated into Han Chinese culture and today are distinguished primarily by their religion, rather than ethnic characteristics. In Chinese, they are called the Huí (回). **Niú Jiē Mosque**, originally built in AD 996, is the oldest and largest mosque in Běijīng, and the spiritual centre for the 10,000 or so Huí Muslims living in the vicinity.

Survival Guide

Transport

ARRIVING IN BĚIJĪNG

Běijīng can be reached by plane, train, bus, car or a combination of a ship and train, but most travellers coming from overseas fly into the city, arriving at Běijīng Capital International Airport. The only trains from overseas to Běijīng come from Mongolia, North Korea, Russia and Vietnam, as well as Hong Kong and Lhasa in Tibet. It is possible to drive to Běijīng from other countries, either by car or motorbike, but it requires permits that take a couple of months to arrange and travel by car or motorbike comes with many conditions. The nearest major port is at Tiānjīn, a 30-minute train ride from Běijīng. At the time of research, the only international route by ship to Tiānjīn was from Incheon in South Korea. There are no international bus routes to Běijīng, but the city can be accessed from many Chinese cities by bus, as well as by train and plane from all major cities. Flights, cars and tours can be booked online at lonely planet.com/bookings.

Air

Most travellers will fly into Běijīng. Average flight times include: London 10 hours, New York 14 hours and Sydney 12 hours. Běijīng's international airport is Běijīng Capital International Airport (PEK). If coming from elsewhere in China, you may also fly into the small Nány-uàn Airport (NAY).

Flights, cars and tours can be booked online at www.lonelyplanet.com.

For good deals on flights to and from Běijīng, try Ctrip (www.ctrip.com) or eLong (www.elong.net).

Běijīng Capital International Airport

Currently the world's second busiest airport, **Běijīng Capital International Airport** (北京首都国际机场; Běijīng Shǒudū Guójì Jīchǎng, PEK; ☑010 6454 1100; www.en.bcia.com.cn) has three terminals. **Terminal 3** (三号航站楼; sān hào háng-zhànlóu) deals with most long-haul flights, although international flights also use **Terminal 2** (二号航站楼; èr hào hángzhànlóu). Both are connected to the slick Airport Express, which links to Běijīng's subway system. The smaller **Terminal 1** (一号航站楼; yī hào hángzhànlóu) is a 10-minute walk from

Terminal 2. Free 24-hour shuttle buses connect all three terminals.

FACILITIES
All terminals have ATMs, money-changing facilities, information desks with English-speaking staff, booths selling local SIM cards, plenty of eating options and shops galore (although much less so at Terminal 1).

SLEEPING
If you need to stay by the airport, **Langham Place** (北京首都机场朗豪酒店; Lǎngháo Jiǔdiàn; ☑010 6457 5555; www.beijingairport.langham placehotels.com; 1 Erjing Lu, terminal 3; 北京首都机场三号航站二径路1号; r from ¥1608; ❋@⊛) lays on a free shuttle bus and is well regarded.

AIRPORT EXPRESS
The **Airport Express** (机场快轨; Jīchǎng Kuàiguǐ; Map p282; one way ¥25; Ⓢ Lines 2, 13 to Dongzhimen, exit B), also written as ABC (Airport Běijīng City), is quick and convenient and links terminals 2 and 3 to Běijīng's subway system at Sanyuanqiao station (Line

TAKEN FOR A RIDE
A well-established illegal taxi operation at the airport attempts to lure weary travellers into a ¥300-plus ride to the city, so be on your guard. If anyone approaches you offering a taxi ride, ignore them and join the queue for a taxi outside.

CLIMATE CHANGE & TRAVEL

Every form of transport that relies on carbon-based fuel generates CO_2, the main cause of human-induced climate change. Modern travel is dependent on aeroplanes, which might use less fuel per kilometre per person than most cars but travel much greater distances. The altitude at which aircraft emit gases (including CO_2) and particles also contributes to their climate change impact. Many websites offer 'carbon calculators' that allow people to estimate the carbon emissions generated by their journey and, for those who wish to do so, to offset the impact of the greenhouse gases emitted with contributions to portfolios of climate-friendly initiatives throughout the world. Lonely Planet offsets the carbon footprint of all staff and author travel.

10) and Dōngzhímén station (Lines 2 and 13). Train times are as follows: Terminal 3 (6.21am to 10.51pm); Terminal 2 (6.35am to 11.10pm); Dōngzhímén (6am to 10.30pm).

BUS
There are 17 different routes for the airport **shuttle bus** (机场巴士; Jīchǎng Bāshì; one way ¥15.50-30), including those listed here. They all leave from all three terminals and run from around 5am to midnight. Note that you may have to show a valid photo ID when buying your ticket.

Line 1 To Fāngzhuāng (方庄), via Dàběiyáo (大北窑) for the CBD (国贸; guó mào)

Line 2 To Xīdàn (西单)

Line 3 To Běijīng train station (北京站; Běijīng Zhàn), via Dōngzhímén (东直门), Dōngsì Shítiáo (东四十条) and Cháoyángmén (朝阳门)

Line 7 To Běijīng west train station (西站; xī zhàn)

Line 10 To Běijīng south train station (南站; nán zhàn)

Coach service to Tiānjīn (天津; ¥82, 2½ hours, 7.30am to 11pm hourly)

TAXI
A taxi should cost ¥90 to ¥120 from the airport to the city centre; bank on it taking 40 minutes to one hour to get into town. Ignore unofficial drivers who may approach you as you exit customs and join the line for an official cab. When you get into the taxi, make sure the driver uses the meter (打表; dǎ biǎo). Have the name of your hotel written down in Chinese to show the driver. Very few drivers speak any English.

CAR
The Vehicle Administration Office on the 1st floor of Terminal 3 – look for the 'Traffic Police' sign – issues temporary driving licences for use in Běijīng municipality. Applicants must be between the ages of 18 and 70, and must hold a temporary Chinese visa (three months or less). The straightforward process involves checking out your home driving licence and undergoing a simple medical test (including an eye-sight test). You'll also need two passport photos and copies and translations of your documents, although it can arrange this for you at the office. The whole procedure takes about 30 minutes and costs ¥10. Once you have the licence, you can hire a car from Hertz (www.hertz.cn), which has an office just along the corridor. Self-drive hire cars (自驾; zìjià) start from ¥279 per day (unlimited mileage). A car-with-driver service (代驾; dàijià) is also available (from ¥1100 per day).

Nányuàn Airport
The very small **Nányuàn Airport** (南苑机场; Nányuàn Jīchǎng, NAY; ☎ 010 6797 8899; Jingbeixi Lu, Nányuàn Zhèn, Fēngtái District; 丰台区 南苑镇警备西路, 警备东路口) feels more like a provincial bus station than an airport, but it does service quite a few domestic routes. Airport facilities are limited to a few shops and snack stalls, and don't expect to hear much English.

BUS
The shuttle bus (机场巴士; jīchǎng bāshì) goes to Xīdàn (西单; ¥18, 1½ hours, 9am to last flight arrival) via Qiánmén (前门). You can pick up the subway at either destination.

TAXI
A taxi costs around ¥60 to ¥70 to the Tiān'ānmén Sq area. Ignore drivers who approach you. Use the taxi queue. Make sure the driver uses the meter.

Train
Běijīng has three major train stations for long-distance travel (Běijīng station, Běijīng west station and Běijīng south station). Běijīng north station is used much less.

There are international train routes to and from Mongolia, North Korea, Russia and Vietnam, as well as trains to and from Hong Kong and Lhasa in Tibet.

Train Ticket Types
It is possible to upgrade (补票; bǔpiào) your ticket once aboard your train, but only on the rare occasions that a better option is available.

BĚIJĪNG TRAIN INFORMATION

Běijīng Train Station

The most central of Běijīng's four main train stations, **Běijīng Train Station** (北京站; Běijīng Zhàn), which has its own subway stop, is mainly for T-class trains (tèkuài), slow trains and trains bound for the northeast; most fast trains heading south now depart from Běijīng south train station and Běijīng west train station. Slower trains to Shànghǎi also go from here.

Approximate travel times and typical train fares are as follows (all soft sleeper unless otherwise indicated).

DESTINATION	SCRIPT	CATEGORY	DURATION	DEPARTURES	FARE (¥)
Dàlián	大连	Z-series	10½ hours	8.27pm	372
Dàlián	大连	K-series hard sleeper	12 hours	4.46am, 8.06pm	239-244
Dàtóng	大同	K-series hard seat	six hours	2.49am, 10.57am, 3.45pm	99
Harbin	哈尔滨	D-series soft seat	10 hours	6.58am, 10.02am, 1.51pm, 3.15pm	306-313
Harbin	哈尔滨	T-series hard sleeper	12 hours	5.10am, noon, 6.57pm, 9.24pm	261-268
Jílín	吉林	Z-series hard sleeper	12 hours	4.55pm	244
Shànghǎi	上海	T-series	14 hours	7.33pm	476-879

Běijīng South Train Station

The ultramodern **Běijīng South Station** (南站; Nán Zhàn), which is linked to the subway system on Line 4, accommodates very high-speed 'bullet' trains to destinations such as Tiānjīn, Shànghǎi, Hángzhōu and Qīngdǎo.

DESTINATION	SCRIPT	CATEGORY	DURATION	DEPARTURES	FARE (¥)
Fúzhōu	福州	D-series	15 hours	regular	765-2389
Hángzhōu	杭州	G-series, 2nd-class seat	six hours	regular	538
Jǐ'nán	济南	G-series, 2nd-class seat	1½ hours	regular	184
Nánjīng	南京	G-series, 2nd-class seat	four hours	regular	443
Qīngdǎo	青岛	G-series, 2nd-class seat	five hours	regular	249-314
Shànghǎi (Hóng-qiáo station)	上海虹桥	G-series, 2nd-class seat	5½ hours	regular	553
Sūzhōu	苏州	G-series, 2nd-class seat	five hours	regular	523
Tiānjīn	天津	C-series, 1st/2nd class	30 minutes	regular	54/93

Běijīng North Train Station

The smaller **Běijīng North Station** (北站; Běi Zhàn) can be accessed from Xizhimen subway station.

DESTINATION	SCRIPT	CATEGORY	DURATION	DEPARTURES	FARE (¥)
Hohhot	呼和浩特	K-series, hard sleeper	nine hours	7.29pm and 11.47pm	72-222
Bādǎlíng Great Wall	八达岭	hard seat	75 minutes	regular (6.12am-1.35pm)	6

Běijīng West Train Station

The gargantuan **Běijīng West Station** (西站; Xī Zhàn) accommodates fast Z-series trains, such as the following (fares are soft sleeper unless indicated).

DESTINATION	SCRIPT	CATEGORY	DURATION	DEPARTURES	FARE (¥)
Chángshā	长沙		13 hours	regular	504
Fúzhōu	福州		20 hours	2.45pm	673

Hànkǒu (Wǔhàn)	汉口		10 hours	11.32am, 5.43pm and 6.02pm	409
Lánzhōu	兰州	Z-and T-series	17 hours	five daily	322-363
Nánchāng	南昌	Z-, T- and K-series, hard sleeper	11½ hours	eight daily	296-322
Wǔchāng (Wǔhàn)	武昌	T- and K-series	10 hours	seven daily	261
Xī'ān	西安	Z- and T-series	11 to 12 hours	six daily	214-268
Kowloon (Hong Kong)	九龙		24 hours	train Q97, 1.08pm	707-738

Other typical train fares for hard sleeper tickets, and travel times

DESTINATION	SCRIPT	CATEGORY	DURATION	DEPARTURES	FARE (¥)
Chángshā	长沙	T- and K-series	14 hours	regular	322
Chéngdū	成都	Z-, T- and K-series	26 to 31 hours	7.53am, 11.32am, 11.46am, 4.32pm and 10.16pm	399-456
Chóngqìng	重庆	T- and K-series	25 to 30 hours	7.16am, 10.31am, 3.12pm and 9.23pm	381-389
Guǎngzhōu	广州	T- and K-series	21 hours	5.15am	426
Guìyáng	贵阳	T- and K-series	29 hours	4.10pm, 9.13pm and 9.23pm	434-463
Kūnmíng	昆明	Z-series	38 hours	8.55am and 1.06pm	536
Shēnzhèn	深圳	K-series	24 to 29 hours	11.21pm	434
Shíjiāzhuāng	石家庄	D-series, 2nd-class seat	two hours	7.58am, 1.18pm, 3.29pm and 9.16pm	86
Ūrümqi	乌鲁木齐	Z-series	34 hours	10am	536
Xīníng	西宁	T-series	20 to 24 hours	1.12pm	353
Yíchāng	宜昌	G-series, 2nd-class seat	21½ hours	8.30am, 9.32am and 12.51pm	605

SOFT SLEEPER

Soft sleepers (软卧; *ruǎn wò*) are very comfortable, with four air-conditioned bunks in a closed compartment. Often, they cost as much as discounted airfares to the same destination.

All Z-class trains are soft-sleeper trains with up-to-date berths. A few T-class trains also offer two-berth compartments, with their own toilet. Tickets on upper berths are slightly cheaper than lower berths.

HARD SLEEPER

About half the price of soft sleepers, hard sleepers (硬卧; *yìng wò*) are the golden ticket everyone wants and are the hardest to obtain: book them well in advance. Normally comprised of six air-conditioned bunks in an open-ended doorless compartment, there is less room than in soft sleepers, but they are still comfortable (clean bedding is provided). There is a small price difference between berths, with the lowest bunk (下铺; *xiàpù*) the most expensive, then the middle (中铺; *zhōngpù*), then the highest bunk (上铺; *shàngpù*).

As with all other classes, smoking is prohibited. Lights and speakers go out at around 10pm. Each compartment is equipped with its own hot-water flask.

SEATS

Soft-seat class (软座; *ruǎn zuò*) is more comfortable but not nearly as common as hard-seat class. First-class (一等; *yīděng*) and 2nd-class (二等; *èrděng*) soft seats are available in C-, D-, and G-series high-speed trains. First class comes with TV, mobile-phone and laptop-charging points, and seats arranged two abreast.

Second-class soft seats are also very comfortable, with courteous staff. On older trains, soft-seat carriages are often double-decker, and are not as plush as on the faster and more modern high-speed express trains.

INTERNATIONAL TRAINS

Mongolia

Two direct weekly trains leave from Běijīng train station to the Mongolian capital of Ulaanbaatar (乌兰巴托; Wūlánbātuō): the **Trans-Mongolian Railway train** (K3; hard sleeper/soft sleeper/deluxe ¥1670/2252/2436, 27 hours, 11.22am) goes via Ulaanbaatar en route to Moscow, and leaves every Wednesday. Meanwhile the **K23** service has a train which leaves on Tuesdays (¥1670/2252/2436, 27 hours, 11.22am). In the other direction, the **K4** leaves Ulaanbaatar at 7.15am on Tuesday and arrives in Běijīng at 11.40am on Wednesday. The **K24** departs from Ulaanbaatar at 7.15am on Thursday and reaches Běijīng the following day at 11.40am.

Russia

The Trans-Siberian Railway runs from Běijīng to Moscow (莫斯科; Mòsīkē) via two routes: the Trans-Mongolian Railway train (K3; hard sleeper/soft sleeper/deluxe ¥4270/6280/6876, 8.05am) and the Trans-Manchurian Railway train (K19; hard sleeper/deluxe ¥4715/7322, 11pm). The K19 leaves Běijīng train station every Saturday at 11pm. It arrives in Moscow on Friday at 5.58pm. The return **K20** leaves Moscow at 11.45pm on Saturday and arrives in Běijīng on Friday at 5.46am.

Vietnam

There are two weekly trains from Běijīng to Hanoi (河内; Hénèi). The **Z5** (M2 in Vietnam) leaves Běijīng west train station at 3.45pm on Thursday and Sunday, arriving in Hanoi at 8.10am on Saturday and Tuesday. In the other direction, the **Z6** (M1 in Vietnam) leaves Hanoi at 9.40pm on Tuesday and Friday and arrives at Běijīng west at 9.55am on Thursday and Friday. Only soft-sleeper tickets (¥2063) are available.

North Korea

There are four weekly services to Pyongyang (平壤; Píngrǎng; hard/soft sleeper ¥1017/1476). The **K27** and **K28** both leave twice a week from Běijīng train station, meaning there's a train on Monday, Wednesday, Thursday and Saturday. Each train leaves at 5.27pm and arrives the following day at 7.30pm. Return trains leave from Pyongyang at 10.10am on Monday, Wednesday, Thursday and Saturday, and arrive the following day in Běijīng at 8.31am.

Visas, Tickets & Tours

Visas are not available at the border crossings to/from Mongolia, North Korea, Russia and Vietnam. Ensure you arrange one beforehand.

You can only buy international tickets through travel agencies in Běijīng, not at train stations. For Mongolia, Russia and North Korea, buy tickets at the helpful office of the state-owned **CITS** (China International Travel Service; 中国国际旅行社; Zhōngguó Guójì Lǚxíngshè; Map p270; ☎010 6512 0507; 9 Jianguomennei Dajie, Běijīng International Hotel, Dōngchéng; ⏲9am-noon & 1.30-5pm Mon-Fri, 9am-noon Sat; [S]Lines 1, 2 to Jianguomen, exit A) housed round the back of the left-hand side of the lobby of the Běijīng International Hotel (北京国际饭店; Běijīng Guójì Fàndiàn), one block north of Běijīng train station. Trans-Siberian/Mongolian/Manchurian tickets can be bought from home, using Intourist Travel (www.intourist.com), which has branches in the UK, the USA, Canada, Finland and Poland.

For Vietnam, buy tickets at the office of **CRTS** (China Railway Travel Service; 中国铁道旅行社; Zhōngguó Tiědào Lǚxíngshè; ☎010 5182 6541; 20 Beifengwo Lu; 北蜂窝路20号; ⏲9am-4pm; [S]Military Museum). There's no English sign, but it's opposite the easy-to-spot Tiānyòu Hotel (天佑大夏; Tiānyòu Dàxià). Walk straight out of Exit C1 of Military Museum subway station, take the first right and CRTS will be on your left (10 minutes).

For help with booking a tour to North Korea, Běijīng's leading tour company to the area is **Koryo Tours** (Map p282; ☎Běijīng 010 6416 7544; www.koryogroup.com; 27 Beisanlitun Nan; [S]Line 2 to Dongsi Shitiao, exit C, or Line 10 to Tuanjiehu, exit A).

Hard-seat class (硬座; *yìng zuò*) is not available on the faster and more comfortable C-, D- and G-series trains, and is only found on T-, K- and N-series trains and trains without a number prefix; a handful of Z-series trains have hard seats. Hard-seat class generally has padded seats, but it's a strain: unsanitary and noisy, packed to the gills and painful on long journeys.

You should get a ticket with an assigned seat number, but if seats have sold out, ask for a standing ticket (无座、站票; *wúzuò* or *zhànpiào*), which gets you on the train, where you may find a seat, but will otherwise have to stand in the carriage or between carriages (with the smokers). Hard-seat sections on newer trains are air-conditioned and less crowded.

Buying Train Tickets
TICKET COUNTERS
There are no longer dedicated ticket offices for foreigners at the main stations in Běijīng, although there is sometimes a ticket window with a temporary 'for foreigners' sign attached to it. Otherwise, join any queue, but arm yourself with a few key Chinese phrases, or better still have a local write down what you want so you can show the ticket seller. Increasingly, ticket sellers at the three main stations speak a bit of English, but don't count on it.

PLANNING AHEAD
Never aim to get a hard-sleeper or soft-sleeper ticket on the day of travel – plan ahead. Most tickets can be booked in advance between two and 20 days prior to your intended date of departure. Buying hard-seat tickets at short notice is usually no hassle, but it may be a standing ticket rather than a numbered seat. It's normally no problem getting a same-day ticket on high-speed G,

D and C-category trains to nearby destinations such as Tiānjīn. Tickets can only be purchased with cash, and you will need to show your passport to get them.

RETURN TICKETS
Tickets are one way only. If you want to buy tickets for a train between two destinations beyond the city you are buying your ticket in, it is often better to go to an independent ticket office that charges a commission.

BUSY PERIODS
As with air travel, buying train tickets around the Lunar New Year and during the 1 May and 1 October holiday periods ranges from very hard to impossible. At these times, touts swarm around the train stations selling black-market tickets; be wary of buying them as foreigners frequently get ripped off. You're better off trying one of the many independent train-ticket offices dotted around the city – they charge a ¥10 mark-up per ticket. Or else ask at your hotel or hostel – they will usually take a mark-up of up to ¥50 per ticket.

ONLINE BOOKINGS
Tickets can be bought online at China DIY Travel (www.china-diy-travel.com/en), or at China Trip Advisor and Ctrip, although the last two charge a hefty commission. If you read Chinese, or know someone who does, you can book online at the of-

ficial Chinese ticket website www.12306.cn without paying any commission.

BULLET TRAIN TO TIĀNJĪN
You can book tickets in advance for the C-class 'bullet train' from Běijīng south station to Tiānjīn, but trains are so frequent that you rarely have to wait more than half an hour for a train (except during public holidays) anyway.

Bus
There are numerous long-distance bus stations, but no international bus routes to Běijīng.

Bāwángfén Long-Distance Bus Station
Bāwángfén Long-Distance Bus Station (八王坟长途客运站; Bāwángfén Chángtú Kèyùnzhàn; 17 Xidawang Lu) is in the east of town, 500m south of Dawanglu subway station. Destinations include the following.

Bāotóu 包头; ¥181, 12 hours, 6pm

Chángchūn 长春; ¥288 to ¥362, 12 hours, 6pm and 9pm

Dàlián 大连; ¥326, 8½ hours, 10am, noon and 10pm

Harbin 哈尔滨; ¥375, 14 hours, 5.30pm

Shěnyáng 沈阳; ¥165 to ¥227,

TRAIN CATEGORIES

CATEGORY	MEANING	TYPE
C	chengjí gāosù (城际高速)	ultra-high-speed express
D	dòngchē, héxiè hào (动车和谐号)	high-speed express
G	gāotiě (高铁)	high-speed
K	kuàisù (快速)	fast train
T	tèkuài (特快)	express
Z	zhídá tèkuài (直达特快)	direct express (overnight)

LEFT LUGGAGE

Left-luggage counters (行李寄存; xíngli jìcún) and lockers can be found at all the main Běijīng train stations. Prices are ¥5 to ¥10 per bag per day. They tend to be open from around 6am to 11pm.

nine hours, regular (8am to 10.30pm)

Tiānjīn 天津; ¥35, two hours, regular (7.30am to 6.30pm)

Sìhuì Long-Distance Bus Station

Sìhuì Long-Distance Bus Station (四惠长途汽车站; Sìhuì Chángtú Qìchēzhàn; Jianguo Lu) is in the east of town, 200m east of Sihui subway station. Destinations include the following.

Bāotóu 包头; ¥180, 12 hours, 10.30am

Chéngdé 承德; ¥85, four hours, regular (6am to 5.50pm)

Dāndōng 丹东; ¥270, 12 hours, 4pm and 5.40pm

Jìxiàn 蓟县; ¥30, two hours, regular (5.10am to 7.30pm)

Liùlǐqiáo Long-Distance Bus Station

Liùlǐqiáo Long-Distance Bus Station (六里桥长途站; Liùlǐqiáo Chángtúzhàn) is in the southwest of town, adjacent to Liuliqiao subway station. Destinations include the following.

Dàtóng 大同; ¥133 to ¥150, 4½ hours, regular (7.10am to 6pm)

Héféi 合肥; ¥380, 13 hours, 1.45pm

Luòyáng 洛阳; ¥148, 10 hours, 5pm and 7.30pm

Shíjiāzhuāng 石家庄; ¥83, 3½ hours, regular (6.30am to 6.30pm)

Xiàmén 厦门; ¥580, 30 hours, 11am

Xī'ān 西安; ¥278, 12 hours, 5.45pm

Zhèngzhōu 郑州; ¥130 to ¥158, 8½ hours, regular (8.30am to 9pm)

Liánhuāchí Long-Distance Bus Station

Liánhuāchí Long-Distance Bus Station (莲花池长途汽车站; Liánhuāchí Chángtú Qìchēzhàn) is a short walk north of Liùlǐqiáo long-distance bus station and close to Liuliqiao subway station. Destinations include the following.

Ānyáng 安阳; ¥100, 6½ hours, six daily (8am to 5.30pm)

Luòyáng 洛阳; ¥150, 11 hours, 5pm and 6.30pm

Yán'ān 延安; ¥256, 14 hours, 2.30pm

Zhàogōngkǒu Long-Distance Bus Station

Zhàogōngkǒu Long-Distance Bus Station (赵公口汽车站; Zhàogōngkǒu Qìchēzhàn) is in the south, 10 minutes walk west of Liujiayao subway station. Destinations include the following.

Shànghǎi 上海; ¥340, 16 hours, 4.30pm

Jǐna\n 济南; ¥129, 5½ hours, regular (6am to 7.30pm)

Ferry

The nearest major port is **Tiānjīn International Cruise Home Port** (天津国际游轮母港; Tiānjīn Guójì Yóulún Mǔgǎng). Express trains leave from **Běijīng south train station** (北京南站; Běijīng Nánzhàn; Ⓢ Beijing South Railway Station) to Tiānjīn every half hour (¥54 to ¥93, 30 minutes). From there, take subway Line 9 to Citizen Plaza station (市民广场; Shìmín Guǎngchǎng; ¥12, one hour), then take bus 513 to the last stop (东疆游轮母港; Dōngjiāng Yóulún Mǔgǎng; ¥2, 40 minutes, 7am to 5pm).

At the time of writing, ferry services to Dàlián (大连; ¥260 to ¥880, 12 hours, 8pm) in Liáoníng province were running only between June and October, but check as the service is frequently suspended. It leaves on even-numbered days (the return comes back on odd numbers). Boarding starts at 6pm and tickets can be bought on the day of travel. You can also catch a ferry from here to Incheon (¥888 to ¥1590, 24 hours) in South Korea. Ferries leave twice a week, on Sundays and Thursdays; departure times vary. Check www.jinchon.cn for more details.

GETTING AROUND BĚIJĪNG

Bicycle

Cycling is the most enjoyable way of getting round Běijīng. The city is as flat as a mahjong table and almost every road has a bike lane, even if cars invade them. The quiet, tree-lined hútòng (alleys) are particularly conducive to cycling.

Bike Rental

The following are good options for renting bicycles (租自行车; zū zìxíngchē):

Bike Běijīng (康多自行车租赁; Kāngduō Zìxíngchē Zūlìn; Map p270; ✆ 010 6526 5857; www.bikebeijing.com; 81 Beiheyan Dajie; 北河沿大街81号; ⏰ 8am-8pm; Ⓢ Lines 6, 8 to Nanluoguxiang, exit B, or Line 5 to Zhangzizhonglu, exit D)

Giant (捷安特; Jié'āntè; Map p274; ✆010 6403 4537; www. giant.com.cn; 4-18 Jiaodaokou Dongdajie; 交道口东大街4-18 号; ⏰9am-7pm; Ⓢ Line 5 to Beixinqiao, exit A)

Natooke (娿（自行车店）; Shuǎ (Zìxíngchē Diàn); Map p274; ✆010 8402 6925; www. natooke.com; 19-1 Wudaoying Hutong; 五道营胡同19－1 号; ⏰11am-7pm; Ⓢ Lines 2, 5 to Yonghegong-Lama Temple, exit D)

Bike stands around the Hòuhǎi Lakes also rent bikes (per hour ¥10). Hostels typically charge ¥30 to ¥50 per day for a standard town bike.

Buying a Bike

Giant (捷安特; Jié'āntè; Map p274; ✆010 6403 4537; www. giant.com.cn; 4-18 Jiaodaokou Dongdajie; 交道口东大街4-18 号; ⏰9am-7pm; Ⓢ Line 5 to Beixinqiao, exit A) For new bikes and equipment.

Bike-Sharing Scheme

Běijīng has a bike-sharing scheme for both locals and foreigners. To use the bikes, you must have an ordinary Běijīng travel card (refundable deposit ¥20) that is activated for bike-rental use.

To do that, head to either Exit A2 of Tiāntán Dōngmén subway station or Exit A of Dōngzhímén subway station. Both desks are only open Monday to Friday from 9.30am to 11.30am and from 2pm to 4pm. You will need your passport and to fill out an English-language application form.

You have to pay a ¥200 deposit to activate the card for bike use, and then ensure it has at least ¥30 on it.

Bike-sharing kiosks are dotted around the city. Swipe your card at one of them to get a bike; then swipe it again when you put it back. Note that when swiping your card, don't remove

it until you hear a click. Bike use is free for the first hour, so if you use them cleverly, swapping bikes at another kiosk before your hour is up, it means free bikes. After the first hour, it's ¥1 per hour to begin with, before it starts rising in price to ¥2, ¥3 or ¥4 per hour, depending on how long you keep the bike for.

Subway

Massive and getting bigger every year, with another 12 lines set to be in operation by 2021, the **Běijīng subway system** (地铁; Dìtiě; www. bjsubway.com; per trip ¥3-8; ⏰6am-11pm) is modern, safe, cheap and easy to use. It does get crowded, though. Fares are ¥3 to ¥8, depending on how far you are travelling. Get hold of a travel card (refundable deposit ¥20) if you don't want to queue for tickets each time you travel. The travel card also gets you a 50% discount on all bus journeys within the municipality of Běijīng.

To recognise a subway station (地铁站; dì tiě zhàn), look for the subway symbol, which is a blue English capital 'D' with a circle around it.

The Metroman smartphone app reveals the Běijīng subway map in all its ever-expanding glory, with stations listed in both English and Chinese.

Taxi

Taxis (出租车; chūzūchē) are everywhere, although finding one can be a problem during rush hour, rainstorms and between 8pm and 10pm – prime time for people heading home after eating out.

Flag fall is ¥13, and lasts for 3km. After that it's ¥2 per kilometre. Rates increase slightly at night.

It's rare for drivers to speak any English, so it's important to have the name

and address of where you want to go written down in Chinese characters. Remember to keep your hotel's business card on you so you can get home at the end of the night.

Most Běijīng taxi drivers are honest and use the meter (打表; dǎ biǎo). If they refuse, get out and find another cab. The exception is for long, out-of-town trips to, say, the Great Wall, where prices are agreed (but not paid for) beforehand.

Taxi Drivers & Car Hire Companies

Miles Meng (✆137 1786 1403; www.beijingenglish driver.com) Friendly, reliable, English-speaking driver. See his website for prices.

Mr Sun (孙先生; Sūn Xiānsheng; ✆136 5109 3753) Only speaks Chinese but is dependable and can find other drivers if he's busy. Round trips to the Great Wall from ¥600.

Hertz (赫兹; Hèzī; ✆400 888 1336; www.hertz.cn; 8am-8pm Mon-Fri, 9am-6pm Sat & Sun) Has an office at Terminal 3 of Běijīng airport, as well as at 10 other locations around town. Self-drive hire cars (自驾; zìjià) from ¥279 per day. Car with driver (代驾; dàijià) from ¥1100 per day.

Bus

Běijīng's buses (公共汽车; gōnggòng qìchē) have always been numerous and cheap (from ¥2), but they're now easier to use for non-Chinese speakers, with swipe cards, announcements in English and bus-stop signs written in Pīnyīn as well as Chinese characters. Nevertheless, it's still a challenge to get from A to B successfully, and the buses are as packed as ever, so you rarely see foreigners climbing aboard.

If you use a travel card, you get 50% discount on all journeys.

Useful Routes

1 Runs along Chang'an Jie, Jianguomenwai Dajie and Jianguomennei Dajie: Sìhuìzhàn, Bāwángfén, Yǒngānlǐ, Dōngdān, Xīdān, Mùxīdì, Jūnshì Bówùguǎn, Gōngzhǔfén, Mǎquányíng

4 Runs along Chang'an Jie, Jianguomenwai Dajie and Jianguomennei Dajie: Gōngzhǔfén, Jūnshì Bówùguǎn, Mùxīdì, Xīdān, Tiān'ānmén West, Dōngdān, Yǒngānlǐ, Bāwángfén, Sìhuìzhàn

5 Déshèngmén, Diànmén, Běihǎi Park, Xīhuámén, Zhōngshān Park, Qiánmén

15 Běijīng Zoo, Fùxīngmén, Xīdān, Hépíngmén, Liúlíchǎng, Tiānqiáo

20 Běijīng south train station, Tiānqiáo, Dashilar, Tiān'ānmén Sq, Wángfǔjǐng, Dōngdān, Běijīng train station

44 Outer ring Xīzhímén, Fùchéngmén, Fùxīngmén, Chángchūnjiē, Xuānwǔmén, Qiánmén, Tàijíchǎng, Chóngwénmén, Dōngbiánmén, Cháoyángmén, Dōngzhímén, Āndìngmén, Déshèngmén, Xīnjiēkǒu

52 Běijīng west train station, Mùxīdì, Fùxīngmén, Xīdān, Gate of Heavenly Peace, Dōngdān, Běijīng train station, Jiànguómén

103 Běijīng train station, Dēngshìkǒu, China Art Gallery, Forbidden City (north entrance), Běihǎi Park, Fùchéngmén, Běijīng Zoo

332 Běijīng Zoo, Wèigōngcūn, Renmin Daxue, Zhongguāncūn, Hǎidiàn, Běijīng University, Summer Palace

These double-decker routes may also be useful:

2 Qiánmén, north on Dongdan Beidajie, Dongsi Nandajie, Dongsi Beidajie, Lama Temple, Zhōnghuá Mínzú Yuán (Ethnic Minorities Park), Asian Games Village

3 Jijia Miao (the southwest extremity of the 3rd Ring Rd), Grand View Garden, Lèyóu Hotel, Jìnguāng New World Hotel, Tuánjiēhú Park, Agricultural Exhibition Center, Lufthansa Center

4 Běijīng Zoo, Exhibition Center, 2nd Ring Rd, Holiday Inn Downtown, Yuètán Park, Fuxingmen Dajie flyover, Qianmen Xidajie, Qiánmén

Rickshaw

Rickshaws (三轮车; *sānlúnchē*) are less common these days, but you will still see them (both the cycle-powered ones and the motorised ones), especially around major tourist sights. Generally speaking they're more expensive than taxis, and foreign tourists are often heavily overcharged, so we don't advise using them.

Hútòng Tours

Rickshaw tours (one hour, per person ¥100) can be taken around the Hòuhǎi Lakes and around the alleys by the Drum Tower, although they are aimed mostly at tour groups, and riders don't speak English.

Tours

There are a number of tour operators who can take you around Běijīng and/or the Great Wall. Tours can range from a half-day trip through the *hútòng*, to multiday tours taking in numerous locations that can be tailored to individuals or groups, so you only see what you are interested in. Tours can be done on foot, by bike, in cars and taxis, or even in a motorcycle sidecar.

Hútòng tours are especially useful because the best ones, like those run by the **China Culture Center** (Kent Center; Map p282; ☎weekdays 010 6432 9341, weekends 010 8420 0671; www.chinaculturecenter.org; Victoria Gardens D4, Chaoyang Gongyuan Xilu; 朝阳公园西路, 维多利亚花园D4; [S]Line 14 to Zaoying or Line 10 to Tuanjiehu, exit C) or **Bike Běijīng** (康多自行车租赁; Kāngduō Zìxíngchē Zūlìn; Map p270; ☎010 6526 5857; www.bikebeijing.com; 81 Beiheyan Dajie; 北河沿大街81号; ⏲8am-8pm; [S]Lines 6, 8 to Nanluoguxiang, exit B, or Line 5 to Zhangzizhonglu, exit D), will take you to places you're unlikely to stumble upon by just walking around on your own.

Popular with visitors are the numerous tours to the Great Wall offered by most hostels. Typically, they are day trips that leave early in the morning, allowing you to spend proper time exploring the Wall (although some tours involve overnight stays near the Wall), before returning in the late afternoon. These tours are often the easiest and most convenient way to get out to the Wall.

Directory A–Z

Customs Regulations

Chinese customs generally pay tourists little attention. There are clearly marked 'green channels' (nothing to declare) and 'red channels' (something to declare) at the airport.

Duty Free You're allowed to import 400 cigarettes or the equivalent in tobacco products and 1.5L of alcohol. Importation of fresh fruit and meat is prohibited. There are no restrictions on foreign currency; however, you should declare any cash that exceeds US$5000 (or its equivalent in another currency).

DVDs Pirated DVDs and CDs are illegal exports from China as well as illegal imports into most other countries. If they are found, they will be confiscated.

Antiques Objects considered antiques require a certificate and red seal to clear customs. To get the proper certificate and seal, your antiques must be inspected by the **Relics Bureau** (Wénwù Jiàndìng; ☎010 6401 4608), where no English is spoken. Anything made before 1949 is considered an antique and needs a certificate, and if it was made before 1795 it cannot legally be taken out of the country.

Discount Cards

Student Cards An International Student Identity Card (ISIC; www.isic.org) may be useful as you could get half-price entry to most sights. Chinese signs at most sights clearly indicate that students pay half price – so push the point. If you are studying in China, your school will issue you with a student card, which is more useful for discounts on admission charges.

Seniors People over the age of 65 are frequently eligible for a discount, so make sure you take your passport as proof of age when visiting sights.

Free Sights Tickets must be purchased for most sights in Běijīng, although more and more museums are now free (you will need to show your passport, though).

Travel Card (交通一卡通; jiāotōng yīkǎtōng; refundable deposit ¥20) Saves you 50% on all bus fares. Can be used on the subway for convenience, but without any discounts. Obtained from subway stations.

Beijing on a Budget Smartphone app for cost-conscious travellers.

BĚIJĪNG MUSEUM PASS

If you're staying in the capital for a while, the **Běijīng Museum Pass** (博物馆通票; Bówùguǎn Tōngpiào; ☎010 6222 3793; www.bowuguan.com.cn; annual pass ¥120) – website and phone service in Chinese only – is a decent investment that will save you both money and queuing for tickets. For ¥120 you get either complimentary access or discounted admission (typically 50%) to 112 tourist attractions, including some 61 museums, plus temples and tourist sights in and around Běijīng. Attractions covered include the Great Wall at Bādàlǐng, Front Gate, the Drum Tower, the Bell Tower, the Confucius Temple, the Botanic Gardens, the Railway Museum, Dōngyuè Temple, White Cloud Temple and Zhìhuà Temple. Not all the sights are worth visiting, but you only have to visit a small selection to make it worth the money. The pass comes in the form of a booklet (Chinese with minimal English), valid from 1 January to 31 December in any one year. The pass, which is harder to obtain as the year goes on, can be picked up from participating museums and most post offices – see its website for locations.

Electricity

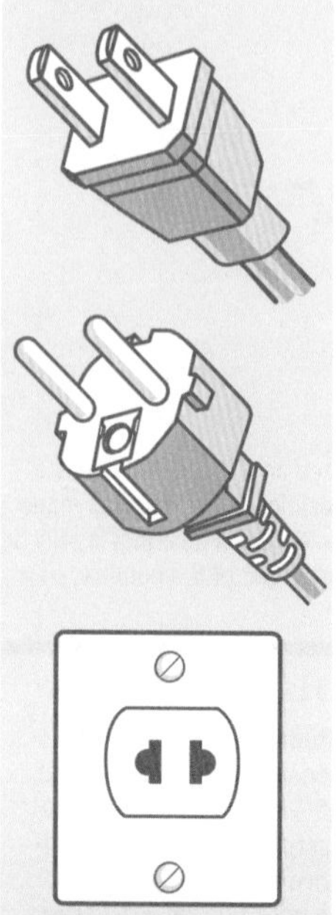

220V/50Hz

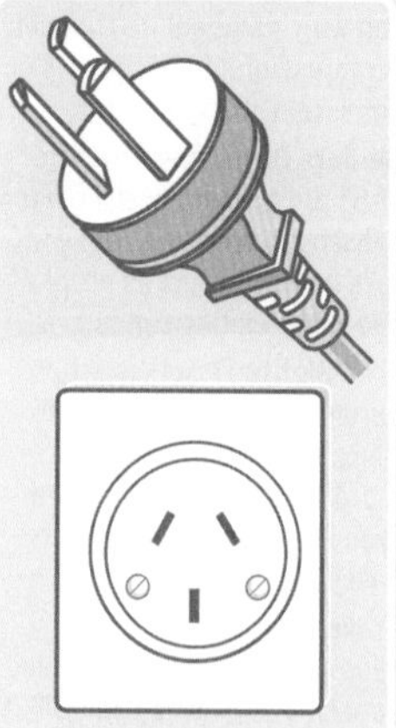

220V/50Hz

Embassies & Consulates

Embassies (大使馆; *dàshǐguǎn*) in Běijīng are open from 9am to noon and from 1.30pm to 4pm Monday to Friday; visa departments, which are often in separate office blocks these days, are sometimes only open in the morning. There are three main embassy areas: Jiànguóménwài, Sānlǐtún and Liàngmǎqiáo.

It has become increasingly common in recent years for embassies to turn down visa applications from foreigners who do not live in China. It's always best to arrange visas in your home country.

Jiànguóménwài Area

Irish Embassy (爱尔兰大使馆; Ài'ěrlán Dàshǐguǎn; Map p282; ☎010 8531 6200; www.irishembassy.cn; 3 Ritan Donglu; 日坛东路3号; 🕒9am-12.30pm & 2-5pm Mon-Fri; [S]Line 1 to Yonganli, exit A1)

Mongolian Embassy (蒙古大使馆; Ménggǔ Dàshǐguǎn; Map p282; ☎010 6532 1203; www.beijing.mfa.gov.mn; 2 Xiushui Beijie; 秀水北街2号; [S]Line 1 to Yonganli, exit A1) There is a separate **visa section** (Map p282; ☎010 6532 6512, 010 6532 1203; www.beijing.mfa.gov.mn; 2 Xiushui Beijie; 秀水北街2号; 🕒visa application 9am-noon Mon-Fri, passport collection 4-5pm Mon-Fri; [S]Line 1 to Yonganli, exit A1).

Singapore Embassy (新加坡大使馆; Xīnjiāpō Dàshǐguǎn; Map p282; ☎010 6532 1115; www.mfa.gov.sg/beijing; 1 Xiushui Beijie; 秀水北街1号; 🕒8.30am-noon & 1-5pm Mon-Fri; [S]Line 1 to Yonganli, exit A1)

Thai Embassy (泰国大使馆; Tàiguó Dàshǐguǎn; Map p282; ☎010 6532 1749; www.thaiembbeij.org; 40 Guanghua Lu; 光华路40号; 🕒8.30am-noon & 2-5.30pm; [S]Lines 1, 2 to Jianguomen, exit B)

UK Embassy (联合王国大使馆; Liánhé Wángguó Dàshǐguǎn; Map p282; ☎010 5192 4000; www.gov.uk; 11 Guanghua Lu; 光华路11号; 🕒9am-noon Mon, Tue, Thu & Fri; [S]Line 1 to Yonganli, exit A1); **Consular Section** (英国大使馆; Map p282; ☎010 8529 6600; www.gov.uk; 21st fl, Kerry Center, 1 Guanghua Lu; 光华路1号家里中心21层; 🕒8.30am-noon & 1.30-4pm Mon-Fri; [S]Line 10 to Jintaixizhao, exit D)

Vietnamese Embassy (越南大使馆; Yuènán Dàshǐguǎn; Map p282; ☎010 6532 1155; http://vnemba.org.cn; 32 Guanghua Lu; 光华路32号; [S]Line 1 to Yonganli, exit A1)

Sānlǐtún Area

Australian Embassy (澳大利亚大使馆; Àodàlìyǎ Dàshǐguǎn; Map p282; ☎010 5140 4111; www.china.embassy.gov.au; 21 Dongzhimenwai Dajie; 东直门外大街21号; 🕒9am-noon & 2-3.30pm Mon-Fri; [S]Line 2 to Dongzhimen, exit B)

Cambodian Embassy (柬埔寨大使馆; Jiǎnpǔzhài Dàshǐguǎn; Map p282; ☎010 6532 1889; camemb.chn@mfa.gov.kh; 9 Dongzhimenwai Dajie; 东直门外大街9号; [S]Line 10 to Agricultural Exhibition Center)

Canadian Embassy (加拿大大使馆; Jiānádà Dàshǐguǎn; Map p282; ☎010 5139 4000; www.china.gc.ca; 19 Dongzhimenwai Dajie; 东直门外大街19号; 🕒8:30-11am Mon-Fri & 1.30-3pm Tue & Thu; [S]Line 2 to Dongzhimen, exit B)

German Embassy (德国大使馆; Déguó dàshǐ guǎn; Map p282; ☎010-8532 9000; www.china.diplo.de; 17 Dongzhimenwai Dajie; 东直门外大街17号; [S]Line 2 to Dongzhimen, exit B)

Italian Embassy (意大利大使馆; Yìdàlì Dàshǐguǎn; Map p282; ☎010 6532 2131; www.ambasciata.net; 2 Sanlitun Dong'erjie; 三里屯东二街; [S]Line 10 to Tuanjiehu, exit A)

PRACTICALITIES

DVDs China is still a big market of pirated foreign movies and TV shows, as well as home-grown ones. Bear in mind that some countries, especially the USA and Australia, will confiscate them and can impose large fines.

Newspapers & Magazines China's print media is state-run and subject to rigid controls. There are two main English-language newspapers, *China Daily* and *Global Times*. *China Daily* is a broadsheet, the *Global Times* a tabloid. Neither are exciting reads. Běijīng has a number of listings magazines in English – *Time Out Beijing*, *The Beijinger* and *City Weekend* – which are useful for finding out the latest bar, club and restaurant hot spots.

Smoking While the dark days of people lighting up in hospitals are mostly a distant memory, and many venues in Běijīng are much more rigorous about enforcing the no-smoking law, China has an estimated 400 million smokers and some people do still smoke in bars and restaurants.

TV & Radio China has a dedicated English-language channel – CCTV News – as well as the English-language China Radio International. Both follow the CCP line and are an uncontroversial mix of news, current-affairs shows and documentaries.

Weights & Measures China employs an approximation of the metric system, using kilometres instead of miles, for example. The most common unit of weight travellers will encounter is the *jīn* (斤). One *jīn* is roughly half a kilo.

Laotian Embassy (老挝大使馆; Lǎowō Dàshǐguǎn; Map p282; 010 6532 1224; laoemcn@public.east.cn.net; 11 Sanlitun Dongsijie; 三里屯东
二街11号; S Line 10 to Agricultural Exhibition Center, exit D2)

Nepalese Embassy (尼泊尔大使馆; Níbó'ěr Dàshǐguǎn; Map p282; 010 6532 1795; www.nepalembassy.org.cn; 1 Sanlitun Xiliujie; 三里屯东六街1号; 10am-noon & 3-4pm Mon-Fri; S Line 10 to Agricultural Exhibition Center or Liangmaqiao, exit D)

New Zealand Embassy (新西兰大使馆, Xīnxīlán Dàshǐguǎn; Map p282; 010 8531 2700; www.mfat.govt.nz; 3 Sanlitun Dongsanjie, 三里屯东三街3号; 8.30am-5pm Mon-Fri; S Line 10 to Agricultural Exhibition Center, exit D2)

South African Embassy (南非洲大使馆; Nán Fēizhōu Dàshǐguǎn; Map p282; 010 5864 1360; www.southafricavac-cn.com; 9th Fl, 5 Dongzhimenwai Dajie; 东直门外大街5号; 8am-3pm Mon-Fri; S Line 10 to Agricultural Exhibition Center, exit A)

Liàngmǎqiáo Area

Indian Embassy (印度大使馆; Yìndù Dàshǐguǎn; Map p282; 010 8531 2500; www.indianembassy.org.cn; 5 Liangmaqiao Beijie; 亮马桥北街5号; visa office 9.30-10.30am Mon-Fri; S Line 10 to Liangmaqiao, exit B)

Japanese Embassy (日本大使馆; Rìběn Dàshǐguǎn; Map p282; 010 8531 9800; www.cn.emb-japan.go.jp; 1 Liangmaqiaodong Jie; 亮马桥东街1号; 9-11.30am & 1-4.30pm; S Line 10 to Liangmaqiao, exit B)

Netherlands Embassy (荷兰大使馆; Hélán Dàshǐguǎn; Map p282; 010 8532 0200; http://china.nlembassy.org/; 4 Liangmahe Nanlu; 亮马河南路4号; 9am-12.30pm & 2-5.30pm Mon-Fri; S Line 10 to Liangmaqiao, exit B)

South Korean Embassy (南韩大使馆; Nánhán Dàshǐguǎn; Map p282; 010-8531 0700; www.cn.mofat.go.kr; North Lu, 7 Liangmaqiao Lu; 北京市朝阳区亮马桥北小街7号; S Line 10 to Liangmaqiao, exit B)

US Embassy (美国大使馆; Měiguó Dàshǐguǎn; Map p282; 010 8531 3300; http://beijing.usembassy-china.org.cn; 55 Anjialou Lu, off Liangmaqiao Lu; 亮马桥安家楼路55号; S Line 10 to Liangmaqiao, exit B)

Other Areas

Russian Embassy (俄罗斯大使馆; Èluósī Dàshǐguǎn; Map p274; 010 6532 1381, visa section 2-6pm Mon-Fri 010 6532 1267; www.russia.org.cn; 4 Dongzhimen Beizhongjie; 东直门内大街东直门北中街4号, off Dongzhimennei Dajie; 9:30-11:30am Mon-Fri; S Lines 2, 13 to Dongzhimen, exit A)

Emergency

AMBULANCE	120
FIRE	119
POLICE	110
PUBLIC SECURITY BUREAU (FOREIGNERS' SECTION)	010 8402 0101

Gay & Lesbian Travellers

Although the Chinese authorities take a dim view of homosexuality, which was officially classified as a mental disorder until 2001, a low-profile gay and lesbian scene exists in Běijīng. For an informative and up-to-date lowdown on the latest gay and lesbian hotspots in Běijīng, have a look at Utopia (www.utopia-asia.com). Another useful publication is the **Spartacus International Gay Guide**, a bestselling guide for gay travellers.

Health

Apart from the thick layer of air pollution that sometimes blankets the city, Běijīng is a reasonably healthy place and you needn't fear tropical diseases such as malaria. Your greatest health and safety issue is likely to be crossing the road. Bear in mind that if you do require immediate treatment, taking a taxi to hospital will often be quicker than waiting for an ambulance.

It's worth taking your own medicine kit. It is also advisable to take your own prescription drugs with you, because they could be more expensive or hard to find in the capital. Antibiotics (*kàngjūnsù*) and sleeping pills (*ānmiányào*) are no longer prescription-free in Běijīng. If you require a specific type of drug, ensure you take an adequate supply. When looking for medications in Běijīng, take along the brand and the generic name so that pharmacy staff can locate it for you.

Recommended Vaccinations

Proof of vaccination for yellow fever is required if entering China within six days of visiting an infected country. If you are travelling to China from Africa or South America, check with a travel-medicine clinic about whether you need the vaccine.

The following vaccinations are recommended for those travelling to China.

Adult diphtheria/tetanus (ADT) A booster is recommended if it is more than 10 years since your last shot. Side effects include a sore arm and fever.

Hepatitis A One shot provides almost 100% protection for up to a year; a booster after 12 months provides another 20 years' protection. Mild side effects include a sore arm, fever and headaches.

Hepatitis B Now considered a routine vaccination for most travellers. Given as three shots over six months, this vaccine can be combined with Hepatitis A (Twinrix). In most people the course gives lifetime protection. Mild side effects include a sore arm and headaches.

Measles/mumps/rubella (MMR) Two lifetime doses of MMR are recommended unless you have had the diseases. Many adults under the age of 35 require a booster. Occasionally a rash and flulike illness occur about a week after vaccination.

Typhoid Needed if spending more than two weeks in China. A single injection provides around 70% protection for two to three years.

Varicella (chickenpox) If you haven't had chickenpox, discuss this vaccine with your doctor. Chickenpox can be a serious disease in adults and has such complications as pneumonia and encephalitis.

Under certain circumstances, or for those at special risk, the following vaccinations are recommended. Discuss these with a doctor who specialises in travel medicine.

Influenza If you are over 50 years of age or have a chronic medical condition such as diabetes, lung disease or heart disease, you should have an influenza shot annually.

Japanese encephalitis There is risk only in the rural areas of China. Recommended if travelling to rural areas for more than a month during summer.

Pneumonia (Pneumococcal) This vaccine is recommended for travellers over 65 or those with chronic lung or heart disease. A single shot is given, with a booster in five years.

Rabies Recommended if spending more than three months in China. Three injections given over a one-month period are required.

If you are pregnant or breast-feeding, consult a doctor who specialises in travel medicine before having any vaccines.

Diseases

BIRD FLU

'Bird flu' or Influenza A (H5N1) is a subtype of the type A influenza virus. This virus typically infects birds and not humans; however, in 1997 the first documented case of bird-to-human transmission was recorded in Hong Kong. The virus has been eliminated from most of the 63 countries infected at its peak in 2006, which

---

HEALTH ADVISORIES

It's a good idea to consult your government's travel-health website before departure.

➡ **Australia** (www.dfat.gov.au/travel)

➡ **Canada** (www.travelhealth.gc.ca)

➡ **New Zealand** (www.safetravel.govt.nz)

➡ **UK** (www.gov.uk/foreign-travel-advice)

➡ **US** (www.cdc.gov/travel)

saw 4000 outbreaks across the globe, but it remains endemic in China. Other variants of the virus, like H7N9, have emerged in China too.

Very close contact with dead or sick birds is the principal source of infection and bird-to-human transmission does not easily occur.

Symptoms include high fever and typical influenza-like symptoms with rapid deterioration, leading to respiratory failure and often death. It is not recommended for travellers to carry antiviral drugs such as Tamiflu; rather, immediate medical care should be sought if bird flu is suspected.

There is currently no vaccine available to prevent bird flu. For up-to-date information, check the website www. who.int/en.

HEPATITIS A

This virus is transmitted through contaminated food and water, and infects the liver, causing jaundice (yellow skin and eyes), nausea and extreme tiredness. There is no specific treatment available; you just need to allow time for the liver to heal, which might take many weeks.

HEPATITIS B

This disease is common in China and is transmitted via infected body fluids, including through sexual contact. The long-term consequences can include liver cancer and cirrhosis.

HIV & SEXUALLY TRANSMITTED INFECTIONS

The Chinese government takes HIV seriously, and overall HIV prevalence is low in the country. However, among certain high-risk groups – gay men, sex workers, intravenous drug users – prevalence of HIV and other sexually transmitted infections is comparatively high, reaching 20% among some groups in some areas. Consistently using condoms during any sexual encounter is an effective way to protect yourself

from becoming infected and never, ever share needles.

If you have engaged in any risky behaviour while travelling, including unprotected sex or injecting drugs, you should get a check-up immediately. You can do this at most major Chinese hospitals or at any Centre for Disease Control (疾控中心; jíkòng zhōngxīn). There's one in every district of the city, including this one just off Nanluogu Xiang: **Dōngchéng Disease Prevention & Control Centre** (东城疾控中心; Dōngchéng Jíkòng Zhōngxīn;; Map p274; ☑010 6404 0807; 5 Beibingmasi Hutong; 东城区交道口南大街北兵马司胡同5号, off Nanluogu Xiang; Ⓢ Lines 6, 8 to Nanluoguxiang, exit F).

For up-to-date information on HIV in China, visit the website of UNAIDS China (www.unaids.org.cn).

INFLUENZA

Flu is common in Běijīng in winter. This virus gives you high fevers, body aches and general symptoms, such as a cough, runny nose and sore throat. Antibiotics won't help unless you develop a complication, such as pneumonia. Anyone travelling in winter could think about vaccination, but it is particularly recommended for the elderly or those with underlying medical conditions.

TRAVELLER'S DIARRHOEA

This is the most common problem faced by travellers in Asia. Most traveller's diarrhoea is caused by bacteria and thus responds rapidly to a short course of appropriate antibiotics. How soon you treat your diarrhoea will depend on individual circumstances, but it is a good idea to carry treatment in your medical kit.

TUBERCULOSIS (TB)

This is a rare disease in travellers that's contracted after prolonged close exposure to a person with an active TB infection. Symptoms include a cough, weight loss, night sweats and fevers. Children

under the age of five spending more than six months in China should receive BCG (Bacillus Calmette-Guérin) vaccination. Adults are rarely immunised.

TYPHOID

This serious bacterial infection is contracted from contaminated food and water. Symptoms include high fever, headache, a cough and lethargy. The diagnosis is made via blood tests, and treatment is with specific antibiotics.

Environmental Hazards

AIR POLLUTION

Běijīng is one of the most polluted cities in the world. Although the government improved the situation prior to the 2008 Olympics and kept certain measures in place after the games (eg restricting car use), those with chronic respiratory conditions should ensure they have adequate personal medication with them in case symptoms worsen.

WATER

Don't drink the tap water or eat ice. Bottled water (but check the seal is not broken on the cap), soft drinks, alcohol and drinks made from boiled water (tea, coffee) are fine.

Health Insurance

Healthcare in Běijīng is not free and bills can quickly mount up if you do require treatment, especially if you have to be admitted to hospital. If you already have health insurance, check with your provider to see if you are covered when you are in China. If not, make sure that your travel-insurance policy includes medical coverage. Ideally, any policy should cover all costs if you are admitted to hospital and provide emergency evacuation to your home country if needed.

Internet Access

Hotels Almost all hotels and guesthouses provide either wi-fi or broadband internet access (or both), although some charge a daily rate. Youth hostels have free wi-fi as well as computer terminals, but levy a small internet charge (around ¥10 per hour) to use them.

Internet Cafes Internet cafes (网吧; *wǎngbā*) are generally easy to find, although some are tucked away down side streets and above shops. They are generally open 24 hours. Standard rates are ¥3 to ¥5 per hour, although there are usually different priced zones within each internet cafe – the common area (*pǔtōng qū*) is the cheapest. Many internet cafes do not allow the use of a USB stick. Internet cafes are required to see your passport before allowing you to go online, and a record of your visit may be made. You will be filmed or digitally photographed at reception by a rectangular metal box that sits on the counter of each licensed internet cafe in town. Usually you will then be given a card with a number (*zhèngjiànhào*) and password (*mìmǎ* or *kǒuling*) to enter into the on-screen box before you can start.

Wi-fi Cafes Almost all cafes and most Western-style bars offer free wi-fi.

Censorship Some politically sensitive websites and many of the most popular social-media websites, such as Twitter, Facebook and YouTube, are blocked in China, as is Gmail. To access such websites while here you will need to run your laptop or smartphone through a VPN (virtual private network).

Legal Matters

Drugs China's laws on the use of illegal drugs are harsh, and foreign nationals have been executed for drug offences (trafficking in more than 50g of heroin can result in the death penalty).

Judicial System The Chinese criminal justice system does not ensure a fair trial, and defendants are not presumed innocent until proven guilty. China conducts more judicial executions than the rest of the world combined; up to 10,000 per year (27 per day), according to some estimates. If arrested, most foreign citizens have the right to contact their embassy.

Medical Services

Clinics

A consultation with a doctor in a private clinic will cost ¥500 and up, depending on where you go. It will cost ¥10 to ¥50 in a state hospital.

Bayley & Jackson Medical Center (庇利积臣医疗中心; Bìlì Jīchén Yīliáo Zhōngxīn; Map p282; ☎010 8562 9998; www.bjhealthcare.com; 7 Ritan Donglu; 🕒dental 9am-4pm Mon-Fri, medical 8.30am-6pm Mon-Sat; [S]Line 1 to Yonganli, exit A1 or Line 6 to Dongdaqiao, exit D) Full range of medical and dental services; attractively located in a courtyard next to Rìtán Park. Dental check-up ¥456; medical consultation ¥500.

Běijīng Union Hospital (PUMCH; 协和医院; Xiéhé Yīyuàn; Map p270; ☎010 6915 6699, emergency 010 6915 9180; www.pumch.cn; 1 Shuaifuyuan; 东城区 王府井帅府园1号; 🕒24hr; [S]Lines 1, 5 to Dongdan, exit A) A recommended hospital, open 24 hours and with a full range of facilities for inpatient and outpatient care, plus a pharmacy. Head to International Medical Services, a wing reserved for foreigners which has English-speaking staff and telephone receptionists.

Běijīng United Family Hospital (和睦家医疗; Hémùjiā Yīliáo; ☎4008 919191, 24hr emergency hotline 010 5927 7120; http://beijing.ufh.com.cn; 2 Jiangtai Lu; 将台路2号; 🕒24hr; [S]Line 14 to Jiangtai, exit A or B) Can provide alternative medical treatments, along with a comprehensive range of inpatient and outpatient care. There is a critical-care unit. Emergency room staffed by expat physicians.

Hong Kong International Medical Clinic (北京香港国际医务诊所; Běijīng Xiānggǎng Guójì Yīwù Zhěnsuǒ; Map p282; ☎010 6553 2288; www.hkclinic.com/en; 9th fl, Office Tower, Hong Kong Macau Center, Swissôtel, 2 Chaoyangmen Beidajie; 朝阳门北大街2号 港澳中心-瑞士酒店办公楼9层, Cháoyáng; 🕒9am-9pm, dental 9am-7pm; [S]Line 2 to Dongsi Shitiao, exit C) Well-trusted dental and medical clinic with English-speaking staff. Includes obstetric and gynaecological services and facilities for ultrasonic scanning. Immunisations can also be performed. Prices are more reasonable than at International SOS. Full medical check-ups start from ¥3000 for men, ¥3500 for women and ¥2200 for children. Dental check-up ¥350; medical consultation ¥690. Has night staff on duty too, so you can call for advice round the clock.

International SOS (国际SOS医务诊所; Guójì SOS Yīwù Zhěnsuǒ; Map p282; ☎24hr alarm centre 010 6462 9100, clinic appointments 010 6462 9112, dental appointments 010 6462 0333; www.internationalsos.com; Suite 105, Wing 1, Kunsha Bldg, 16 Xinyuanli, off Xin Donglu, Cháoyáng; 🕒8am-8pm; [S]Line 10 to Liangmaqiao, exit D) Offering 24-hour emergency medical care, with a high-quality clinic with English-speaking staff. Dental check-up ¥620; medical consultation ¥1320.

Pharmacies

Pharmacies (药店; *yàodiàn*) are identified by a green cross. Several sizeable pharmacies on Wangfujing Dajie stock both Chinese (*zhōngyào*) and Western medicine (*xīyào*). As with many large shops in Běijīng, once you have chosen your item you are issued with a receipt that you take to the till counter (*shōuyíntái*) where you pay, then you return to the counter where you chose your medicine to collect your purchase. Note that many chemists are effectively open 24 hours and have a small window or slit through which you can pay for and collect medicines through the night.

Money

Rénmínbì (RMB), or 'people's money', is issued by the Bank of China. The basic unit of Chinese currency is the *yuán*, usually written in shops and on signs with its Chinese character (元). *Yuán* is also referred to colloquially as *kuài* or *kuàiqián*. There are also smaller denominations of *jiǎo* and *fēn*. Ten *jiǎo* – in spoken Chinese, it's known as *máo* – make up one *yuán*. Ten *fēn* make up one *jiǎo*, but these days *fēn* are rare because they are worth next to nothing.

ATMs

Most ATMs (取款机; *qǔkuǎnjī*) in Běijīng accept foreign credit cards and bank cards connected to Plus, Cirrus, Visa, MasterCard and Amex; a small withdrawal charge will be levied by your bank.

The following banks have extensive ATM networks.

Agricultural Bank of China (ABC; 中国农业银行; Zhōngguó Nóngyè Yínháng)

Bank of China (中国银行; Zhōngguó Yínháng)

China Construction Bank (中国建设银行; Zhōngguó Jiànshè Yínháng)

Industrial & Commercial Bank of China (ICBC; 工商银行; Gōngshāng Yínháng)

ATM screens almost always offer the choice of English or Chinese operation. There are ATMs in the arrivals hall at Běijīng Capital International Airport, and in many large department stores and hotels.

Banks

Bank of China (中国银行; Zhōngguó Yínháng; Map p270; ☎010 6513 2214; 19 Dong'anmen Dajie, 东城区东安门大街19号) One of dozens of branches around Běijīng with money-changing facilities.

HSBC (汇丰银行; Huìfēng Yínháng; Map p270; www.hsbc.com.cn; 1st fl, Block A, COFCO Plaza, 8 Jianguomennei Dajie, Dōngchéng; ⏰9am-5pm Mon-Fri, 10am-6pm Sat) One of 26 branches and ATMs in the capital.

Changing Money

Foreign currency can be changed at large branches of banks, such as the Bank of China, CITIC Industrial Bank, ICBC and the China Construction Bank; and at the airport, hotel money-changing counters and at several department stores, as long as you have your passport. You can normally change foreign currency into rénmínbì at foreign-exchange outlets and banks at large international airports outside China, but rates may be poor. Hotels usually give the official rate, but some will add a small commission. Some upmarket hotels will change money for their own guests only.

Keep at least a few exchange receipts if you want to change any remaining rénmínbì back into another currency at the end of your trip.

Counterfeit Bills

Counterfeit notes are a problem across China, Běijīng included. Very few shopkeepers will accept a ¥50 or ¥100 note without first running it under an ultraviolet light or through a machine. If you receive a note that doesn't seem right, hand it straight back.

Credit Cards

Credit is not big in China. The older generation doesn't like debt, however short-term, and while it is increasingly fashionable for young Chinese to use credit cards, numbers remain low compared to the West. In Běijīng, credit cards are relatively straightforward to use, but don't expect to be able to use them everywhere, and always carry enough cash. Where they are accepted, credit cards often deliver a slightly better exchange rate than in banks. Money can also be withdrawn at most ATMs on credit cards such as Visa, MasterCard and Amex. Credit cards can't be used to buy train tickets, but Civil Aviation Administration of China (CAAC; 中国民航; Zhōngguó Mínháng) offices readily accept international Visa cards for buying air tickets.

Money Transfers

If you need cash in a dash, **Western Union** (Map p282; ☎010 8442 9005; www.westernunion.com; 5 Sanlitun Lu; 三里屯路5号; ⏰9am-4pm; ⓈTuanjiehu) arranges money transfers that arrive in just 15 minutes. Counters can be found all over town at branches of China Post and the Agricultural Bank of China.

Tipping

Almost no one in Běijīng asks for tips. Many midrange and top-end eateries include their own (often huge) service charge; cheap restaurants do not expect a tip. Taxi drivers do not ask for or expect tips.

Travellers Cheques

Travellers cheques cannot be used everywhere; as with credit cards, always ensure you carry enough ready cash. You should have no problem cashing them at top-end tourist hotels, but they are of little use in budget hotels and restaurants. Most hotels will only cash the cheques of their guests. If cashing them at banks, aim for the larger banks such as the Bank of China or ICBC. Some banks won't change travellers cheques at the weekend.

Sticking to the major companies such as Thomas Cook, Amex and Visa is advisable, particularly if you plan to travel outside Běijīng. Keep your exchange receipts so you can change your money back to its original currency when you leave.

Opening Hours

China officially has a five-day working week, but much remains open at weekends.

Banks, offices & government departments Normally 9am to 5pm or 6pm (some close for two hours at midday), Monday to Friday. Some banks open weekends.

Bars To 2am, sometimes later. Some bars close one day of the week.

Internet Cafes Usually 24/7.

Museums Most close Mondays. Museums stop selling tickets half an hour before close.

Parks 6am to 9pm or later, shorter hours in winter.

Restaurants 11am to 11pm, some close 2pm to 5.30pm. Some open for breakfast (6am–8.30am).

Shops 10am to 9pm.

Post

Large post offices are generally open daily between 9am and 6pm. You can post letters via your hotel reception desk, or at green post boxes around town.

Letters and parcels marked 'Poste Restante, Běijīng Main Post Office' will arrive at the **International Post Office** (Zhōngguó Yóuzhèng; Map p282; ☑010 6512 8114; Jianguomen Beidajie; 建 国门北大街; ☺8.30am-6pm; Ⓢ Lines 1, 2 to Jianguomen, exit B), 200m north of Jianguomen station. Outsized parcels going overseas should be sent from here (packaging can be bought at the post office); smaller parcels (up to around 20kg) can go from smaller post offices. Both outgoing and incoming packages will be opened and inspected. If you're sending a parcel, don't seal the package until you've had it inspected.

Letters take around a week to reach most overseas destinations. China charges extra for registered mail, but offers cheaper postal rates for printed matter, small packets, parcels, bulk mailings and so on.

Express Mail Service (EMS; 快递; kuàidì) is available for registered deliveries to domestic and international destinations from most post offices around town. Prices are very reasonable.

Courier Companies

Several private couriers in Běijīng offer international express posting of documents and parcels, and have reliable pick-up services as well as drop-off centres.

DHL (敦豪快递, Dūnháo Kuàidì; ☑800 810 8000, 010 5790 5288, 010 6780 6680; www.cn.dhl.com; Unit C18, 9 Jiuxianqiao Beilu, Cháoyáng; 朝阳区酒仙桥北路9号; ☺10am-10pm Mon-Fri, 10.30am-9pm Sat) This branch, beside Běijīng's 798 Art District, is one of five, all on the outskirts of town.

FedEx (Federal Express; 联邦快递, Liánbāng Kuàidì; ☑010 6464 8855, toll-free landline 800 988 1888, toll-free mobile phones 400 886 1888; www.fedex.com/cn; Room 101, Tower C, Lonsdale Center, 5 Wanhong Lu, Cháoyáng; 朝阳区万红路5号蓝涛中心C座101; ☺9am-9pm Mon-Sat; Ⓢ Line 14 to Jiangtai, exit A) Also has self-service counters in Kodak Express shops around town.

Public Holidays

China has 11 national holidays:

New Year's Day 1 January

Lunar New Year January or February

International Women's Day 8 March

Tomb Sweeping Festival 5 April

International Labour Day 1 May

Youth Day 4 May

International Children's Day 1 June

Birthday of the Chinese Communist Party 1 July

Anniversary of the Founding of the People's Liberation Army 1 August

Moon Festival September

National Day 1 October

Many of the national holidays are nominal holidays that do not result in leave. The 1 May holiday is a three-day holiday, while National Day marks a week-long holiday from 1 October; the Lunar New Year is also a week-long holiday for many. It's not a great idea to arrive in China or go travelling during these holidays as the country tends to grind to a halt. Hotel prices rapidly shoot up during the May and October holiday periods.

Relocating

The following international companies can help you move house in Běijīng. Rates are typically around US$500 to US$1000 per cubic metre.

Asian Express (亚洲捷运(国际)货运代理; Yàzhōu Jiéyùn; Map p282; ☑010 8580 1471; www.aemovers.com.hk; Room 1612, Tower D, SOHO New Town, 88 Jianguo Lu, Cháoyáng; Ⓢ Lines 1, 14 to Dawanglu, exit C)

Crown Worldwide (Crown 国际货运代理; Crown Guójì Huòyùndàilǐ; ☑400 8213 129; www.crownworldwide.com; 16 Xingmao Yijie, Tōngzhōu Logistics Park, Tōngzhōu District;

通州区马驹桥兴贸一街16号; ◎9am-5.30pm) Located in southeast Běijīng.

Safe Travel

Generally speaking, Běijīng is very safe compared to other similarly sized cities. Serious crime against foreigners is rare, although on the rise.

➡ Guard against pickpockets, especially on public transport and in crowded places.

➡ Use a money belt to carry valuables, particularly on buses and trains.

➡ Hotels are usually secure places to leave your stuff and older establishments may have an attendant watching who goes in and out.

➡ Staying in dormitories carries its own risks, and while there have been some reports of thefts by staff, the culprits are usually other guests. Use lockers as much as possible.

Loss Reports

If something of yours is stolen, report it immediately to the nearest Foreign Affairs Branch of the Public Security Bureau (PSB). Staff will ask you to fill in a loss report before investigating the case. If you have travel insurance, it is essential to obtain a loss report so you can claim compensation. Be prepared to spend many hours, perhaps even several days, organising it. Make a copy of your passport in case of loss or theft.

Road Safety

The greatest hazard may well be crossing the road, a manoeuvre that requires alertness and dexterity. It can seem like a mad scramble on the streets as vehicles squeeze into every available space. Traffic often comes from all directions (bikes, in particular, frequently ride the wrong way down streets), and a seeming reluctance to give way holds sway. If right

of way is uncertain, drivers tend to dig in their heels. Ignore zebra crossings; cars are not obliged to stop at them, and never do. And take care at traffic-light crossings: the green 'cross now' light doesn't necessarily mean that traffic won't run you down, as cars can still turn on red lights and bicycles, electric bikes and motor bikes rarely stop at red lights.

Scams

Teahouse Invitations Refuse invitations to teahouses from sweet-talking girls around Tiān'ānmén Sq or Wangfujing Dajie – it's an expensive scam.

Art Exhibitions Similar invitations by 'art students' see tourists pressured into buying overpriced art.

Rickshaws Riders at the North Gate of the Forbidden City are particularly unscrupulous. The ¥3 trip really is too good to be true – it'll end up costing you ¥300!

Taxis Always use official taxis. If any city-centre driver refuses to dǎ biǎo (use the meter), get out and find another taxi. Note, for long journeys, such as to the Great Wall, you'll have to negotiate a nonmetered fee.

Departure Tax Note that there is no departure tax at the Capital Airport, so ignore fraudsters who try and sell it to you.

Taxes & Refunds

China does have a value-added tax (VAT), but it is always included in the price of any item you buy and you won't see a separate mention of it on the receipt. Visitors are not able to claim tax refunds on items bought in China when they leave.

Telephone

International and domestic calls can be made easily

from your hotel room or from public telephones, which are plentiful. Local calls from hotel-room phones are usually free, while international calls are expensive. If making a domestic phone call, public phones at newspaper stands (报刊亭; bàokāntíng) and hole-in-the-wall shops (小卖部; xiǎomàibù) are useful; make your call and pay the owner (a local call is around 5 jiǎo). Most public phones take IC (Integrated Circuit; IC kǎ) cards. When making domestic long-distance or international calls in China, it's cheapest to use an IP (Internet Phone; IP kǎ) card. Domestic long-distance and international phone calls can also be made from main telecommunications offices or 'phone bars' (huàbā). The country code to use to access China is 🖉86; the code for Hong Kong is 🖉852 and Macau is 🖉853. To call a number in Běijīng from abroad, dial the international access code (🖉00 in the UK, 🖉011 in the USA and so on), dial the country code (🖉86) and then the area code for Běijīng (🖉010), dropping the first zero, and then dial the local number. For telephone calls within the same city, drop the area code (qūhào). Important city area codes within China include the following:

CITY	AREA CODE
Běijīng	🖉010
Chéngdū	🖉028
Chóngqìng	🖉023
Guǎngzhōu	🖉020
Hángzhōu	🖉0571
Hāěrbīn	🖉0451
Hong Kong	🖉852
Jǐnán	🖉0531
Kūnmíng	🖉0871
Nánjīng	🖉025
Qīngdǎo	🖉0532
Shànghǎi	🖉021
Shíjiāzhuāng	🖉0311
Tiānjīn	🖉022
Xiàmén	🖉0592

Mobile Phones

Mobile-phone shops (手机店; *shǒujīdiàn*) such as China Mobile and China Unicom sell SIM cards, which cost around ¥100 and include ¥50 of credit. Bring your passport, as you'll be registered when you buy a SIM. Note that numbers containing 4s are avoided by the Chinese, making them cheaper. You can top up credit with ¥20 to ¥100 credit-charging cards (充值卡; *chōngzhí kǎ*). Those cards are available from newspaper kiosks and corner shops displaying the China Mobile sign.

The mobile phone you use in your home country should work (as long as it has not been locked by your network – check with your phone company before you go) or you can buy a pay-as-you-go phone locally (from ¥300). China Mobile's local, nonroaming city call charge is 6 *jiǎo* per minute if calling a landline and 1.50 *jiǎo* per minute if calling another mobile phone. Receiving calls on your mobile is free from mobile phones and 6 *jiǎo* from landline phones. Roaming charges cost an additional 1 to 2 *jiǎo* per minute and the call-receiving charge is the same. Overseas calls can be made for ¥8 per minute plus the local charge per minute by dialling ☑17951 – then follow the instructions and add 00 before the country code. Otherwise you will be charged the International Dialling Code call charge plus 6 *jiǎo* per minute.

Mobile phones are particularly useful for communicating messages to non-English speakers. You can phone restaurants and other venues from a taxi and hand the phone to the driver, so he knows where to go, or phone a Chinese-speaking friend and ask them to communicate your message.

Phonecards

For domestic calls, IC cards, available from kiosks, hole-in-the-wall shops, internet cafes and China Telecom offices, are prepaid cards in a variety of denominations that can be used in most public telephones. Note that some IC cards can only be used locally while other cards can be used in phones throughout China, so check this when you purchase one.

For international calls on a mobile phone, or hotel phone and for long-distance domestic calls, buy an IP card. International calls on IP cards are ¥1.80 per minute to the USA or Canada, ¥1.50 per minute to Hong Kong, Macau and Taiwan, and ¥3.20 to all other countries; domestic long-distance calls are ¥0.30 per minute. Follow the instructions on the reverse; English-language service is usually available. IP cards come in various denominations, typically with a big discount (a ¥100 card should cost around ¥40). IP cards can be found at the same places as IC cards. Again, some IP cards can only be used locally, while others can be used nation-wide, so it is important to buy the right card (and check the expiry date).

Time

All of China runs on the same time as Běijīng, which is set eight hours ahead of GMT/UTC (there's no daylight saving time during summer). When it's noon in Běijīng it's 4am the same day in London; 5am in Frankfurt, Paris and Rome; noon in Hong Kong; 2pm in Melbourne; 4pm in Wellington; and, on the previous day, 8pm in Los Angeles and 11pm in Montreal and New York.

Toilets

➡ Over the last decade the capital has made its toilets less of an assault course of foul smells and primitive appliances, but many remain pungent. Make a beeline for fast-food outlets, top-end hotels and department stores for more hygienic alternatives.

➡ Toilet paper is rarely provided in streetside public toilets so keep a stash with you.

➡ Toilets are often squat versions, although most public toilets will have one sit-down toilet for disabled users (and inflexible Westerners).

➡ As a general rule, if you see a wastebasket next to the toilet, that's where you should throw the toilet paper.

➡ The symbol for men is 男 (*nán*) and women is 女 (*nǚ*).

Tourist Information

Staff at the chain of **Běijīng Tourist Information Centers** (北京旅游咨询; Běijīng Lǚyóu Zīxún Fúwù Zhōngxīn; ⊗9am-5pm) generally have limited English-language skills and are not always helpful, but you can grab a free tourist map of town, nab handfuls of free literature and, at some branches, rustle up train tickets. Useful branches include the following:

Běijīng Train Station (Map p270; ☑010 6528 4848; 16 Laoqianju Hutong; tours ¥260-400; ⊗8.30am-6pm; Ⓢ Line 2 to Beijing Railway Station, exit B)

Capital Airport (☑010 6459 8148; Terminal 3, Běijīng Capital International Airport)

Hòuhǎi Lakes (Map p278; 49 Di'anmenxi Dajie; 地安门西大街49号, Hòuhǎi Lakes; ⊗9am-6pm; Ⓢ Line 6 to Beihai North, exit B, or Lines 6, 8 to Nanlu-guxiang, exit E) Has an excellent, very detailed free map of all the *hùtòng* alleys surrounding the lakes of Hòuhǎi. Can also arrange rickshaw tours of the *hùtòng* with English-speaking riders.

The **China National Tourist Hotline** (☑press 2 for English 12301; ⊗24hr) has English-speaking operators available to answer questions and hear complaints. **CITS** (CITS; 中国国际旅行社; Zhōngguó Guójì Lǚxíngshè; Map p270; ☎010 8511 8522; www.cits.net; Room 1212, CITS Bldg, 1 Dongdan Beidajie; ⏰9am-7pm; [S]Line 5 to Dengshikou) is more useful for booking tours, China-wide.

Hotels can offer you advice or connect you with a suitable tour, and some have useful tourist information desks that can point you in the right direction.

The best travel advice for independent travellers is usually dished out at guesthouses and hostels, although be aware that they will sometimes try to sign you up to one of their tours rather than give you impartial advice. Tours run by hostels are generally pretty good, though.

Travellers with Disabilities

If you are wheelchair-bound or have a mobility disability, Běijīng can be a major obstacle course. Pavements are often crowded and in a dangerous condition, with high curbs often preventing wheelchair access. Many streets can be crossed only via underground or overhead walkways with steps. You will also have to stick to the main roads, as parked cars and bicycles often occupy the pavements of smaller alleys and lanes, forcing others on to the road. Escalators in subways normally only go up, but wheelchair lifts have been installed in numerous stations (although you may have to send someone down to find a member of staff to operate them). Getting around temples and big sights such as the Forbidden City and the Summer Palace can be trying for those in wheelchairs. It is recommended that you take a lightweight chair so it can be collapsed easily when necessary, such as to load it into the back of a taxi. Most, but not all, hotels will have lifts, and while many top-end hotels do have rooms for those with disabilities as well as good wheelchair access, hotel restaurants may not.

Those with sight, hearing or mobility disabilities must be extremely cautious of the traffic, which almost never yields to pedestrians.

Download Lonely Planet's free Accessible Travel guide from http://lptravel.to/AccessibleTravel.

Visas

Citizens of 51 countries, including Australia, France, Germany, the UK and the USA, are allowed to stay for up to 72 hours in Běijīng without a visa, as long as they have an onward travel ticket to another country. However, if you are staying longer, citizens of every country, bar Japan, Singapore and Brunei, require a visa. Note that visas do not allow you to travel in areas of China, such as Tibet, that require special permits to visit.

Your passport must be valid for at least six months after the expiry date of your visa and you'll need at least one entire blank page in your passport for the visa. You may be required to show proof of hotel reservations and onward travel from China, as well as a bank statement showing you have $100 in your account for every day you plan to spend in China.

At the time of writing, prices for a single-entry 30-day visa were as follows.

- £85 for UK citizens
- US$140 for US citizens
- US$30 for citizens of other nations

Double-entry visas:

- £85 for UK citizens
- US$140 for US citizens
- US$45 for all other nationals

Six-month multiple-entry visas:

- £85 for UK citizens
- US$140 for US citizens
- US$60 for all other nationals

Most Chinese embassies abroad can issue a standard 30-day single-entry visa in three to five working days. Express visas cost twice the usual fee. In some countries (eg the UK and the US) the visa service has been outsourced from the Chinese embassy to a Chinese Visa Application Service Centre, which levies an extra administration fee. In the case of the UK, a single-entry visa costs £85, but the standard administration charge levied by the centre is a further £66.

A standard 30-day visa is activated on the date you enter China, and must be used within three months of the date of issue. The 60-day and 90-day tourist visas are reasonably easy to obtain in your home country but difficult elsewhere. To stay longer, you can extend your visa in China at least once, sometimes twice.

Visa applications require a completed application form (available at the embassy or downloaded from its website) and at least one photo (normally 51mm x 51mm). You normally pay for your visa when you collect it. A visa mailed to you will take up to three weeks. In the US and Canada, mailed visa applications have to go via a visa agent, at extra cost. In the US, many people use the China Visa Service Center (www.mychinavisa.com), which offers prompt service. The procedure takes around 10 to 14 days.

Hong Kong is a good place to pick up a China visa. However, at the time of writing only Hong Kong residents were able to obtain them direct from the **Visa Office of the People's Republic of China** (☎10-11am & 3-4pm Mon-Fri 852 3413 2424, recorded info 852 3413 2300; www.fmcoprc.gov.hk; 7th fl, Lower Block, China Resources Centre, 26 Harbour Rd, Wan Chai; ⏰9am-noon & 2-5pm Mon-Fri; [M]Wan Chai, exit A3). Single-entry visas processed here cost HK$200, double-entry visas HK$300, while six-month/one-year multiple-entry visas are HK$500. But China Travel Service (CTS) and many travel agencies in Hong Kong can get you a visa in two to three working days. Expect to pay HK$650 for a single-entry visa and HK$750 for a double-entry. Both American and UK passport holders must pay considerably more for their visas.

Be aware that political events can suddenly make visas more difficult to procure or renew.

When asked about your itinerary on the application form, list standard tourist destinations; if you are considering going to Tibet or western Xīnjiāng, just leave it off the form. The list you give is not binding. Those working in the media or journalism should profess a different occupation; otherwise, a visa may be refused or a shorter length of stay may be given. There are many different categories of visa. The eight most common are listed here (most travellers will enter China on an 'L' visa).

Visa Extensions

The Foreign Affairs Branch of the local PSB – the police force – handles visa extensions. The visa office at the **PSB main office** (北京公安局出入境管理处; Běijīngshì Gōng'ānjú Chūrùjìng Guǎnlǐchù; Map p274; ☎ 010 8402 0101, 010 8400 2101; www.bjgaj.gov.cn; 2 Andingmen Dongdajie; 东城区 东城区安定门东大街2号;

⏱ 9am-5pm Mon-Sat; ⓢ Line 2, 5 to Yonghegong-Lama Temple, exit B) is on the 2nd floor, accessed from the North 2nd Ring Rd. You can also apply for a residence permit here. You should apply for your visa extension at least seven days before your current visa expires, but this rule is not always enforced.

First-time extensions of 30 days are usually easy to obtain on single-entry tourist visas; further extensions are harder to get, and may only give you another week. Travellers report generous extensions in provincial towns, but don't bank on this. Popping south to Hong Kong to apply for a new tourist visa is another option.

Extensions to single-entry visas vary in price, depending on your nationality. At the time of writing, US travellers paid the most, ¥960, while Canadians and Australians paid ¥160. Expect to wait up to five days for your visa extension to be processed. You may be asked to prove that you have adequate funds (US$100 per day, or the equivalent in other currencies) for the time you are staying in China.

The penalty for overstaying your visa in China is up to ¥500 per day. Some travellers have reported having trouble with officials who read the 'valid until' date on their visa incorrectly. For a one-month travel (L) visa, the 'valid until' date is the date by which you must enter the

country (within three months of the date the visa was issued), not the date upon which your visa expires.

Residence Permits

Residence permits are available – normally issued for a period of one year at a time as a sticker in your passport – to people resident in China for work, who are married to Chinese citizens (although that doesn't guarantee you will be allowed to work while in China) and long-term students. Requirements are stringent; you will need to be sponsored by a Chinese company or university, or a foreign company with an office in China, and undergo a health check. Long-term residency permits, valid for five years and known as 'green cards', are available but are issued under even more stringent conditions.

Passports

Chinese law requires foreign visitors to carry their passport with them at all times; it is the most basic travel document and all hotels (and internet cafes) will insist on seeing it. You also need it to buy train tickets or to get into some tourist sights, particularly those which are free.

It's a good idea to bring an ID card with your photo in case you lose your passport. Even better, make photocopies, or take digital photos of your passport – your embassy may need these before issuing a new one. You should also report the loss to the local PSB. Be careful who you pass your passport to, as you may never see it again.

Volunteering

Large numbers of Westerners work in China with international development charities such as the following:

Go Overseas (www.gooverseas.com) Places volunteer teachers in Běijīng and elsewhere in China.

VISA TYPES

TYPE	ENGLISH NAME	CHINESE NAME
C	flight attendant	chéngwù; 乘务
D	resident	dìngjū; 定居
F	business, student or person on exchange program	fǎngwèn; 访问
G	transit	guòjìng; 过境
J	journalist	jìzhě; 记者
L	travel	lǚxíng; 旅行
X	long-term student	liúxué; 留学
Z	working	gōngzuò; 工作

Joy in Action (www.joyinaction.org) Establishing work camps in places in need in south China.

VSO (www.vso.org.uk) Provides you with useful experience and the chance to learn Chinese.

World Teach (www.worldteach.org) Volunteer teachers.

Women Travellers

Women travellers generally feel safe in Běijīng. Chinese men are not macho and respect for women is deeply ingrained in Chinese culture. As with anywhere else, you will be taking a risk if you travel alone. Tampons *(wèishēng miántiáo)* can be found almost everywhere. It may be advisable to take supplies of the pill *(bìyùnyào)*, although you will find brands like Marvelon at local pharmacies.

Work

Over the past decade it has become easier for foreigners to find work in Běijīng, although having Chinese-language skills is now increasingly important.

Teaching jobs that pay by the hour are usually quite lucrative. If you have recognised ELT qualifications, such as TEFL, and/or experience, teaching can be a rewarding and profitable way to earn a living in Běijīng. International schools offer salaries in the region of ¥10,000 and up per month to qualified teachers, with accommodation sometimes provided. More basic (and plentiful) teaching positions will offer around ¥200 per hour. Schools regularly advertise in expat magazines, such as *The Beijinger*; you can visit its classified pages online at www.thebeijinger.com. Also hunt for teaching jobs on www.teachabroad.com. You could also try approaching organisations such as the British Council (www.britishcouncil.org), which runs teacher placement programs in Běijīng and beyond.

There are also opportunities in translation, freelance writing, editing, proofreading, the hotel industry, acting, modelling, photography, bar work, sales and marketing, and beyond. Most people find jobs in Běijīng through word of mouth, so networking is the key.

Doing Business

Difficulties for foreigners attempting to do business have eased up, but the China work environment can still be frustrating. Renting properties, getting licences, hiring employees and paying taxes can generate huge quantities of red tape. Most foreign business people who have worked in China say that success is usually the result of dogged persistence and finding cooperative officials.

If you are considering doing business in China, plenty of preliminary research is recommended. In particular, talk to other foreigners who are already working here. Alternatively, approach a firm of business consultants for advice, or approach one of the following Běijīng business associations.

American Chamber of Commerce (中国美国商会; Zhōngguó Měiguó Shānghuì; Map p282; ☎010 8519 0800; www.amchamchina.org; The Office Park, Tower AB, 6th fl, 10 Jintongxi Lu, Cháoyáng; 朝阳区金桐西路10号远洋光华国际AB座6层; [S]Line 1 to Yong'anli, exit B)

British Chamber of Commerce (中国英国商会; Zhōngguó Yīngguó Shānghuì; Map p282; ☎010 8525 1111; www.britishchamber.cn; Room 1001, China Life Tower, 16 Chaoyangmenwai Dajie, Cháoyáng; 朝阳门外大街16号中国人寿大夏1001室; [S]Lines 2, 6 to Chaoyangmen, exit A)

Canada-China Business Council (加中贸易理事会; Jiāzhōng Màoyì Lǐshìhuì; Map p282; ☎010 8526 1820; www.ccbc.com; Suite 11A16, Tower A, Hanwei Plaza, 7 Guanghua Lu, Cháoyáng; 朝阳区光华路7号汉威大夏A座; [S]Lines 1, 2 to Jianguomen, exit B or Line 1 to Yong'anli, exit A1)

China-Australia Chamber of Commerce (中国澳大利亚商会; Zhōngguó Àodàlìyà Shānghuì; Map p282; ☎010 8561 5005; www.austcham.org; 1005, Tower A, U-Town Office Bldg, 1 Sanfengbeili, Cháoyáng; 朝阳区三丰北里1号 悠唐写字楼A座910室; [S]Lines 2, 6 to Chaoyangmen, exit A)

China-Britain Business Council (CBBC; 英中贸易协会; Yīngzhōng Màoyì Xiéhuì; Map p282; ☎010 8525 1111; www.cbbc.org; Room 1001, China Life Tower, 16 Chaoyangmenwai Dajie, Cháoyáng; 朝阳区朝阳门外大街16号, 中国人寿大夏1001室; [S]Lines 2, 6 to Chaoyangmen, exit A)

European Union Chamber of Commerce in China (中国欧盟商会; Zhōngguó Ōuméng Shànghuì; Map p282; ☎010 6462 2066; www.europeanchamber.com.cn; Room C-412, Lufthansa Center, 50 Liangmaqiao Lu, Cháoyáng; 朝阳区亮马桥路50号, 燕莎中心写字楼C-412室; [S]Line 10 to Liangmaqiao, exit B)

French Chamber of Commerce & Industry (中国法国工商会; Zhōngguó Fǎguó Gōngshānghuì; Map p282; ☎010 6461 0260; www.ccifc.org; Ste 201-222, 2nd Fl, Bldg 81, 4 Gongti Beilu; 工体北路4号 81号楼二层201－222室 邮政编码; [S]Line 10 to Tuanjiehu, exit A or D)

US-China Business Council (美中贸易全国委员会; Měizhōng Màoyì Quánguó Wěiyuánhuì; Map p282; ☎010 6592 0727; www.uschina.org; CITIC Bldg, Suite 10-01, 19 Jianguomenwai Dajie, Cháoyáng; 朝阳区建国门外大街19号, 国际大夏10-01室; [S]Lines 1, 2 to Jianguomen, exit B or Line 1 to Yong'anli, exit A1)

Language

Discounting its many ethnic minority languages, China has eight major dialect groups: Pǔtōnghuà (Mandarin), Yue (Cantonese), Wu (Shanghainese), Minbei (Fuzhou), Minnan (Hokkien-Taiwanese), Xiang, Gan and Hakka. Each of them also divides into subdialects.

It's the language spoken in Běijīng which is considered the official language of China. It's usually referred to as Mandarin, but the Chinese themselves call it Pǔtōnghuà (meaning 'common speech'). Pǔtōnghuà is variously referred to as Hànyǔ (the Han language), Guóyǔ (the national language) or Zhōngwén or Zhōngguóhuà (Chinese). You'll find that knowing a few basics in Mandarin will not only come in handy in Běijīng, but also in many other parts of the country (although it may be spoken there with a regional accent).

Writing

Chinese is often referred to as a language of pictographs. Many of the basic Chinese characters are highly stylised pictures of what they represent, but around 90% are compounds of a 'meaning' element and a 'sound' element.

A well-educated, contemporary Chinese speaker might use between 6000 and 8000 characters. To read a Chinese newspaper you need to know 2000 to 3000 characters, but 1200 to 1500 would be enough to get the gist.

Theoretically, all Chinese dialects share the same written system. In practice, Cantonese adds about 3000 specialised characters and many dialects don't have a written form at all.

WANT MORE?

For in-depth language information and handy phrases, check out Lonely Planet's *China Phrasebook* and *Mandarin Phrasebook*. You'll find them at **shop.lonelyplanet.com**.

Pinyin & Pronunciation

In 1958 the Chinese adopted Pinyin, a system of writing Mandarin using the Roman alphabet. The original idea was to eventually do away with Chinese characters, but over time this idea was abandoned.

Pinyin is often used on shop fronts, street signs and advertising billboards. However, in the countryside and the smaller towns you may not see a single Pinyin sign anywhere, so unless you speak Chinese you'll need a phrasebook with Chinese characters.

In this chapter we've provided Pinyin alongside the Mandarin script. Below is a brief guide to the pronunciation of Pinyin letters.

Vowels

a	as in 'father'
ai	as in 'aisle'
ao	as the 'ow' in 'cow'
e	as in 'her' (without 'r' sound)
ei	as in 'weigh'
i	as the 'ee' in 'meet' (or like a light 'r' as in 'Grrr!' after c, ch, r, s, sh, z or zh)
ian	as the word 'yen'
ie	as the English word 'yeah'
o	as in 'or' (without 'r' sound)
ou	as the 'oa' in 'boat'
u	as in 'flute'
ui	as the word 'way'
uo	like a 'w' followed by 'o'
yu/ü	like 'ee' with lips pursed

Consonants

c	as the 'ts' in 'bits'
ch	as in 'chop', with the tongue curled up and back
h	as in 'hay', articulated from further back in the throat
q	as the 'ch' in 'cheese'
sh	as in 'ship', with the tongue curled up and back
x	as the 'sh 'in 'ship'
z	as the 'ds' in 'suds'
zh	as the 'j' in 'judge', with the tongue curled up and back

The only consonants that occur at the end of a syllable are n, ng and r. In Pinyin, apostrophes are occasionally used to separate syllables in order to prevent ambiguity, eg the word píng'ān can be written with an apostrophe after the 'g' to prevent it being pronounced as pín'gǎn.

Tones

Mandarin is a language with a large number of words with the same pronunciation but a different meaning. What distinguishes these homophones (as these words are called) is their 'tonal' quality – the raising and the lowering of pitch on certain syllables. Mandarin has four tones – high, rising, falling-rising and falling, plus a fifth 'neutral' tone that you can all but ignore. Tones are important for distinguishing meaning of words – eg the word ma has four different meanings according to tone: mā (mother), má (hemp, numb), mǎ (horse), mà (scold, swear). Tones are indicated in Pinyin by the following accent marks on vowels: ā (high), á (rising), ǎ (falling-rising) and à (falling).

Basics

When asking a question it is polite to start with qǐng wèn – literally, 'May I ask?'.

Hello.	你好。	Nǐhǎo.
Goodbye.	再见。	Zàijiàn.
How are you?	你好吗？	Nǐhǎo ma?
Fine. And you?	好。你呢？	Hǎo. Nǐ ne?
Excuse me.	劳驾。	Láojià.
Sorry.	对不起。	Duìbùqǐ.
Yes./No.	是。/不是。	Shì./Bùshì.
Please ...	请……	Qǐng ...
Thank you.	谢谢你。	Xièxie nǐ.
You're welcome.	不客气。	Bù kèqi.

What's your name?
你叫什么名字？ Nǐ jiào shénme míngzi?

My name is ...
我叫…… Wǒ jiào ...

Do you speak English?
你会说英文吗？ Nǐ huìshuō Yīngwén ma?

I don't understand.
我不明白。 Wǒ bù míngbái.

Accommodation

Do you have a single/double room?
有没有(单人/ Yǒuméiyǒu (dānrén/
套)房？ tào) fáng?

How much is it per night/person?
每天/人多少钱？ Měi tiān/rén duōshǎo qián?

KEY PATTERNS

To get by in Mandarin, mix and match these simple patterns with words of your choice:

How much is (the deposit)?
(押金)多少？ (Yājīn) duōshǎo?

Do you have (a room)?
有没有(房)？ Yǒuméiyǒu (fáng)?

Is there (heating)?
有(暖气)吗？ Yóu (nuǎnqì) ma?

I'd like (that one).
我要(那个)。 Wǒ yào (nàge).

Please give me (the menu).
请给我(菜单)。 Qǐng gěiwǒ (càidān).

Can I (sit here)?
我能(坐这儿)吗？ Wǒ néng (zuò zhè'er) ma?

I need (a can opener).
我想要(一个 Wǒ xiǎngyào (yīge
开罐器)。 kāiguàn qì).

Do we need (a guide)?
需要(向导)吗？ Xūyào (xiàngdǎo) ma?

I have (a reservation).
我有(预订)。 Wǒ yǒu (yùdìng).

I'm (a doctor).
我(是医生)。 Wǒ (shì yīshēng).

air-con	空调	kōngtiáo
bathroom	浴室	yùshì
bed	床	chuáng
campsite	露营地	lùyíngdì
guesthouse	宾馆	bīnguǎn
hostel	招待所	zhāodàisuǒ
hotel	酒店	jiǔdiàn
window	窗	chuāng

Directions

Where's a (bank)?
(银行)在哪儿？ (Yínháng) zài nǎr?

What's the address?
地址在哪儿？ Dìzhǐ zài nǎr?

Could you write the address, please?
能不能请你 Néngbunéng qǐng nǐ
把地址写下来？ bǎ dìzhǐ xiě xiàlái?

Can you show me where it is on the map?
请帮我找它在 Qǐng bāngwǒ zhǎo tā zài
地图上的位置。 dìtú shàng de wèizhi.

Go straight ahead.
一直走。 Yīzhí zǒu.

Turn left/right.
左/右转。 Zuǒ/Yòu zhuǎn.

LANGUAGE EATING & DRINKING

Question Words

What?	什么?	Shénme?
When?	什么时候	Shénme shíhòu?
Where?	哪儿	Nǎr?
Which?	哪个	Nǎge?
Who?	谁?	Shéi?
Why?	为什么?	Wèishénme?

at the traffic lights	在红绿灯	zài hónglǜdēng
behind	背面	bèimiàn
far	远	yuǎn
in front of ...	……的前面	... de qiánmian
near	近	jìn
next to	旁边	pángbiān
on the corner	拐角	guǎijiǎo
opposite	对面	duìmiàn

Eating & Drinking

What would you recommend?
有什么菜可以推荐的? — Yǒu shénme cài kěyǐ tuījiàn de?

What's in that dish?
这道菜用什么东西做的? — Zhèdào cài yòng shénme dōngxī zuòde?

That was delicious.
真好吃。 — Zhēn hǎochī.

The bill, please!
买单! — Mǎidān!

Cheers!
干杯! — Gānbēi!

I'd like to reserve a table for ...	我想预订一张……的桌子。	Wǒ xiǎng yùdìng yìzhāng ... de zhuōzi.
(eight) o'clock	(八)点钟	(bā) diǎn zhōng
(two) people	(两个)人	(liǎngge) rén

I don't eat ...	我不吃……	Wǒ bùchī ...
nuts	果仁	guǒrén
pork	猪肉	zhūròu
red meat	牛羊肉	niúyángròu

Key Words

bar	酒吧	jiǔbā
bottle	瓶子	píngzi
bowl	碗	wǎn
breakfast	早饭	zǎofàn
cafe	咖啡屋	kāfēiwū
(too) cold	(太)凉	(tài) liáng
dinner	晚饭	wǎnfàn
food	食品	shípǐn
fork	叉子	chāzi
glass	杯子	bēizi
hot (warm)	热	rè
knife	刀	dāo
local specialties	地方小吃	dìfāng xiǎochī
lunch	午饭	wǔfàn
market	菜市	càishì
menu (in English)	(英文)菜单	(Yīngwén) càidān
plate	碟子	diézi
restaurant	餐馆	cānguǎn
(too) spicy	(太)辣	(tài) là
spoon	勺	sháo
vegetarian food	素食食品	sùshí shípín

Meat & Fish

beef	牛肉	niúròu
chicken	鸡肉	jīròu
duck	鸭	yā
fish	鱼	yú
lamb	羊肉	yángròu
pork	猪肉	zhūròu
seafood	海鲜	hǎixiān

Fruit & Vegetables

apple	苹果	píngguǒ
banana	香蕉	xiāngjiāo
carrot	胡萝卜	húluóbo
celery	芹菜	qíncài
cucumber	黄瓜	huángguā
fruit	水果	shuǐguǒ
grape	葡萄	pútáo
green beans	扁豆	biǎndòu
mango	芒果	mángguǒ
mushroom	蘑菇	mógu
onion	洋葱	yáng cōng
orange	橙子	chéngzi

Signs

入口	Rùkǒu	**Entrance**
出口	Chūkǒu	**Exit**
问讯处	Wènxùnchù	**Information**
开	Kāi	**Open**
关	Guān	**Closed**
禁止	Jìnzhǐ	**Prohibited**
厕所	Cèsuǒ	**Toilets**
男	Nán	**Men**
女	Nǚ	**Women**

pear	梨	lí
pineapple	凤梨	fènglí
plum	梅子	méizi
potato	土豆	tǔdòu
radish	萝卜	luóbo
spring onion	小葱	xiǎo cōng
sweet potato	地瓜	dìguā
vegetable	蔬菜	shūcài
watermelon	西瓜	xīguā

Other

bread	面包	miànbāo
butter	黄油	huángyóu
egg	蛋	dàn
herbs/spices	香料	xiāngliào
pepper	胡椒粉	hújiāo fěn
salt	盐	yán
soy sauce	酱油	jiàngyóu
sugar	砂糖	shātáng
tofu	豆腐	dòufu
vinegar	醋	cù
vegetable oil	菜油	càiyóu

Drinks

beer	啤酒	píjiǔ
coffee	咖啡	kāfēi
(orange) juice	(橙)汁	(chéng) zhī
milk	牛奶	niúnǎi
mineral water	矿泉水	kuàngquán shuǐ
red wine	红葡萄酒	hóng pútáo jiǔ
rice wine	米酒	mǐjiǔ
soft drink	汽水	qìshuǐ
tea	茶	chá
(boiled) water	(开)水	(kāi) shuǐ
white wine	白葡萄酒	bái pútáo jiǔ
yoghurt	酸奶	suānnǎi

Emergencies

Help!	救命！	Jiùmìng!
I'm lost.	我迷路了。	Wǒ mílù le.
Go away!	走开！	Zǒukāi!

There's been an accident.
出事了。   Chūshì le.

Call a doctor!
请叫医生来!   Qǐng jiào yīshēng lái!

Call the police!
请叫警察!   Qǐng jiào jǐngchá!

I'm ill.
我生病了。   Wǒ shēngbìng le.

Where are the toilets?
厕所在哪儿？   Cèsuǒ zài nǎr?

Shopping & Services

I'd like to buy ...
我想买……   Wǒ xiǎng mǎi ...

I'm just looking.
我先看看。   Wǒ xiān kànkan.

Can I look at it?
我能看看吗？   Wǒ néng kànkan ma?

I don't like it.
我不喜欢。   Wǒ bù xǐhuān.

How much is it?
多少钱？   Duōshǎo qián?

That's too expensive.
太贵了。   Tàiguì le.

Can you lower the price?
能便宜一点吗？   Néng piányí yīdiǎn ma?

There's a mistake in the bill.
帐单上有问题。   Zhàngdān shàng yǒu wèntí.

ATM	自动取款机	zìdòng qǔkuǎn jī
internet cafe	网吧	wǎngbā
post office	邮局	yóujú
tourist office	旅行店	lǚxíng diàn

Time & Dates

What time is it?
现在几点钟？   Xiànzài jǐdiǎn zhōng?

It's (10) o'clock.
(十)点钟。   (Shí) diǎn zhōng.

Half past (10).
(十)点三十分。   (Shí) diǎn sānshífēn.

morning	早上	zǎoshang
afternoon	下午	xiàwǔ
evening	晚上	wǎnshàng

yesterday	昨天	zuótiān
today	今天	jīntiān
tomorrow	明天	míngtiān

Monday	星期一	xīngqī yī
Tuesday	星期二	xīngqī èr
Wednesday	星期三	xīngqī sān
Thursday	星期四	xīngqī sì
Friday	星期五	xīngqī wǔ
Saturday	星期六	xīngqī liù
Sunday	星期天	xīngqī tiān

Numbers

1	一	yī
2	二/两	èr/liǎng
3	三	sān
4	四	sì
5	五	wǔ
6	六	liù
7	七	qī
8	八	bā
9	九	jiǔ
10	十	shí
20	二十	èrshí
30	三十	sānshí
40	四十	sìshí
50	五十	wǔshí
60	六十	liùshí
70	七十	qīshí
80	八十	bāshí
90	九十	jiǔshí
100	一百	yībǎi
1000	一千	yīqiān

Transport

boat	船	chuán
bus (city)	大巴	dàbā
bus (intercity)	长途车	chángtú chē
plane	飞机	fēijī
taxi	出租车	chūzū chē
train	火车	huǒchē
tram	电车	diànchē

I want to go to ...
我要去…… Wǒ yào qù ...

Does it stop at ...?
在……能下车吗？ Zài ... néng xià chē ma?

At what time does it leave?
几点钟出发？ Jǐdiǎnzhōng chūfā?

At what time does it get to ...?
几点钟到……？ Jǐdiǎnzhōng dào ...?

I want to get off here.
我想这儿下车。 Wǒ xiǎng zhè'er xiàchē.

When's the first/last (bus)?
首班/末班(车) Shǒubān/Mòbān (chē)
几点走? jǐdiǎn zǒu?

A ... ticket to (Dàlián). 一张票到(大连)。 Yī zhāng piào dào (Dàlián).
　1st-class 头等 tóuděng
　2nd-class 二等 èrděng
　one-way 单程 dānchéng
　return 双程 shuāngchéng

aisle seat 走廊的座位 zǒuláng de zuòwèi
ticket office 售票处 shòupiàochù
timetable 时刻表 shíkè biǎo
window seat 窗户的座位 chuānghù de zuòwèi

bicycle pump 打气筒 dǎqitóng
child seat 婴儿座 yīng'ér zuò
helmet 头盔 tóukuī

I'd like a taxi to depart at (9am)
我要订一辆出租车, Wǒ yào dìng yīliàng chūzū
(早上9点钟)出发。 chē, (zǎoshàng jiǔ diǎn zhōng) chūfā.

I'd like a taxi now.
我要订一辆出租车, Wǒ yào dìng yīliàng chūzū
现在。 chē, xiànzài.

I'd like a taxi tomorrow
我要订一辆出租车, Wǒ yào dìng yīliàng chūzū
明天。 chē, míngtiān.

Where's the taxi rank?
在哪里打出租车? Zài nǎli dǎ chūzū chē?

Is this taxi free?
这出租车有人吗? Zhè chūzū chē yǒurén ma?

Please put the meter on.
请打表。 Qǐng dǎbiǎo.

How much is it (to this address)?
(到这个地址) (Dào zhège dìzhǐ)
多少钱? duōshǎo qián?

Please take me to (this address).
请带我到 Qǐng dàiwǒ dào
(这个地址)。 (zhège dìzhǐ).

GLOSSARY

arhat – Buddhist, especially a monk, who has achieved enlightenment and passes to nirvana at death

běi – north; the other points of the compass are *nán* (south), *dōng* (east) and *xī* (west)
bīnguǎn – tourist hotel
bìxì – mythical tortoise-like dragons often depicted in Confucian temples
bodhisattva – one worthy of nirvana but who remains on earth to help others attain enlightenment
bówùguǎn – museum
bǔpiào – upgrade

cāntīng – restaurant
CCP – Chinese Communist Party, founded in Shànghǎi in 1921
Chángchéng – the Great Wall
CITS – China International Travel Service; the organisation deals with China's foreign tourists

dàjiē – avenue
dàshà – hotel, building
dàxué – university
dìtiě – subway
dōng – east; the other points of the compass are *běi* (north), *nán* (south) and *xī* (west)
dòngwùyuán – zoo

fàndiàn – hotel or restaurant

gé – pavilion, temple (Taoist)
gōng – palace, temple
gōngyuán – park
gùjū – house, home, residence

hé – river
hú – lake
Huí – ethnic Chinese Muslims
hútòng – a narrow alleyway

jiāng – river
jiǎo — see *máo*
jiē – street
jié – festival
jīn – unit of measurement equal to 500g
jiǔdiàn – hotel

kǎoyādiàn – roast duck restaurant
kuài – colloquial term for the currency, *yuán*
Kuomintang – Chiang Kaishek's Nationalist Party, the dominant political force after the fall of the Qing dynasty

líng – tomb
lóu – tower
lù – road
luóhàn – see *arhat*

máo – colloquial term for *jiǎo*, 10 of which equal one *kuài*
mén – gate
miào – temple

nán – south; the other points of the compass are *běi* (north), *dōng* (east) and *xī* (west)

páilou – decorated archway
Pinyin – the official system for transliterating Chinese script into the Roman alphabet
PLA – People's Liberation Army

PRC – People's Republic of China
PSB – Public Security Bureau; the arm of the police force set up to deal with foreigners

qì – flow of vital or universal energy
qiáo – bridge
qílín – a hybrid animal that only appeared on earth in times of harmony

rénmín – people, people's
renminbi – literally 'people's money', the formal name for the currency of China; shortened to RMB

shān – hill, mountain
shìchǎng – market
sì – temple, monastery
sìhéyuàn – courtyard house

tíng – pavilion

wǔshù – martial arts

xī – west; the other points of the compass are *běi* (north), *nán* (south) and *dōng* (east)

yáng – positive, bright and masculine; the complementary principle to *yīn*
yīn – negative, dark and feminine; the complementary principle to *yáng*
yuán – the Chinese unit of currency; also referred to as RMB (see also *renminbi*)

zhōng – middle, centre

Behind the Scenes

SEND US YOUR FEEDBACK

We love to hear from travellers – your comments keep us on our toes and help make our books better. Our well-travelled team reads every word on what you loved or loathed about this book. Although we cannot reply individually to your submissions, we always guarantee that your feedback goes straight to the appropriate authors, in time for the next edition. Each person who sends us information is thanked in the next edition – the most useful submissions are rewarded with a selection of digital PDF chapters.

Visit **lonelyplanet.com/contact** to submit your updates and suggestions or to ask for help. Our award-winning website also features inspirational travel stories, news and discussions.

Note: We may edit, reproduce and incorporate your comments in Lonely Planet products such as guidebooks, websites and digital products, so let us know if you don't want your comments reproduced or your name acknowledged. For a copy of our privacy policy visit lonelyplanet.com/privacy.

OUR READERS

Many thanks to the travellers who used the last edition and wrote to us with helpful hints, useful advice and interesting anecdotes:

Ann Alderson, Christer Ferm, Cindy Poole, David Hildebrand, Joella Jacobs, Kevin Samuels, Lotte Oostebrink, Mingga Anggawan, Patrick Teunissen, Ulrich Giebel

WRITER THANKS

David Eimer

Thanks to Daniel McCrohan for his sterling work on previous editions. Thanks also to Megan Eaves and Julie Sheridan at Lonely Planet. Special gratitude to Emi Yang for her invaluable assistance.

Trent Holden

First up a massive thanks to Megan Eaves for commissioning me on this title. A massive honour indeed to cover a city of this magnitude. Also wanted to say a big thank you to fellow LP colleagues based in the Běijīng office, including Vega Liu for all your great tips, beers and assistance along the way, and Guan 'Coco' Yuanyuan for letting me use the office as a temporary workspace – a big help! A shout out to everyone who I shared a beer with, and the tips on places to check out. As always lots of love to my girlfriend, Kate Morgan, and all my family and friends in Melbourne and London.

ACKNOWLEDGEMENTS

Cover photograph: Traditional dancers leaving the stage at the Summer Palace, Matt Munroe/Lonely Planet ©
Illustrations p58–9 by Michael Weldon

THIS BOOK

This 11th edition of Lonely Planet's *Beijing* guidebook was researched and written by David Eimer and Trent Holden. The previous two editions were written by David Eimer, Damian Harper and Daniel McCrohan. This guidebook was produced by the following:

Destination Editor Megan Eaves
Product Editors Grace Dobell, Genna Patterson
Senior Cartographer Julie Sheridan
Book Designers Fergal Condon, Katherine Marsh
Assisting Editors Janet Austin, Melanie Dankel, Carly Hall, Paul Harding, Helen Koehne, Kellie Langdon

Assisting Cartographer Anthony Phelan
Cover Researcher Naomi Parker
Thanks to Jane Atkin, Cheree Broughton, Jennifer Carey, Neill Coen, Daniel Corbett, Jane Grisman, Coco Guan, Kate James, Lauren Keith, Kate Kiely, Chris LeeAck, Vega Liu, Laura Noiret, Tom O'Malley, Kirsten Rawlings, Ellie Simpson

See also separate subindexes for:

✕ **EATING P263**

🍷 **DRINKING & NIGHTLIFE P263**

☆ **ENTERTAINMENT P264**

🛍 **SHOPPING P264**

🏃 **SPORTS & ACTIVITIES P264**

🛏 **SLEEPING P265**

Index

Běijīng Maps

Sights

- Beach
- Bird Sanctuary
- Buddhist
- Castle/Palace
- Christian
- Confucian
- Hindu
- Islamic
- Jain
- Jewish
- Monument
- Museum/Gallery/Historic Building
- Ruin
- Shinto
- Sikh
- Taoist
- Winery/Vineyard
- Zoo/Wildlife Sanctuary
- Other Sight

Activities, Courses & Tours

- Bodysurfing
- Diving
- Canoeing/Kayaking
- Course/Tour
- Sento Hot Baths/Onsen
- Skiing
- Snorkelling
- Surfing
- Swimming/Pool
- Walking
- Windsurfing
- Other Activity

Sleeping

- Sleeping
- Camping

Eating

- Eating

Drinking & Nightlife

- Drinking & Nightlife
- Cafe

Entertainment

- Entertainment

Shopping

- Shopping

Information

- Bank
- Embassy/Consulate
- Hospital/Medical
- Internet
- Police
- Post Office
- Telephone
- Toilet
- Tourist Information
- Other Information

Geographic

- Beach
- Gate
- Hut/Shelter
- Lighthouse
- Lookout
- Mountain/Volcano
- Oasis
- Park
- Pass
- Picnic Area
- Waterfall

Population

- Capital (National)
- Capital (State/Province)
- City/Large Town
- Town/Village

Transport

- Airport
- Border crossing
- Bus
- Cable car/Funicular
- Cycling
- Ferry
- Metro/MTR/MRT station
- Monorail
- Parking
- Petrol station
- Skytrain/Subway station
- Taxi
- Train station/Railway
- Tram
- Underground station
- Other Transport

Note: Not all symbols displayed above appear on the maps in this book

Routes

- Tollway
- Freeway
- Primary
- Secondary
- Tertiary
- Lane
- Unsealed road
- Road under construction
- Plaza/Mall
- Steps
- Tunnel
- Pedestrian overpass
- Walking Tour
- Walking Tour detour
- Path/Walking Trail

Boundaries

- International
- State/Province
- Disputed
- Regional/Suburb
- Marine Park
- Cliff
- Wall

Hydrography

- River, Creek
- Intermittent River
- Canal
- Water
- Dry/Salt/Intermittent Lake
- Reef

Areas

- Airport/Runway
- Beach/Desert
- Cemetery (Christian)
- Cemetery (Other)
- Glacier
- Mudflat
- Park/Forest
- Sight (Building)
- Sportsground
- Swamp/Mangrove

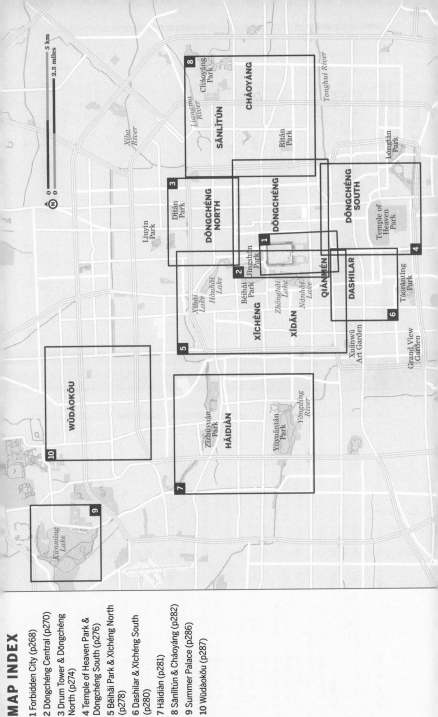

MAP INDEX

0 — 5 km
0 — 2.5 miles

WŪDÀOKǑU (10)

HǍIDIÀN (7)

Kūnmíng Lake (9)

Zǐzhúyuàn Park

Yùyuāntán Park

Yǒngdìng River

Xība River

Liángmǎ River

Liuyin Park

DŌNGCHÉNG NORTH (3)

Dìtán Park

SĀNLǏTÚN

Cháoyáng Park (8)

CHÁOYÁNG

Rìtán Park

DŌNGCHÉNG (1)

Jǐngshān Park

XĪCHÉNG

Xīhǎi Lake

Hòuhǎi Lake

Běihǎi Park

Zhōnghǎi Lake

Nánhǎi Lake (2)

XĪDĀN

QIÁNMÉN

DASHILAR (6)

Xuānwǔ Art Garden

Grand View Garden

DŌNGCHÉNG SOUTH (4)

Temple of Heaven Park

Táorántíng Park

Lóngtán Park

Tōnghuì River

(5)

500 m
0.25 miles

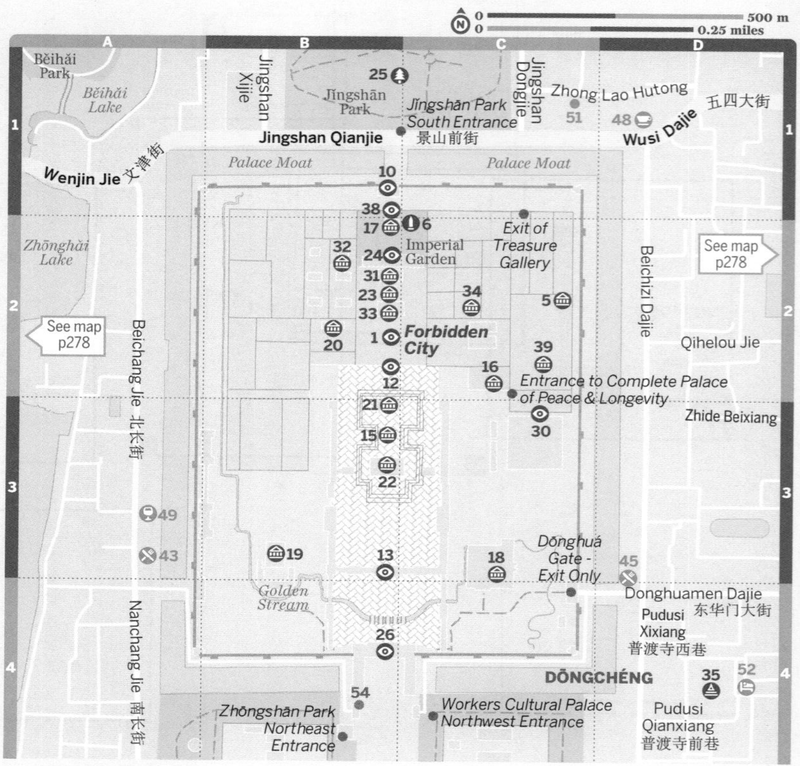

See map p278

See map p278

Beihai
Lake

Beihai
Park

Zhōnghǎi
Lake

Wenjin Jie 文津街

Beichang Jie 北长街

Nanchang Jie 南长街

Jingshan
Xijie

Jingshan
Dongjie

Jingshan Park

Jingshan Qianjie

Jingshan Park
South Entrance
景山前街

Palace Moat

Palace Moat

Palace Moat

Wusi Dajie

五四大街

Zhong Lao Hutong

Beichizi Dajie

Qihelou Jie

Zhide Beixiang

Entrance to Complete Palace
of Peace & Longevity

Donghuámen Dajie 东华门大街

Pudusi
Qianxiang
普渡寺前巷

Pudusi
Xixiang
普渡寺西巷

DŌNGCHÉNG

Workers Cultural Palace
Northwest Entrance

Donghuá
Gate -
Exit Only

Exit of
Treasure
Gallery

Imperial
Garden

Forbidden
City

Golden
Stream

Zhongshan Park
Northeast Entrance

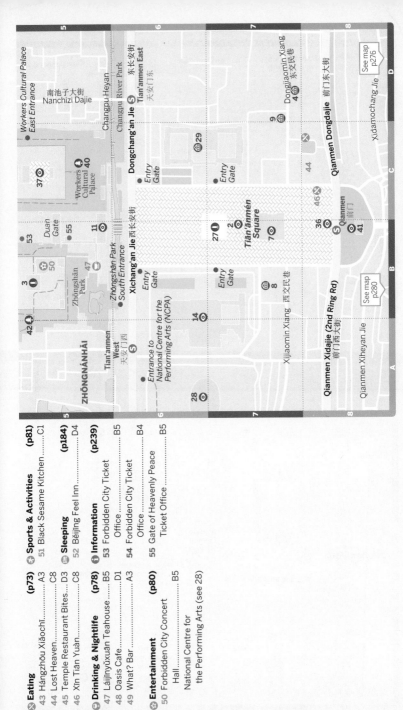

FORBIDDEN CITY

DŌNGCHÉNG CENTRAL

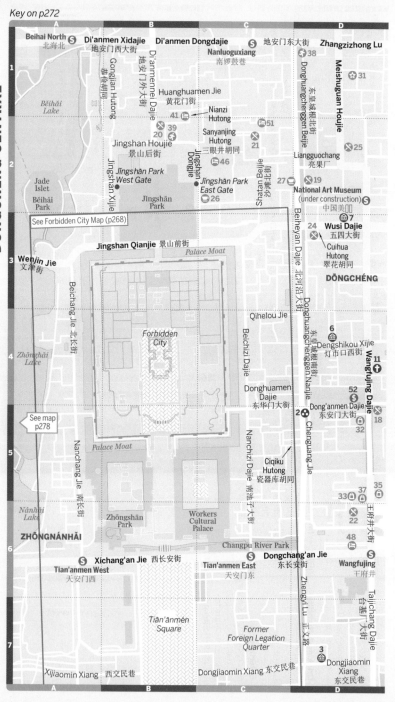

Beihai North Ⓢ
北海北

Di'anmen Xidajie
地安门西大街

Di'anmen Dongdajie
地安门东大街

地安门东大街

Nanluoguxiang
南锣鼓巷

Zhangzizhong Lu

Gongjian Hutong

Di'annennei Dajie
地安门内大街

🚇38

Dōnghuangchenggen Beijie
东皇城根北街

Meishuguan Houjie

☆31

Běihǎi
Lake

Huanghuamen Jie
黄花门街

41 🏛

Nianzi
Hutong

🏛51

20 🏛
39

Sanyanjing
Hutong
三眼井胡同

21 🍴

🍴25

Jingshan Houjie
景山后街

Jingshan
Dongjie

🏛46

Liangguochang
亮果厂

Jingshan Xijie

Jīngshān Park
West Gate

Jingshan Park
East Gate

🍴19

27 🚇

Jade
Islet

Jīngshān
Park

🚇26

National Art Museum
(under construction) Ⓢ
中国美🏛🏛

Shatan Beijie

☆7

Běihǎi
Park

24
🍴

Wusi Dajie
五四大街

3
Wenjin Jie
文津街

See Forbidden City Map (p268)

Jingshan Qianjie 景山前街

Palace Moat

Cuihua
Hutong
翠花胡同

DŌNGCHÉNG

Beichang Jie 北长街

Forbidden
City

Qihelou Jie

Beiheyan Dajie 北河沿大街

Dōnghuangchenggen Nanjie 东皇城根南街

6 🏛
Dengshikou Xijie
灯市口西街

4
Zhōnghǎi
Lake

Beichizi Dajie

11 🚇

Wangfujing Dajie 王府井大街

52 🍴
Ⓢ

See map
p278

Donghuamen
Dajie
东华门大街

Dong'anmen Dajie
东安门大街

🍴18

2 🚇

32 🔒

Nanchang Jie 南长街

Palace Moat

Nanchizi Dajie 南池子大街

Chenguang Jie

5

Nánhǎi
Lake

Ciqiku
Hutong
瓷器库胡同

35 🔒

33 🔒
37 🔒

Wangfujing Dajie 王府井大街

ZHŌNGNÁNHĂI

Zhōngshān
Park

Workers
Cultural
Palace

🍴22

48 🏛

Changpu River Park Ⓢ

6
Xichang'an Jie 西长安街

Dongchang'an Jie
东长安街

Wangfujing
🍴
Ⓢ

Tian'anmen West
天安门西

Tian'anmen East
天安门东

Wangfujing
干府井

Zhengyi Lu 正义路

Taijichang Dajie 台基厂大街

Tiān'anmén
Square

Former
Foreign Legation
Quarter

3 🏛
Dongjiaomin
Xiang

7
Xijiaomin Xiang 西交民巷

Dongjiaomin Xiang 东交民巷

东交民巷

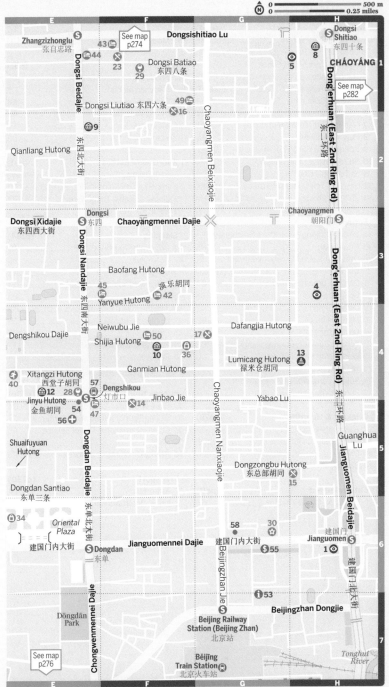

0   500 m
0   0.25 miles

DŌNGCHÉNG CENTRAL

Zhangzizhonglu
张自忠路

Dongsishitiao Lu

Dongsi
Shitiao
东四十条

CHÁOYÁNG

See map
p274

43
44
23

Dongsi Batiao
东四八条

29

5

8

Dongsi Beidajie

See map
p282

Dongsi Liutiao 东四六条

49
16

9

Qianliang Hutong

东四北大街

Chaoyangmen Beixiaojie

Dongsi Xidajie
东四西大街

Dongsi
东四

Chaoyangmennei Dajie

Chaoyangmen
朝阳门

Dongsi Nandajie

Baofang Hutong

45

Yanyue Hutong

滨乐胡同
42

4

Dafangjia Hutong

东四南大街

Dengshikou Dajie

Neiwubu Jie

Shijia Hutong

50

10

17
36

Lumicang Hutong
禄米仓胡同

13

Dong erhuan (East 2nd Ring Rd)   东二环路

Ganmian Hutong

Xitangzi Hutong
西堂子胡同

40

12   28

57

Dengshikou
灯市口

Jinbao Jie

Yabao Lu

Jinyu Hutong
金鱼胡同

54

14

47

56

Shuaifuyuan
Hutong

Dongdan Beidajie

Dongdan Santiao
东单三条

Dongzongbu Hutong
东总部胡同

15

东单北大街

Guanghua
Lu

Jianguomen Beidajie

34

Oriental
Plaza

建国门内大街

Chongwenmennei Dajie

Dongdan
东单

Jianguomennei Dajie

Beijingzhan Jie

建国门内大街

58

30

55

Jianguomen
建国门

1

**Dōngdān
Park**

Jianguomen Beidajie

建国门北大街

See map
p276

53

Beijingzhan Dongjie

**Beijing Railway
Station (Beijing Zhan)**
北京站

**Běijīng
Train Station**
北京火车站

*Tonghui
River*

DŌNGCHÉNG CENTRAL *Map on p270*

DŌNGCHÉNG CENTRAL

DRUM TOWER & DŌNGCHÉNG NORTH *Map on p274*

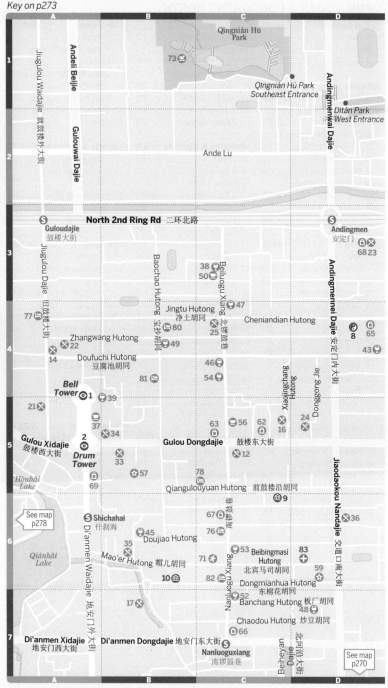

Qīngnián Hú Park

73

Qīngnián Hú Park
Southeast Entrance

Andingmenwai Dajie

Dìtán Park
West Entrance

Jiugulou Waidajie 旧鼓楼外大街

Andeli Beijie

Gulouwai Dajie

Ande Lu

North 2nd Ring Rd 二环北路

Guloudajie
鼓楼大街

Andingmen
安定门

68 23

Jiugulou Dajie 旧鼓楼大街

Baochao Hutong 宝钞胡同

38
50

Beiluogu Xiang 北锣鼓巷

47

Jingtu Hutong
净土胡同
80

25

Cheniandian Hutong

Andingmennei Dajie 安定门内大街

77

8

65

Zhangwang Hutong
22

49

43

14

Doufuchi Hutong
豆腐池胡同

46

54

Xiaojingchang Hutong

Douggougou Jie

81

**Bell
Tower** 1

39

63

56

62

16

24

21

37

34

33

12

Gulou Dongdajie

鼓楼东大街

Gulou Xidajie
鼓楼西大街

2

**Drum
Tower**

57

78

Hòuhǎi
Lake

69

Qianguloyuan Hutong 前鼓楼沿胡同

9

See map
p278

Qiánhǎi
Lake

Shichahai
什刹海

45

35

Nanluoguxiang 南锣鼓巷

67

76

53

Beibingmasi
Hutong
北宾马司胡同

83

59

Doujiao Hutong

71

Mao'er Hutong 帽儿胡同

10

82

Dongmianhua Hutong
东棉花胡同

Di'anmen Waidajie 地安门外大街

52

48

17

Banchang Hutong 板厂胡同

66

Chaodou Hutong 炒豆胡同

Jiaodaokou Nandajie 交道口南大街

36

Di'anmen Xidajie
地安门西大街

Di'anmen Dongdajie 地安门东大街

Nanluoguxiang
南锣鼓巷

Beiheyan Dajie

北河沿大街

See map
p270

0   500 m
0   0.25 miles

7

Dìtán
Park

Hépíngli Xijie

Hépíngli Dōngjie

Dìtán Park
South Entrance

20

North 2nd Ring Rd 二环北路

S
29 72 44 5 Yonghegong
30 Lama Temple
Wudaoying 雍和宫
Hutong
五道营胡同

26 Jianchang
新一胡同
Hutong
60

31
4
40 **15**

6
Guozijian Jie
国子监街

Yonghegong Dajie 雍和宫大街

84

Paoju Toutiao
炮局头条

3 *Lama*
Temple

Dongzhimen Beixiaojie

85

Nánguān
Park

Dongzhimen Beizhongjie

Fangjia Hutong 方家胡同
58 **79** **55**

19

28
Beixinqiao Santiao Hutong 北新桥三条
13   **75**

11

32

Jiaodaokou Dongdajie

64

Beixinqiao
S 北新桥

Dongzhimennei Dajie 东直门内大街

51   **18**

70

27   **41**

74

Dongsi Beidajie 东四北大街

Dongzhimen Nanxiaojie

See map
p282

42

61

S Zhangzizhonglu
张自忠路

Zhangzizhong Lu

Dongsishitiao Lu

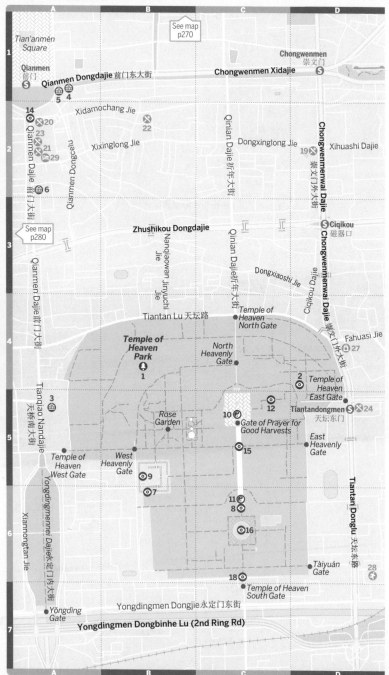

Tian'anmén Square

Qianmen
前门 Ⓢ

See map p270

Chongwenmen
崇文门 Ⓢ

Qianmen Dongdajie 前门东大街

Chongwenmen Xidajie

Xidamochang Jie

22 ✕

14

20 ✕

23 ✕

21 ✕
29

6

Xixinglong Jie

Qianmen Dongdajie 前门大街

Qianmen Dongdajie

Qinian Dajie 祈年大街

Dongxinglong Jie

Xihuashi Dajie

19 ✕

Chongwenmenwai Dajie 崇文门外大街

Zhushikou Dongdajie

Nanqiaowan Jinyuchi Jie

Ciqikou
磁器口 Ⓢ

Dongxiaoshi Jie

Chongwenmenwai Dajie 崇文门外大街

Qianmen Dajie 前门大街

Qinian Dajie 祈年大街

Tiantan Lu 天坛路

Temple of Heaven North Gate

Fahuasi Jie

27

Temple of Heaven Park
1

North Heavenly Gate

Tianqiao Nandajie 天桥南大街

3

Rose Garden

10

Gate of Prayer for Good Harvests

12

2

Temple of Heaven East Gate

Tiantandongmen
天坛东门 Ⓢ 24

15

East Heavenly Gate

West Heavenly Gate

9

Temple of Heaven West Gate

7

11
8

16

Tàiyuán Gate

28

Yongdingmennei Dajie 永定门内大街

Xiannongtan Jie

Tiantan Donglu 天坛东路

18

Temple of Heaven South Gate

Yŏngdìng Gate

Yongdingmen Dongjie 永定门东街

Yongdingmen Dongbinhe Lu (2nd Ring Rd)

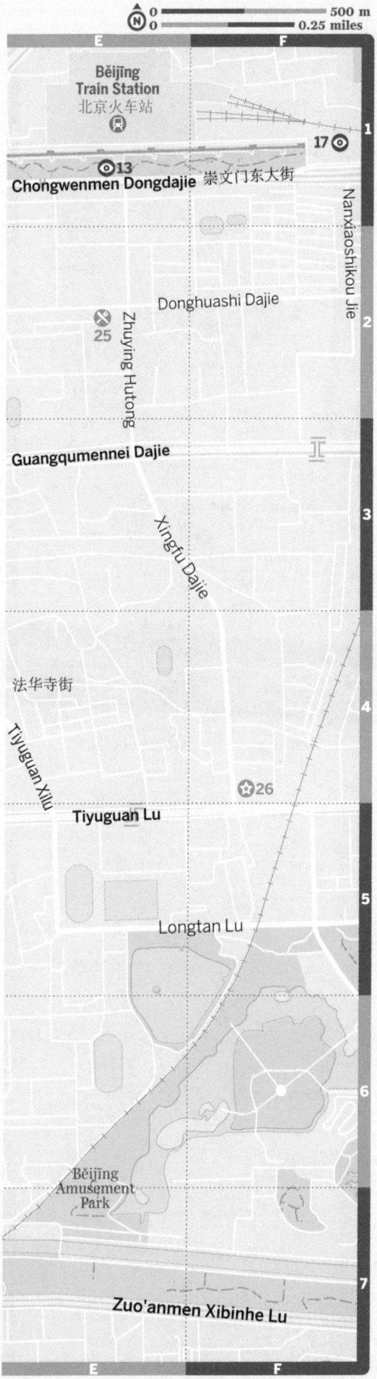

TEMPLE OF HEAVEN PARK & DŌNGCHÉNG SOUTH

Map

Běijīng Train Station 北京火车站

13 Chongwenmen Dongdajie 崇文门东大街

17

Donghuashi Dajie

25 Zhuying Hutong

Guangqumennei Dajie

Xingfu Dajie

法华寺街

Tiyuguan Xilu

Tiyuguan Lu

26

Longtan Lu

Nanxiaoshikou Jie

Běijīng Amusement Park

Zuo'anmen Xibinhe Lu

BĚIHǍI PARK & XĪCHÉNG NORTH

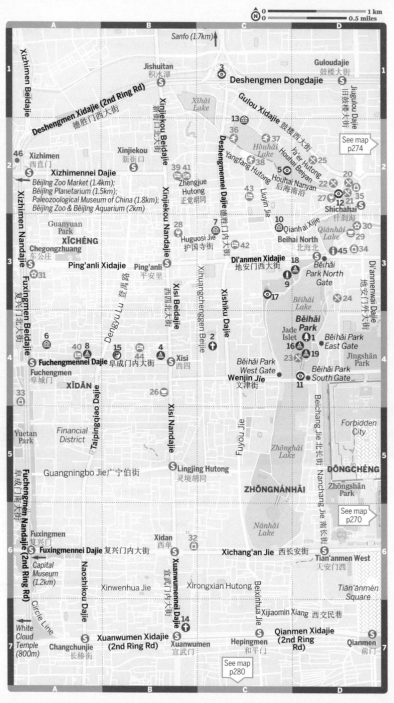

Sanfo (1.7km)

A

B

C

D

Xizhimen Beidajie
西直门北大街

Deshengmen Xidajie (2nd Ring Rd)
德胜门西大街

Xinjiekou Beidajie
新街门北大街

Jishuitan
积水潭

3

Deshengmen Dongdajie

Guloudajie
鼓楼大街

Gulou Xidajie 鼓楼西大街

Jiuguloudajie
旧鼓楼大街

See map
p274

Xīhǎi
Lake

13

36
37
Hòuhǎi
Lake
38
Houhai Beiyan

25
20
22
27
35
21
12
Shichahai
什刹海

Xizhimen
西直门
46

Xizhimennei Dajie
Běijīng Zoo Market (1.4km);
Běijīng Planetarium (1.5km);
Paleozoological Museum of China (1.8km);
Běijīng Zoo & Běijīng Aquarium (2km)

Xinjiekou
新街口

S

Deshengmennei Dajie 德胜门内大街

Yangfang Hutong

Liuyin Jie

Houhai Nanyan
后海南沿

5

Qianhai Xijie
前海西街
10

Qiánhǎi
Lake
29
30
45
34

Guanyuan
Park

Chegongzhuang
车公庄
S

XĪCHÉNG

Ping'anli Xidajie

39 41

Zhengjue
Hutong
正觉胡同

28

Huguosi Jie
护国寺街

7

42

Di'anmen Xidajie
地安门大街

Beihai North
北海北

18

Běihǎi
Park North
Gate

i 45

Fuxingmen Beidajie 复兴门北大街

31

Xinjiekou Nandajie

Ping'anli
平安里

Dengyu Lu 登禹路

Xisi Beidajie 西四北大街

Xihuangchenggen Beijie

Xishiku Dajie

2

17

9

Běihǎi
Lake

24

Di'anmennei Dajie 地安门外大街

Běihǎi
Park

Jade
Islet

16
1
19
23

Běihǎi Park
East Gate

Jingshān
Park

6
40
8
15
44
4

Fuchengmennei Dajie 阜成门内大街

Xisi
西四

Běihǎi Park
West Gate

Beichang Jie 北长街

Nanchang Jie 南长街

Fuchengmen
阜城门

XĪDĀN

26

Wenjin Jie
文津街

11

Běihǎi Park
South Gate

33

Yuetan
Park

Financial
District

Taipingqiao Dajie

Xisi Nandajie

Fuyou Jie

Zhōnghǎi
Lake

Forbidden
City

DŌNGCHÉNG

Guangningbo Jie 广宁伯街

Lingjing Hutong
灵境胡同
S

ZHŌNGNÁNHǍI

Zhōngshān
Park

See map
p270

Fuxingmen
复兴门

Fuxingmennei Dajie 复兴门内大街

Xidan
西单

32

Xichang'an Jie 西长安街

Nánhǎi
Lake

Tian'anmen West
天安门西

Tiān'ānmén
Square

Fuchengmen Nandajie (2nd Ring Rd) 阜成门南大街

Capital
Museum
(1.2km)

Naoshikou Dajie

Xinwenhua Jie

Xuanwumennei Dajie 宣武门内大街

Xirongxian Hutong

Beixinhua Jie

Xijiaomin Xiang 西交民巷

Circle Line

White
Cloud
Temple
(800m)

Changchunjie
长椿街

14

Xuanwumen Xidajie
(2nd Ring Rd)

Xuanwumen
宣武门

Hepingmen
和平门

Qianmen Xidajie
(2nd Ring
Rd)

Qianmen
前门
S

See map
p280

BĚIHǍI PARK & XĪCHÉNG NORTH

500 m
0.25 miles

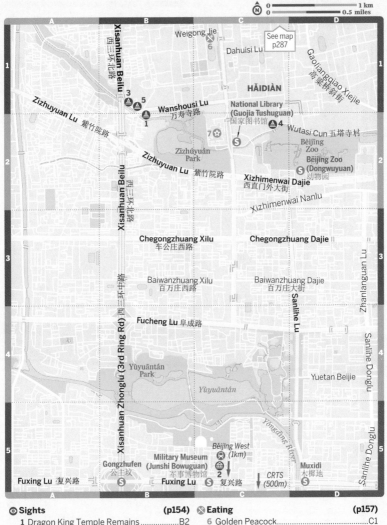

HĂIDIÀN

⦿ Sights	(p154)
1 Dragon King Temple Remains	B2
2 Military Museum	C5
3 Wànshòu Temple	B1
4 Wŭtă Temple	C2
5 Yánqìng Temple Remains	B1

🍴 Eating	(p157)
6 Golden Peacock	C1

★ Entertainment	(p159)
7 National Library Arts Centre	C2

SĀNLĬTÚN & CHÁOYÁNG

Key on p284

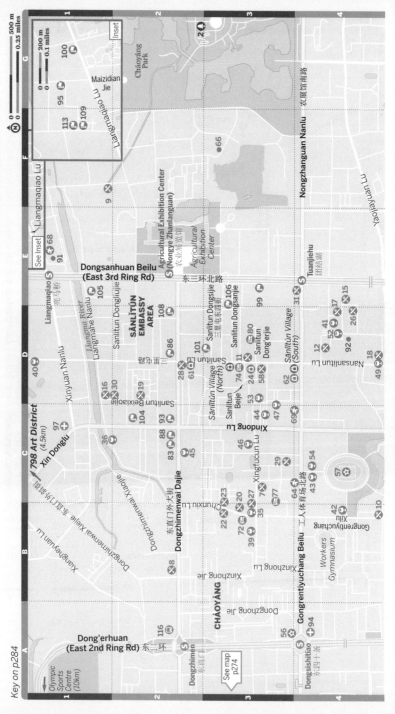

500 m
0.25 miles

Inset

200 m
0.1 miles

Liangmaqiao Lu

See Inset

Maizidian Jie

Cháoyáng Park

100
95
109
113

66

Nongzhanguan Nanlu

Yabaolou m

Liangmaqiao Lu

68
91

Liangmaqiao 联马桥

105

Liangma River
Liangmahe Nanlu

Xinyuan Nanlu

Dongsanhuan Beilu
(East 3rd Ring Rd)

Agricultural Exhibition Center
(Nongye Zhanlanguan)
农业展览馆

东三环北路

Agricultural
Exhibition
Center

SĀNLĬTÚN
EMBASSY
AREA

Sanlitun Dongliujie
Sanlitun Dongsijie
三里屯东四街
Sanlitun Dongsanjie

108
106
99

Tuanjiehu
团结湖

31
15
17
41
52
92
26
18
49

40

Sanlitun Beixiaojie

86
101
28
61

Sanlitun Dong'erjie
Sanlitun Dong'erjie

80
11
74
24
58

12

Nansanlitun Lu

16
30
19

Sanlitun Village
(North)
三里屯 北街

Sanlitun
Beijie

Sanlitun Village
(South)

62

104
93
88
83
45
36

53
44
47
69

Xindong Lu

Xin Donglu

798 Art District
(4.5km)

97

46

Xingfucun Lu

29

54

57

Gongti Beilu 工人体育场北路

43

Chunxiu Lu

Dongzhimenwai Xiejie 东直门外斜街

Dongzhimenwai Dajie
东直门外大街

22
23
20
27
72
39
35
9
7
77
64

42
Gongrentiyuchang
Xilu

10

Xinzhong Jie

8

Xiangheyuan Lu

Xinzhong Lu

Workers
Gymnasium

Gongrentiyuchang Beilu
工人体育场北路

Dong'erhuan
(East 2nd Ring Rd) 东二环

116

Dongzhimen
东直门

See map
p274

CHÁOYÁNG

Dongzhong Jie

56

94

Dongsishitao
东四十条

Olympic
Sports
Centre
(10km)

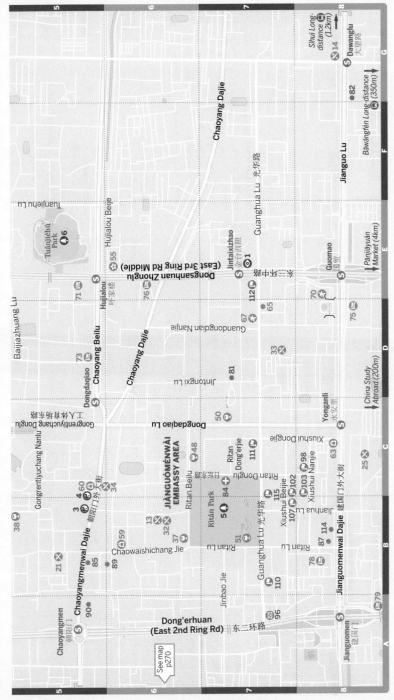

Tuánjiéhú Park

Tuánjiéhú Lu

Chaoyang Dajie

Guanghua Lu 光华路

Jianguo Lu

Sihui Long-distance (1.2km)

Dawanglu 大望路

Bawàngfén Long-distance (350m)

Panjiayuán Market (4km)

Guomao 国贸

Jintaixizhao 金台夕照

Dongsanhuan Zhonglu (East 3rd Ring Rd Middle) 东三环中路

Hujialou Beijie

Hujialou 呼家楼

Chaoyang Beilu

Chaoyang Dajie

Guandongdian Nanjie 光中三环

Dongdaqiao 东大桥

Baijiazhuang Lu

Jintongxi Lu

Yonganli 永安里

China Study Abroad (200m)

Dongdaqiao Lu

Gongrentiyuchang Donglu 工人体育场东路

JIÀNGUÓMÉNWÀI EMBASSY AREA

Ritan Beilu

Ritan Park

Ritán Park

Ritan Donglu

日坛东路

Ritan Dong'erjie

Ritan Dong'erjie

Xiushui Dongjie

Xiushui Nanjie

Xiushui Beijie

Jianguomenwai Dajie 建国门外大街

Jianguomenwai Dajie

Jianhua Lu 建华路

Ritan Lu

Ritan Lu

Jianhua Lu

Guanghua Lu 光华路

Gongrentiyuchang Nanlu

Chaoyangmenwai Dajie

Chaoyangmen 朝阳门

Chaowaishichang Jie

Jinbao Jie

Dong'erhuan (East 2nd Ring Rd) 东二环路

Jianguomen 建国门

See map p270

SUMMER PALACE

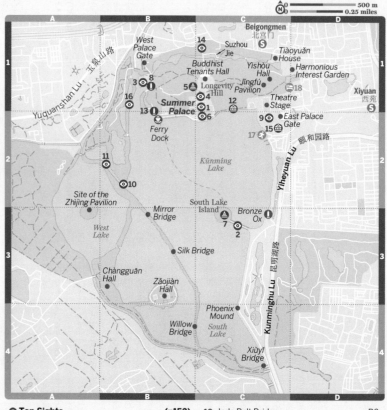

500 m
0.25 miles